A HISTORY
of the
PORT TALBOT RAILWAY & DOCKS COMPANY
and the
SOUTH WALES MINERAL RAILWAY COMPANY
Volume 1: 1853–1907

PTR 0-8-2T No. 20 after being fitted with a GWR standard No. 4 boiler and modified firebox, circa August 1908. The locomotive is finished in the livery originally specified apart from no brass numerals on the chimney, and carries the Port Talbot Company's armorial device.

A HISTORY
of the
PORT TALBOT RAILWAY & DOCKS COMPANY
and the
SOUTH WALES MINERAL RAILWAY COMPANY
Volume 1: 1853–1907

Robin G. Simmonds

Lightmoor Press

This map accompanied a Boundary Commission Report of 1832 on proposed changes in the Aberavon district and depicts Aberavon Harbour, the original course of the River Avon, the town of Aberavon and the villages of Taibach and Cwmavon. Also marked are the industries at Taibach and Cwmavon, and the early "rail roads" *Author's collection*

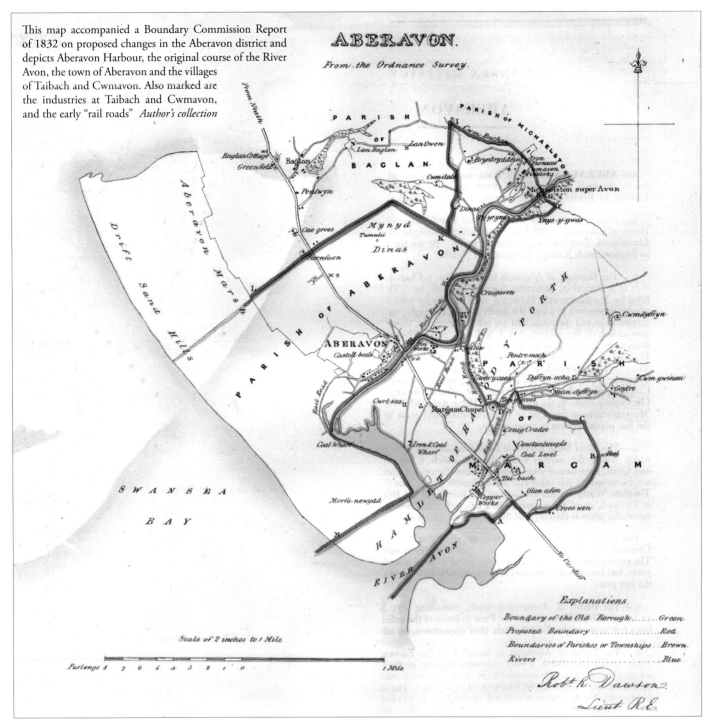

ABERAVON.

From the Ordnance Survey.

LIGHTMOOR PRESS
Unit 144B, Lydney Trading Estate, Harbour Road, Lydney, Gloucestershire GL15 5EJ
www.lightmoor.co.uk
Lightmoor Press is an imprint of Black Dwarf Lightmoor Publications Ltd.
Printed by TJ International, Padstow, Cornwall.

Contents

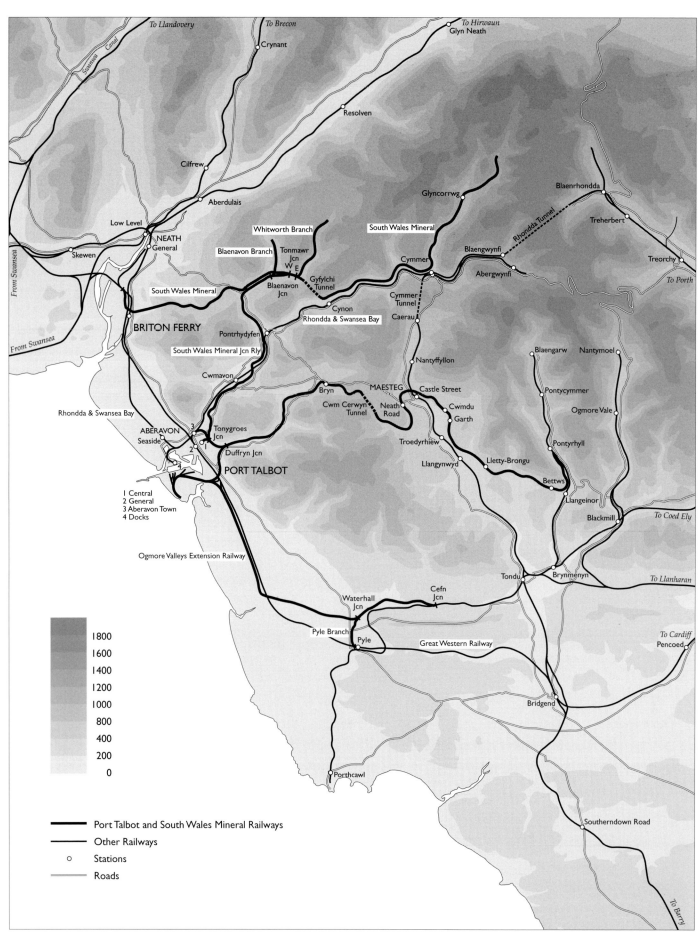

Introduction

The Port Talbot Railway & Docks Company was one of the few to be conceived as an integrated undertaking from the outset, and was one of the last standard gauge, mainline railway companies to be incorporated in the UK. Its origins, however, go back to 1834 when local industrialists obtained an Act of Parliament to form the Aberavon Harbour Company. This Act was soon realised to be inadequate and in 1836 a further Act was obtained authorising the formation of the Port Talbot Company, named after the local landowner, Christopher Rice Mansel Talbot, with powers to build an enclosed dock, the first in South Wales. When Mr Talbot died in 1890 the dock possessed only modest facilities, despite several approaches by other interested parties with schemes to improve them, and was regarded as a very inadequate port. Mr Talbot was succeeded by his eldest daughter, Miss Emily Charlotte Talbot, who inherited *inter alia* the Penrice Estate on the Gower peninsula and the Margam Estate, which included Port Talbot Dock. It was the development of the mineral and industrial potential of the latter estate which interested Miss Talbot. Miss Talbot and her enthusiastic and forceful agent, Edward Knox, conceived a scheme of a new dock at Port Talbot served by a railway running up the Duffryn Valley, which bisected the estate, and continued through a tunnel to Maesteg in the Llynvi Valley, parts of which also lay within the estate. This proposed line was extended to the Garw Valley following representations from coal owners there. Miss Talbot insisted that both the railway and dock parts of this scheme were essential and vigorously opposed a rival scheme promoted by the Great Western Railway, seemingly as a spoiling move, to construct a similar railway to Maesteg but without a new dock. The outcome was the Port Talbot Railway & Docks Act 1894, "to dissolve and reincorporate and confer further powers upon the Port Talbot Company and to authorise them to construct an additional dock and railways and for other purposes." Thus the Port Talbot Co. evolved into an integrated railway and docks undertaking and both aspects are covered in this history.

By 1894 the Margam Estate was already surrounded by railways: the South Wales Railway along the coast, the GWR in the Llynvi

Although entitled "Copper Works, A View Near Aberavon, Glamorganshire, South Wales", this 1798 hand-coloured aquatint by Francis Jukes actually depicts Lower or Afan Forge on the River Avon. There had been a forge here since 1717 supplying local needs. Margam Tinplate Works was built on the site in 1822 and was served by sidings off the lower part of the Mynydd Bychan Tramroad, later the Oakwood Railway, which passed to the rear of the works.

Courtesy Barrie Flint

1

Valley, and the Rhondda & Swansea Bay Railway up the Avon Valley, the latter two lines meeting at Cymmer in the upper Avon Valley. All of these railways took some time to become fully established, and an account of them is included here to set the scene. Despite their presence, most of the original Port Talbot line and its later extensions remained in use until the 1960s. A further railway, the South Wales Mineral Railway, ran from Briton Ferry to Cymmer and terminated at Glyncorrwg. An extension of the Port Talbot Railway made a junction with this line at Tonmawr in 1898. This route provided a better outlet to a seaport than via the incline at Briton Ferry. In 1908 three of the Port Talbot directors, with help from the GWR, acquired the share capital, rolling stock and other assets of the SWMR, and this line was then worked by the PT Co. Accordingly a concise account of the SWMR is included to provide the background to this acquisition.

The initial antagonism of the GWR soon changed to a spirit of mutual cooperation. A traffic agreement of 1903 resulted in the withdrawal of PTR mineral trains in the Garw Valley in exchange for a share of the receipts, and provided for the GWR to route more traffic to Port Talbot Docks. This presaged an agreement of 1908 for the GWR to work the railway portion of the PT Co.'s undertaking, leaving the directors, and to some extent the officers, to concentrate on dock side of the business. The most significant addition to the dock facilities post 1908 was the erection of three electric coal conveyors, the first in South Wales, for the rapid loading of steamers. Furthermore, this period saw the development at the docks of firstly Port Talbot Steelworks and then Margam Steelworks, which were the foundation of what was to become Port Talbot's dominant industry.

SPELLINGS

The spelling of place names always causes difficulties when writing accounts of Welsh railways. Throughout, this work uses the Anglicised spellings which predominated during the principal period it covers, i.e. up to 1922. Likewise, money is expressed in pounds (£), shillings (s) and pence (d), and distances in miles (m), furlongs (f) and chains (ch).

SOURCES

This history is based on primary sources, most of which are held by The National Archives (TNA): Public Record Office (PRO) at Kew. Other primary sources consulted were the Parliamentary Archives (PA), the National Library of Wales, Penrice & Margam Collection (NLW P&M), the National Museums & Galleries of Wales (NM&GW), Glamorgan Record Office (GRO), West

An artist's view of Bridgend circa 1840, with what is believed to be the Bridgend Railway in the foreground.

Glamorgan Archive Service (WGAS), the Science Museum Library (SML) and Wiltshire & Swindon History Centre (W&SHC). These primary sources are complemented by contemporary newspapers, particularly *The Cambrian*, an online index for which is held by WGAS, and *The London Gazette*, which is fully available online. Background information on industrial developments in and around Port Talbot and the neighbouring valleys has been obtained from accounts written by local historians, as noted in the references. Information on distances and dates has been obtained from the series of *Track Layout Diagrams of the Great Western Railway and BR Western Region* by R A Cooke. The sections consulted were 49A *Tondu Branches*; 50A *Neath to Port Talbot*; 50B *Margam to Bridgend*; and 51 *Port Talbot & Cymmer Branches*.

All significant courses of action taken by the PTR&D and the SWMR were authorised by their boards of directors, and their Minute Books (TNA: PRO RAIL 574/1–5 and RAIL 639/1–3 respectively) provide the basis of this history of the companies during their independent existence. To avoid the lists of references becoming even longer, allusion to these Minutes Books is limited to citations of dates in the text, which is sufficient to identify them. Otherwise, references are collected at the end of each chapter.

ACKNOWLEDGEMENTS

I should like to acknowledge the help of all those who have contributed in various ways, and without whose input this history could not have been written. Special thanks are due to Colin Chapman, Michael Hale, John Lyons, Harold Morgan, Ian Pope, Arthur Rees, Paul Reynolds, and members of the Welsh Railways Research Circle.

*This book is dedicated to my wife Judy
in appreciation of her support and understanding throughout.*

1

Tramroad and Railway Developments in the Avon, Llynvi and Garw Valleys

THE RIVER AVON RISES about two miles east of Blaengwynfi. Unusually for a river in South Wales, the upper Avon runs in a westerly direction through Cymmer, where the River Corrwg enters, to Pontrhydyfen, the junction of the River Pelenna. At Pontrhydyfen the Avon turns south-west and flows through Cwmavon towards the sea at Aberavon. In pre-industrial times, at a point about one mile from the coast, the river turned south-east towards Taibach. Here it was fed by the River Ffrwdwyllt, which flows down the Duffryn Valley. A little further on the Avon turned south-west again to meet the sea. The lower three miles of the river were tidal and coastal trade was possible.

The River Llynvi rises on Mynydd-y-Caerau north-east of Maesteg, about a mile from the source of the Avon, and runs south through the Llynvi Valley to meet the River Ogmore at Aberkenfig. The River Garw rises a short distance further east and also runs south to join the Ogmore at Brynmenyn. The Ogmore downstream from here is a lowland river and flows through Bridgend to enter the sea at Ogmore-by-Sea. These valleys were never canalised unlike the neighbouring Vale of Neath. The closest a canal got to this area was the proposed extension of the Neath Canal from Briton Ferry to Aberavon, based on a survey made by William Kirkhouse, which was considered in December 1836.[1] This extension was presumably intended to run into the new dock, construction of which was about to begin, but seems not to have progressed beyond the discussion stage.

The area drained by these rivers straddles the southern boundary of the South Wales coalfield. Steam coal occurs under most of this area, but bituminous coal outcrops along the southern edge, and anthracite occurs towards the north-west.[2] Deposits of iron ore and ironstone also occur in workable quantities. It was these natural resources which principally drove the industrial development of the area.

Although railways were constructed along these river valleys as the network expanded to meet the needs of growing industrialisation, it was not until the 1890s that a company was incorporated to build a railway connecting the Avon, Duffryn, Llynvi and Garw valleys and to provide a major new outlet for the export of coal. This was the Port Talbot Railway and Docks Company, one of the last standard gauge, mainline railways to be incorporated in the United Kingdom.

TRAMROADS IN THE LOWER AVON VALLEY

In medieval times, these valleys were sparsely populated and supported a pastoral economy. There are records of coal and iron mining at least back to the thirteenth century, but the products of these activities were primarily for local use. By the middle of the eighteenth century change was afoot, and tramroads started to appear in the area. The first was recorded circa 1740 for the transport of coal being worked at Craig y Constant above Taibach, for shipment at a small wharf on Groeswen Pill near the then mouth of the Avon.[3] Further impetus to industrialisation of the Taibach area came from Messrs Cartwright and Newton, who in 1757 obtained a lease of all the land around Groeswen Pill with the specific intention of erecting a copper works. They also obtained leases of land up the Avon Valley and opened levels at Craigavon, Lletty Harry and Mynydd Bychan, as well as acquiring Greoswen Colliery.[4] By 1769, a horse tramroad had been constructed from Mynydd Bychan to a quay in the harbour on the Avon estuary.[5] This tramroad had wooden rails and ran along the mountain side to Penycae, where the trams were lowered down an incline to Tydraw, and thence on level ground to the quay.[6] It is shown as a waggon way on Yates' 1799 map of Glamorgan. In 1768, Cartwright and Newton surrendered their leases of land and collieries to the Governor and Company of Copper Miners in England, usually known as the English Copper Company, who commenced building the copper works in 1770.[7] The existing Mynydd Bychan Tramroad was extended from Penycae across the river Ffrwdwyllt to Taibach.[8] The copper works started production circa 1774, using ore imported at the pill from Cornwall, Anglesey, Scotland and Ireland. A branch of the Mynydd Bychan Tramroad was constructed in 1808 to take coal from Goytre level in the lower Duffryn Valley to the works. This tramroad was also used to carry corn to Duffryn Mill.[9]

The establishment of what became the Cwmavon Works occurred in 1811, when Samuel Lettsom obtained a lease of the area and built the first blast furnace there in 1819.[10] Iron ore and coal were available locally, and power was obtained by a wheel fed by a watercourse from Pontrhydyfen further up the valley. Initially, at least, limestone was carried from Taibach along the Mynydd Bychan Tramroad on the mountainside opposite and then transferred to horse-drawn carts and taken down the hill to the valley floor.[11] Lettsom failed before his blast furnace could be brought into use, and in 1820 Messrs Vigurs, Smith & Co. took possession of the works and started production.[12] Products were taken over the parish road to Aberavon for shipment at a wharf near the then mouth of the River Avon. Increased trade rendered this method of transport inadequate, and in 1824 a three mile long horse-drawn tramroad was laid, despite local objections,[13] over the parish road, which ran along the right bank of the river, to the old harbour.[14] This tramroad, which became known as the Cwmavon Tramroad, was authorised by a lease dated 7th December 1818 which granted Lettsom "liberty to make a single line of railway from Ynis-Pant-Du through

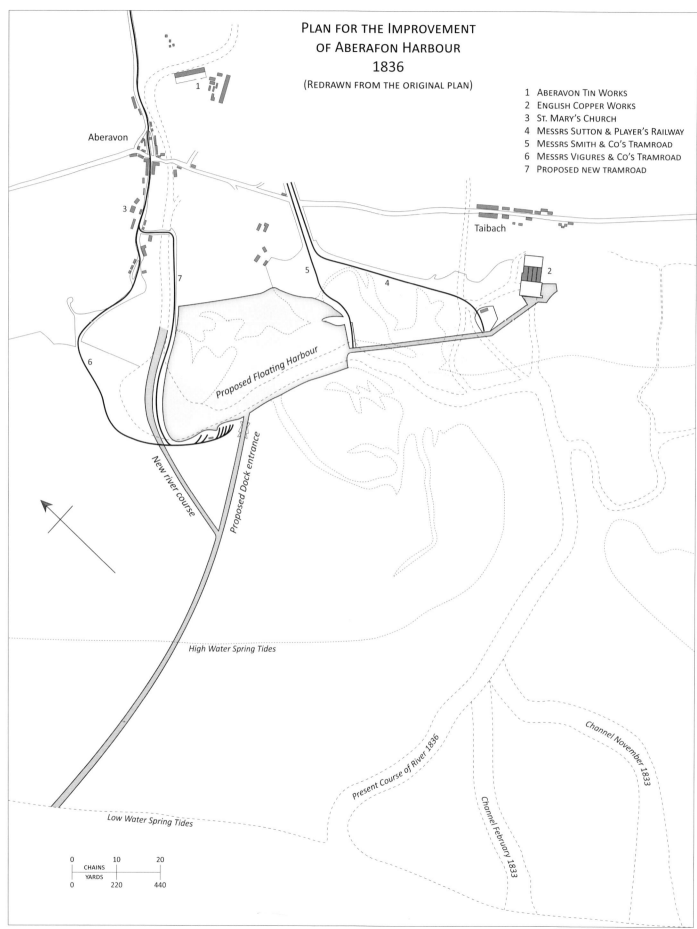

PLAN FOR THE IMPROVEMENT
OF ABERAFON HARBOUR
1836
(REDRAWN FROM THE ORIGINAL PLAN)

1 ABERAVON TIN WORKS
2 ENGLISH COPPER WORKS
3 ST. MARY'S CHURCH
4 MESSRS SUTTON & PLAYER'S RAILWAY
5 MESSRS SMITH & CO'S TRAMROAD
6 MESSRS VIGURES & CO'S TRAMROAD
7 PROPOSED NEW TRAMROAD

Aberavon

Taibach

Proposed Floating Harbour

New river course

Proposed Dock entrance

High Water Spring Tides

Present Course of River 1836

Channel November 1833

Channel February 1833

Low Water Spring Tides

0   10   20
CHAINS
YARDS
0   220   440

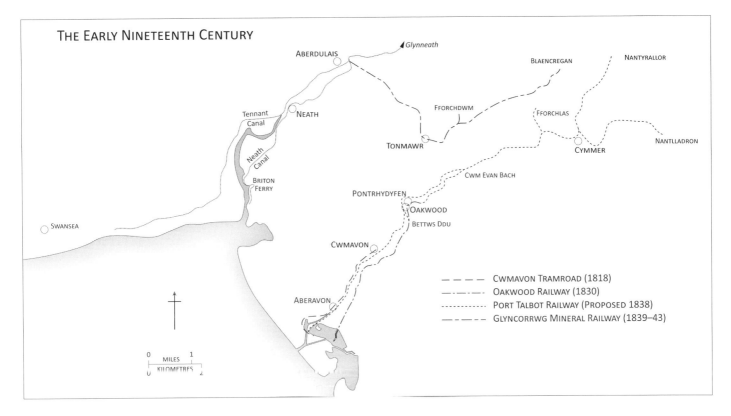

THE EARLY NINETEENTH CENTURY

---- CWMAVON TRAMROAD (1818)
-·-·- OAKWOOD RAILWAY (1830)
········· PORT TALBOT RAILWAY (PROPOSED 1838)
----- GLYNCORRWG MINERAL RAILWAY (1839–43)

Aberavon over the marshes across the Avon above the Sawpit at the entrance to Port Talbot to the stables on the wharf commonly called Docky-Llonga."[15] A second blast furnace, a tinplate works and a chemical works were added to the Cwmavon Works in 1825. Smith left Cwmavon in 1835,[16] the company now being known as Vigurs & Co. Copper smelting started at Cwmavon in 1838.[17]

Meanwhile, John Reynolds and Robert Smith had in 1822 established the Margam Tinplate Works on adjacent sites known as the Upper and Lower Forges on the left bank of the River Avon.[18] These two gentlemen parted company in 1824, Smith retaining the tinplate works. Reynolds proceeded to erect a large ironworks at Oakwood, Pontrhydyfen.[19] Power for the blast was generated by a waterwheel fed from the river Avon over an aqueduct, completed in 1827, which still exists. The works were connected by a tramroad to the existing line running from Mynydd Bychan to Taibach, where Reynolds built his own wharf near the river mouth.

OAKWOOD RAILWAY

In January 1830 an advertisement appeared in *The Cambrian* stating that several veins of coal at Gyfylchi above Pontrhydyfen were available to be let and that a railway to the port of Aberavon was in progress.[20] This new line, which became known as the Oakwood Railway, was built by Reynolds under the terms of a lease of 1824[21] to extend his existing tramroad at Oakwood Ironworks to Aberavon Harbour. The new line ran from Oakwood along the left bank of the Avon to Upper Forge, beyond which it made use of and followed the Mynydd Bychan Tramroad and continued to the harbour, terminating at a point later known as Llewellyn's Quay. This lower section was named as belonging to Messrs Smith & Co. on the Deposited Plan for the forthcoming Port Talbot Dock,[22] suggesting that it had been adapted by them to serve their Margam Tinplate Works. A separate line running into the copper works was

shown as being in the possession of Messrs Sutton & Player, who at the time were working coal in Cwm Evan Bach near Oakwood for the English Copper Company.[23] Reynolds was advertising coal for sale at his wharf in 1831.[24]

Reynolds' venture at Oakwood was a financial disaster. In 1838, after the works had been idle for some years, he sold his interests to the Oakwood & Argoed Coal & Iron Co.,[25] who soon had them back in full production.[26] Two years later the company was advertising for blocklayers and contractors to keep in repair the railroad from their works to Port Talbot, a distance of about five miles.[27] The Governor & Company of Copper Miners in England were re-formed under the same name in 1841.[28] The English Copper Company, as it was still known, became the proprietor of the Oakwood Railway when it took over the lease of the Oakwood Ironworks and Colliery in that year,[29] and kept it in repair until the Oakwood Works were finally abandoned in 1870. The Oakwood Wharf, the blast furnaces and some coal at Oakwood were not returned to Mr Talbot, the landowner, until Michaelmas 1883.[30]

In addition to the Oakwood Railway, a tramroad of 3 foot 3 inch gauge running from Margam Tinplate Works to the docks was in existence by 1848.[31] These two lines, being already in existence, were crossed on the level by the South Wales Railway (SWR) just south of Port Talbot station. This crossing was maintained under the terms of Deeds of Covenant by the SWR (1854) and the GWR (1868). Following the closure of the Oakwood Ironworks, the Oakwood Railway deteriorated to such an extent that the line over the crossing could not be used, and it had been removed by the time of the gauge conversion of the South Wales main line in 1872. The narrow gauge line, by now owned by Messrs Byass & Co., was widened to the standard gauge at this time and a connection made at Byass' expense to a siding in Port Talbot goods yard to facilitate the exchange of traffic.[32] Signals and catch points were added to the Byass line by October 1877,[33] as required by the Board of Trade Inspector.[34] No locomotives used the crossing until March 1878 when Messrs Byass gave notice of their intention to do so.

Messrs Byass & Co. had acquired the Margam Tinplate Company in 1864[35] and paid Mr Talbot 6d per ton wayleave to bring coal the three miles from Tewgoed Colliery over the Oakwood Railway to their works. In turn the English Copper Company received 3d per ton from Mr Talbot up to Michaelmas 1883 when their lease expired. Latterly Messrs Byass had to repair the line themselves as Mr Talbot declined to do so, and later used the R&SB route when that line opened in 1885.[36] Margam Tinplate Works closed in 1893 and production was concentrated on the company's Mansel Tinplate Works which had been opened in 1874 at a site further down the river near the docks. Byass & Co. gave up their lease of the Oakwood Railway at Michaelmas 1893,[37] the upper part not having been used since 1882.[38]

By 1833 it had become apparent that the old Aberavon Harbour was totally inadequate to serve the needs of the area, and steps were taken that were to result in the construction of a new dock.[39] Among the provisions of the new company's second Act of 1836 was one that changed its name to the Port Talbot Company (PT Co.), thereby establishing a new, and permanent, name for the locality. In June 1838, before the new dock was finished, the English Copper Co. gave up the Taibach Copper Works as access by vessels bringing copper ore was impeded by the new floating dock and the diversion of the river, and the works were sold to the landowner, Mr Talbot, only to be sold on later that year by auction to Vivian & Sons. To overcome problems with coal supply, Vivian & Sons replaced the earlier horses and wagons with a horse-drawn tramroad which ran from their levels in the Brombil area to the Constant, where the wagons were let down the incline by rope directly into the works. This tramroad was in use until 1883.[40] The copper works restarted in 1839, now being known as the Margam Copper Works. Also in 1838, the Mynydd Bychan Tramroad, apart from the section that led from Taibach to the Goytre level, was abandoned,[41] and the materials and twenty-three draught horses offered for sale.[42] The tramroad to Goytre was sold to Vivian & Sons for £400.[43] Vivian & Sons also obtained coal from the English Copper Co.,[44] which presumably came from Oakwood Colliery and was transported over the Oakwood Railway.

PORT TALBOT RAILWAY

None of the foregoing tramroads had a statutory basis. All were built on land leased from the local landowners, principally the Talbots of Margam, and the Earls of Jersey. However, early in 1838 the first tentative steps were taken to build a railway in the Avon Valley which would be authorised by an Act of Parliament. In February of that year notices appeared in *The Cambrian*[45] and *The London Gazette*[46] stating that an application would be made in the next session of Parliament for leave to bring in a Bill for making a railway from Nantyrallor, opposite Glyncorrwg in the Corrwg Valley, down the Avon Valley to Port Talbot. There were to be branches to Fforchlas above Abercreggan and to what is now Blaengwynfi, in the upper Avon Valley, as well as two connections to the Oakwood Railway. Powers were also sought to purchase this railway and the Cwmavon

Oakwood Colliery at Pontrhydyfen was established by John Reynolds circa 1827 to serve his new ironworks nearby. The colliery was at the inland end of the Oakwood Railway about five miles from Port Talbot. This much later view shows the colliery towards the end of its life circa 1926. Postcard, postally used 11th September 1929.

Author's collection

The appropriately named Incline Row, Taibach, down which coal was lowered by rope to Vivian & Sons' Margam Copper Works. The coal was brought by tramroad from the Brombil area off to the right, to a point near the white painted Constant, or Constant Row. Postcard, postally used 14th November 1917.
Author's collection

Tramroad. The notices were published in the name of William Llewellyn, a solicitor and one of the brothers of Griffith Llewellyn, who at the time was agent to the Margam Estate. The plans and other documents were deposited with the Clerk of the Peace for Glamorgan,[47] but there is no evidence that they ever reached the Private Bill office of Parliament. Although no title was given for the proposed line in either notice, the deposited plan indicated that it was intended to be called the Port Talbot Railway. This abortive scheme seems to have been an attempt by a party closely associated with the principal shareholder of the PT Co. to attract trade to its new dock which was approaching completion and to encourage the development of the upper Avon Valley. There is no mention of it in that company's minute books.[48]

TRAMROADS IN THE UPPER AVON VALLEY

In 1832 the Houghton brothers made preparations to work the coal that lay under their Fforchdwm Estate in Cwm Pelenna, one of the Avon's side valleys.[49] A tramroad 3,960 yards long was constructed from Abertwrch in the Neath Valley over Mynydd Pelenna and down to Blaen Pelenna. Coal was first raised in 1833, but the venture failed and the level was abandoned in 1836. A subsequent attempt to win the coal from the eastern side of the Neath Valley also failed.

GLYNCORRWG MINERAL RAILWAY
By 1839 the Fforchdwm Estate coal had been leased to Robert Parsons and Charles Strange who had announced a grandiose scheme to work all the coal on the north side of the Avon Valley from Tonmawr to Glyncorrwg.[50] They acquired 5,756 acres of coal leases and, starting in 1839, built a tramroad seven and a half miles in length from Aberdulais on the Neath canal to Blaencregan, about two miles north of Cymmer, to take out the coal. There was also a short branch up to the Fforchdwm level, which was situated half a mile down from the Blaen Pelenna level in Cwm Pelenna. Aberdulais was seemingly chosen over a shorter downhill route to Aberavon because it offered easier access to the industries and shipping ports of Neath, Briton Ferry and Swansea, rather than the unproven advantages of the new dock at Port Talbot. The engineer was William Kirkhouse (1776–1866).[51] The gauge was 3ft.[52] The line became known as the Glyncorrwg Mineral Railway, sometimes unjustly referred to as Parsons' Folly, and boasted seven inclined planes, six of which descended with the load and worked on the self-acting principle. The ascending incline out of Cwm Gwenffrwd required a fixed engine, bought from Neath Abbey Iron Co. The four miles of level railroad were worked by horse, although it was intended to replace these with two locomotives. Parsons and Strange did not succeed in working all the coal they had leased, and in 1843 were in severe financial difficulties. They were obliged to surrender their leases to the Houghton brothers, and in 1845 lost control of the Aberdulais–Cwm Gwenffrwd section of their tramroad, although they regained it by 1850. The Blaengregan–Fforchdwm section was dismantled in 1852. The portion between Fforchdwm and Cwm Gwenffrwd was made redundant by the opening of the broad gauge South Wales Mineral Railway (SWMR) to Tonmawr on 1st September 1861, although a short section apparently remained in use to serve collieries in Cwm Gwenffrwd. The western incline down to Aberdulais remained in use for a further twenty years to take out coal from the Wenallt and Wenallt Merthyr Collieries.

7

ABOVE: A lithograph of Cwmavon based on sketches by Edgar MacCulloch, engraved by G Hawkins and published by Day & Haghe in 1838. The view is from the south-east towards Mynydd y Foel on the right, with the River Avon running across the foreground. On top of the Foel is the stack through which noxious fumes from the copper works at the foot of the mountain were dispersed via a mile-long flue. To the right of the copper works is St. Michael's church, and prominent in the centre is the lower tinplate works. Four journeys of trams are visible on the Cwmavon Tramroad in the middle distance, which connected the works at Cwmavon initially to shipping points in Aberavon Harbour and latterly to a wharf in the new Port Talbot Dock. At the bottom right is a partial view of a journey of trams on the Oakwood Railway conveying what looks like coal from the pits near Pontrhydyfen to Margam. One of Edgar MacCulloch's pencil sketches of Aberavon Harbour is reproduced on page 60.   *Courtesy Barrie Flint*

LEFT: The aqueduct over the River Avon built by John Reynolds in 1827 to provide water from higher up the river to drive the wheel which powered the blast at his Oakwood Ironworks about a quarter of a mile off to the left. The PTR Viaduct can be discerned through the arches. Postcard, postally used 24th January 1910.

Author's collection

As well as regaining the Fforchdwm level, Dugdale Houghton opened up another level slightly further up the valley, and a third called, confusingly, Nantybar level or Fforchdwm Draw, the coal being originally sent out via the Glyncorrwg Mineral Railway.[53] The authorised branch of the SWMR to Fforchdwm was never constructed, the lessees of the line, the Glyncorrwg Coal Co. and its successors, being more interested in developing their own interests. Instead, Houghton built his own tramroad, or quite possibly made use of remnants of the old one, to a transshipment point alongside the SWMR near the western end of Gyfylchi Tunnel. Traffic was worked in this way by the Fforchdwm Colliery Co. until November 1865. The Fforchdwm Estate passed to the Ton Mawr Co. Ltd, in reality Edmund Parsons, the son of Robert Parsons, in September 1865, who worked the Fforchdwm level until 1867 when he was declared bankrupt.[54] The property eventually passed to the Welsh Freehold Coal & Iron Co., who in 1873 laid in a standard gauge branch line from the SWMR, itself by now converted to this gauge, to serve two collieries, Fforchdwm level, which was renamed Welsh Freehold Colliery, and Whitworth Colliery. The engineer for the line was Sidney William Yockney, the future engineer of the Rhondda & Swansea Bay Railway (R&SBR).[55] The traffic was initially worked by the SWMR, but this detracted from its own operations and the colliery company acquired its own locomotive, a converted L&NWR tender engine.[56] The collieries ceased working

in June 1875 because the poor quality coal could not be sold at a profit. The company went into liquidation and the branch railway was dismantled. After a further period of inactivity the whole estate passed into the hands of the South Wales Whitworth Mineral Estate Ltd which was registered in 1889.[57] This company commenced relaying the Fforchdwm Branch in 1890, and in February 1891 the first coal was brought down the Whitworth Railway from Whitworth Colliery, which had been established at Blaen Pelenna. Again the SWMR provided the initial locomotive power, but the Whitworth company soon provided its own engines.[58]

By 1863 the lease of some of the Fforchdwm minerals had been acquired by the Neath & Pelenna Colliery Company Ltd,[59] which had been formed that year with a capital of £65,000.[60] The N&PC initially worked the Wenallt level, almost certainly Houghton's level at Blaen Pelenna,[61] and in 1864 started the Rhondda No. 3 level which outcropped higher up the valley side.[62] The two levels had a combined output of 600–800 tons per day. Coal was taken by horse-drawn cart down to the SWMR[63] at Tonmawr for onward shipment. As a consequence of the high rates charged by the SWMR, between 9d and 12d per ton, and the damage and loss caused by transshipment, it was announced that a separate company was to be formed to build a narrow (standard) gauge line to connect the levels to the Vale of Neath Railway (VoNR).[64] The local contractor

Fforchdwm Viaduct photographed on 19th October 1969. This viaduct was built circa 1840 to carry the Glyncorrwg Mineral Railway across the Pelenna Valley. The incline up to Blaencregan commenced on the far side and ran up to the right of the house. The track bed of the Whitworth Branch in the foreground ran through the left-hand arch. The viaduct was later considered to be a danger to the public and was blown up the Army on 14th July 1979.

Courtesy J A Peden

John Dickson was prepared to build the line, but required an outlay of £3,000 from the N&PC and a guarantee of 300 tons per day to make it pay.[65] These were not forthcoming and, as the coal could not be sold at an economic price, operations were suspended in July 1865. The N&PC went into liquidation in December 1865 and was dissolved in August 1873. The company had its own broad gauge wagons, nineteen of which were offered for sale at Court Sart siding, SWMR.[66]

The initiative for the proposed railway was taken up by George Bedford who had a lease on the Gnoll Estate north of Fforchdwm.[67] Bedford planned a single track, standard gauge, line from Clyne on the Neath Canal to Blaenycwm using Houghton's wharf and incline, with a branch into Cwm Pelenna to serve the N&PC. His intention was not so much to work Gnoll coal as to carry coal across the estate from Cefn Mawr and Fforchdwm. Prolonged negotiations resulted in an initial agreement for wayleaves not being made until March 1866, which by then incorporated a junction with VoNR near Resolven. The Vale of Neath & Cefn Mawr Junction Railway Company Ltd was registered on 5th May 1866 with a capital of £20,000. Construction started in 1867, but little more than the relaying of Houghtons' incline was achieved. The company was eventually wound up on 31st August 1883. The wayleave for the railway passed in 1869 to the Neath Merthyr Colliery Company who built the line to serve their Blaenycwm Colliery.

CWMAVON RAILWAY

In May 1838, three interrelated agreements were made which were to lead to the lower section of the original Cwmavon Tramroad from the harbour to Pant-du being replaced by a railway independent of the parish road:

- Mr Talbot leased from Robert Smith & Co. a portion of the Forge Field in which stood their Lower Forge Works, with powers to build a railway towards Cwmavon and a branch into the works.[68]
- John Vigurs & Co. leased from Robert Smith & Co. the Pant-du meadows and the land between the parish road from Aberavon to Cwmavon and the River Avon, for the purpose of making a railway.[69]
- Mr Talbot consented to John Vigurs & Co. making and using the railway to be built on his lands, and to Robert Smith & Co. using them.[70]

Also in May 1838, John Vigurs and Co. granted Robert Smith & Co. liberty to make a railway from their collieries at Tewgoed and Pwll-y-glau to connect with their line at Cwmavon, with reciprocal rights over each other's lines.[71] The new railway built on the two pieces of land crossed the Avon by a new bridge at Velindre, and was opened circa 1839. The upper section of the original tramroad, which skirted the hills to the north from Pant-du to Cwmavon Works, continued in use.

The English Copper Company took over the whole of Cwmavon Works (coal, iron, tinplate copper) from John Vigurs & Co. on 29th May 1841, thereby becoming proprietors of the new Cwmavon Railway and the remaining section of the old tramroad.[72] The works were developed considerably over the next few years, by the addition

ABOVE: Cwmavon and the Avon Valley circa 1848. English Copper Co.'s works in the centre and the hamlet of Pant-du in the bottom left, through which the Cwmavon Tramroad once passed. The recently constructed Cwmavon Railway runs diagonally across the view. The Oakwood Railway is just discernible following the left bank of the River Avon. The loop in the river crossed by the Cwmavon Railway was eliminated when the R&SBR Co. cut a new channel.

NM&GW

BELOW: Locomotives on the Cwmavon Railway, circa 1880. All Saints' Church, Cwmavon, is on the left. *Courtesy Arthur Rees*

ABOVE: The 1839 Cwmavon Railway was built to replace the earlier tramroad which followed the parish road. This railway was purchased in its entirety by the R&SBR Co. in 1882 to provide the basis of its line to Port Talbot. The view shows the R&SBR passing through the defile at Blackwells alongside the River Avon with the former Oakwood Railway, by now part of the Port Talbot Railway, on the other bank. The chimneys of Cwmavon Works are visible in the middle distance *Author's collection*

BELOW: Cwmavon Works saw many changes over the years. This view circa 1908 shows the out of use blast furnaces in the centre with the still operational tinplate works to the left. *Author's collection*

CWMAVON, GLAM

Port Talbot & Aberavon station GWR circa 1905, looking up the line towards Cardiff. Oakwood Crossing was just beyond the platforms and apparently still operational as evidenced by the signal on the right of the view, although probably little used. *Author's collection*

of three more blast furnaces, a rail mill, and a large engineering works known as the "Depot". The company also acquired the blast furnaces at Pontrhydyfen and the coal and ironstone properties at Oakwood and Mynydd Bychan further up the valley.

First to be developed, in 1841, was coal working at Bryn in the Duffryn Valley.[73] Coal and ironstone were brought two miles over the high ground by tramroad, then lowered by a 600 yard long self-acting incline to a new bridge over the Avon at Ynys Avon and thence into the works.[74]

A locomotive was introduced to the upper section of this tramroad in 1845, having the distinction of the being the first in the district.[75] The gauge is unknown, but was probably the same as the rest of the works lines. A second locomotive was at work on the line from Cwmavon to Port Talbot by the end of 1845. At least one of these engines was built by the Neath Abbey Iron Co.[76] One of them, named *Redruth*, was involved in a fatal accident near Velindre in June 1848.[77] This incident is also noteworthy for the large number of men, twenty-five, riding on the trams. The company owned three locomotives and 2,250 trams and wagons in 1849.[78]

Sometime around 1847 a new direct line to the works was built, crossing the river twice by wooden bridges.[79] It proceeded up the valley to cross the Bryn Tramroad, where a connection allowed access to the blast furnaces and copper works, continued to Tymaen where it intersected with the Oakwood Railway, and terminated in the Oakwood Works.

The Cwmavon Railway survived the period when the English Copper Company was in financial difficulties and the Bank of England, as mortgagees, took possession of Cwmavon Works from April 1848 to May 1852.[80] The Oakwood Works and collieries were brought to a standstill.[81] One of the outstanding issues was the arrears of rent and royalties of £15,000 due to Mr Talbot. He threatened to take possession of the collieries at Bryn and the tramroad connecting them to Cwmavon if payment was not made

and the furnaces at Oakwood kept in use. The bank was forced to hand over *Redruth* and 100 new coal trams, which were sent to Bryn. Common sense prevailed, Mr Talbot having agreed to an advance of £5,000,[82] and the works and collieries were soon back in operation.[83]

Further prosperity followed the resulting reorganisation of the English Copper Company in 1852, but it failed again in August 1876 and was compelled to go into liquidation.[84] In April 1877 all the company's property and assets were sold to James Shaw, managing director of the Cwmavon Estate & Works Co. Ltd. By now the length of the Cwmavon Railway was 6,230 yards (about 3½ miles), 2,800 belonging to Lord Jersey, 2,030 to the Talbot Estate and 1,400 to the PT Co.[85] Those parts belonging to Mr Talbot and the PT Co. were leased in 1878 for sixty-one years to Messrs Shaw & Co. Later that year the tinplate section of Cwmavon Works was sold on to the Copper Miners' Tinplate Co. Ltd.[86] The Cwmavon Estate & Works Co. continued to operate the copper works, blast furnaces and collieries until it was forced into liquidation in June 1882 by the depressed state of the metal market. The business was eventually acquired by a new undertaking styled the Cwmavon Works Proprietors under the management of Samuel Danks.[87] A steelworks was added to the complex at Cwmavon, but the copper works remained idle. By 1889 the blast furnaces, steelworks and collieries had passed to Messrs Wright, Butler & Co. Ltd, whose chairman was John Roper Wright.[88] Col Wright was later to play a prominent role in the promotion and development of the Port Talbot Railway & Docks Company.

No contemporary record of the original gauges of the Oakwood and Cwmavon railways has been found. In documents of the 1890s, the gauge of the Oakwood Railway is given variously as 4ft 3ins[89] and 4ft 5ins,[90] whereas that of the Cwmavon Railway, with which it at one time connected, is stated as being 4ft 5ins.[91] One might surmise that the true gauge of both lines was 4ft 4ins.

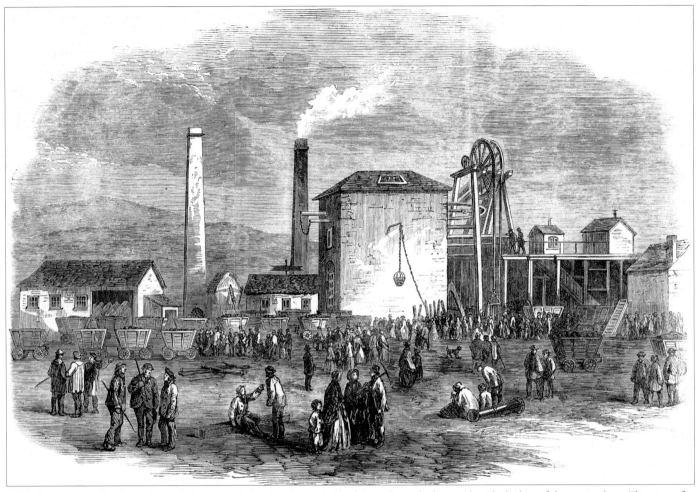

Morfa Colliery suffered a major explosion on 17th October 1863, the third since the pit had opened, with the loss of thirty-nine lives. This view of the scene at the pithead during rescue operations was published in *The Illustrated London News* on 31st October 1863. The wagons appear to be too big to have been used underground, and were probably those employed to transport coal to Messrs Vivian's works and wharves about one and a half miles away.

Author's collection

The opening in 1850 of the SWR, which crossed the Cwmavon Railway on the level, offered improved communication from Cwmavon Works to inland destinations, but the gauge difference necessitated transshipment at Port Talbot, and most traffic still passed through the dock, being handled at the company's wharf (later Talbot Wharf), and shipped coastwise for distribution.[92] A good deal of locomotive-hauled works traffic used the crossing in 1854–57.[93] The GWR Board approved additional accommodation for the interchange of traffic with the English Copper Company at Port Talbot in August 1869.[94] The Copper Company had one siding 200 yards in length for interchange of traffic at Port Talbot in 1871.[95] The Cwmavon Railway was converted to standard gauge, presumably at or shortly after the gauge conversion in 1872. A single west to south connection with the GWR was in place by July 1875,[96] and two more by October 1877.[97] The Oakwood line was not converted, being virtually moribund at the time.

Although the Cwmavon Railway was used primarily for the conveyance of exports and imports to and from the dock, a carriage ran between Cwmavon and Port Talbot for the convenience of the public.[98] It usually travelled down the gradient alone and was worked back to Cwmavon attached to goods trains.[99]

MORFA RAILWAY

Meanwhile, Margam Copper Works had expanded with the introduction of new machinery and processes. More coal was needed than was available from the Brombil district. In 1849 the first coal was raised from the Albion Pit of Morfa Colliery, situated on Margam Moors close to the sea on land leased by Messrs Vivian & Sons from Mr Talbot. A contemporary writer noted that a locomotive was working on the connecting railway shortly after the colliery opened.[100] This engine may have preceded the two built by the Neath Abbey Iron Co. to a gauge of 4ft 4ins in 1855 and 1859.[101] Morfa Colliery proved to be very productive, and a considerable proportion of the output was exported from Port Talbot.[102] In 1854, of the 77,000 tons of Morfa coal shipped, 40,000 tons went to Devon and Cornwall, and in 1869 20,000 tons went to Ireland. To expedite the shipment of coal Vivians erected four wooden tips alongside the channel leading to their works. These were of the type designed to minimise coal breakage by lowering wagons or iron boxes into a ship's hold. This method of loading was in use until 1895 when work started on improving the dock.[103]

The SWR, which was opened in 1850, ran through the middle of the copper works, separating the mill from the smelters, and was utilised to exchange traffic with Vivian's Works at Swansea. In 1866,

Neath Abbey Ironworks locomotive built for Vivian & Sons' Morfa Colliery, possibly *Tubal Cain* supplied new by Neath Abbey Ironworks in 1859. *Courtesy Arthur Rees*

the 2.40 pm Swansea to Paddington goods train was instructed to load sufficiently lightly to take Messrs Vivian & Sons' trucks from Hafod siding, Swansea, to Margam siding. Return traffic was to be taken by the 8.30 am Stormy and the 2.40 pm Llantrissant to Swansea coal trains.[104]

Morfa Colliery was connected to the SWR at Margam siding near milepost 201. In 1871 the colliery siding was described as mixed gauge,[105] presumably the original 4ft 4ins and the broad gauge. Indeed, the colliery had advertised for 10-ton broad gauge trucks in 1857[106] and narrow gauge colliery wagons in 1862.[107] The colliery siding was not included in the 1872 gauge conversion scheme,[108] Vivian's having to do this work themselves. However, Vivian's sand siding off the SWR north-west of Port Talbot and a lengthy siding from near Port Talbot station to the copper works were converted by the GWR. Vivian's two 4ft 4 ins gauge locomotives were converted in 1872,[109] and presumably worked mixed gauge trains over the colliery branch until then. Morfa Colliery closed in 1913 and the Morfa Railway was acquired by Baldwins Ltd to access a tipping ground on which the Abbey Works were eventually constructed.

Thus by 1850 there were four railways operational in the Avon Valley. Three served the dock and growing industries in the Port Talbot area, whilst Parsons and Strange's tramroad was conveying coal from the Tonmawr area to Aberdulais for shipment on the Neath Canal and the VoNR. In June that year the SWR opened from Chepstow to Swansea, the first step to the opening, in June 1852, of through rail communication from Port Talbot via Gloucester to the whole of Great Britain.

SOUTH WALES MINERAL RAILWAY

In May 1851 a report appeared in *The Cardiff & Merthyr Guardian* of a projected railway to Port Talbot.[110] The route was alleged to be from Maesteg through a tunnel under Blaen Llynvi to the Avon Valley where a junction would be made with a contemplated railway down to Port Talbot. Its purpose was to provide a cheap outlet for the works in the upper Llynvi Valley, and to circumvent the manifold deficiencies of the Duffryn Llynvi & Porthcawl

Railway (DL&PR). The writer had probably become aware of, and misunderstood, plans that were soon to become embodied in the Maesteg, Glyncorrwg & Briton Ferry Railway (MG&BFR), but were then at an early stage. In December 1851 *The Cambrian* reported that a prospectus had been issued for the construction of this railway, fifteen miles in length, from a junction with the SWR at Briton Ferry Dock to serve the Avon, Llynvi and Corrwg valleys.[111] An Act authorising the construction of this dock had been passed in the previous July.[112] The distance of the new line to the Avon Valley was stated to be seven miles, at which point two branches each four miles long were to lead to Maesteg and Glyncorrwg. The capital required was estimated to be £150,000. The major landowners were willing to proved the necessary land for free.

A public meeting of local landowners and businessmen to discuss the proposed railway was held on 16th July 1852,[113] although not before an anonymous correspondent had suggested that Port Talbot would be a better terminus than Briton Ferry.[114] The chairman, Nash Edwards-Vaughan, declared that the area to be served was rich in steam coal and iron ore and deserved better means of communication. No engineering problems for the broad gauge line were expected despite the need for two tunnels. Robert Parsons was a prominent speaker, and predicted a traffic of 545,000 tons per annum from the three valleys, which would generate a return of 7½ per cent on the capital outlay. Charles Hampton, the manager of the Llynvi Ironworks, spoke in favour of the scheme, and pointed out that the only reason some works in the Llynvi Valley were currently idle was the cost of conveyance to Porthcawl, at 3s 4d per ton, whereas to Briton Ferry would be 9d per ton. Dugdale Houghton of Fforchdwm near Tonmawr was elected chairman of the provisional committee.[115]

Another meeting was held on 4th September 1852, the chairman this time being Viscount Villiers, chairman of the VoNR.[116] Robert Parsons, described as a very active promoter of the line, informed the meeting that a group of wealthy capitalists from Liverpool were prepared to work the coal in the Glyncorrwg area if a means of transport could be assured. This involvement marked the beginning of the transfer of the controlling interests to outside parties. For

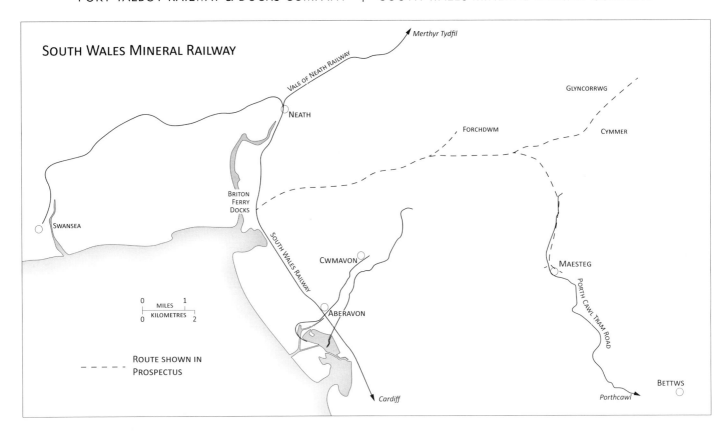

the first time the question of gradients was raised. William Rosser, who had surveyed the line, stated that apart from the first mile at Ynysmaerdy the next seven miles were level, followed by 1 in 80 up to Glyncorrwg. Houghton found it necessary to remind the meeting that although he had personally expended a good deal of money in preparing the plans, this was to be a public railway, respectable in every way.

The proposed line was put to the public at a meeting on 18th September 1852. Two months later a Parliamentary Notice dated 4th November 1852 was published.[117] In the meantime a significant change had occurred. The line was now called the South Wales Mineral Railway, although its proposed routes remained the same. These were:

- a main line, length 11m 3f 4ch, which commenced at a point adjacent to the SWR about three-quarters of a mile west of Briton Ferry station and terminated at Glyncorrwg, and which was connected by a back-shunt to a facing siding off the Down SWR main line,
- a branch railway, length 3m 2f 8ch, leaving the main line at 7m 7f and running through a 1,760 yard long tunnel under Mynydd Caerau into the Llynvi Valley and terminating near Maesteg Ironworks,
- a short branch railway from the above, length 1f 8ch, terminating near the Llynvi Ironworks,
- a branch railway from Tonmawr on the main line, length 7f 2ch, terminating at Fforchdwm Colliery.

The engineer was Isambard Kingdom Brunel (1806–59), whose estimate for the construction of these works was £77,500.[118] The South Wales Mineral Railway Company had been registered

in October 1852 to make and maintain these railways, the sole promoter being named as Dugdale Houghton.[119]

The prospect of a line into the upper Llynvi Valley, taking traffic from the works there, was not appealing to the directors of the Llynvi Valley Railway (LVR). At their meeting on 25th November they resolved to instruct their solicitors to take the necessary steps to oppose the Bill in Parliament.[120] The officers of the LVR were instructed to ensure the continuance of traffic from the various works in return for the contemplated improvements of their line. At this time these consisted of easing some of the curves of the erstwhile DL&PR and the introduction of locomotives,[121] as described below.

A new prospectus was issued in January 1853, this time in the name of the South Wales Mineral Railway Company.[122] Of the twenty-three directors listed, about one half were recognisably local men, the remainder residing in London or the Midlands. Robert Parsons was named as secretary. Capitalisation was put at £150,000, in shares of £10 each. The estimated cost of the works had risen to £130,000, the balance of £20,000 of the capital being available for the construction of branches to other ironworks and collieries. The railways proposed to be built were necessarily as described above, but with one significant addition. This was for a proposed junction with the improved LYR at Blaen Llynvi, which would allow easy access of Glyncorrwg steam coal to the valuable Cardiff market.

The LVR directors reaffirmed their opposition to the SWMR Bill until the Llynvi Valley Branch was withdrawn.[123] They also rejected a proposed amalgamation of the two lines which was supported by a SWMR deputation, Messrs Houghton, Knox and Parsons, who had attended the Board. However, it became apparent at a special meeting of LVR proprietors later that day that the Board was split on the matter.[124] The majority of the directors were in favour of the position stated above. The minority faction, led by Mr MacGreggor, the deputy chairman, was in favour of an amalgamation of the two broad gauge companies, and had gone so far as to draw up heads of an agreement with the SWMR for that purpose. After a spirited discussion the majority view prevailed in a vote. Houghton attended the LVR Board meeting on 31st March 1853 and informed the directors that it was the intention of the promoters of the SWMR to withdraw the branch to the Llynvi Valley, provided the LVR withdrew its opposition to the remainder of the Bill. This was agreed, thereby saving the SWMR promoters the expense of a Parliamentary contest, and the first attempt to link the upper Avon and Llynvi valleys by a railway came to nothing.

Thus modified, the SWMR Bill had an uneventful passage through Parliament, the only other significant amendment being the deletion of powers for the line to be worked by the SWR, VoNR and Briton Ferry Floating Dock Co. as these not been approved by the respective proprietors.[125] The resulting South Wales Mineral Railway Act, 1853, received the Royal Assent on 15th August 1853.[126] The line to Glyncorrwg was eventually opened in March 1863.[127]

AFON VALLEY RAILWAY

During the 1860s a second scheme to join the Avon and upper Llynvi valleys by a railway was promoted. In October 1864 *The Cambrian* reported that a deputation of local dignitaries had had an interview with Mr Talbot regarding the construction of a railway though the Avon Valley on the Margam side of the river to Cymmer and to Mynydd Caerau in the Llynvi Valley, and had gained his approval.[128] The scheme seems to have originated with the contractor John Dickson,[129] who had surveyed the route,[130] and was supported by Sir John Pelly, David Thomas and William Struvé, respectively governor, colliery manger and works manager of the Cwmavon Works of the English Copper Company.[131]

The route of the proposed line, to be known as the Afon Valley Railway (AVR), became clearer with the publication of a Parliamentary Notice dated 14th November 1864.[132] The intended line consisted of a railway just over eight miles long, leaving the SWR main line at or near Port Talbot station and curving north-east parallel with the left bank of the River Avon. After crossing the river twice, it passed through a 242 yard long tunnel under Craig Avon and followed the river to Oakwood. It then passed through a second tunnel, 275 yards long, and continued up Avon Valley, before curving away, somewhat short of Cymmer, up alongside Nant Trafael, crossing over to the Llynvi Valley and terminating at Blaencaerau. Here a second railway, two miles long, commenced by a trailing junction and proceeded down the Llynvi Valley to a junction with the LVR near Maesteg Ironworks. The maximum gradient was 1 in 40. The engineer was James Gordon McKenzie.[133] An essay extolling the advantages of this scheme was awarded a prize at the Eisteddfod held at Aberavon in 1865.[134]

Not surprisingly, the LVR was not happy with this scheme, and petitioned against the AVR Bill claiming that the preamble was incapable of proof, as the existing railways (the Cwmavon Railway, SWMR, LVR) served the needs of the district adequately, and also on account of the gradients and shortage of space at the site chosen for the junction with its line.[135] The LVR was successful to the extent that Railway No. 2 was deleted from the Bill, and gained a concession that should the AVR in the future be connected to any part of its line the LVR could use the AVR and all its facilities. A SWMR petition against the Bill was withdrawn.[136] The Afon Valley Railway Act, 1865, gained the Royal Assent on 6th July 1865.[137]

The authorised capital of the new company was £130,000, in shares of £10, and up to £43,000 could be borrowed on mortgage. The gauge of the new line was not specified, although a clause in the Act suggests it was to be to the standard gauge. This clause authorised the AVR and GWR to lay down an additional line of rails to the narrow (standard) gauge on the SWR main line between the Oakwood Railway Crossing and Port Talbot Dock Junction. Quite what was intended by this provision is not clear, although it would have allowed AVR trains access to Port Talbot Dock if the Dock Branch was also so modified. Alteration of the Dock Branch did not require Parliamentary approval as it was a private railway. There is no mention of the Oakwood Railway in the Act, suggesting that the new line was intended to run parallel to it and not over any part of its course.

At their first meeting the AVR directors offered the contract for the construction of their railway to an "eminent" contractor,[138] this presumably being John Dickson. They were also planning three short extensions to their authorised line, including a different route to the Llynvi Valley, which were revealed in a Parliamentary Notice dated 14th November 1865.[139]

The proposed railways consisted of a one mile long branch from New Wharf (later known as North Bank) in Port Talbot Dock, which joined the authorised line near Margam Tinplate Works, and a two mile long connection from near Pontrhydyfen on the authorised line to a point on the SWMR seven miles from Briton Ferry. The company also proposed an alternative route into the Llynvi Valley, this time commencing with a facing junction on the authorised line near Blaen Llynvi and terminating near the Llynvi Ironworks.[140] The engineer was again James McKenzie. The AVR also planned to buy or lease the Cwmavon Railway from the English Copper Company, and to abandon so much of it as would be made unnecessary by the construction of its own line, to make agreements with the PT Co. regarding the management and use of the facilities at Port Talbot Dock, and to rearrange its share capital. There must have been considerable opposition to this Bill, or the company had a change of heart, as the Afon Valley Railway Act, 1866, which gained the Royal Assent on 18th May 1866,[141] was restricted to financial matters, whereby the company was authorised to divide its shares into half shares so as to raise funds more easily. Later that year the AVR announced its intention to apply to Parliament in the next Session for powers similar to those asked for in 1866, the principal difference being the omission of a branch to the SWMR.[142] Perhaps reflecting its lack of achievement, nothing was done to further this application.

As little or no progress had been made in constructing the AVR, the company intended to return to Parliament in 1868 to seek an extension of time and modification of its powers. This time a much more modest line was proposed, being a railway from Port Talbot to a junction with the SWMR.[143] This was to be achieved by a short link from the authorised railway near Port Talbot to the Cwmavon Railway, purchase or lease of the latter, and by the construction of a three mile extension of the Cwmavon Railway to a junction with the SWMR just east of Gyfylchi Tunnel. The engineer was again

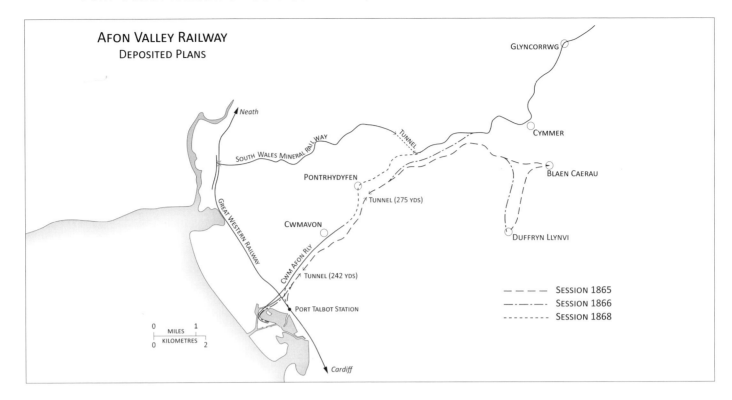

AFON VALLEY RAILWAY
DEPOSITED PLANS

— — — — SESSION 1865
—·—·— SESSION 1866
– – – – – SESSION 1868

James McKenzie, who estimated the cost of the new lines to be £34,000. The remainder of the line authorised in 1865 was to be abandoned.[144]

Although the Petition for the Bill was deposited in the Private Bill Office of Parliament, there were no further proceedings. Nevertheless, *The Cambrian* reported that the AVR had applied to the Board of Trade on 16th July 1868 for an extension of time of two years – that is, to 6th July 1870 for compulsory purchase and 6th July 1872 for completion.[145] This was agreed to, but then withdrawn due to objections made by landowners.[146] In the meantime Richard Hanbury Miers, a shareholder and director of the AVR, and one of the sureties to the Bond conditional for the completion of the railway, had applied for authority to abandon the railway. The grounds given were that nothing had been done towards its construction, there were no funds, only £21,000 of the share capital had been issued, solely as security for services rendered, and there was no prospect of the company making the railway within the prescribed time. On enquiry, the Board of Trade found that a contract for the construction of the line for £173,000 had been sealed, to be paid in shares and debentures, but before any work was done the contractor became insolvent, John Dickson being declared bankrupt on 30th September 1867.[147] Nothing had been paid on any of the shares. Consequently, the Board of Trade agreed to the abandonment of the AVR, the warrant being dated 13th July 1870.[148] A hearing into the liquidation of the company was held on 20th March 1871.[149]

PORT TALBOT HARBOUR & RHONDDA VALLEY RAILWAY

The next attempt to construct a railway up the Avon Valley came in 1871. This time the objective was the upper Rhondda Valley, where coal had been proved in the mid-1850s. The route of the aptly named Port Talbot Harbour & Rhondda Valley Railway (PTH&RVR) was in effect an extension of the AVR scheme of

1868.[150] It used the Cwmavon Railway as far as Cwmavon Works, then followed the river upstream to eventually make a junction with the SWMR near the east end of Gyfylchi Tunnel. From here a new line ran parallel to the SWMR, effectively a widening of the latter, to Cymmer. It then ran up to the head of the valley at Blaenavon Farm and through a 3,663 yard long tunnel on a 1 in 50 down gradient to make a triangular junction with the Taff Vale Railway (TVR) near Treorchy.[151] The engineer was Frederick Barry, who estimated the cost to be £352,631. The new company also sought powers to lease or purchase the Port Talbot Railway (*sic*, probably the Oakwood Railway) and the Cwmavon Railway together with all their facilities, and also the wharves and other property of the PT Co. Reciprocal running powers were to be sought over the GWR between Port Talbot and Briton Ferry, the SWMR, and several branches of the TVR north of Pontypridd. The promoters of this ambitious scheme are not known, but the solicitors for the Bill were the London firm of Messrs Baxter, Rose, Norton & Co., who were involved with a number of railway schemes in the second half of the nineteenth century, including an interest in the SWMR.[152] According to *The Cambrian*, colliery proprietors in the Rhondda were expected to support the scheme as it would be of considerable advantage to them.[153] The Bill was deposited but withdrawn before any proceedings had taken place.

PORT TALBOT & RHONDDA RAILWAY

The PTH&RVR scheme was a pointer to future railway developments in the Avon Valley. In September 1879 Yockney produced a report on the proposed Port Talbot & Rhondda Railway (PT&RR) for which he was engineer.[154] The intention was to give the Rhondda Valley collieries access to Port Talbot, which had recently been much improved by Mr Talbot.[155] Mr Talbot was reported to support the scheme,[156] but was not one of the promoters and could not consent to be one of the committee.[157] The line would also bring Swansea to

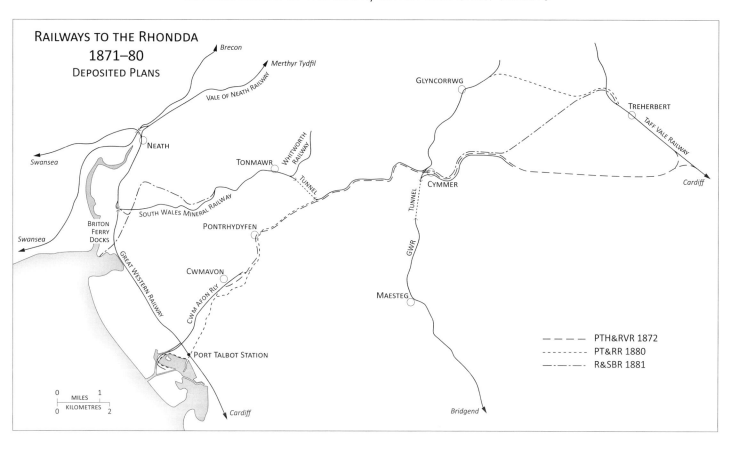

the same distance from the Rhondda as Cardiff. The Parliamentary Notice was dated 13th November 1879.[158]

The proposed route commenced with a short connection with the Cwmavon Railway on Talbot Wharf at Port Talbot and then made use of the Oakwood Railway as far as Oakwood Colliery, whence a new line three miles long was to cross the River Avon by a viaduct and proceed up the hillside to make a junction with the SWMR near the eastern end of Gyfylchi Tunnel. From here it was proposed to use the SWMR to Glyncorrwg, a distance of five and a half miles. From Glyncorrwg the line passed through a 3,266 yard long tunnel on a slight down gradient to a junction at Blaencwm with a line authorised by the TVR Act of 1873. There were also to be short connections with the GWR towards Swansea near Port Talbot station, with the Cwmavon Railway, to Tewgoed Colliery and to the Express Tinplate Works, Cwmavon. Yockney's estimate for the works was £293,354.[159] Yockney's report also considered an alternative route, leaving the SWMR at Cymmer, passing up the Avon Valley, and through a tunnel to a junction with the TVR near Treochy, much as the PTH&RVR scheme of 1871–72. However, he found the Glyncorrwg route to be £37,000 cheaper, and had more favourable gradients against the load, 1 in 85 compared to 1 in 50.

The promoters were Philip William Flower, George Henry Davey, Richard Phillips and William Jones. These gentlemen and seventeen others formed a provisional committee under the chairmanship of William Llewellyn. The secretary was H S Ludlow,[160] who was later the first secretary of the R&SBR. However, all was not plain sailing. Early in January 1880, Messrs Byass & Co., who, as noted above, were making use of the Oakwood Railway, informed the committee that they would require the use of the new railway without any

kind of restriction as if no railway company was in existence. Furthermore, some who agreed to join the committee had now decided not to do so. Consequently Yockney recommended the committee not to proceed. The Bill, which sought Parliamentary authorisation for a capital of £300,000, had been deposited in the Private Bill Office, but no-one appeared on behalf of the promoters and it was struck out as dead.

RHONDDA & SWANSEA BAY RAILWAY[161]

Swansea had long agitated for better railway connections and to be able to participate in the export of coal from the Rhondda Valley.[162] Originally the city was served by an awkward branch off the SWR main line at Landore, which was eased only partially by the opening of the Swansea & Neath Railway (S&NR) in 1863.[163] By 1880, this situation was becoming intolerable, and there was mounting clamour for a railway crossing of the River Neath estuary at Briton Ferry. The subject was aired at a meeting in Swansea on 12th October 1880.[164] At this meeting John Richardson Francis stated that an economic course of action would be to utilise the SWMR from Briton Ferry to Glyncorrwg, followed by a tunnel through the mountain to Treherbert, apparently overlooking the drawback of the rope-worked Ynysmaerdy Incline.[165] This proposal employed elements of the PT&RR scheme of 1879–80.

Further rapid planning ensued, and a Parliamentary Notice dated 18th November 1880 was published.[166] This announced the intention to apply to Parliament for the incorporation of a company to be known as the Rhondda & Swansea Bay Railway (R&SBR) Company, and for powers to build a railway from Briton Ferry to the Rhondda. The proposed route commenced at a junction with the SWMR where it crossed the SWR main line at Briton Ferry

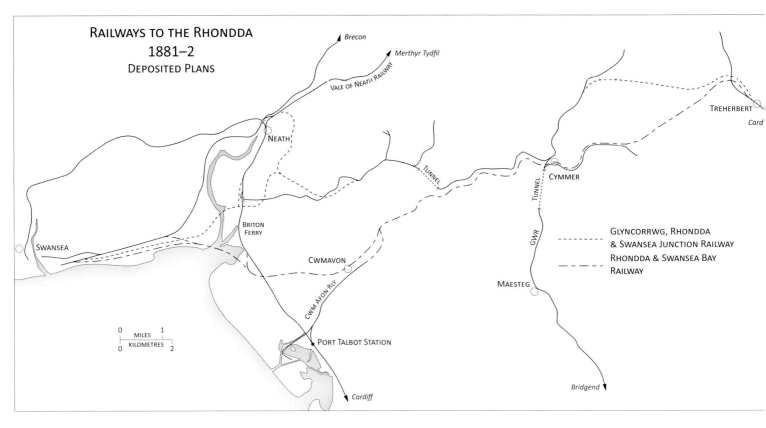

and headed north and then east, up alongside Nant Crythan to rejoin the SWMR near its milepost 3¼, thus bypassing the incline. The SWMR was then followed for six miles to Cymmer, where a new line was to branch off up the Avon Valley to Abergwynfi and through a 3,364 yard long tunnel to terminate by a junction with a siding belonging to Thomas Joseph at Dunraven Colliery in the Rhondda Valley. There was also to be a branch from near the bottom of the old incline to Briton Ferry Docks. The engineers were Sidney William Yockney and his father Samuel Hansard Yockney, who estimated the cost of the works to be £315,000.[167] The new company proposed to take out of use the bypassed section of the SWMR, seemingly ignoring the collieries situated along it, to take over all or part of the SWMR, and if necessary to require the SWMR Company to lay additional lines of rails and to adapt its line for use by passenger trains. There was no application for powers to cross the River Neath, the intention seemingly being to make a start on part of the line.

The Bill named the Earl of Jersey, Charles Bath, Thomas Cory, John Richardson Francis and Thomas Joseph as the promoters, and put the capital at £330,000, with powers to borrow a further £110,000.[168] Petitions against the Bill came from the GWR, the TVR, the SWMR and the Marquis of Bute. The Swansea Harbour Trust and the inhabitants of Briton Ferry and the Rhondda Valley petitioned in favour.[169] The Bill came before a committee of the House of Lords in March 1881.[170] It soon became apparent that there was an insurmountable technical issue regarding the siding connection at Dunraven Colliery, and on 4th March the promoters, rather than forego the railway from Cymmer to the Rhondda, decided to withdraw their Bill.

The same promoters announced their intention to bring in a much modified Bill in the 1882 Session in *The London Gazette*.[171]

This time the line was to run from a junction with the TVR near Treherbert through a tunnel to Abergwynfi, then down the Avon Valley to Cwmavon and through a tunnel under Mynydd Dinas to Baglan between Aberavon and Briton Ferry. From here the main line continued over the River Neath and on to Swansea. There were to be connections to the GWR near Briton Ferry, to the S&NR near Jersey Marine, from Pontrhydyfen to the Cwmavon Railway, and to the Tewgoed Branch of the Oakwood Railway. Messrs Yockney were again the engineers, who estimated these works to cost £467,736.[172] The new company also sought powers to purchase the Cwmavon Railway and use it as part of their undertaking,.

The same issue of *The London Gazette* also announced a rival scheme, to be known as the Glyncorrwg, Rhondda & Swansea Junction Railway (GR&SJR). This line also commenced near Treherbert, but ran through a tunnel to Glyncorrwg, in a similar fashion to the PTH&RVR scheme of 1880, and then made use of the SWMR to beyond Tonmawr. From here a new line was to skirt round the high ground to avoid Ynysmaerdy Incline, reminiscent of the R&SBR 1881 route, to make a junction with the GWR between Briton Ferry and Neath. Swansea was to be reached by a connecting line from near the bottom of the incline. There were also to be connections to the GWR near Swansea and to the VoNR near Neath, the latter providing an alternative route to Swansea via the S&NR. In effect, this proposal amounted to an extension of the SWMR. The engineers were William Morris (1836–86) and Trevor Thomas, who estimated the coast of the works to be £452,750.[173] As with the R&SBR scheme of 1881, this new company proposed to acquire the SWMR and to abandon its incline. The promoters of the GR&SJR were Samuel Laing, Sir Philip Rose, William Perch and Thomas Walker, and the solicitors were Messrs Norton, Rose, Norton & Brewer, with whom Sir Philip was once a partner.[174]

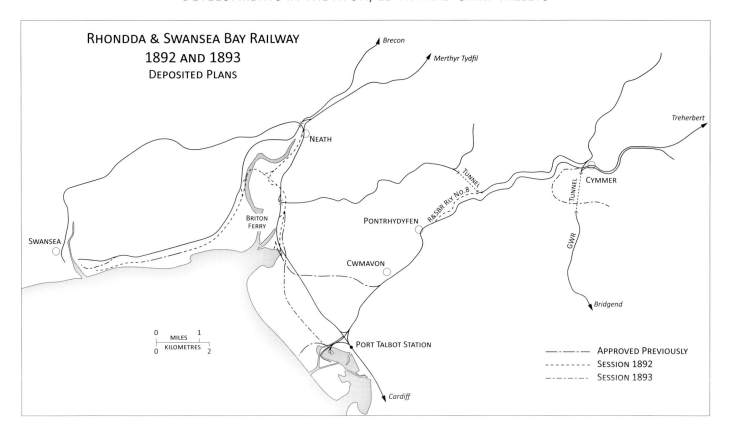

William Perch was one of the trustees of the Glyncorrwg Colliery Co. which leased the SWMR. By the time the GR&SJR Bill was printed the promoters had reached agreement with the SWMR regarding running powers over and repairs to its line, acquisition of that undertaking having been abandoned.[175] Two reports extolling the merits of the GR&SJR scheme were prepared, one by the engineer Trevor Thomas comparing it to the R&SBR scheme of 1881,[176] the other anonymously comparing it to the latest R&SBR proposal.[177] Both favoured the GR&SJR, the principal reasons being that it made use of an existing railway, it served more collieries, and it connected with other local railways.

The competing Bills were considered by a House of Lords Committee in March 1882, the GR&SJR proposal being taken first.[178] After two weeks of legal argument the committee found on 30th March that the preamble to the GR&SJR Bill had not been proved and that the preamble to the R&SBR Bill had been proved, subject to a discussion of a clause relating to the Cwmavon Tramway and one or two other minor points. The next day the GR&SJR's application seeking approval of its SWMR incline avoiding line was rejected, and its Bill was reported as not being expedient to proceed with.[179]

During the hearing it became apparent that one of the problems was putting a bridge across the River Neath. The promoters of the R&SBR case therefore removed all reference to their line from Briton Ferry to Swansea from their Bill, thereby enabling it to be passed. After amendment by the House of Lords and further amendment by the House of Commons, the R&SBR Act gained the Royal Assent on 10th August 1882.[180] Building a railway across the River Neath proved to be a protracted business, not being resolved until the passing of the R&SBR Act of 1892. The capital of the new company was set at £450,000, with powers to borrow up

to £150,000. Powers to purchase, maintain and use the Cwmavon Railway were confirmed, with the restriction that no R&SBR train was to run over the level crossing at Port Talbot within fifteen minutes of a non-stop GWR passenger train being due. The new company also undertook to pay half the cost of obviating the level crossing if the GWR gained powers for this purpose. A schedule attached to the Act granted special rates to the Cwmavon Estate & Works Co. Ltd for traffic carried to Port Talbot on the Cwmavon Railway over which they hitherto had right of use. A similar agreement was made with Messrs Byass & Co. on 25th March 1882 for goods conveyed between Tewgoed Colliery, Margam Tinplate Works, Mansel Tinplate Works and Port Talbot Docks.[181] Messrs Byass were also empowered to lay a third rail along the length of the R&SBR's branch to Tewgoed Colliery so as to correspond with that of the Oakwood Railway, and to require the promoters to lay in a connection with their Margam Tinplate Works.

The 1882 Act provided the basis for the route of the R&SBR along the length of the Avon Valley and through to Treherbert. The only modification was a slight alteration to the point of connection to the Cwmavon Railway, which was authorised retrospectively by its 1886 Act.[182] The 1882 Act required the R&SBR to purchase, within three years of its passing, that part of the Cwmavon Railway lying between the junction of the proposed branch to Tewgoed Colliery and its termination in Port Talbot Docks, including the junctions with the GWR at Aberavon, a total 5,850 yards.[183] A total of £65,000 was paid for what Yockney described as three and a half miles of very indifferent line, of which £53,000 went to Mr Talbot and Messrs Shaw & Co., the then owners of Cwmavon Works.[184] A further £60,000 was spent in remaking the Cwmavon Railway, which included some doubling to facilitate Wright, Butler's traffic, and the diversion of the River Avon for about quarter of a mile between

A general view of the railways at Cymmer circa 1910 showing on the far left the SWMR heading up to Glyncorrwg, and the 1878 viaduct across the River Avon carrying the short railway connecting the SWMR and LVR. The R&SBR climbs up from the bottom of the picture on its was to the Rhondda Tunnel and passes under the viaduct to reach its two platform station left of centre. The LVR emerges from Cymmer Tunnel on the far right, curving round to its single platform station in the centre of the view and continuing up the valley to Abergwynfi. Glyn Cymmer Colliery at the bottom was connected to both the LVR and the R&SBR. *Author's collection*

Pantdu and Cwmavon Works to eliminate two timber bridges over the river. The improved Cwmavon Railway was the cheapest part of the R&SBR and gave it easy access to Port Talbot Docks.

The 1886 Act also authorised the company to abandon its line through Mynydd Dinas to Baglan as the intended route towards Swansea. On 13th August 1885 the company had concluded an agreement whereby the GWR would convey its traffic thence. Consequently, the 1886 Act provided for a west to north connection with the GWR at Aberavon, and also with the GWR at Cymmer, thereby giving access to the Llynvi Valley. The first section of the R&SBR from Aberavon to Pontrhydyfen was opened on 25th June 1885,[185] but it was not until 14th July 1890 that the line to Treherbert was finished. Following the termination of the agreement with the GWR as allowed by the company's 1891 Act,[186] the R&SBR upgraded the Cwmavon Railway to Talbot Wharf in Port Talbot Dock and opened its Port Talbot Docks station there on 25th July 1891. This station was closed to the public 14th March 1895 when the coastal route towards Swansea opened, but remained in use for workmen's trains for many years.[187]

In 1891 the R&SBR, ever looking for ways to increase the traffic on its railway, announced the first proposal for a new line to provide a westward outlet for coal and other traffic from the upper Avon Valley.[188] Among other provisions, the company was authorised by its 1892 Act[189] to make Railway No. 8 from Pontrhydyfen to Nantybar on the SWMR, a distance of one and three quarter miles. This railway was estimated to cost £12,012 and featured a gradient of 1 in 40/47 up to a junction with the SWMR near the east end of Gyfylchi Tunnel.[190] This line would have provided an alternative to the SWMR to Briton Ferry via Ynysmaerdy Incline,

but as the dock at Port Talbot was still in a poor state, its advantages are not clear. It was also related to an offer from the R&SBR to the SWMR directors, reported on 17th March 1892, to work their line for 70 per cent of the receipts, to put that line in order, and pay off the loans.[191] Terms could not be agreed, however, and the offer was withdrawn in May 1892. The R&SBR directors reviewed their offer in July 1895 and in the December revised the terms to 60 per cent of the receipts, having decided on 28th November to proceed with their 1892 Railway No. 8.[192] The SWMR, however, aligned itself with the PT Company in January 1896,[193] and in September and October 1896 announced its intention to resist any attempt by the R&SBR to make a junction with its railway.[194] Time was running out for the completion of Railway No. 8 and the R&SBR obtained an extension of two years in its 1897 Act.[195] Although it had by now lost its opportunity to tap SWMR traffic, the R&SBR let a contract for the construction of Railway No. 8 in November 1897.[196] The SWMR directors relented in April 1898 and approved the plan for the junction provided their line was not moved.[197] Progress was slow and the connection was not reported to be completed until June 1899.[198] Despite being built there is no evidence that the connection ever saw any revenue earning traffic. It was reported on 5th February 1909 that the easement for the junction should include an arrangement whereby the R&SBR would not open the junction for coal traffic provided the SWMR did not cross the River Avon (presumably at Cymmer) and divert traffic now served by the R&SBR,[199] a condition easily complied with. The junction was taken out in December 1917 as a cost saving measure,[200] and Railway No. 8 was eventually abandoned under the GWR's 1929 Act.[201]

The R&SBR's Port Talbot (Aberavon) station looking up the line towards Cwmavon circa 1910. The R&SBR through here from Cwmavon to Port Talbot Docks was built over the route of the Cwmavon Railway. The engine, R&SBR No. 30, is ex-GWR No. 1834 which was transferred to the R&SBR between April 1907 and January 1922, and is carrying lamps indicating it is engaged in shunting operations. *Author's collection*

Cwmavon Station, R&SBR, looking up the valley ca. 1908. The passenger station consisted of typical Up and Down platforms on the otherwise single line. The track on the left was a half mile long bidirectional loop which served reception sidings for the extensive works off to the left. At this date, these consisted of the Copper Miners Tin Plate Co., the Express Steel Co., and the Rio Tinto Co. The short goods siding on the right also served the Cwmavon Brick Works Co. which occupied part of the site of the defunct Cwmavon Iron Works, whose chimney dominates the view. Cwmavon opened on 25th June 1885 and closed 3rd December 1962.
Author's collection

The R&SBR's final expansionist move in the upper Avon Valley was to include in the Parliamentary Notice for its Bill for the 1893 Session a scheme for a railway from Cymmer to Blaen Caerau in the Llynvi Valley, reminiscent of the AVR schemes of 1865 and 1866.[202] This line commenced at a west-facing junction with the existing railway at Cymmer, described a wide semicircle over 1 in 40 gradients, passed over the GWR tunnel at Caerau and terminated near Caerau Colliery. The hope, presumably, was to tap traffic from the new colliery being developed there. The cost of this line was estimated by Yockney to be £32,892.[203] The GWR petitioned against this proposed line on the grounds that it would be deprived of traffic, and on 10th March 1893 it was announced to the House of Lords Committee that the line was withdrawn.[204] However, the 1893 Act[205] did sanction the coastal route from Aberavon to Baglan as built, and opened fully for traffic on 14th March 1895, and also empowered the company to subscribe to the PT Company.[206]

THE LLYNVI AND GARW VALLEYS

The development of railways in the Llynvi and Garw valleys followed a different pattern to the Avon Valley. A tramroad running the length of the Llynvi Valley and on to the coast at Porthcawl was in use by 1830. This line formed the basis of later main line railway schemes, first in the Llynvi Valley, followed in turn by the Ogmore and Garw valleys.

Exploitation of the coal and ironstone seams in the upper Llynvi Valley began in the early 1770s.[207] Both were supplied to John Bedford's largely unsuccessful Cefn Cribbwr Ironworks under the terms of a lease of 1772.[208] Transport was by horse and cart. Thirty years later these mineral leases were acquired by Thomas Jones, although his venture was not initially successful.[209] Nevertheless, *The Cambrian* of 22nd October 1814 published a notice announcing a meeting to consider that a tramroad from the hills north of Bridgend to Ewenny might be of great public utility. The meeting, held on 26th November under the chairmanship of Wyndham Quinn MP,[210] approved the project and decided on a route from Ewenny, on the Neath to Cardiff turnpike, to Dyffryn Llynvi, with a branch through Tyr Gunter and Cefn Cwsc to Taibach. This tramroad would have provided an outlet for the ironworks in the Cefn Cribbwr area,[211] then inactive, and the fledgling industries in the Llynvi Valley. The need for a proper survey was discussed at a meeting on 21st February 1815,[212] as a result of which an alternative route to the mouth of the River Ogmore was presented to the subscribers.[213] On 23rd November it was resolved to apply to Parliament for the necessary powers.[214] Plans were prepared and deposited locally[215] and at the Private Bill Office of Parliament. The necessary arrangements were not completed until 23rd December. Despite not complying with Standing Orders, the Bill, which named the proposed line as the Ewenny Railway, was allowed to proceed and given a first reading on 21st March 1816.[216] There were

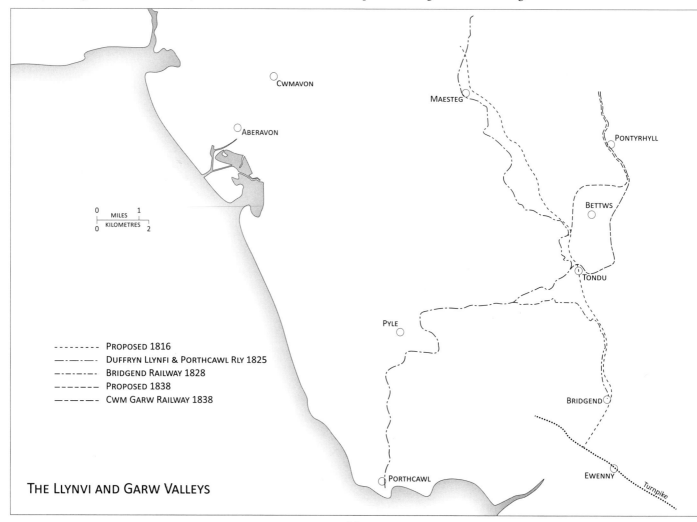

THE LLYNVI AND GARW VALLEYS

no further proceedings, the scheme having been abandoned at a meeting of the promoters on 16th April 1816 as conditions were not right for such a venture.[217] Another meeting was held on 19th September 1818[218] in an attempt to revive the River Ogmore route, but to no avail.

Thomas Jones renewed his interest in 1824 when demand for iron was increasing, and with his brother Charles set about raising capital and finding partners. Thomas died before the partnership could be formalised, but Charles and a third brother, William, pressed on and formed the Maesteg Company in 1826, with the intention of building an ironworks on the east bank of the Llynvi Valley near Maesteg Uchaf Farm. The first blast furnace was in use by 1828, a second was added in 1830 and a third in 1845.[219] After thirty-one years of fluctuating fortunes, Maesteg Ironworks ceased production in 1859. An attempt in 1860 to refloat the enterprise as the Maesteg Iron & Coal Company Ltd failed and the works were acquired by the Llynvi Vale Iron Company in 1862. The site was finally abandoned in 1873.

THE DUFFRYN LLYNVI & PORTHCAWL RAILWAY AND THE BRIDGEND RAILWAY

No doubt in anticipation of Jones' intentions, brief notices appeared in *The Cambrian*[220] and *The London Gazette*[221] announcing the impending application to Parliament for powers to build a railway or tramroad from Duffryn Llynvi to Porthcawl, and to improve the port. A meeting to discuss the proposed Bill was held on 21st January 1825 under the chairmanship of Wyndham Lewis MP, and a committee formed, which included the Earl of Dunraven and Mr Talbot, the two largest landowners in the area.[222]

Porthcawl was seemingly chosen as the coastal terminus as nearby Newton was an established shipping place.[223] The route proceeded north towards the ironworks at Bryndu, avoiding the highest ground by means of a wide loop, then headed east past the ironworks at Cefn before turning north again to closely follow the mountainside on the west side of the Llynvi Valley up to Duffryn Llynvi.[224] The average gradient for the sixteen mile course as set out by John Hodgkinson was 1 in 200. The Bill for the DL&PR had an uneventful passage through Parliament. The resulting Act, which received the Royal Assent on 10th June 1825,[225] named an impressive list of fifty-seven proprietors, who included English as well as local interests and were headed by the Earl of Dunraven. The capital of the new company was set at £40,000. Further financial powers were granted by Acts of 1829[226] and 1840.[227] The gauge of this horse-worked tramroad was 4ft 7ins.[228] According to one report the wheels had outside flanges.[229] The undertaking opened without ceremony in 1828, following the issue of a Justices certificate dated 2nd April 1828 that Porthcawl Harbour had been completed.[230] Although locomotive haulage was considered in 1834 and 1837,[231] the line remained horse-drawn throughout its life. Short branches over the River Llynvi connected Maesteg Ironworks to the DL&PR.

The market town of Bridgend had been bypassed by the DL&PR. A meeting was held on 25th May 1827 to discuss a proposed branch railway, to be called the Bridgend Railway, from the DL&PR to Bridgend, plus, if the Earl of Dunraven required it, a branch to Tregunter Coal Park.[232] The requisite notice was published later that year.[233] The ensuing Act, which received the Royal Assent on

19th June 1828,[234] provided for a capital of £6,000. The proprietors were mostly the same as those of the DL&PR, and the engineer was again John Hodgkinson. The four and a half mile route left the DL&PR near Cefn Cwsc Ironworks and headed east and then south along the east bank of the River Ogmore to terminate to the east of Bridgend town centre.[235] Despite some delay caused by the need to borrow additional funds, the Bridgend Railway was opened with due ceremony on 22nd October 1830.[236]

These two tramroads served the local area for more than a quarter of a century, carrying coal and iron from the Llynvi Valley to Porthcawl and Bridgend. A regular service was run – in 1855 the Down trains were taking about six hours and Up trains eight hours[237] – despite frequent complaints about the state of the line.[238] Passengers were occasionally carried in adapted wagons. Little traffic was generated by the Cefn Cribbwr Ironworks.[239] In July 1836 Esther Williams and her companions travelled from Brombil near Margam to visit the ironworks at Maesteg using the DL&PR for part of the journey.[240]

The first proposal for a tramroad or railway in the neighbouring Garw Valley was made in 1837. A preliminary notice appeared in *The London Gazette* for 21st February, followed by the full notice in the 17th September issue. This line, to be called the Cwm Garw Railway, was intended to run from Braich y Cymmer, above present-day Pontyrhyll, to a junction with the DL&PR at Pentwyn Bayden. The route of approximately five miles followed the River Garw as far as Llangeinor, then turned north-west and passed through a half mile long tunnel (under the route of the later Port Talbot Railway) to reach Cwm Cedfyw and thence down to the Llynvi Valley. After crossing the river, a short inclined plane brought the new line up to the level of the DL&PR.[241] Early in 1838 an amended route was announced.[242] The Deposited Plan[243] shows the intended five and a half mile route following the River Garw to Brynmenyn where it turned west to join the DL&PR about half a mile below Pentywn Bayden, again by an upwards inclined plane. The latter notice also referred to a connection with the Bridgend Railway, not shown on the Deposited Plan.

Although there were no proceedings in Parliament, the western part of the original scheme had been constructed as early as 1828 by Nash Vaughan Edwards-Vaughan to connect his drift colliery at Bettws in Cwm Cedfyw to the DL&PR.[244] The mineral properties in the Bettws area and the tramroad were sub-leased to Sir Robert Price in 1837, who might well have been one of the promoters of the Cwm Garw Railway. Also in 1837 Sir Robert formed the Glamorgan Iron & Coal Company with the intention of completing his ironworks at Tondu, construction having started in 1836.[245] Sir Robert later built his own line from the bottom of the incline near Pentwyn Bayden to Tondu, thereby avoiding the tolls of the DL&PR, and continued it to join the Bridgend Railway.[246] Mounting losses forced Sir Robert Price to dispose of his interests around Tondu. By June 1855 John Brogden & Sons had acquired all the works and leases, the first step in their involvement in the industries of Mid-Glamorgan.[247]

Stimulated by the high price of iron and the ready availability of raw materials, the construction of a second ironworks in the upper Llynvi Valley began in 1838, with the formation of the Cambrian Iron & Spelter Company.[248] The Llynvi Ironworks were built on a site on the west bank of the river opposite Maesteg Ironworks.

The bridge carrying the PTR over the GW Llynvi Valley, originally built to carry across the valley a tramroad linking the Llynvi and Maesteg ironworks. An Abergwynvi-bound train headed by a '4500' Class 2-6-2T has just left Maesteg (GW) station which was opened in 1897. *GRO*

The bridge built in 1827 to carry a short spur off the DL&PR over the River Llynvi into Maesteg Ironworks. It fell out of such use in 1860s, but remained and was widened as a public thoroughfare in the 1960s.

Author's collection

Although two blast furnaces were constructed initially, limited activity before 1843 had an adverse effect on the fortunes of the DL&PR.[249] The incomplete works were sold to Dr John Bowring and his brother Charles in 1844, who named their new enterprise the Llynvi Iron Company.[250]

GLAMORGAN CENTRAL MINERAL RAILWAY

The years 1844–47 were a period of excessive railway speculation in the UK. The Llynvi and Garw Valleys were not immune from this activity and in 1845 three schemes were promoted which had the potential to have a profound effect on the railway map of the area.

The first of these schemes was the Glamorgan Central Mineral Railway (GCMR). The directors of the DL&PR received a letter from the Llynvi Iron Company in April 1845 stating that it was contemplating using the Cwmavon Railway to take its iron to Port Talbot for shipment and asking what improvements were likely to be made to the tramroad before making any final arrangement.[251] The directors replied that the road was to be relaid in the shortest possible time, their solution being the GCMR.

A preliminary announcement was published in October 1845 of the intention to rebuild the entire length of the DL&PR and the Bridgend Railway, to construct branches into the Garw and Ogmore valleys and to Cwmdu in the Llynvi Valley, to make junctions with the recently incorporated SWR, and to improve Porthcawl Harbour.[252] A company with a capital of £500,000 was provisionally registered in October 1845.[253] The engineer of this ambitious locomotive-worked scheme with a combined length of twenty-six miles was Joseph Locke (1805–60).[254] A prospectus was published, naming a large provisional committee headed by Sir Digby Mackworth, Bart. and Sir Robert Price, Bart.,[255] which received favourable press comment.[256] Progress appeared to be being made when it was announced that the DL&PR shareholders had agreed to convert their shares into those of the new company.[257] A Parliamentary Notice was published[258] and a Bill deposited. Time was running out for such schemes, however, and on 26th January 1846 the provisional committee announced that the application to Parliament had been abandoned owing to the default of numerous parties in paying deposits on shares allotted to them.[259]

OGMORES & GARW VALES AND PORT OF CARDIFF UNION RAILWAY

The second of these schemes was the grandly titled Ogmores & Garw Vales and Port of Cardiff Union Railway, which published a provisional prospectus in October 1845.[260] The line, whose title defined its purpose, was planned to commence by a junction with the Bridgend Railway at Aberkenfig and to terminate by a junction with the SWR at Llandaff.[261] Included in its proposals was a branch railway three miles long from Bryncethyn into the Garw Valley, terminating at Nant Hir near Blaengarw.[262] A Parliamentary Notice was published,[263] and a Bill deposited, but this was another casualty of the railway mania, and nothing further was done.

LLYNVI VALLEY RAILWAY

The third scheme was destined to have far-reaching consequences in the Llynvi and Garw valleys. In September 1845 a consortium of

One clear reminder of the DL&PR is the width of Commercial Street, Maesteg. As this town grew properties were built so as allow room for the tramroad and the public highway. Postcard, postally used 13th September 1910. *Author's collection*

representatives of local railways and industrial concerns provisionally registered the Llynvi Valley & South Wales Junction Railway,[264] with a capital of £200,000 in £20 shares. The group included Dr Bowring of the Llynvi Iron Company, William Malins, proprietor of a new ironworks at Garth near Maesteg[265] and the existing works at Cefn Cwsc, and a total of seven directors of the GWR, the SWR and the English Copper Company. The preliminary notice drew attention to the shortcomings of the DL&PR and announced an intended locomotive-worked broad gauge line from the head of the Llynvi Valley to a junction with the recently sanctioned SWR near Margam.[266] The proposed line ran directly down the Llynvi Valley rather than follow the tortuous curves of the DL&PR to Tondu, then followed the tramroad route westwards to Pyle and continued to Margam.[267] Joseph Cubitt (1811–72), the engineer, estimated the cost of the fifteen mile route to be £180,000. The DL&PR and local landowners including Mr Talbot petitioned against the Bill when it came before the select committees of both Houses of Parliament, the latter on the grounds that it was injurious to his property. In the event all the petitions were withdrawn,[268] the promoters of the new company and the DL&PR having reached an agreement on 24th July.[269] The House of Commons decided that the name of the new company should be the Llynvi Valley Railway (LVR) Company. The ensuing Act, which gained the Royal Assent on 7th August 1846,[270] included clauses for the lease or sale of the LVR to the SWR.

The agreement between the LVR and the DL&PR called for the amalgamation of the two companies, and Parliamentary Notice to this effect appeared in *The London Gazette* for 28th November 1846. The resulting Act,[271] which received the Royal Assent on 22nd July 1847, vested the DL&PR and all its property, effects, powers and liabilities in the LVR. In exchange the DL&PR's stockholders received a total of £50,000 in new LVR shares.

Also in 1846 the LVR announced plans to extend its recently authorised railway.[272] The SWR intended to extensively deviate its authorised line between Margam and Coychurch, as described below, and a more convenient junction of the LVR with the SWR was possible. The LVR's line from Pyle to Margam was abandoned, no doubt to Mr Talbot's satisfaction, and replaced by a three mile broad gauge extension from Tondu to a triangular junction with proposed SWR deviation line north of Bridgend. Cubitt estimated the cost of this new line to be £50,000, replacing lines estimated to cost £72,000.[273] Despite objections from the Bridgend Railway and the Earl of Dunraven,[274] the LVR Extension Act received the Royal Assent on 2nd July 1847.[275]

This period of railway mania benefited the Llynvi Iron Company and a third blast furnace was added in 1845 to cope with the increase in demand for iron. This situation did not last, and by 1847 the company was trading at a loss.[276] Although Dr Bowring departed in 1848, operations continued and a fourth blast furnace was added in 1849. With another upturn in the iron trade in prospect, the enterprise was reconstituted in 1852 as the Llynvi Vale Iron Company and the works further developed.[277] Transport still relied on the horse-drawn DL&PR with its high tolls. The company survived a trade recession in the late 1850s, principally because the ready accessibility of black-band iron ore led to low production costs. Acquisition of the neighbouring Maesteg Works in 1862 further increased the reserves of coal and ironstone. The company was re-formed as the Llynvi Coal & Iron Company Ltd in 1866 at a time of industrial turmoil.[278]

John Brogden & Sons had developed mineral interests in the upper Llynvi Valley and at Cwmdu since 1854.[279] The levels at Blaen Cwmdu, one and a half miles east of Maesteg, were connected by a tramway to the LVR at Llwydarth. Brogdens sank the first deep

This engraving appeared in the *Illustrated London News* dated 31st July 1858 to illustrate a short article on cutting the first turf for the Llynvi Valley Railway on 15th July 1858. Although difficult to make out, the ceremony is taking place in the centre of the view near the white flag. This is the only known view of Llynvi Ironworks, on the left, and Maesteg Ironworks, in the centre, in operation. *Author's collection*

pit in the valley at nearby Garth in 1864.[280] In December 1871 Brogdens made an agreement to purchase the Llynvi Coal & Iron Company,[281] and in 1872 both concerns were merged into a new venture, the Llynvi, Tondu & Ogmore Coal & Iron Company Ltd, with works at Tondu and Llynvi, as well as collieries in the Ogmore Valley. The early 1870s saw the final boom period of the South Wales wrought iron trade, competition coming in the form of the Bessemer steel process and the importation of high-grade Spanish ore. 1874 was the watershed year. By 1877 the company was unable to pay interest to its debenture holders and in January 1878 it went into receivership.[282] The receiver re-formed the enterprise as the Llynvi & Tondu Company in 1880, but this too failed in 1885,[283] and apart from Garth Colliery it was eventually bought up by Col John North and his associates.[284]

A short south to east connection between the DL&PR and the SWR at Stormy near Pyle was authorised by the LVR's 1851 Act,[285] a restriction being that steam power was not to be used over it. The wording is unusual in that the new line commenced at a point on the DL&PR and terminated at a point on the SWR. The connection to the SWR, known as the South Wales Junction Branch Railway[286] was constructed, to the broad gauge, almost immediately, and may have originally been intended as a transshipment siding. In November 1851 Messrs G S Ford & Sons, proprietors of Bryndu Colliery, Pyle, requested an additional third

rail to be laid down from the junction railway to their works.[287] Their intention was to eliminate damage to the coal and other goods which were being transshipped at the northern extremity of the new junction railway.[288] This creation of a broad gauge line from Bryndu Colliery to the SWR main line was confirmed by an agreement which stipulated a minimum traffic of 500 tons per week and the works to be completed within six weeks.[289] In June 1855 representatives of the Cefn Cwsc Coal & Iron Company requested that the broad gauge be extended from Messrs Ford's works to the point at which their siding left the branch, a distance of about a quarter of a mile.[290] According to the agreement between the parties dated 18th September 1855, the Cefn Cwsc Company had already built their branch line to the broad gauge.[291] The extension was completed in December 1855.[292] This section of the DL&PR was probably unique in being mixed 4ft 7ins and 7ft gauge.[293]

The LVR Board had already rejected plans to sanction an outlay of £72,800 to convert its line to a locomotive-worked broad gauge railway.[294] Instead, the LVR announced plans to make twelve deviation railways so as to eliminate the sharper curves in the DL&PR main line and to construct a branch to Porthcawl Harbour.[295] It also sought powers to construct five deviations on the Bridgend Railway, to convert both railways to mixed gauge, to make a connection with the SWR at Bridgend, and to work the railways by steam locomotives. In the event, the resulting Act of

1853[296] restricted the LVR to the branch at Porthcawl and four deviations at Tondu and Pyle, constructed to either gauge.

In March 1853 the LVR Board succeeded in fighting off a proposal of the SWMR to construct a branch line to the upper Llynvi Valley, as previously recounted. However, none of the authorised improvements to its line except the broad gauge connection near Pyle had been carried out and there was still a great need for better communications in the area. A public meeting had been held on 19th March to consider the expediency of having a lower-level broad gauge line from Blaen Llynvi to Bridgend.[297] Such a line would also bring benefits to the neighbouring Garw and Ogmore valleys. The LVR Board viewed this development favourably at its meeting the following month, and resolved to withdraw from their 1853 Bill all clauses affecting their line between Tondu and Blaen Llynvi.[298] The promoters of the Maesteg, Bridgend and South Wales Junction Railway registered a company of this name on 25th October 1853, the stated purpose being to make a railway from Blaen Llynvi to the SWR at or near the town of Bridgend.[299] Brunel was engaged as the engineer.[300] The LVR Board met representatives of the promoters on 15th November to discuss the terms of an agreement. It was decided to confine attention to improving the line from Ffos to Blaen Llynvi. The heads of an agreement between the parities were finally settled on 25th November 1853.[301] The outcome was a Parliamentary Notice[302] announcing a proposal to build an eight and a half mile broad gauge railway from Tywith via Tondu to Ffos Toll House on much the same route as authorised by the 1846 Act, and to convert the remainder of the DL&PR to broad gauge.[303] The Notice also mentioned two proposed connections to the SWR, but these did not appear on the deposited plans. The estimated cost of this line, which was nearer the valley bottom than the DL&PR, was £84,000.[304] The Bridgend Railway did not figure in these proposals. Some Parliamentary progress was made, but the Bill was withdrawn on 24th February 1854, and the replacement Bill rejected on 29th June, on the grounds that the preamble had not been proved.[305]

A notice announcing a revised scheme appeared later that year.[306] This proposal retained the line from Tywith to Ffos Toll House, and in addition incorporated a new railway three miles in length from Tondu to a junction with the SWR near Bridgend station, all to the broad gauge.[307] Joseph Cubitt, the engineer, estimated the cost of these works to be £100,000. The comprehensive LVR Act of 1855[308] authorised the re-incorporation of the company with a capital of £200,000, with powers to borrow on mortgage not more than £66,600. In addition to making the new railways, the company was empowered to discontinue the use of existing unnecessary lines except where they served works at Tondu. The LVR was also authorised to purchase the Bridgend Railway for £3,000, and to enter into working arrangements with the SWR.

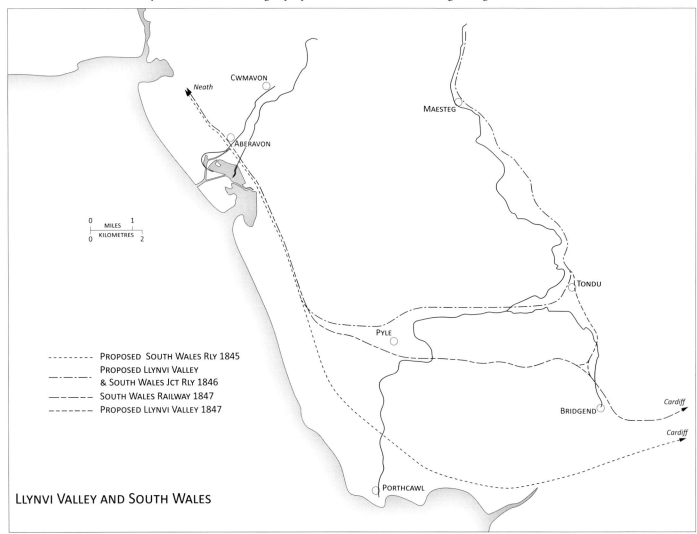

LLYNVI VALLEY AND SOUTH WALES

- - - - - - - PROPOSED SOUTH WALES RLY 1845
- · - · - · - PROPOSED LLYNVI VALLEY & SOUTH WALES JCT RLY 1846
———— SOUTH WALES RAILWAY 1847
- - - - - - PROPOSED LLYNVI VALLEY 1847

This view shows Glannant siding which joined the LVR just beyond the bridge at Bettws Colliery Junction, about one mile north of Tondu. At one time this short siding extended for about one mile up Cwm Cedfwy and was originally a tramway serving the collieries owned by Sir Robert Price. In Price's time the tramway continued down the valley to Tondu to eventually join the Bridgend Railway, which possibly accounts for the wide span of this bridge.   *Author's collection*

The scheme, when it came to fruition, was to be of great benefit to the Llynvi Vale Iron Co. Progress was slow, however, and in June 1857 the Llynvi Vale Iron Company prosecuted the LVR over the poor condition of the existing track.[309] It was probably this state of affairs that prompted the Iron Company in September 1857 to contemplate a route to Briton Ferry via the SWMR.[310] At the same time an extension of the Ely Valley Railway from Gellyrhaidd to Maesteg was considered, but not pursued.[311] It appears that Cubitt had fallen out with the LVR Board, which was informed in January 1857 that Brunel had accepted the position of consulting engineer for the construction of the line.[312] Due to difficulties in raising the necessary capital there was a delay until June 1858, when the contract was awarded to Messrs Baldwin of Kent. Robert Pearson Brereton (1818–94), Brunel's assistant, was appointed supervising engineer in August 1858, and took over as the LVR engineer following the latter's death in September 1959. It was not until July 1858 that the first sod on the new LVR was cut by William Mitcalfe (*sic*), the principal shareholder in the Llynvi Vale Iron Company and father of the then chairman, Stephen Metcalfe.[313] The LVR was opened for mineral traffic on 10th August 1861, worked initially by locomotives hired from the GWR.[314] The LVR Act of 1862[315] empowered the company to raise additional capital to enable it to complete the works authorised by the 1855 Act. Passenger services between Bridgend and Maesteg commenced on 25th February 1864. The short South Wales Junction Branch Railway at Stormy was removed after the opening of the LVR, the only connection

with the SWR then being at Bridgend.[316] It was recommended that a new junction should be made at Tydraw near Pyle, and Brereton was instructed to prepare plans.[317] In the event, nothing was done until 1876 when a new junction was laid in at Pyle by the GWR.

OGMORE VALLEY RAILWAYS

In the early 1860s John Brogden & Sons extended their coal mining operations by leasing mineral properties in the Ogmore Valley from the Duchy of Lancaster. Levels at Nantymoel at the head of the valley were developed first, followed in 1865 by the sinking of the Wyndham pit. The Brogdens promoted the Ogmore Valley Railways (OVR) to provide an outlet for their coal.[318] The engineer was W H Woodhouse.[319] The OVR Act of 1863[320] incorporated the new company, with John Brodgen, two of his sons, and Stephen Metcalfe among the first directors. The capital was set at £90,000, with a borrowing limit of £30,000. The cost of the new works was estimated to be £70,000. The authorised line commenced with a junction with the LVR just north of Tondu, and terminated at Nantymoel, a distance of seven and three-quarter miles. Also authorised, but never constructed, was a branch up Cwm Nant y Ci. The OVR agreed not to build a branch into Tondu Ironworks, having been granted powers to run over the LVR from the junction point to the works entrance, and also to Bridgend and Porthcawl.

The OVR Act of 1863 specified that its railways were to be laid to the broad gauge, and might also be laid to the narrow gauge.

Later that year the LVR and OVR announced a joint application to Parliament for powers to abandon the broad gauge on the OVR, to lay down standard gauge rails on parts of the LVR, and to enlarge Porthcawl Harbour.[321] The engineer, Robert Pearson Brereton, estimated that the railway works would cost £6,000 and the other works £55,000.[322] The Llynvi & Ogmore Railways Act 1864[323] stipulated that Porthcawl Harbour was to become joint property, administered by a committee of four with two nominees from each company. The LVR was empowered to lay down a third rail from a point 600 yards north of the OVR junction at Tondu to the harbour, and the OVR was authorised to be constructed to the narrow gauge. To pay for these works each company was authorised to raise additional capital of not more than £30,000. The OVR was opened as a narrow (standard) gauge railway in August 1865. The upper section of the LVR was converted to mixed gauge in 1868.[324]

The DL&PR Act of 1840 had authorised that company to raise not more than £20,000 for the completion and maintenance of its railway, pier and other works. By 1863, Porthcawl Harbour was no longer adequate for the trade now on offer following the opening of Brogden's new collieries. The 1864 Act authorised the construction of an inner dock with a gated entrance from the old harbour, and the extension of the existing breakwaters. The new dock, which had four coal hoists and covered 7½ acres, was served by two new branch railways. It opened in July 1867, and prospered immediately, exporting over 165,000 tons of coal in 1871.[325]

The mid-1860s were another period of railway mania. *The London Gazette* for 24th November 1865 published three announcements of intentions to apply to Parliament for powers to extend the LVR to Blaen Llynvi and to the SWMR, to construct extensions of the OVR including a branch into the Garw Valley, and to amalgamate

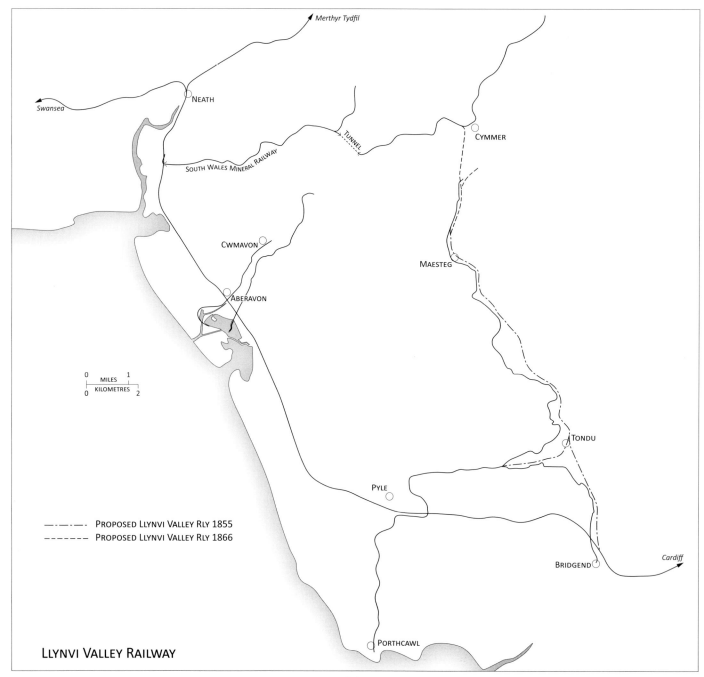

LLYNVI VALLEY RAILWAY

ABOVE: Oakwood or Maesteg Merthyr Colliery was sunk in 1868, and outlet and inlet connections were put in at 7m 25ch and 7m 56ch on the LVR. By the date of this view it was owned by Elder's Navigation Collieries Ltd. Postcard, postally used 1922. *Author's collection*

The first Maesteg station on the LVR was provided with a single platform, an engine shed and a turntable and opened on 25th February 1864. The line through here was doubled in 1885 and in July 1897, possibly in anticipation of competition from the nearby PTR, the GWR opened a new station about 200 yards further up the valley and nearer the town centre. Improved goods and siding accommodation was provided, just visible in this view looking south. The station was renamed Maesteg Castle Street on 1st July 1924 and closed on 22nd June 1970. *Author's collection*

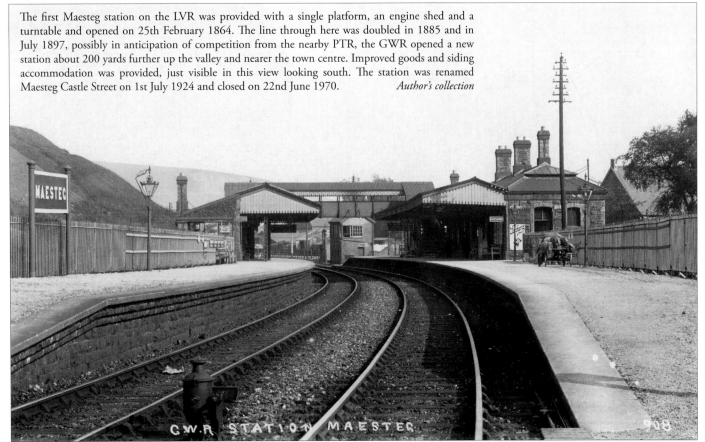

A typical Up local passenger train consisting of an 0-6-0 saddle tank engine and three non-corridor coaches heading down the LVR at Nantyffyllon. Postcard, postally used 23rd September 1910. *Author's collection*

Nantyffyllon station opened as Tywith on 19th July 1880 when passenger services started on the new line through Cymmer Tunnel to Cymmer and beyond. This line branched to the right off the original LVR about 100 yards beyond the platforms. As can just be made out in this view, the old line continued in use as a goods line serving Caerau Goods just beyond the site of the original LVR station, which seemingly was named Coynant. Tywith station was renamed Nantyffyllon on 1st January 1903 and closed on 22nd June 1970.
Author's collection

the two companies. The proposed LVR extension commenced at the Tywith terminus and ran through a 1,507 yard long tunnel to emerge into the Avon Valley at Cymmer, where it crossed the river and made a trailing connection with the SWMR in the direction of Briton Ferry, a distance of just over two miles. Also planned was a half mile branch from the new line at Blaen Llynvi up to Blaen Caerau.[326] The LVR Act of 1866[327] empowered the company to make these railways and to raise not more than £133,000 to pay for their construction. Furthermore, the Llynvi & Ogmore Railway (L&OR) Act of 1867[328] authorised that company to enter into agreements to maintain, manage and use the SWMR. This was the second attempt to connect the Llynvi and Avon valleys by a railway, but again it came to nothing, and the powers were abandoned by the L&OR Act of 1869.[329]

Coal had been worked on a small scale in the Garw Valley for a number of years.[330] By 1863 the Brogdens were taking coal by tramroad from Fforch-las in Cwm Fforch-wen on the eastern side of the valley south of Pontycymmer, over the mountain to reach the OVR.[331] A little further down the valley the contractors building the Garw Branch started in 1874 to work seams at Braichycymmer, later to become the Braichycymmer Colliery Company.[332] Meanwhile, Edward Plummer, the manager of the Glyncorrwg Collieries, had leased the minerals at Ffaldau and by 1878 two pits were working. Ffaldau Colliery was taken over by Pyman, Watson & Co. in 1881. The largest collieries were established at the head of the valley on the old Pwllcarn farm. The International commenced

in 1873 when leases of the seams worked in earlier times were obtained.[333] The final venture was the Ocean Colliery consequent to a lease obtained by David Davies of Llandinam in 1886.[334] Apart from Ocean Colliery, which was part of the Ocean Coal Company Ltd, the other collieries did not amalgamate, unlike those in the neighbouring Llynvi valley.

The proposed Garw Valley Branch of the OVR commenced by a junction with the existing railway at Brynmenyn and terminated at Pwllcarn near the farmhouse called Blaen Garw just over five and a half miles distant. Also proposed was a short link at Brynmenyn to make a triangular junction with the OVR main line. Samuel Dobson, the engineer, estimated the cost of these two lines to £36,296.[335] These works were authorised by the OVR Act 1866.[336] The failure of the Overend, Gurney & Co. bank in May 1866 and the panic which ensued severely curtailed railway speculation and construction.[337] The 1866 Act allowed five years for the construction of the Garw Branch, but because of the lack of progress the L&OR Act of 1869 provided for a further three years. The plans deposited for the L&OR Bill of 1873, prepared in late 1872, show the line apparently constructed as far as Pontyrhyll, but the complete branch was not opened until October 1876.[338] Powers for the construction of the triangular junction at Brynmenyn were allowed to expire.

LLYNVI & OGMORE RAILWAY

The arrangements for the joint administration of Porthcawl Harbour made under the terms of the Llynvi & Ogmore Railways Act 1864

Porthcawl Inner Dock was opened in 1867 and is shown here in its heyday, circa 1885. On the nearest siding are wagons lettered for the Llynvi, Tondu & Ogmore Coal & Iron Co. Ltd (1872–78) and its eventual successor, the Llynvi & Tondu Co. (1880–85).   *Author's collection*

Caerau station was a latecomer to the LVR, being opened by the GWR on 1st April 1901, presumably to serve the growing township associated with the new colliery. The southern portal of Cymmer Tunnel was just beyond the far end of the platform. This station closed on 22nd June 1970. Postcard, postally used 29th June 1911.

Author's collection

presaged the amalgamation of the two companies. This was duly authorised by the Llynvi & Ogmore Railways (Amalgamation) Act of 1866.[339] The OVR itself had absorbed the broad gauge Ely Valley Extension Railway the previous year[340] as a consequence of the Brogdens taking over the works from the contractor and completing the line.[341] Under the 1866 Act the OVR Company was dissolved and amalgamated with the LVR Company to create the L&OR Company with a capital of £402,000 and borrowing powers of £133,900. Insufficient funds were available to complete the works at Porthcawl, resulting in these amounts being raised by £100,000 and £33,300 respectively by the L&OR Act of 1867. Circumstances required the company to rearrange its finances in 1869. Abandonment of the line through to the Avon Valley authorised by the LVR Act of 1866 made it expedient to reduce the share capital by £80,000. The contractor was owed £16,500 for

the construction of the new dock and over £50,000 was committed for locomotives and rolling stock. Consequently the company was authorised to borrow a further £60,000 by the L&OR Act of 1869.

The early 1870s saw the L&OR preoccupied with an attempt to connect its isolated narrow gauge lines to the wider world by means of a line from Blackmill to a junction with the Rhymney Railway near Walnut Tree Junction.[342] The Bill was withdrawn during its passage through the House of Lords[343] as result of the GWR's decision to convert its lines in South Wales from broad to narrow gauge, which took place in 1872.

No doubt encouraged by the demise of the broad gauge in South Wales, the L&OR again looked towards extending its lines northwards as well as eastwards.[344] The new railways proposed at the upper end of the LVR, for which the engineers were Messrs Dobson, Brown & Adam,[345] were a line just over two and a quarter

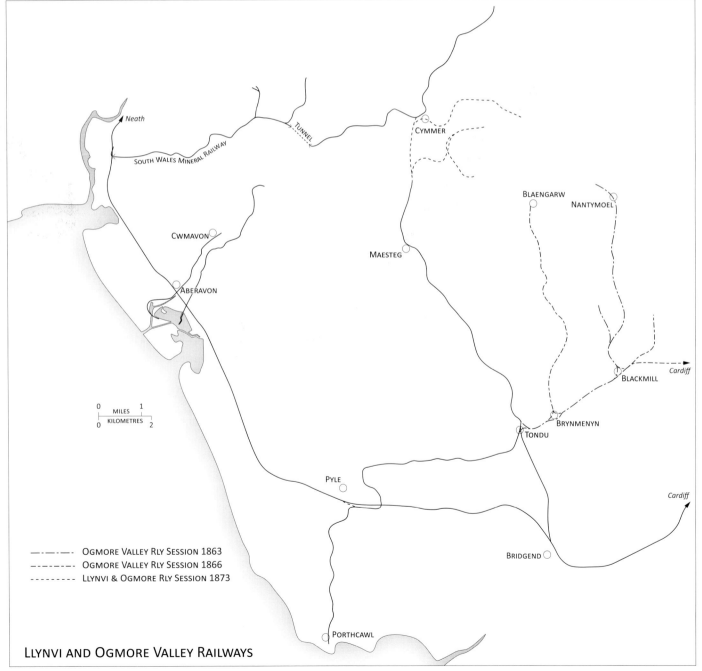

LLYNVI AND OGMORE VALLEY RAILWAYS

—·—·— OGMORE VALLEY RLY SESSION 1863
-------- OGMORE VALLEY RLY SESSION 1866
-------- LLYNVI & OGMORE RLY SESSION 1873

Its 1863 Act authorised the OVR to construct a railway from Tondu to Nantymoel, opened in 1865. In time Tondu became an important junction with a large engine shed opened in 1889 replacing earlier sheds provided by the OVR and L&OR. This view from the station footbridge shows the OVR branching off to the right and the LVR to the left. Below the photographer's feet, the Porthcawl Branch via Cefn Junction and Pyle heads left with the line to Bridgend on the right. Both branches had two platform faces. Tondu Middle signal box is on the far left. The nearer of three saddle tank engines is shunting on the goods reception road; the engine to its right with the long goods train is standing on the Down line to Maesteg, and thus on the wrong road. Postcard, postally used 21st August 1908.   *Author's collection*

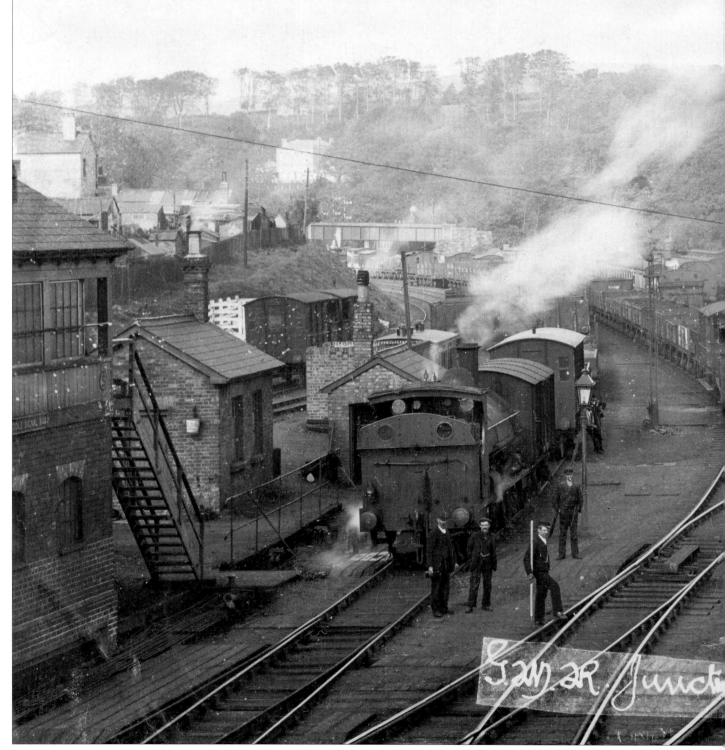

The Garw Valley Branch was authorised by the OVR Act 1866 and left the OVR main line at Brynmenyn Junction, about three-quarters of a mile from Tondu. Each line was double track with two platform faces at the junction, but both became single track beyond the station. Otherwise the facilities were minimal, with one short siding off each of the branches. Brynmenyn station closed on 5th May 1958. *Author's collection*

miles long commencing at a junction with the existing line north of the site of the future Nantyffyllon station, passing through a 1,496 yard long tunnel and over the River Avon to a junction with the SWMR at Cymmer, and a three mile extension up the Avon Valley commencing at the north end of the tunnel and terminating at Blaenavon. These lines would provide an alternative outlet to traffic from the upper part of the SWMR and serve the site of the mineral leases at Abergwynfi which Alexander Brogden secured in 1873. These leases were in turn conveyed to Sir Daniel Gooch and others who were acting as trustees for the GWR. The GWR's colliery at Abergwynfi was sunk between 1877–82.[346]

Also proposed was a steeply graded switchback line, two and a half miles long, commencing at a junction with the proposed SWMR junction line near Blaen Llynvi which followed the River Llynvi eastwards, then turned northwards and passed through a 357 yard long tunnel to terminate in Cwm Nant-y-fedw high above the River Avon, with a trailing branch line one mile long commencing at the north end of this tunnel and looping back over it to terminate on the flanks of Mynydd Caerau. The L&OR also sought running powers and facilities over the SWMR, and also the lease, sale or transfer of its undertaking to the GWR.

The Bill was opposed by the major landowners concerned, the Earl of Dunraven and John P Traherne, and was extensively amended by the House of Lords select committee. The resulting Llynvi & Ogmore Railways Act, 1873[347] authorised only the construction of the railways through to the SWMR at Cymmer and up the Avon Valley. Thomas Joseph, who had mineral interests in the upper Avon Valley, was authorised to make a connection to reach his mineral interests at Blaengwynfi and another with the SWMR near Cymmer, this presumably being a modification of the tramway authorised by the SWMR's 1864 Act.[348] The connection to the SWMR was not to be opened before the line up the Avon Valley without the consent of Joseph. Running powers over the SWMR were rejected, but an agreement dated 16th May 1873 for the GWR to work in perpetuity the undertaking of the L&OR as from 1st July 1873 was sanctioned.

The line to Cymmer and the connection to the SWMR, which involved a high bridge over the River Avon, opened for goods traffic in July 1878. Passenger traffic to Cymmer commenced in July 1880, but the line to Abergwynfi was not opened until March 1886. The GWR had experienced much difficulty in working its colliery there, and in 1910 assigned its lease to the Ocean Coal Company.[349] The GWR worked the L&OR for ten years. The amalgamation of the two companies on 1st July 1883 was authorised by the Great Western and Llynvi & Ogmore Railways Amalgamation Act, 1883.[350] The GWR also took over Porthcawl Docks, which were in a state of decline, brought about principally by the impending demise of the Llynvi & Tondu Company in 1885. A brief revival saw the peak of exports of 227,000 tons in 1892, but following the opening of Barry Dock in 1889, the opening of new Port Talbot Dock in 1898 was the final straw, and Porthcawl Dock closed in 1906.[351] Starting in 1913 the inner dock was filled in, and Porthcawl began to transform itself into a major holiday resort.

COASTWISE[352]

A better means of transport through South Wales was clearly a desirable objective, both to encourage trade in manufactured goods and to improve communication with Ireland. The roads were inadequate, particularly in wet weather, and sailing ships were subject to the vagaries of the wind.

The depression at the end of the Napoleonic wars was followed by a short period of promotion of highly speculative joint stock companies. Among these was the London & South Wales Railroad

Company of 1824–25.[353] A prospectus dated 28th December 1824 was issued,[354] pointing out that unfavourable sailing conditions caused much delay in bringing goods from the Bristol Channel ports to London. Apart from coal, these amounted to 30,000–40,000 tons of iron, 10,000 tons of copper, and 5,000 tons of tinplates annually. The proposed remedy was a railroad from Glamorganshire to London, passing through Gloucester and Oxford, and capitalised at £1 million. A meeting on 30th December 1824 resolved to press on with the scheme,[355] and appointed fourteen gentlemen, mainly from families who were active in the London or South Wales iron trades, to be directors of the company. The scheme was announced in *The Cambrian*,[356] but generated little local interest and nothing more was heard of it. A quarter of a century was to pass before such a railway came into being.

All the existing tramroads in the area ran inland from coastal termini. In November 1829 a notice appeared announcing the intention to apply to Parliament for powers to build a tramroad or railway along the coast from Pyle to Briton Ferry with a branch from Aberavon to Pontrhydyfen.[357] The solicitors were William & Griffith Llewellyn, both of whom acted in turn as agents for C R M Talbot and the Margam Estate.[358] This was the first of several schemes announced by the agents which would have increased the trade at Aberavon Harbour and later Port Talbot Docks. Plans were deposited with the Clerk of the Peace for Glamorganshire showing the line running from a junction with the DL&PR at the toll house south of Cornelly via the English Copper Company's works at Taibach to terminate by the ferry over the River Neath at Briton Ferry. The branch followed the Oakwood Railway to opposite Cwmavon, then crossed over the River Avon and followed the right bank of the river up to near its junction with the River Pelenna.[359]

The engineer was William Kirkhouse. The application to Parliament did not materialise and nothing more was heard of this line, which would have formed a useful link between the new dock at Porthcawl and the Neath Canal and the wharves at Neath.

A rather more grandiose scheme was announced by William Llewellyn in November 1835, on the same date as his publication of the intention to apply for powers to build an enclosed dock at Aberavon.[360] The intended railway or tramroad was to commence at Taibach, presumably at the site of the proposed dock, cross the River Neath by means of a bridge at Giant's Grave upstream from Briton Ferry and proceed via Llansamlet to Tyr Llandwr on the left bank of the River Tawe in Swansea where wharves and quays were to be built. There was also to be a branch to Port Tennant on the Tennant Canal. In addition, it was intended to purchase the Cwmavon Tramroad and the Oakwood Railway and to combine them with new line to create a united public railway. No plans were deposited for public inspection, and nothing more was heard of this scheme. Crossing the River Neath in the vicinity of Briton Ferry would have been a major difficulty, as the R&SBR was to find to its cost in the 1880s.[361]

Meanwhile, efforts to promote a railway from South Wales to England had resumed. The first was the Cambrian, London & Gloucester Railway, whose line from Gloucester was proposed to go via Usk, Newport, Cardiff, Briton Ferry and Swansea, to terminate at Milford,[362] and promoted by a Mr Wooddeson. The engineer was William Brunton.[363] Meetings were held in Merthyr Tydfil and Swansea where committees were formed of leading industrialists and landowners, including Mr Talbot of Margam.[364] Birmingham was added to the title at a meeting in Gloucester on 6th November 1833.[365] However, a week later *The Cambrian* reported that very

The Down platform (GWR terminology) of Pontyrhyll station looking up the valley towards Pontycymmer and Blaengarw. The siding connection was for Llest Colliery which was short distance up the valley off to the right. Despite the line being finished in 1876, Pontyrhyll station was not opened until 25th October 1886 and closed on 9th February 1953.

Author's collection

serious objections had arisen to the proposed route of the Cambrian, Gloucester, Birmingham & London Railway. It subsequently reported that a general impression prevailed among influential men of business that such a scheme could only be effected by Government.[366]

Two weeks later *The Cambrian* reported a meeting held in Swansea on 14th April 1834 to consider a proposal for a railway from Llanelly to Cardiff to be known as the Grand Cambrian and Western Railway. The engineer was Henry Habberley Price, who had been involved with early schemes for a railway between London and Bristol,[367] and with improving Aberavon Harbour.[368] Price proposed a double line from the port of Cardiff through Llantrissant, St. Bride's Minor (Bridgend), near Cefn Cribbwr Ironworks, along the flats to Aberavon, across the River Neath near Briton Ferry and River Tawe at Swansea and thence to Llanelly Docks and the Carmarthenshire Railway. Mr Talbot was again prominent on the committee that was formed. This scheme was well received and it was resolved that if a railway was brought from London across the River Severn by means of a bridge at or near to Sharpness Point it may become expedient to make the intermediate thirty-six miles of railway on from Cardiff. It was also resolved to confine immediate efforts to the Llanelly–Cardiff line, which would be a profitable investment for the transport of coal alone, and to give every encouragement to those parties endeavouring to bring a railway from London across the Severn. Surprisingly, nothing further was heard of this scheme.

A Supplementary Prospectus to the ultimately successful Great Western Railway Bill of 1835 noted that "the [proposed] line has been preferred on account of … its offering the greatest facilities for a junction … through Gloucester with South Wales".[369] Meetings of landed and manufacturing interests were held in London and Gloucester in March 1836 to raise funds for making a preliminary survey for a line from Gloucester to Swansea.[370] A meeting of the Gloucester & South Wales Railway (G&SWR) committee held on 16th April 1836 rejected this survey and resolved to appoint a new engineer to survey a line from Gloucester to Milford Haven. Isambard Kingdom Brunel was appointed to the post on 23rd April 1836.[371] Brunel's report, which contemplated routes from Gloucester to Newport by either Chepstow or Monmouth, with a preference for the former, was considered at a meeting on 21st September 1836.[372] Brunel estimated the expenses to be £1 million to Cardiff via Chepstow and a further £1 million on to Swansea. A further £200,000 would be needed for a route via Monmouth. In view of these figures, the meeting resolved that for the present it was not expedient to extend the line beyond Cardiff, and that a route via Chepstow was preferable. A further meeting on 10th October resolved to form a company with a capital of £900,000 to construct this railway.[373] A subscriber to this scheme pointed out in *The Cambrian* in March 1840 that nothing further was done following the general fall the value of railway stock which occurred in late 1836, but also extolled the virtues of a South Wales railway.[374] A meeting was called in November 1840 to consider what action to take over unpaid subscriptions.[375] Another writer in June 1844 reiterated the case for the coastwise G&SWR, apparently unaware of what was about to unfold.[376]

In fact it was not until 1844 that conditions were deemed favourable to take up Brunel's proposal. In that year the GWR issued a prospectus in the name of the South Wales Railway Company,[377] proposing a railway from Fishguard, via Carmarthen, Swansea, Neath, Bridgend, Cardiff, Newport and thence via a

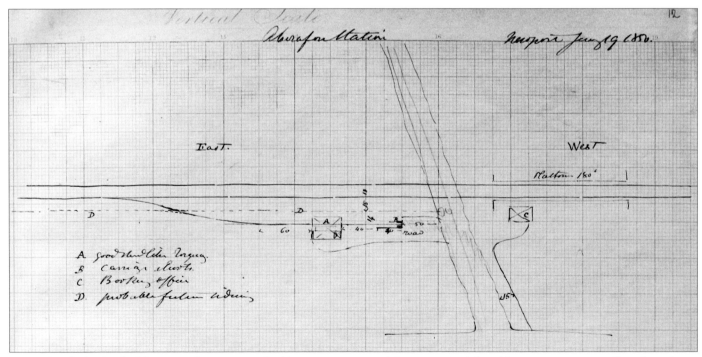

Brunel made this sketch of the proposed arrangements for Aberavon station on 19th January 1850 whilst at Newport, unconventionally with north at the bottom. The platforms and goods shed are shown in what was to become their familiar positions, to the west and east of the Oakwood Crossing respectively. A carriage dock is shown at the end of the goods siding, as is a probable further siding between this and the Up line. A surprising omission is a crossover between the running lines to permit wagons from Down trains to be worked into the goods yard. *Courtesy of the Brunel Institute – a collaboration of the SS Great Britain Trust and the University of Bristol, reference DM162/8/1/1/Large Sketchbook 1/folio 12*

What could be a typical train of the period, consisting of a '45xx' Class 2-6-2T and seven close-coupled 4- or 6-wheeled coaches, approaching Pontycymmer from the Tondu direction. Postcard, postally used 1916. Although a miners' service started in 1877, the station did not open until 1st June 1889 and closed on 9th February 1953.
Author's collection

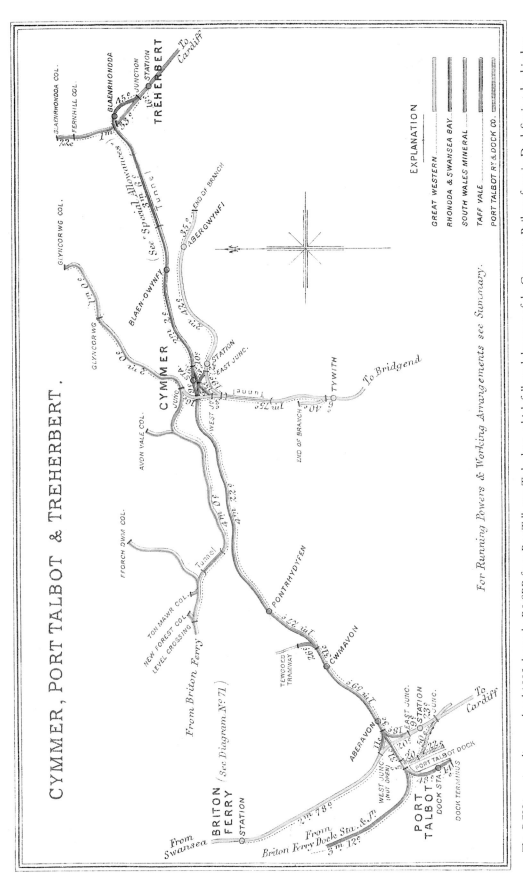

CYMMER, PORT TALBOT & TREHERBERT.

This RCH junction diagram dated 1895 shows the R&SBR from Port Talbot to Treherbert, which followed the route of the Cwmavon Railway from its Dock Station, by this date closed, as far as the junction with the Tewgoed Tramway. The short-lived west to north connection to the SWR at West Junction was closed in December 1893. The diagram also shows the short branch line from the SWR to the old dock, but there is no representation of the Oakwood Railway which crossed the SWR by Port Talbot station.

Author's collection

bridge over the River Severn to a junction with its Cheltenham Branch at Standish between Stroud and Gloucester. There was also to be a branch to Pembroke. The importance of communication with Ireland was emphasised, and the provisional committee consisted of representatives of Irish and South Welsh interests, as well as GWR directors. This time real progress was be made and the usual Parliamentary Notice appeared.[378] Brunel estimated the total cost of building this broad gauge railway to be £2,500,000.[379] There was little local objection to the line between Fishguard and Newport, but from there eastwards there was considerable opposition. Monmouthshire and Gloucester interests objected to the coastal route, but most importantly the Admiralty effectively vetoed the bridge across the Severn.[380] Consequently, the Bill was extensively amended by Parliament, which sanctioned the line of the South Wales Railway (SWR) only as far east as Chepstow. Royal Assent to the resulting Act was given on 8th August 1845.[381] Capital was set at £2.8 million in £50 shares with powers to borrow up to £933,333. The chairman of the GWR, Charles Russell, became chairman of both companies.

From Briton Ferry the authorised line hugged the coast as far as Porthcawl before turning across Merthyr Mawr Warren and following the Ewenny River south of Bridgend to Pencoed. Despite the fact that the route of the line inevitably crossed the Margam Estate between Aberavon and Kenfig Burrows, Mr Talbot chose initially not to involve himself financially with the new company. He did not take up the option of converting his contribution to the Parliamentary expenses into shares, and in September 1845 only

acquired a nominal holding of 100 shares.[382] A further 1,000 shares were purchased in late 1847.[383]

The SWR was soon proposing alterations and extensions to its authorised lines.[384] These included crossing the Severn by a higher bridge or a tunnel, an extension of the Gloucester & Forest of Dean Railway to Gloucester, branches to Swansea and Haverfordwest, and two extensive deviations of the main line. The first of these deviations was between Carmarthen and Kidwelly to improve the gradients, and the second was between Margam and Llantrissant. The proposed route of this thirteen and a half mile deviation, which included a 352 yard long tunnel, turned away from the coast at Margam to pass north of Cefn Cribbwr and Cefn Cwsc works, and follow the line of the DL&PR eastwards to Cwm Ffos. It then crossed the River Ogmore and passed north and east of Bridgend to rejoin the authorised line at Coity. The reasons given for this deviation were that it shortened the railway by two miles, it reduced the costs of maintenance by avoiding the shifting sands of Norton (*sic*, presumably Newton) and Kenfig, and it passed close to iron and coal works, affording a direct means of communication with ports and shipping places. The gradients would be more severe than those of the authorised line but easily worked.[385] Brunel estimated the additional cost of all these works to be £70,000, no breakdown being given.[386] The first Bill was not proceeded with.[387] Mr Talbot petitioned against parts of the second, revised, Bill that was presented to Parliament, on the grounds that it interfered with his property,[388] presumably referring to his newly built mansion, Margam Castle, and his works at Bryndu. The citizens of Bridgend also wished

A view of Pyle goods yard looking along the South Wales main line towards Cardiff circa 1962. The C&PR entered the yard and reached the junction with the main line from just behind the telegraph pole to the left of the goods shed. In the middle distance are the exchange sidings initially laid in circa 1863 for traffic generated by the works at Bryndu and Cefn, and remodelled in 1900 to the layout seen here. These sidings saw little traffic after 1914 when Marshall Stonehouse abandoned their slag works at Cefn, and were taken out of use in 1964. In the far distance are the junction signals for the Tondu–Porthcawl branch. *Author's collection*

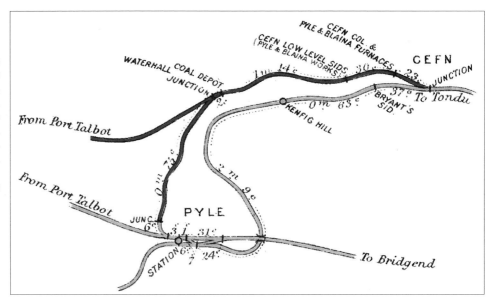

This 1909 junction diagram shows the OVER from Margam following the route of the C&PR from what became known as Waterhall Junction to Cefn Colliery, and then making a new connection to the Porthcawl Branch of the GWR at Cefn Junction. The other half of the C&PR southwards from Waterhall Junction became the PTR&D's Pyle Branch.

Author's collection

the original route to be retained.[389] All reference to this deviation was deleted from the Bill, as was any crossing of the Severn below Gloucester. The SWR's Amendment Act of 1846, which obtained the Royal Assent on 27th July,[390] increased the capital to £3 million and the borrowing limit to £1 million.

Powers to construct a modified Margam to Coychurch deviation, together with others elsewhere, and further branches, including one to the wharves at Briton Ferry, were sought in the 1847 Session.[391] This deviation was planned to leave the authorised route north of Kenfig Burrows and head east through Tydraw just south of Pyle village, over Stormy Down, before turning south to pass east of Bridgend then east again to rejoin the authorised line at Coychurch, a distance of just over fourteen and a half miles. Brunel estimated the total cost of all the proposed new works to be £465,000, again no breakdown being given.[392] This deviation, which was supported by Mr Talbot,[393] survived Parliamentary scrutiny[394] and was included in the SWR's Amendment Act of 1847, which gained the Royal Assent on 2nd July 1847.[395]

It was always the intention that the GWR would lease and work the SWR at a guaranteed rent on the share and loan capital plus a share of the surplus profits. The first provisional agreement was made on 21st October 1846, to commence when the line from Fishguard to Gloucester was completed and opened.[396] This agreement was to cause endless disputes between the two companies, and was modified a number of times.[397]

Mr Talbot was invited to join the Board of the SWR in November 1848, replacing Col Owen who had resigned.[398] According to *The Cambrian*, he held more shares than any other proprietor.[399] The appointment was announced at the half-yearly meeting of the SWR held on 28th February 1849, the directors feeling "that his large interest in the undertaking and his great local knowledge and influence will render him a most important and valuable acquisition in the management of your affairs."[400] Charles Russell resigned as chairman of the SWR on 2nd May 1849 because of the conflict of interest with the GWR, and Mr Talbot was elected in his place.[401] He was destined to guide the company through fourteen years of troubled relations with the GWR until amalgamation in 1863.[402]

Construction of the line started in the summer of 1846, but before long the general shortage of finance obliged the directors to concentrate on the line east of Swansea. By 1849 the famine in Ireland and economic conditions in general predicated that a railway to Fishguard was a hopeless undertaking, and its abandonment was proposed. This course of action would have prevented the operation of the guarantee, but the GWR declined to modify the agreement, and the original plan was adhered to for the time being. Eventually a new western terminus was agreed on the north side of Milford Haven, and abandonment of the line from Fishguard was authorised by the SWR Act 1852.[403] This Act also authorised the construction of a line to Milford Haven (renamed New Milford in 1859 and Neyland in 1906) via Haverfordwest, which was opened throughout in April 1856.

When construction was halted temporally in 1849 due to a lack of funds, Mr Talbot is reputed to have presented the company with a cheque for £500,000 to complete the line,[404] a sum which, if exchanged for shares or debenture stock, would have generated a substantial income for him. A year later the first portion of the line, from Chepstow West to Swansea, was complete and Mr Talbot led the official party which travelled on the opening train on 18th June 1850. At the celebration banquet that evening Mr Talbot welcomed the numerous benefits the railway would bring, and went on to observe that he would not be satisfied until the whole of South Wales was joined together.[405] Public services began on 19th June. Less than two months later an excursion from Swansea to Chepstow Horticultural Fete on 5th September was advertised.[406] Although the line from Chepstow East to Gloucester was opened in September 1851, it was not until 19th July 1852 that a single line over the new bridge across the River Wye was opened for traffic, thereby completing the through route from Swansea to London and bringing into effect the GWR guarantee. The second line over the Wye bridge was not brought into use until 18th April 1853. An excursion from Swansea to London and Windsor was advertised shortly afterwards.[407]

The differences between the SWR and GWR companies were finally settled by a lease and agreement dated 21st February 1862 and confirmed by the GWR (South Wales Amalgamation) Act 1863.[408]

This Act provided for the dissolution of the SWR Company and its amalgamation on 1st August 1863 with the recently amalgamated GWR and West Midland Railway companies.[409] Mr Talbot, who by now had £200,000 invested in the SWR, became a long-serving GWR director. William Owen (1810–85), the SWR's engineer, continued in that position for this division of the GWR until 1868 when he became chief engineer of the GWR.

Port Talbot station was situated near to the dock, between the Cwmavon and Oakwood railways, which were crossed on the level without any physical connection, as noted above. A junction for a branch railway to the dock was ready for use in June 1863 and formally opened in September 1864.[410] Also in June 1863 a junction and sidings at Pyle, put in quarter of a mile east of the original station by Mr Talbot at cost of £1,268 16s 1d, were certified by the divisional engineer.[411] The cost was reimbursed by a rebate of 20 per cent of the receipts on the traffic passing over the branch, and the junction became the property of the GWR. This junction provided a connection for what became known as the Cefn & Pyle Railway (C&PR).

CEFN & PYLE RAILWAY

By about 1862 Bryndu Colliery and the colliery and ironworks at Cefn Cwsc[412] were back in Mr Talbot's hands.[413] The removal of the South Wales Junction Branch Railway at Stormy meant that the only outlet for traffic from these works to the SWR was via Bridgend.[414] Bryndu and Cefn Collieries were going concerns and this seems to have encouraged Mr Talbot to construct in 1863 his own broad gauge railway from Pyle to Bryndu, a distance of about one mile,

and to continue it to Cefn over the route of an earlier tramroad which had connected these works with the DL&PR. A further extension eastwards to a new slip was made in 1874.[415] For thirty years there was no connection at Cefn to the nearby LVR, which ensured that Mr Talbot enjoyed maximum benefit from the rates generated by the traffic. In May 1892 Miss Talbot gave permission for the connection to be made, a restriction in use being that it was to facilitate traffic towards Tondu only.[416] There is no evidence that a junction was made at the time, it having to wait until the Ogmore Valleys Extension Railway opened in December 1898.[417] The two collieries were operated as Bryndu Coal & Coke Works until sold by Miss Talbot in 1898.[418] The GWR supplied Mr Talbot with 75 tons of rails in 1863 "for your branch".[419] Bryndu Coal & Coke Works operated at least one broad gauge engine – as evidenced by an invoice from the GWR in October 1868 for putting steel tyres on a colliery engine, and one was involved in a fatal accident on the line in June 1870.[420] Cefn Ironworks were idle until 1873 when Mr Talbot expended over £18,000 on improvements,[421] he then leased them and the right to use the C&PR to William Henry Forester and William Morgan who operated as the Cefn Iron Co.[422] This attempt to resurrect the works was unsuccessful[423] and the business was acquired in 1880 by the newly formed Pyle Works Ltd to manufacture ferromanganese alloys.[424] This firm got into financial difficulties and in 1889 the High Court ordered that it be wound up. That year the liquidator sold the business to another newly formed company, Pyle & Blaina Works Ltd.[425]

In 1871 the GWR listed the C&PR as far as Bryndu as one of the lines belonging to other companies which had to be narrowed as

The first station at Pyle was opened by the SWR on 19th June 1850 and closed on 1st July 1886 when a new station was opened a quarter of a mile to the east near the exchange sidings and connection with the C&PR. The L&OR had its own station at Pyle, opened on 1st August 1865. Later realignment of the L&OR brought about the combined station seen here, with the Porthcawl Branch on the right. An Up GWR goods train is starting the climb up to Stormy on the skyline. The connection to the C&PR was behind the trees on the left. Further alterations in 1912 resulted in revised connections between the two main routes and provided two platform faces on the branch. *Author's collection*

General View. Port Talbot. 502.

Port Talbot station looking towards Cardiff circa 1915. R&SBR cattle wagons are stabled in the sidings on the left which led off an array of loops connected to the R&SBR near Aberavon station, the first of which was installed in 1875 after the SWR and Cwmavon Railway had been converted to narrow gauge in 1872. Prior to that, sidings were provided for the transshipment of goods between the two railways. The flat crossing of the R&SBR over the GWR is about quarter of a mile behind the photographer.

Author's collection

part of the gauge conversion in South Wales in 1872.[426] The length so designated, including sidings, was one and a half miles, Mr Talbot having to convert the remaining two miles plus sidings at his own expense. Also in 1872 the exchange sidings at Pyle were extended to cope with the hoped-for traffic generated by the rejuvenated ironworks at a cost of £778 to Mr Talbot, and the amount was allowed to him by a rebate on the traffic.[427]

The GWR continued to do work for the Bryndu Coal & Coke Works after the gauge conversion. Mr Talbot received invoices for the repairs to "No. 1" and "No. 2" engines in 1873, these two eventually being replaced by *Derby* and *Penylan*.[428] He was also charged that year for the hire of an unidentified engine, and in November 1873 for the repair of a narrow gauge engine.[429] This might have referred to the locomotive sold by the GWR to the Bryndu Coal & Coke Works the previous October which became *Bryndu No. 3*.[430] Although the C&PR owned at least three locomotives, no buildings in the vicinity of the colliery or railway are marked on the Ordnance Surveys of 1875 or 1897 as being an engine shed. The most likely candidate was at Bryndu,[431] where there was a building shown on the 1897 survey approximately 50 feet wide by 25 feet deep, into which three short sidings ran.[432] Edward Knox, Miss Talbot's agent, was the general manager of the C&PR in 1895.[433]

Eighty-two Bryndu Coal & Coke Co. broad gauge wagons were registered with the GWR in 1872.[434] The fate of these is not known, but by April 1880 the company had seventy-five wagons on hire from the Gloucester Wagon Co.[435]

GAUGE CONVERSION

The break in gauge had long been the major obstruction to exchanging goods traffic between the GWR and its neighbours. In March 1866 the directors received a memorial signed by 296 traders, land and mineral proprietors, and others interested in South Wales, urging the adaption of the narrow gauge (that is, standard gauge) along the whole length of the South Wales main line.[436] A deputation representing this group was informed that if the application then before Parliament was successful, the company proposed to start laying narrow gauge over parts of their line, of which one part would be South Wales. Consequently, the directors were able to announce at the next half-yearly meeting the proposals to convert portions of the South Wales mainline as soon as funds permitted.[437] Another financial crisis prevented anything being done at the time.

At the March 1867 meeting the directors announced the following:

A special arrangement has, however, been entered into for the laying of a third rail between Neath and Port Talbot, by which the Copper and Tin plate Works of Margam and Aberavon, and the extensive works at Cwmavon will be brought into Narrow Gauge communication with the Vale of Neath Railway, and thus with the whole Narrow Gauge system of the kingdom. The directors have been enabled to effect this arrangement by the assistance of a gentleman, who, being locally interested in the district and desirous of securing the increased accommodation for it, has agreed to provide the capital required for the purpose at the rate of 4 per cent. per annum for four years, with the option to the Company, at the expiration of that time, either to

payoff the sum advanced or to issue to him an amount of the last created stock of the Company equal to that sum.

The identity of the gentleman was not disclosed, although Mr Talbot would certainly have fitted the description. This special arrangement was not carried out and the section remained broad gauge until the conversion of all the South Wales lines five years later. A second petition regarding the narrow gauge, this time between Neath and Briton Ferry, was received in March 1869, and referred to the general manager.[438]

Nothing was done until February 1871 when the GWR Board considered Joshua Williams' report on three schemes for converting all or parts of the lines between Stonehouse in Gloucestershire and New Milford.[439] The directors decided on the comprehensive option, involving conversion from broad to narrow gauge of the entire main line from New Milford to Grange Court and from Gloucester to Swindon, removal of broad gauge rails between Grange Court and Gloucester and on the Vale of Neath Railway, and laying mixed gauge from Didcot to Swindon, thereby providing a narrow gauge line throughout from London to New Milford. The total cost of this scheme, including new locomotives and rolling stock, was put at £511,295.[440] This was not before time, as in July 1871 Mr Talbot found it necessary to call the attention of the directors to the shortage of broad gauge trucks in South Wales and delays caused by goods awaiting transfer at junctions with the narrow gauge.[441] The GWR chairman, Daniel Gooch, met a deputation of colliery proprietors and owners of broad gauge stock in October 1871 regarding compensation for the cost of altering their wagons and lines to narrow gauge. This request was not entertained, the GWR having no powers to make such payments, and such wagons were worked to their homes prior to conversion. Over 1,600 broad gauge private owner wagons, including 128 operated by the Glyncorrwg Colliery Co. on the SWMR, were based in South Wales and registered with the GWR in 1871.[442]

General powers to convert their broad gauge railways to the narrow gauge were contained in the GWR (Further Powers) Act 1866.[443] In addition, powers to make arrangements with South Wales railway companies affected by the change, but not the SWMR, made up part of the GWR's omnibus 1872 Act.[444] The change was organised with military precision, the South Wales main line being dealt with over the weekend of 11–12th May 1872, although much preliminary work had been done earlier.[445] The work was inspected by Capt. H W Tyler, RE, whose report dated 4th June 1872 noted that the conversion was generally well done, although there were a large number of minor matters still to attend to.[446] Locally, locking frames were required at Pyle Sidings and Margam Sidings, and the signalling and sidings at Port Talbot needed to be carefully arranged. The sidings required to be locked and worked in connection with the two tramway crossings. Capt. Tyler noted that most of these works were in hand.[447]

In 1881, one further railway was proposed by the GWR between Port Talbot and Bridgend, a short east to north connection just over one mile in length with the L&OR at Pyle.[448] This line was planned to commence just west of the first Pyle station and to cross the Cefn & Pyle Railway on the level.[449] It was included in the GWR (No. 2) Act of 1882,[450] apparently without any opposition from Mr Talbot, but nothing was done and the power was allowed to expire.

NOTES

1. Charles Hadfield, *The Canals of South Wales and the Border* (David & Charles 1967), p. 72.
2. Arthur H John and Glanmor Williams (eds), *Glamorgan County History*, vol. 5 *Industrial Glamorgan* (Glamorgan County History Trust 1980).
3. A Leslie Evans, *The History of Taibach and District* (Alun Books 1963), p. 41.
4. Martin Phillips, *The Copper Industry in the Port Talbot District* (Guardian Press 1935), p. 11.
5. Arthur Rees, 'Notes on the Early Development of Taibach', *Trans of the Port Talbot Historical Society*, 4/1 (1990), p. 44.
6. Richard Morgan, *A History of Taibach to 1872* [Gemau Margam] (trans. A Leslie Evans) (Port Talbot Historical Society 1987), p. 6.
7. Phillips, *Copper*, p. 14.
8. Evans, *Taibach*, p. 47.
9. Morgan, *Taibach to 1872*, p. 12.
10. A Leslie Evans, *Cwmavon Then and Now* (Port Talbot Historical Society 1992), p. 10.
11. Ibid., pp. 12–13.
12. Ibid., p. 11.
13. James O'Brien, *Old Afan and Margam* (the author 1926), p. 96.
14. Phillips, *Copper*, p. 45.
15. Frank Jux, 'South Wales Snippets, Part 32: More Notes on Cwmavon', *The Industrial Locomotive*, 12/4 (2007), p. 101.
16. Evans, 'Cwmavon', pp. 13–14.
17. Phillips, *Copper*, p. 44.
18. Martin Phillips, 'Early Developments of the Iron and Tinplate Industries in the Port Talbot District', *Trans Aberafan and Margam District Historical Society*, 5 (1932–3), p. 20.
19. Ibid., p. 22.
20. *The Cambrian*, 23 January 1830; Paul Reynolds, 'Coal Mining in the Upper Afan, Part 3: The Collieries below Cymmer', *Afan Uchaf*, 7 (1984), pp. 24–6.
21. Quoted in NLW P&M 8927.
22. PA HC/CL/PB/6/plan1836/1.
23. TNA: PRO C 109/124.
24. *The Cambrian*, 10 September 1831.
25. Phillips, 'Early Developments', p. 22.
26. *The Cambrian*, 10 November 1838.
27. *The Cambrian*, 19 September 1840.
28. RO Roberts, 'The Bank of England, the Company of Copper Miners, and the Cwmavon Works, 1847–1852', *Welsh History Review*, 4/3 (1969), p. 222.
29. Phillips, 'Early Development', p. 24.
30. TNA: PRO RAIL 1057/2514.
31. TNA: PRO RAIL 258/421.
32. TNA: PRO RAIL 250/24.
33. TNA: PRO RAIL 252/742; TNA: PRO MT 6/256/9.
34. TNA: PRO RAIL 253/699.
35. Phillips, 'Early Development', p. 21.
36. TNA: PRO RAIL 1066/2506.
37. TNA: PRO RAIL 1057/2514.
38. TNA: PRO RAIL 1066/2505.
39. See Chapter 2.
40. Robert R Toomey, *Vivian and Sons, 1809–1924: A Study of the Firm in the Copper and Related Industries* (Garland Publishing Inc. 1985), p. 132.
41. Phillips, *Copper*, pp. 26–7.
42. *The Cambrian*, 8 December 1838.
43. D John Adams, *Glimpses of Margam Life 1830–1918* (West Glamorgan County Council 1986), p. 56.
44. Toomey, *Vivian*, p. 129.
45. *The Cambrian*, 17 February 1838.
46. *The London Gazette*, 23 February 1838.
47. GRO Q/DP 75.
48. Paul Reynolds, 'The First Port Talbot Railway (1838)', *Railway & Canal Historical Society Tramroad Group Occasional Paper*, 30 (1985); Paul Reynolds, 'Parsons, the First Port Talbot Railway (1838) and the Upper Afan Valley', *Afan Uchaf*, 8 (1985), pp. 1–11.
49. Paul Reynolds, 'Where was the First Fforchdwm Level?', *Railway & Canal Historical Society Tramroad Group Occasional Paper*, 14 (1982).
50. Reynolds, 'Coal Mining Part 3', pp. 2–5; Harry Green, 'Parsons' Folly – the Glyncorrwg Mineral Railway', *Trans Neath Antiquarian Society* (1977), pp. 78–88.
51. Stephen Hughes, *The Brecon Forest Tramroads* (Royal Commission on Ancient and Historical Monuments in Wales 1990), pp. 127–31.
52. *Mining Journal*, 19 June 1847.
53. Reynolds, 'Coal Mining Part 3', pp. 20–21.
54. TNA: PRO RAIL 1057/1539; *The Times*, 2 May 1864; TNA: PRO BT 31/1167/2502C.
55. TNA: PRO RAIL 1057/1551.
56. M Potts and GW Green, *Industrial Locomotives of West Glamorgan* (Industrial Railway Society 1996), p. 128.
57. TNA: PRO BT 31/4679/30808.
58. TNA: PRO RAIL 1057/1539.
59. *Mining Journal*, 7 January 1865
60. TNA: PRO BT 31/793/496C
61. Reynolds, 'The First Fforchdwm Level'.
62. *Mining Journal*, 28 January 1865.
63. See Chapter 7.
64. *The Cambrian*, 8 July 1864.
65. *Mining Journal*, 28 January 1865.
66. *The Cambrian*, 12 January 1866.
67. Paul Reynolds, 'The Vale of Neath and Cefn Mawr Junction Railway', *Welsh Railways Archive*, 5/2 (November 2010), pp. 27–30.
68. NLW P&M 8746.
69. NLW P&M 8747.
70. NLW P&M 8748.
71. NLW P&M 8749.
72. Phillips, *Copper*, p. 48 et seq.
73. Ibid., p. 40.
74. Evans, 'Cwmavon', p. 16.
75. Ibid., p. 19.
76. Laurence Ince, *Neath Abbey in the Industrial Revolution* (Tempus 2001), p. 170; Paul Reynolds, 'A Dreadful Accident on the Port Talbot Railway (1848)', *South West Wales Industrial Archaeology Society Bulletin*, 68 (March 1997).
77. *The Cambrian*, 23 June 1848.
78. Quoted in Phillips, *Copper*, p. 62.
79. Evans, 'Cwmavon', p. 21.
80. Roberts, 'Bank of England', pp. 219–34.
81. *The Cambrian*, 2 June 1848.
82. Roberts 'Bank of England', p. 229.
83. *The Cambrian*, 9 June 1848.
84. See Chapter 2.
85. TNA: PRO RAIL 1066/2505; TNA: PRO RAIL 1057/1551.
86. Phillips, *Copper*, pp. 70–71.
87. Ibid., pp. 71–5.
88. Ibid., pp. 75–6.
89. TNA: PRO RAIL 258/421.
90. TNA: PRO RAIL 1057/1551.
91. TNA: PRO RAIL 1066/2506.
92. Phillips, *Copper*, p. 65.
93. TNA: PRO RAIL 258/421.
94. TNA: PRO RAIL 250/22.
95. TNA: PRO RAIL 253/520.
96. TNA: PRO MT 6/141/7.
97. TNA: PRO MT 6/256/9.
98. *Post Office Directory*, 1871, p. 316.
99. Phillips, *Copper*, p. 74.
100. Morgan, *Taibach to 1872*, p. 17.

101. Ince, *Neath Abbey*, p. 170.
102. Evans, *Taibach*, p. 64.
103. Toomey, *Vivian*, p. 131; Phillips, *Copper*, p. 30.
104. *GWR Service Time Tables*, South Wales Section, February 1866, (repr. Dragonwheel Books 2004).
105. TNA: PRO RAIL 253/520.
106. *The Cambrian*, 8 July 1857.
107. *The Cambrian*, 31 January 1862.
108. TNA: PRO RAIL 253/520.
109. Potts and Green, *Industrial Locomotives*, p. 144.
110. *The Cardiff & Merthyr Guardian*, 31 May 1851.
111. *The Cambrian*, 9 December 1851.
112. 14 & 15 Vict. c.xlix.
113. *The Cambrian*, 23 July 1852.
114. *The Cambrian*, 9 July 1852.
115. *The Cambrian*, 8 August 1852.
116. *The Cambrian*, 10 September 1852.
117. *The London Gazette*, 23 November 1852.
118. PA HL/PO/PB/3/plan1852-1853/S2.
119. TNA: PRO BT 41/905/5472.
120. TNA: PRO RAIL 383/3.
121. *The London Gazette*, 31 November 1852.
122. *The Cambrian*, 21 January 1853.
123. TNA: PRO RAIL 383/3 22 March 1853.
124. *The Railway Times*, 26 March 1853.
125. *House of Lords Journal*, 1853.
126. 16 & 17 Vict. c.cxcvii.
127. See Chapter 7.
128. *The Cambrian*, 14 October 1864.
129. Paul Reynolds, 'Cast Iron and India Rubber: an Outline of the Life of John Dickson, Railway Contractor', *South West Wales Industrial Archaeology Society Bulletin*, 89 (2004), p. 6.
130. *The Cambrian*, 14 October 1864
131. Charles Wilkins, *The History of the Iron, Steel, Tinplate and Other Trades of Wales* (Joseph Williams 1903), p. 342.
132. *The London Gazette*, 25 November 1864.
133. GRO Q/DP 271.
134. Thos C Watkins, 'Prize Essay on the Propriety of having a Railway from Aberavon to Mynydd-y Caerau, Cwmcorrwg & Maesteg', Aberavon Eisteddfod 1865.
135. TNA: PRO RAIL 1057/1530/10.
136. *House of Lords Journal*, 1865.
137. 28 & 29 Vict. c.ccclxxvi.
138. *The Cambrian*, 8 September 1865.
139. *The London Gazette*, 24 November 1865.
140. GRO Q/DP 300.
141. 29 & 30 Vict. c.xlv.
142. *The Cambrian*, 16 November 1866.
143. *The London Gazette*, 29 November 1867.
144. PA HL/PO/PB/3/plan1867-1868/A2.
145. *The Cambrian*, 17 July 1868.
146. TNA: PRO MT 6/75/10.
147. Reynolds 'Cast Iron', p. 7.
148. TNA: PRO MT 6/75/10.
149. *The Cambrian*, 24 February 1871.
150. *The London Gazette*, 24 November 1871.
151. PA HL/PO/PB/3/plan1872/P6.
152. See Chapter 7.
153. *The Cambrian*, 8 December 1871.
154. TNA: PRO RAIL 1057/1540.
155. See Chapter 2.
156. *Western Mail*, 27 October 1879.
157. TNA: PRO RAIL 1507/1540.
158. *The London Gazette*, 25 November 1879.
159. PA HL/PO/PB/3/plan1880/P5.
160. TNA: PRO RAIL 1057/1540.
161. This account is restricted to the establishment of the R&SBR in the Avon Valley.
162. Paul Reynolds, 'The Neath River Railway Tunnel', *Trans Neath Antiquarian Society*, 1980–81, pp. 7–9.
163. Gwyn Briwnant Jones and Denis Dunstone, *The Vale of Neath Line*, Gomer 1996, pp. 52–3.
164. *The Cambrian*, 15 October 1880.
165. See Chapter 7.
166. *The London Gazette*, 26 November 1880.
167. PA HL/PO/PB/3/plan1881/R11.
168. PA HL/PO/JO/10/9/1025.
169. *House of Lords Journal*, 1881.
170. TNA: PRO RAIL 1066/619.
171. *The London Gazette*, 25 November 1881.
172. PA HL/PO/PB/3/plan1882/R5.
173. PA HL/PO/PB/3/plan1882/G8.
174. Andrew St George, *A History of Norton Rose* (Granta Editions 1995), pp. 14–25, 118.
175. PA HL/PO/JO/10/9/1053.
176. TNA: PRO RAIL 1057/1544.
177. TNA: PRO RAIL 1066/974.
178. TNA: PRO RAIL 1066/973.
179. *House of Lords Journal*, 1882.
180. 45 & 46 Vict. c.cci.
181. TNA: PRO RAIL 581/65, 1057/1530/18.
182. 49 & 50 Vict. c.xliv.
183. TNA: PRO RAIL 1057/1551.
184. TNA: PRO RAIL 1066/2506.
185. *The Cambrian*, 26 June 1885.
186. 54 & 55 Vict. c.clxxvii.
187. Michael Quick, *Railway Passenger Stations in Great Britain: A Chronology* (Railway & Canal Historical Society 2009).
188. *The London Gazette*, 24 November 1891.
189. 55 & 56 Vict. c.clxxix.
190. PA HL/PO/PB/3/plan1892/R3. A similar, shorter connection about 1,200 yards long between the two railways further up the valley had been included in R&SB Co.'s 1885 Bill (*The London Gazette*, 23 November 1884), but was withdrawn following opposition from the SWMR Co.
191. TNA: PRO RAIL 639/2.
192. TNA: PRO RAIL 581/4.
193. See Chapter 5.
194. TNA: PRO RAIL 581/4.
195. 60 & 61 Vict. c.cv.
196. *The Railway Times*, 12 February 1898.
197. TNA: PRO RAIL 639/2.
198. *The Railway Times*, 5 August 1899.
199. TNA: PRO RAIL 639/3.
200. TNA: PRO RAIL 581/7.
201. 19 & 20 Geo. 5 c.xliii.
202. *The London Gazette*, 19 November 1892.
203. PA HL/PO/PB/3/plan1893/R3.
204. TNA: PRO RAIL 1066/2568.
205. 56 & 57 Vict. c.lxiv.
206. See Chapter 2.
207. DA Lewis, *A Cambrian Adventure: A History of the Iron Industry in Maesteg* (Goldleaf Publishing 2001), p. 3.
208. Philip Riden, *John Bedford and the Ironworks at Cefn Cribwr* (the author 1992), p. 27.
209. Lewis, *Cambrian Adventure*, p. 4.
210. *The Cambrian*, 3 December 1814.
211. Riden, *John Bedford*, p. 84.
212. *The Cambrian*, 11 February 1815.
213. *The Cambrian*, 18 September 1815.
214. *The Cambrian*, 6 December 1815.
215. GRO Q/DP 17.
216. *House of Commons Journal*, 1816.
217. *The Cambrian*, 20 April 1816.
218. *The Cambrian*, 26 September 1818.
219. Lewis, *Cambrian Adventure*, pp. 3–10.

220. *The Cambrian*, 13 October 1824.
221. *The London Gazette*, 13 November 1824.
222. *The Cambrian*, 29 January 1825.
223. Riden, *John Bedford*, p. 88.
224. PA HL/PO/PB/3/plan39.
225. 6 Geo. 4 c.civ.
226. 10 Geo. 4 c.xxxviii.
227. 3 & 4 Vict. c.lxx.
228. LVR Act 1853.
229. *Cardiff Times*, 5 October 1866.
230. *The Cambrian*, 3 May 1828.
231. Riden, *John Bedford*, p. 103.
232. *The Cambrian*, 2 June 1827.
233. *The Cambrian*, 27 October 1827.
234. 9 Geo. 4 c.xcii.
235. PA HC/CL/PB/6/plan1828/13, HL/PO/PB/3/plan62.
236. *The Cambrian*, 30 October 1830.
237. Thomas Bevan, 'Industrial Development of the Llynfi, Ogmore & Garw Valleys' (unpublished MA Thesis University of Wales 1928), Appendix 5.
238. Riden, *John Bedford*, p. 103.
239. Ibid., p. 102.
240. Martin Phillips, 'Early Itineraries', *Trans Aberafan & Margam Historical Society*, 4 (1933–4), p. 1.
241. PA HL/PO/PB/3/plan197.
242. *The London Gazette*, 20 February 1838.
243. PA HL/PO/PB/3/plan236.
244. Arthur John Flint, 'Sir Robert Price, Bart., MP,' in *Glamorgan Historian*, 11 (Stewart Williams nd), pp, 82–7.
245. Ibid., p 89.
246. Ibid., p 93.
247. Leonard S Higgins, 'John Brogden & Sons,' in *Glamorgan Historian*, 10 (Stewart Williams 1974), p 149.
248. Lewis, *Cambrian Adventure*, p. 11.
249. Ibid., p. 12–13.
250. Ibid., p. 14.
251. TNA: PRO RAIL 161/1.
252. *The Cambrian*, 3 October 1845.
253. *The Cambrian*, 10 October 1845; TNA: PRO BT 41/827/4694.
254. PA HL/PO/PB/3/plan1846/G36, GRO Q/DP 93.
255. *The Cambrian*, 24 October 1845.
256. *The Cambrian*, 31 October 1845.
257. *The Cambrian*, 7 and 14 November 1845.
258. *The London Gazette*, 19 November 1845.
259. *The Cambrian*, 30 January 1846.
260. *The Cambrian*, 24 October 1845.
261. *The Times*, 25 October 1845.
262. PA HL/PO/PB/3/plan1846/O7, GRO Q/DP 99.
263. *The London Gazette*, 20 November 1845.
264. TNA: PRO BT 41/856/4987.
265. Lewis, *Cambrian Adventure*, p. 35.
266. *The London Gazette*, 18 November 1845.
267. PA HL/PO/PB/3/plan1846/L64, GRO Q/DP 90.
268. *House of Commons Journal*, 1846; *House of Lords Journal*, 1846.
269. *The London Gazette*, 28 November 1846.
270. 9 & 10 Vict. c.ccliii.
271. 10 & 11 Vict. c.ccxcv.
272. *The London Gazette*, 28 November 1846.
273. PA HL/PO/PB/3/plan1847/172.
274. *House of Commons Journal*, 1847.
275. 10 & 11 Vict. c.lxxix.
276. Lewis, *Cambrian Adventure*, p. 16.
277. Ibid., pp. 19–20.
278. Ibid., pp. 26–7.
279. Higgins, 'Brogden', pp 149–50.
280. Ibid., p. 150.
281. Lewis, *Cambrian Adventure*, p. 31.
282. Higgins, 'Brogden', p 154.
283. Lewis, *Cambrian Adventure*, p. 34.
284. See Chapter 3.
285. 14 & 15 Vict. c.cxxv.
286. LVR Act 1855.
287. TNA: PRO RAIL 383/2.
288. TNA: PRO RAIL 383/47.
289. TNA: PRO RAIL 383/47.
290. TNA: PRO RAIL 383/3.
291. TNA: PRO RAIL 383/79.
292. TNA: PRO RAIL 383/3.
293. Colin Chapman, 'The Duffryn Llynvi and Porth Cawl Railway: Gauge and Mixed Gauge', *Railway & Canal Historical Society Tramroad Group Occasional Paper*, 144.
294. TNA: PRO RAIL 383/3, 30 September 1852.
295. *The London Gazette*, 23 November 1852.
296. 16 & 17 Vict. c.cxlvi.
297. *The Railway Times*, 26 March 1853.
298. TNA: PRO RAIL 383/3 28 April 1853.
299. TNA: PRO BT 41/866/5087.
300. *The Cambrian*, 4 November 1853.
301. TNA: PRO RAIL 383/3.
302. *The London Gazette*, 25 November 1853.
303. PA HL/PO/PB/3/plan1854/L10.
304. *The Cambrian*, 3 March 1854.
305. *House of Commons Journal*, 1854.
306. *The London Gazette*, 24 November 1854.
307. PA HL/PO/PB/3/plan1855/L12.
308. 18 & 19 Vict. c.l.
309. *The Cambrian*, 12 June 1857.
310. TNA: PRO RAIL 639/1.
311. Colin Chapman, *The Ely Valley Railway* (Oakwood Press 2000), p. 26.
312. TNA: PRO RAIL 383/4.
313. Lewis, *Cambrian Adventure*, p. 23.
314. *The Locomotives of the Great Western Railway, Part 3 Absorbed Engines 1854–1921* (Railway Correspondence & Travel Society 1956), p. C49.
315. 25 & 26 Vict. c.cxv.
316. TNA: PRO RAIL 383/7, 21 July 1864.
317. TNA: PRO RAIL 383/7, 11 October 1864.
318. *The London Gazette*, 25 November 1862.
319. PA HL/PO/PB/3/plan1863/O1.
320. 26 & 27 Vict. c.cxxxix.
321. *The London Gazette*, 24 November 1863.
322. PA HL/PO/PB/3/plan1864/L22.
323. 27 & 28 Vict. c.xlviii.
324. ET MacDermot, revised CR Clinker, *History of the Great Western Railway, Vol. 2: 1863–1921* (Ian Allan 1964), p. 328.
325. Higgins, 'Brogden', pp. 151, 153.
326. GRO Q/DP 283.
327. 29 & 30 Vict. c.cxvii.
328. 30 & 31 Vict. c.cxv.
329. 32 & 33 Vict. c.lxi.
330. Bevan, 'Industrial Development', p. 186.
331. Ibid., p. 159.
332. Ibid., p. 188.
333. Ibid., p. 189.
334. Ibid., p. 190.
335. PA HL/PO/PB/3/plan1866/O1.
336. 29 & 30 Vict. c.cclii.
337. Jack Simmons and Gordon Biddle (eds), *Oxford Companion to British Railway History* (OUP 1997), pp 462–4.
338. MacDermot and Clinker, *GWR, Vol. 2*, p. 314.
339. 29 & 30 Vict. c.cxx.
340. 28 & 29 Vict. c.ccv.
341. Chapman, *Ely Valley Railway*, p. 33.
342. *The London Gazette*, 25 November 1870; PA HL/PO/PB/3/plan1871/L5.
343. *House of Lords Journal*, 1872.
344. *The London Gazette*, 26 November 1872.

345. PA HL/PO/PB/3/plan1873/L21.
346. Roger L Brown, 'Coal Mining in the Upper Afan Valley, Part IV: Joseph, Gibb and the Great Western Railway' *Afan Uchaf*, 8 (1985), pp. 22–3.
347. 36 & 37 Vict. c.clxxvii.
348. See Chapter 7.
349. Brown, 'Coal Mining, Part IV', pp. 24–5.
350. 46 & 47 Vict. c.lii.
351. Alun Morgan, *Porthcawl, Newton and Nottage: A Concise Illustrated History* (D Brown 1987), pp. 41–5.
352. This account deals mainly with the history of the SWR between Pyle and Briton Ferry. For more complete accounts of the SWR, see ET MacDermot, revised CR Clinker, *History of the Great Western Railway, Vol. 1: 1833–1863* (Ian Allan 1964), chapter XI; DSM Barrie, *A Regional History of the Railways of Great Britain, Vol. 12: South Wales* (David & Charles 1980); Stephen K Jones, *Brunel in South Wales, Vol. 2: Communications and Coal* (Tempus 2006).
353. Paul Reynolds, 'The London & South Wales Railway Scheme of 1824/25', *South West Wales Industrial Archaeology Society Bulletin*, 95 (February 2006), pp. 3–7.
354. Reproduced in *Herepath's Journal*, 15 May 1847.
355. *The Times*, 31 December 1824.
356. *The Cambrian*, 15 January 1825.
357. *The Cambrian*, 21 November 1829.
358. See Chapter 2.
359. GRO Q/DP 34.
360. *The Cambrian*, 14 November 1835; see also Chapter 2.
361. Reynolds, 'Neath River Tunnel', pp. 7–14.
362. *The Cambrian*, 31 August 1833.
363. *The Cambrian*, 7 September 1833.
364. *The Cambrian*, 19 October 1833.
365. *The Cambrian*, 9 November 1833.
366. *The Cambrian*, 4 April 1834.
367. Jones, *Brunel*, p. 26 et seq.
368. See Chapter 2
369. MacDermot and Clinker, *GWR, Vol. 1*, p. 8.
370. *The Cambrian*, 2 April 1836.
371. *The Cambrian*, 30 April 1836.
372. *The Cambrian*, 1 October 1836.
373. *The Cambrian*, 22 October 1936.
374. *The Cambrian*, 7 March 1840.
375. *The Cambrian*, 21 November 1840.
376. *The Cambrian*, 22 June 1844.
377. TNA: PRO RAIL 1075/222.
378. *The London Gazette*, 9 November 1844.
379. PA HL/PO/PB/3/plan1845/S2.
380. *House of Commons Journal*, 1845.
381. 8 & 9 Vict. c.cxc.
382. A Rees, *CRM Talbot and the Great Western Railway* (West Glamorgan County Council 1985), p. 2.
383. *The Cambrian*, 31 December 1847.
384. *The London Gazette*, 12 November 1845.
385. TNA: PRO RAIL 640/147.
386. PA HL/PO/PB/3/plan1846/S37.
387. *House of Commons Journal*, 1846.
388. *The Cambrian*, 30 April 1847.
389. Jones, *Brunel*, pp. 128–31.
390. 9 & 10 Vict. c.ccxxxix.
391. *The London Gazette*, 11 November 1846.
392. PA HL/PO/PB/3/plan1847/298.
393. *The Cambrian*, 30 April 1847.
394. *The Cambrian*, 7 May 1847.
395. 10 & 11 Vict. c.cix.
396. TNA: PRO RAIL 640/389.
397. TNA: PRO RAIL 640/41, 640/390; MacDermot and Clinker, *GWR, Vol. 1*, chapter XI.
398. TNA: PRO RAIL 640/4, 15 December 1848.
399. *The Cambrian*, 1 December 1848.
400. *The Cambrian*, 2 March 1849.
401. TNA: PRO RAIL 640/4; *The Cambrian*, 4 May 1849.
402. MacDermot and Clinker, *GWR, Vol. 1*, pp. 296–308.
403. 15 & 16 Vict. c.cxvii.
404. John Vivian Hughes, *The Wealthiest Commoner: CRM Talbot 1803–1890* (the author 1977), p. 26.
405. *The Cambrian*, 21 June 1850.
406. *The Cambrian*, 2 August 1850.
407. *The Cambrian*, 29 July 1853.
408. 26 & 27 Vict. c.cxcviii.
409. GWR (West Midland Amalgamation) Act 1863, 26 & 27 Vict. c.cxiii.
410. See Chapter 2.
411. NLW P&M 9430.
412. See Chapter 1.
413. Charles Wilkins, *The South Wales Coal Trade and its Allied Industries* (Daniel Owen & Co. 1888), p. 148.
414. See Chapter 1.
415. *Glamorgan Gazette*, 20 March 1874.
416. Neville Granville, *All Change at Cefn Junction* (the author 1998), p. 10.
417. See Chapter 5.
418. TNA: PRO BT 31/8023/57728; See also Chapter 20.
419. NLW P&M 9428; TNA: PRO RAIL 258/421.
420. *Glamorgan Gazette*, 17 June 1870.
421. NLW P&M 9435.
422. TNA: PRO BT 31/2703/14565.
423. Laurence Ince, *The South Wales Iron Industry 1750–1885* (Ferric Publications 1993), p. 147.
424. TNA: PRO BT 31/15008/29580.
425. TNA: PRO BT 31/15008/29580; see also Chapter 5.
426. TNA: PRO RAIL 253/520.
427. TNA: PRO RAIL 250/4.
428. See Chapter 9.
429. TNA: PRO RAIL 258/421.
430. See Chapter 9.
431. Geoffrey Hill and John Fletcher, 'Auctioneers and Surveyors of Cardiff: part 4, Stephenson & Alexander', *The Industrial Locomotive*, 13/1 (2009), p. 2.
432. The site identified in E Lyons and E Mountford, *An Historical Survey of Great Western Engine Sheds 1837–1947* (Oxford Publishing Co. 1979), p. 140, was the local coal yard.
433. *Kelly's Directory of Monmouthshire and South Wales*, 1895.
434. Geoff Sheppard, 'South Wales Goods Trains – May 1872', *Broad Gauge Society Broadsheet 39* (Spring 1998) pp. 6–7.
435. NLW P&M 9435.
436. TNA: PRO RAIL 250/21.
437. MacDermot and Clinker, *GWR, Vol. 2*, p. 26.
438. TNA: PRO RAIL 250/22.
439. TNA: PRO RAIL 250/23.
440. TNA: PRO RAIL 267/7.
441. TNA: PRO RAIL 250/24.
442. Sheppard, 'South Wales Goods Trains', pp 6–7.
443. 29 & 30 Vict. c.cccvii.
444. 35 & 36 Vict. c.cxxix.
445. MacDermot and Clinker, *GWR, Vol. 2*, Chapter 2.
446. TNA: PRO 253/699.
447. For example, work at Briton Ferry was finished on 29 May, *The Cambrian*, 31 May 1872.
448. *The London Gazette*, 29 November 1881.
449. PA HL/PO/PB/3/plan1882/G14.
450. 45 & 46 Vict. c.cxlviii.

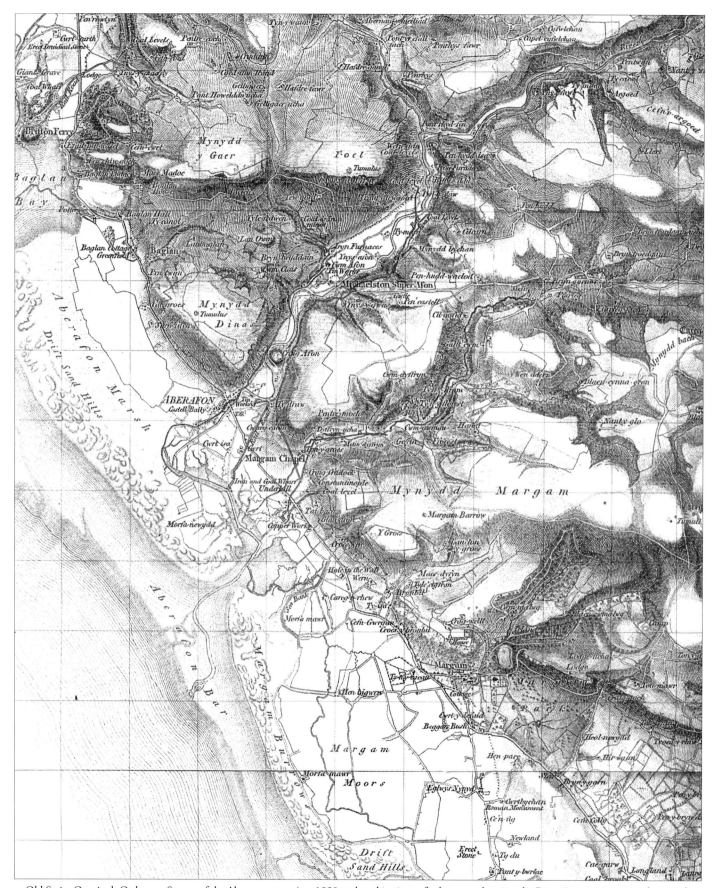

Old Series One-inch Ordnance Survey of the Aberavon area circa 1830, reduced in size to fit the page, showing the River Avon on its original, natural, course and the harbour near its mouth. Both the Cwmavon Tramroad and the Oakwood Railway are marked as Rail Roads, the latter terminating in an Iron and Coal Wharf. Also shown are the various industries referred to in the text.

2

The Port Talbot Company

Christopher Rice Mansel Talbot was born on 10th May 1803. In 1813 he inherited the Penrice and Margam estates, which were held in trust until he attained his majority in 1824.[1] He was educated at Harrow School and then Oxford University, where he obtained a first class degree in mathematics, and was elected a Member of Parliament for one of the seats in the County of Glamorgan in 1830, holding the position until his death in 1890. Mr Talbot's involvement in the promotion of the South Wales Railway and his directorship of the GWR have been already been noted,[2] and it was on his recommendation that the GWR absorbed the Vale of Neath Railway.[3] In 1862 his holdings in the SWR amounted to £85,000 in debentures, £45,000 preference shares, and £70,000 ordinary shares, as well as 13,000 GWR shares.[4]

Penrice was primarily an agricultural estate. The Margam Estate, however, straddled the southern outcrop of the South Wales coalfield and had great potential for industrial development, as Mr Talbot was well aware.[5] It extended from Pontrhydyfen along the south bank of the River Avon to the coast at Aberavon, where it included some land to the north of the river, thence down the coast to Kenfig and inland to include parts of the Llynvi Valley. The major waterway was the River Avon which entered the sea via a somewhat serpentine course and where there had been a port since historic times.

The old Aberavon Harbour was a major obstacle to industrial growth in the locality. Reaching it by sea was difficult, especially in bad weather and in winter, due to the presence of Aberavon Bar. In an attempt to alleviate the problem, a Mr Stephenson was commissioned in about 1830 by Mr Talbot and a small group of local industrialists, consisting of Messrs Vigurs and Smith, John Reynolds, and the English Copper Company, to prepare a report and to suggest possible improvements. One proposal was for a wet dock of four acres with tidal docking for coasters and colliers. The cost, estimated at £34,000, was not acceptable to Mr Talbot, especially as the difficulties outside the port were not considered.

In 1833 Henry Habberley Price, one of the partners of Neath Abbey Ironworks,[6] submitted plans for improvements to the harbour which would give a greater depth than at either Neath or Swansea, and for providing a steam tug and other conveniences. This scheme was estimated to take three years to complete.[7] A notice announcing the intention to apply to Parliament for an Act for the improvement of Aberavon Harbour was published over the name of William Llewellyn, solicitor, in *The Cambrian* on 12th October 1833. Notwithstanding some opposition from the Corporation of Bristol,[8] an Act was obtained in 1834[9] which authorised the formation of the Aberavon Harbour Company, with a capital of £12,000 and powers to raise £9,000 on mortgage. Despite being one of the sponsors of the Act, the English Copper Company was initially reluctant to subscribe to any shares, but by May 1834 they had taken £5,800. John Vigurs took £1,000, Thomas Reynolds £200, and Mr Talbot £5,000. The company's solicitor and secretary was William Llewellyn of Neath.[10]

This modest scheme, which provided for the construction of quays, deepening of the channel and improving access, was soon realised to be totally inadequate. Even before the new company held its first formal Board meeting (on 9th May 1836) another notice appeared in *The Cambrian* on 14th November 1835 stating that application would be made to Parliament in the following Session

Lithograph portrait of Christopher Rice Mansel Talbot (1803–90) dated 1877. Apart from his involvement in the development of the first dock at Port Talbot and chairmanship of the SWR, C R M Talbot was a director of the GWR 1863–90, Liberal MP for Glamorgan 1830–90, and Lord Lieutenant of the county 1848–90.

Courtesy John Vivian Hughes

for a Bill to alter, explain, amend, enlarge and partially repeal the previous Act. Despite some irregularities in Parliamentary procedure resulting from doubt as to the ability to raise the necessary funds, the Bill was allowed to proceed.[11] The second Act, which was passed on 4th July 1836,[12] amended the previous Act, providing for further improvements to the harbour and changing its name to Port Talbot. Henceforth the company was to be known as the Port Talbot Company. Although this provision legalised the name of the area as Port Talbot it was not the first time it had been used. Plans produced in 1784 for C R M Talbot's father for improving the gardens at Margam referred to moving the chapter house "to ye top of Port Talbot",[13] and the 1818 lease for the Cwmavon Tramroad referred to the harbour as Port Talbot. The share capital was raised to £30,000 and the mortgage limit raised to £25,000. A dock was to be made by stopping up the existing river by means of a lock, and fed by water taken from above a weir to be built across the River Avon near Margam Tinplate works. The river was to be diverted through a new cut to take a much more direct route to the sea, and cuts were also to be made for the new dock entrance, and for access to the English Copper Company's premises (see plan, page 4). These alterations meant that the Cwmavon tramroad had to be diverted across the river near Aberavon in order to reach the existing wharf which retained its position in the new dock. The works, which were designed and executed by Henry Robinson Palmer, the first vice-president of the Institution of Civil Engineers, were estimated to cost an additional £18,000, making a total of

£30,000, and to take five years to complete.[14] Most of the required land was owned by Mr Talbot. The area between the right bank of the old river and the right bank of the new cut was owned by the Portreeve, Aldermen and Burgesses of Aberavon and by Henry John Grant, and was conveyed to the new company by them in 1836 and 1839 respectively. This transfer of ownership was confirmed by the Court of Appeal in 1901.[15]

The new course for the River Avon was cut by repeated scouring, a course of action suggested by John Vigurs.[16] This process took five weeks to accomplish and was completed by mid-May 1837.[17] Tenders for the new lock were sought in March 1837.[18] The lock was 140 feet long by 44 feet wide.[19] The old entrance to the port was closed towards the end of October 1840, and tolls were first levied on ships entering the new dock on 30th April 1841. The new dock was known as "The Float" and was the first major enclosed dock in South Wales. Capt Pentreath was appointed the first harbour master in May 1838.

All subscriptions (£30,000) were paid up in full, but by November 1837 it was apparent that the original estimate was far too low, there only being sufficient cash in hand for two week's liabilities. Palmer needed £10,000 for additional works, which was raised by the proprietors as mortgages in proportion to their shareholding, at 5 per cent interest. A further £10,000 was raised similarly the following July. A further Act was required to enable the company to raise additional funds. Belated notices appeared in *The Cambrian*[20] and *The London Gazette*.[21] Despite this failure

This pencil sketch of Aberavon Harbour circa 1834 by Edgar MacCulloch shows the River Avon on its original course from Aberavon in the distance to its mouth opposite Taibach, with one of the wharves in the foreground. The Avon Valley heads into the hills to the left of the mound in the centre known as Craigavon. This sketch was one of a series, some of which were used to create the lithograph of Cwmavon that is reproduced on pages 8–9.
Author's collection

Margam Castle was built by C R M Talbot during 1830–35 to designs by Thomas Hopper (1776–1856). This was his principal residence and after his death in 1890 passed to his eldest daughter Miss Emily Charlotte Talbot.

Author's collection

to comply with Standing Orders, the Bill was allowed to proceed and was unopposed.[22] The resulting Act of 1840[23] raised the share capital by a further £40,000, which proved sufficient to complete the works.

The presence of at least one person holding thirty shares (£3,000 worth), either as a principal or proxy, was necessary to permit meetings to conduct the business of the company, although all shareholders were entitled to vote. Usually three or four persons were present. Mr Talbot attended mainly in the winter months, presumably when he was in residence at Margam or Penrice. At other times he was represented by one of his agents as proxy. Initially this was Griffith Llewellyn (1836–44), who was followed by William Llewellyn and his cousin, also William Llewellyn (1844–56), and then by John Felton, Mr Talbot's bookkeeper (1860–74 or later). The English Copper Company was represented by a succession of managers as proxies, notably William Jones (1836–38), William Gilbertson (1841–44, 1852–60), Thomas Richard Guppy (1846–48), William Price Struvé (1860–70), Edward Pritchard Martin (1871–74) and Thomas Barkworth (1874–75). John Vigurs or his son Louis represented the firm of John Vigurs & Co. for the period up to the time the Cwmavon Works were acquired by the English Copper Company (1836–41). John Rowland was appointed Treasurer at a Board meeting held on 26th July 1836.

The English Copper Company was re-formed in 1841 with a capital of £1,000,000. It expected to make annual profits of £85,875, including £4,000 from its shareholding in the PT Co.[24] The re-formed company took over the Cwmavon and Oakwood works in 1841.[25]

Financial difficulties became apparent as early as March 1843 when the directors of the PT Co. decided that only expenditure authorised by resolution would be allowed, and that the accounts were to be investigated. The shareholders had received no dividends, and no interest had been paid on the mortgages. Matters eventually came to head in January 1856 when the English Copper Company submitted a judgment obtained in March 1850 in their favour for £11,000 due on the mortgages they held. By February 1858, the Copper Company's claim had reached £15,000, and by June 1860, £17,000. In May 1858 the Copper Company obtained a judgment putting the PT Co. into receivership. Henry John Lewis, the harbour master, was appointed the receiver, to be replaced by the new harbour master, Capt. Jenkins, in December 1859.

To compound matters, Mr Talbot's trustees had issued a writ of ejectment in December 1857 on all those occupying his land on which the Port Talbot Dock and associated works had been constructed. No reasons were given, although flooding of his Upper Court and Lower Court Farms nearby almost certainly occurred. The directors resolved to go to arbitration, although nothing was done, and it as not until September 1860 that it was agreed that Mr Talbot and Struvé should meet to try to arrange matters, perhaps spurred on by the former's claim of £4,000 for unpaid interest made the previous month by his bookkeeper John Felton. The initial exchanges were not promising. Struvé wrote to Mr Talbot in February 1861 suggesting that the trade of Port Talbot might be greatly increased if it were connected with the South Wales Railway, some of the dock was filled in, and wharves were created. It would then be possible to ship steam coals. This scheme would also prevent flooding of Mr Talbot's land near the dock. Mr Talbot's rather sharp reply was the these were questions not for the harbour, who did not have the power to do the work, but for himself. If the harbour were properly finished (which it never had been) it might be worth his while. Under existing circumstances it was not prudent for him to expend capital for such a purpose. Nevertheless, with regard to this proposed connection, the English Copper Company did offer to reclaim a portion of the land covered by water (presumably adjacent to the SWR) for about £500 per acre, and this offer was accepted.

By this time the authorised capital (£95,000) was held by Mr Talbot (£10,575 shares, £4,000 mortgages), the English Copper Company (£45,960 shares, £20,000 mortgages) and a Mr Pritchard (£333 6s 8d mortgage), with balance not called up (£3,465 shares) or subscribed to (£10,000 shares, £666 13s 4d mortgages). Following a proposal made at the PT Co.'s annual meeting in May 1861, an arrangement was reached in the November whereby most of the existing mortgages were converted to shares, and Mr Talbot agreed to advance just over £14,000, he being entitled to 5 per cent as a preference charge payable out of the revenues of the company secured by their bonds. The £14,000 was to be used for:

1   Paying for the land required by the PT Co.
2   Paying for the occupation of land covered with water by the PT Co. during the past twenty years.
3   Paying for the damage to the Court farms during twenty years, outside the PT Co.'s limits.
4   Deepening the harbour inside.

5   Formation of new wharves and approaches to the railway at Port Talbot station.
6   Repairing and extending the breakwater.

Mr Talbot further agreed to lump the first three items together and accept £5,000 in satisfaction of all his claims. He also proposed to keep possession of the Copper Company's wharves and to lease them direct. The final result of this financial reorganisation was Mr Talbot held £13,000 as shares and £16,000 as mortgages, and the English Copper Company £57,000 and £9,000 respectively, Pritchard having surrendered his small mortgage in March 1863. The arrangement was approved by the Court of Assistants of the English Copper Company in June 1862 and at the PT Co.'s annual meeting in May 1863. The receiver was released from his obligations in August 1863, and was paid £550 for his services.

After many years of neglect, the port had begun to develop under Struvé. In March 1862 it was reported in *The Cambrian* that the embankment, presumably what was later known as North Bank, was nearing completion, and would provide extensive accommodation for coal shipping. A week later the paper reported that a railway running from the lock gates to the side of the projected breakwater had been completed and had been opened on 12th March in the presence of a party of English Copper Company directors and officials, all of whom rode on the engine, presumably belonging to the Copper Company, to the end of the line and back.[26] At the annual Court of the Copper Company held on 9th April 1863, the Governor, Sir John Pelly, Bart., commented on the rapid progress

The lock entrance to the Old Dock dating from 1837, probably photographed just before construction of the New Dock commenced.
From Port Talbot and its Progress *(PTR&D Co. 1919), Author's collection*

being made, and remarked that the dock, which in the past had given much trouble, would hopefully become a source of profit.

No sooner was the financial rearrangement in place than Struvé reported that money raised by the issue of new bonds was nearly exhausted. Much work needed to be done before the port could be connected to the SWR. Completing the branch railway and erecting three shipping stages of simple design were estimated to cost £5,500. The English Copper Company desired the works to be completed as soon as possible, and were prepared to provide £5,000 at 5 per cent. So far the English Copper Company had been paid £4,000 on account for work done to date, however Mr Talbot required agreed accounts for that work before making a final decision on the financial arrangements for future outlay at the port. At a meeting in March 1864 the English Copper Company agreed to deposit the £9,000 in mortgages held by them with Mr Talbot as security for a loan of £9,000.

This loan was to be applied to the construction and completion of the new branch railway and coal drops and other necessary works, which were designed by Struvé, subject to the approval of Mr Talbot. Mr Talbot had first raised the question of a junction with SWR at a Board meeting on 4th January 1861, he being the chairman.[27] The plans were approved at a meeting on 20th December 1861, but nothing was seemingly done at that time. The plans were re-approved at a GWR Board meeting on 29th October 1862, the cost

to be reimbursed to the PT Co. by an abatement of 20 per cent of the receipts on the traffic passing onto the branch, with the junction, which later became known as Old Dock Junction, becoming the property of the GWR.[28] The works, which cost £1,419 0s 6d, were certified by the GWR's divisional engineer, William Owen, in June 1863.[29] As a further sum was required to complete the new works, Mr Talbot was requested to enquire if the GWR was willing to negotiate for the purchase or leasing of the railway and a portion of the wharves. Progress must have been made, as in July 1864 it was reported that one hoist for tipping coal from broad gauge wagons had been ready for some weeks. Completion of the other had been delayed. The new branch railway was formally opened on 1st September 1864, when an engine and wagons first ran over it.[30] The total length of the Dock Branch and sidings in 1871 was just over one and a half miles and included two turntables,[31] implying that two coal tips were then in use.

The company was still not generating sufficient income. In June 1864 Mr Talbot demanded the interest due on his preference bonds, and again in May 1865. As none was forthcoming, he demanded that the books be audited, John Rowland of Neath being appointed to the task in July 1865. The following March Capt. Jenkins was again appointed receiver as a result of Mr Talbot's application to the Neath Justices, being owed £1,450 interest on these bonds. The English Copper Company resolved not to claim on the bonds it

The Cwmavon Works of the English Copper Co. made a rail bar 62 feet 5 inches long for the Great Exhibition held at Crystal Palace in 1851. At the time it was the longest rolled in one pass. The rail was transported by the Cwmavon Railway to Port Talbot, and is shown on Cwmavon Wharf ready for shipment. Note the wagon carrying a band attached to the engine on the track behind the rail. This engraving appeared in the *Illustrated London News* dated 22nd February 1851.

Author's collection

held until the interest due to Mr Talbot had been paid. Meanwhile in 1865 the company had obtained a further Act[32] enabling it to raise additional share capital not exceeding £80,000 and to borrow up to £25,000. The tonnage and wharfage rates granted in the 1836 Act were repealed and replaced by new rates. The English Copper Company and Vivian & Sons were exempted from paying rates on any goods handled at their own wharves.

The reappointment of a receiver seemingly spurred the English Copper Company into action. In April 1866 the Copper Company and its advisors met in London to consider the financial position of the PT Co. Improvements were deemed to be indispensable and Struvé and Messrs Clark & Barry, Consulting Engineers, were instructed to independently prepare reports, the aim being a large foreign and costal trade. A provisional committee was nominated, mainly in absentia, consisting of, among others, Mr Talbot, H H Vivian, R B Byass and Daniel Gooch. The meeting concluded with the vain hope that Mr Talbot would cooperate. The reports seem not to have survived, but the lock gates were noted as becoming unsafe. The question of replacements was due to be considered at a Board meeting in January 1867, but Mr Talbot's position prevented any progress. A terse letter to R J Gillett, the secretary, reminded the Board that the company was mortgaged to him for £16,000, mostly as preference shares, that a receiver had been appointed for the purpose of satisfying his large claim for arrears of interest, that the first claim was his, and that he did not admit the necessity of new lock gates.

The branch railway from the SWR main line was also falling into disrepair. In April 1871 it was reported that Mr Talbot had suggested that the railway might be sold to the GWR and so provide funds. The conversion of the main line to standard gauge in 1872 also required some action by the company. Contractors were sought and the GWR was to be asked if they would undertake the work on the branch line, and afterwards keep it in working order for five years, or even to purchase it. There is no evidence that the GWR directors ever considered the latter proposals, and it is unlikely they would have been entertained. The Dock Branch and sidings were, however, included in the list of broad gauge lines which were to be narrowed by the GWR.[33] In December 1877, Mr Talbot, by then the sole shareholder in the PT Co., suggested that the GWR should acquire the branch.[34] Instead, and after discussion with the general manager, it was arranged that the GWR would repair the branch, Mr Talbot providing the rails and material, and the GWR the labour. In consideration of this arrangement the GWR was permitted to use the branch for its own shunting purposes free of charge.

It was not until June 1873 that the company sought tenders for the enlargement of the entrance lock and breakwater.[35] A contract with John Dixon was approved on 19th March 1874. The lock gates, which by now were leaking badly, were inspected by a diver on 25th March under the supervision of R Applegarth, submarine and mining engineer, on behalf of Denayonze & Co., London.[36] The works were paid for by Mr Talbot who was compensated by the issue from time to time of Guaranteed Preference Shares Class A, 400 of which at £100 each were created under the terms of the company's 1865 Act at a Board meeting on 2nd April 1874. In addition, 105 Preference Shares Class B of £100 each were created at the same time. Mr Talbot was requested to take general supervision of the works, and Capt. Fitzmaurice, who had been appointed harbour master and receiver in January 1868 following

the death of Capt. Jenkins, was also appointed Clerk of the Works at £100 per annum, as from 1st January 1874. A Mr Brady was appointed resident engineer, his terms being 5 per cent of the cost of the works.

As the improvements would benefit the English Copper Company, an agreement was made on 3rd April whereby the tolls and dues payable were guaranteed to be at least £1,720. A further agreement of that date provided that Mr Talbot would be reimbursed by the issue of mortgages amounting to £9,000 at 5 per cent and the balance as Class A shares.[37] By April 1876 the total expenditure amounted to almost £34,000, for which Mr Talbot had been issued with mortgages totalling £9,000 and 250 Class A shares. Mr Talbot's and the English Copper Company's earlier mortgages had been cancelled in January 1875 in return for which they were issued with fifteen and ninety Class B shares respectively.

It is not clear when the works were finished, although the last (recorded) payment to Dixon was made in April 1876. They took the form of an additional lock 44 feet wide by 150 feet long, making a total length of 290 feet, a 370 yard long extension of the breakwater, extension of the wharfage, and deepening in The Float by dredging. Large stones quarried from Craig Avon, above Aberavon, were used for the breakwater, and small stones were deposited on the embankment on the north side of The Float where coal tips were to be erected, so as to extend the frontage and raise the wharf. The improved dock covered 30 acres and had four wharves: the PT Co.'s own, later known as North Bank, the English Copper Company's 1,000 foot long Cwmavon Wharf, later known as Talbot Wharf, Vivian & Sons wharf near their copper works, and Messrs Byass' wharf on Llewellyn's Quay.[38] Vivian & Sons had been shipping coal from their Morfa Colliery since about 1850. Coal was lowered into ships' holds by the wooden tips either in wagons or in iron boxes, this method lasting until the 1890s.[39]

Meanwhile, all was not well with the English Copper Company. At a special meeting of the proprietors held on 15th May 1872, a committee, which included Mr Talbot, was appointed to look into the company's affairs.[40] The meeting also considered a proposal to guarantee the interest on any outlay on improvements at Port Talbot Dock that would benefit Cwmavon Works. A report critical of mismanagement by the London office appeared in November 1872.[41] Operations continued at a loss and, in spite of the likely benefits resulting from improvements at Port Talbot, the company was ordered to be wound up on 1st August 1876, by which time Mr Talbot was a deputy governor.[42] John Young was appointed official liquidator. By an agreement dated 31st December 1877, made between the English Copper Company, the liquidator and the PT Co., the cross claims between the two companies were settled by the transfer of all the stocks and shares in the dock company held by the Copper Company to the dock company. This left Mr Talbot as sole shareholder in the PT Co., his holding consisting of:

£23,000 in A shares
£1,500 in B shares
£13,000 on ordinary shares, and
£23,500 in mortgages.

Up to 1875 the PT Co. more or less broke even on its working expenses. Liabilities, though, in the form of interest and dividends owed, increased from £18,900 in April 1867 to over £27,700 in April 1875.

The minutes of the PT Co.'s meetings cease in October 1875, although A Beattie, who was appointed secretary in March 1874, continued until September 1880. How the company was run from 1875 onwards is not clear, but one imagines that Mr Talbot coped by supervising the activities of his agent and the harbour master. He was not helped by the death of his son and heir, Theodore Mansel Talbot, on 18th June 1876, aged thirty-seven years, as a result of injuries sustained in a riding accident. This loss affected him deeply and may account for the lack of interest he showed in developing the docks further from then on.[43]

Others, though, were beginning to show some interest. In particular, Sidney William Yockney, the engineer of the R&SBR, then under construction, was involved in a number of schemes from 1884 onwards.[44] The R&SBR had gained access to the west side of the dock by virtue of its purchase of the Cwmavon Railway as authorised by its 1882 Act. After conversion to a modern railway, this first part of its main line was opened to traffic on 2nd November 1885. In August 1884 Yockney noted that a Richard Richards and a William Jones were to ascertain if Mr Talbot would let the harbour and property of the PT Co. in perpetuity, and if so that he was to be appointed engineer. This approach apparently achieved nothing. The following year Yockney produced a plan for improving Port Talbot Dock, including extending the breakwater, providing a new 60 foot wide lock and erecting seven coal tips, at an estimated cost of £150,150. This plan was presented to Mr Talbot's agent, William Llewellyn, in August 1886, with the recommendation that Parliament be asked in the next Session to authorise the raising of the necessary capital. Arguments in favour of the scheme were that the R&SBR was about to reach the Rhondda (this proved to be very optimistic), and the GWR and R&SBR had direct access the dock, as did the Maesteg district via Cymmer Junction.

Mr Talbot was not over-impressed. Some suggestions, for example deepening the dock and erecting coal tips, were very desirable, but he could see no advantage in extending the breakwater, and destruction of the present lock and construction of a new one would only benefit a contractor. If an additional entrance lock was necessary, it could be provided without an Act of Parliament. Nevertheless, draft particulars for a Parliamentary Notice were produced on 9th November 1886:

1 Build training wall on south side of channel and breakwater on north side.
2 Deepen entrance channel.
3 Deepen dock, construct additional lock entrance. Construct additional coal tips, sidings, cranes, warehouses, and other works.
4 Terminate any leases for the exchange or other use of the dock.
5 Create additional £200,000 capital.
6 Enter into arrangements with the GWR and/or the R&SBR for working and management of the undertaking.
7 Extend powers of the harbour master.
8 Enable the company to lease all or part of their undertaking to any individual or company.

9 Purchase lands compulsorily for the purpose of the proposed works.
10 Wholly in the parishes of Aberavon and Margam in the County of Glamorgan.

The R&SBR was evidently closely involved with this scheme. The following day H S Ludlow, the R&SBR's secretary, wrote to Llewellyn that he had heard from Yockney that Mr Talbot was favourably disposed towards the new dock, but that nothing was decided. Just over a week later Mr Talbot produced a typically terse comment on the draft:

1 North side desirable, south side unnecessary.
2 Necessary under any circumstances.
3 Needless expense. Tidal basin would have every advantage for far less cost. If lock became necessary, should be in old harbour entrance.
4 Not desirable.
5 Not desirable.
6 Premature.
7 Of course.
8 Matter of detail.
9 Matter of detail.
10 This is so.

Furthermore, he did not believe that the works required an Act of Parliament.

The deadline for the 1887 Session had of course passed, and in January 1887, in a flurry of exchanges, Yockney informed Mr Talbot that the directors of the R&SBR were disposed to take the matter up if he did not make the improvements himself, if they were granted suitable terms. In reply, Mr Talbot stated he was not prepared to make any offer with respect to improvements at Port Talbot Harbour, but would always be glad to hear the views of the R&SBR on the subject. His and their ideas differed so widely on the engineering part of the matter that it would be a waste of time to discuss details. Yockney rather grovellingly offered to modify his scheme to meet, with advantage, Mr Talbot's views, but Mr Talbot repeated that he did not contemplate any immediate action in the matter of works for the improvement of Port Talbot.

Nevertheless, the R&SBR was still interested in developing the dock. In February 1887, Ludlow reported to Yockney on a long talk he had had with Mr Talbot, by now nearly eighty-four years old and in declining health. He agreed something should be done so as to be prepared to ship large cargoes as soon as the Rhondda Tunnel was completed, but Yockney and he could not agree how this should be done. This had been a pet scheme of Mr Talbot for the last forty to fifty years; he had asked the advice of many engineers, and had concluded that a mistake had been made in altering the entrance to the dock, but that could not well be remedied. He was willing to sell or let the property; several people had been to him in the past few years, but had not received much encouragement. He was disposed to deal with the R&SBR, but they had to conform to his notions, or they would be out of it. He did not appear to be in any hurry, thought the coal in the area was not fit for shipment, and that if the work was ready before the tunnel was finished there would be no increase in shipment.

Encouraged by this, Yockney wrote to Mr Talbot in March 1887 asking if he was disposed to extend the recent arrangement for the R&SBR to use the branch of his railway to the New Wharf (that is, the North Bank) to include acquiring the use of the whole of the dock. Mr Talbot pointed out that this was not possible as the GWR, Vivian & Sons and Messrs Byass all had railway access of their own which could not be interfered with, except by Act of Parliament. Yockney pointed out that the Cwmavon Works Proprietors, both railway companies and both these firms all desired an improvement, but Mr Talbot was unmoved, and there the matter rested for the time being.

Meanwhile the docks continued to deteriorate. In December 1887, Yockney wrote to Samuel Danks, manager of the Cwmavon Works Proprietors, who by now operated blast furnaces at the old English Copper Company's site and who were having great difficulty in importing iron ore due to the bad condition of the port. The rate from Bilbao to Newport was 5s 3d per ton, but shipowners would not accept even 6s 3d per ton for the shorter voyage to Port Talbot. A quicker discharge was required, or soon no boat would go there. Rates would be driven up when their new furnace was in blast again and more ore was required. The Rio Tinto Co. was running its own steamer as it could not get other boats to visit. Many insurance companies were refusing to insure boats going to Port Talbot. Yockney advised Danks to see the owners of the port to have something done to make it more easily accessible.

Danks' partner, a Mr Smith, eventually saw Mr Talbot in October 1888, and came away with a very negative impression. Mr Talbot did not believe in any coal coming down the R&SBR to any extent until all the best steam coal was exhausted, and thus estimates of income at Port Talbot were a deception. He ignored the question of the position of the Cwmavon Works unless the port was improved, and suggested that Vivian & Sons would be very difficult to deal with as they did not want any more than they had. He attached no value to his own coal for export for the next fifty years. Smith reported that he had never had to negotiate with a more selfish man, who did not like to be reminded of any moral or social responsibility; apparently Mr Talbot saw nothing in this matter that would ever realise a pecuniary advantage, except the sale of his interest, and his pride rebelled against an unrepentant Port Talbot. Old age was not treating Mr Talbot well.

Yockney showed his plans to John Aird, senior partner of the contractors Lucas & Aird, in September 1889, with the comment that the docks could be acquired for a very moderate sum or on reasonable terms. Aird's view was that nothing could be done in the next Session of Parliament, and that it would be better to wait until Barry Dock had proved itself, and he had a chance to speak to Mr Talbot. Nevertheless, a Parliamentary Notice appeared in November that year[45] stating that a Bill would be introduced in the 1890 Session enabling the R&SBR to, *inter alia*:

- build a new quay costing an estimated £16,708 at Port Talbot Dock by extending the New Wharf (North Bank) by about 375 yards in a north-westerly direction,
- dredge the dock,
- enter lands on the north-west and north-east sides of Port Talbot Dock adjoining the Cwmavon Railway of the R&SBR, including the branch to the New Wharf,

- enter into arrangements with the PT Co. regarding the docks, accommodation, traffic, rates, employment of officers and servants, and appointment of joint committees.

Yockney was the engineer.[46] The GWR petitioned against those clauses which would affect its access to the existing sidings and coal tips, without success. The PT Co.'s petition against the Bill was withdrawn, it having secured the insertion of a new clause stating that the quay was not to be made or lands taken without consent, thereby giving it a veto over any changes.[47] The amended Bill passed into law as the Rhondda and Swansea Bay Railway Act 1890.[48]

Mr Talbot had died on 17th January 1890, in his eighty-seventh year. He was succeeded by his eldest daughter, Emily Charlotte Talbot (1840–1918), then aged thirty-nine. She inherited an estate worth nearly £6 million, over £3 million being invested in railways with the remainder in property – the approximately 35,000 acres around Port Talbot and in the Gower peninsula generated an annual rental of £44,000, half of this coming from mining leases. She was thus the richest heiress in Great Britain and, as it turned out, a force to be reckoned with.[49] In 1890 James Adair McConnochie (1835–95) was appointed her consulting engineer[50] and Edward Knox (born circa 1861) her agent.[51] Miss Talbot also frequently sought the advice of her cousin Thomas Mansel Franklen (1840–1928), the Clerk of Glamorgan County Council from 1889 until his death.[52]

Early in 1891 the R&SBR began efforts to give effect to its 1890 Act. Yockney was instructed to report on the cost of improving Port Talbot, and he and John David, the traffic manager, were instructed to see McConnochie on the subject of sidings at the dock.[53] The meeting took place on 21st February, and a week later Ludlow, the R&SBR's secretary, wrote to Knox stating that his directors were considering the question of working over the Port Talbot Dock lines to reach the Taibach part of the dock including the works there. The R&SBR were prepared, by arrangement with Miss Talbot under the powers of their 1890 Act, to double the PT Co.'s branch from near Port Talbot station to the new dock so as to improve the means of working the traffic, and also to lay the lines onto Oakwood Wharf (Llewellyn's Quay). Suggested payment was by way-leave over the dock company's lines.

Messrs Knox and McConnochie attended the meeting of the directors of the R&SBR on 4th March 1891 regarding the use of the Oakwood Railway. Knox stated that Miss Talbot was to be recommended to allow 3d per ton to the PT Co. and 1d per ton to herself. The R&SBR was be allowed to lay down a new line of rails to the wharf, no way-leave being paid for traffic over the new line. Knox also stated that Miss Talbot had been advised not to incur any more expenditure in improving Port Talbot Dock. She was prepared to receive an offer for the dock and property of the PT Co. on which £170,000 had been expended. The average balance over working expenses for the past eight years was £1,450, without paying interest on the capital. The suggested terms for the disposal of the property were £60,000 in cash, £20,000 in R&SBR shares, the appointment of a director on the R&SBR Board and royalty of one farthing/ton of coal shipped. The R&SBR's initial reaction to this proposal is not recorded. The directors restricted themselves to ascertaining whether local firms would connect with the proposed new line and send traffic over it. It seems nothing was done, as in June 1891 Knox wrote to Yockney to the effect that other arrangements had been made and that Miss Talbot had been advised that whatever she might have been prepared to agree to three months ago she could not agree to now. Unbeknown to the R&SBR, the dock had first been offered to the GWR, but at their meeting on 9th April its directors declined to entertain the matter.[54]

In fact, Knox had developed a rather more radical scheme, and had circulated a private letter outlining his ideas. He pointed out the present disadvantages of poor access from the sea and lack of the necessary facilities for carrying on an increasing trade. He also drew attention to the "scarcely concealed opposition of the large railway company whose interests, no doubt, have been elsewhere than at Port Talbot." This was a reference to the GWR, and Knox later claimed that the GWR was using the dock connection as a siding for their own convenience and hindering traffic. The traffic could have been worked by the R&SBR, but the GWR threatened that had this been done there would have been no more traffic from the GWR to Port Talbot.[55] The first two disadvantages were to be remedied along the lines suggested by an eminent engineer (McConnochie). To get round the problems with the GWR it was proposed that the PT Co. should apply for powers to construct a railway from Port Talbot to Tondu. This railway would be easy to construct, and would tap the enormous coal fields in the valleys of that district. For two-thirds of its length it would cross the property of Miss Talbot, who would materially assist in promoting the undertaking. At this stage, all that was required from traders were guaranteed shipments of coal. This document was the first to give an idea of how Miss Talbot was planning to develop her estate.

Knox attended the R&SBR Board meeting on 30th June 1891, at which McConnochie's report on the improvement of Port Talbot was read. This report formed the basis of Yockney's proposals which were submitted three weeks later. Knox then submitted to the meeting draft heads of terms for the sale and purchase of the PT Co.'s undertaking. The heads were modified at this meeting leading to a revised version being issued on 7th August:

Port Talbot Dock
Draft heads of terms for the sale and purchase of the Port Talbot Company's Undertaking.

The following gentlemen to purchase the whole of the Shares of the Port Talbot Company: [the names of the gentlemen purchasing the shares were not stated]

1. Miss Talbot as owner of the Margam Estate and sole share-holder of the Port Talbot Company, is party to these terms.
2. The purchase money to be £80,000 payable at the option of Miss Talbot, either by the issue to her of Mortgage debentures of that nominal value bearing interest at 4% constituting a first charge on the whole undertaking of the Company, or by the grant to Miss Talbot, of a rent charge of £3,200 per annum, secured as an absolute first charge on the said undertaking, together with a Royalty of one farthing per ton for all coal shipped in perpetuity at the Port, which, at the option of the purchasers may be commuted into a payment of £20,000 in cash or an additional rent charge of £800 a year, such option to be declared at time of purchase.

3. The boundaries of the property to be extended so as to include all the water space required, and certain land on the south east of the dock, which are to be included on easy terms, the ground so allotted to be for dock purposes only, and a plan to be prepared by McConnochie and Yockney and agreed and attached to the agreement.
4. Miss Talbot to facilitate the construction through her property of such railway lines as the purchasers or their successors may desire as additional approaches to and from the dock, due regard being had in the laying out of the same to the residential value and character of Margam Abbey, and the limitation of such to be defined previous to the final completion of the purchase, provided always that no line shall come nearer to Margam Abbey than the Great Western Railway Company's lines do at present.
5. Miss Talbot in letting her mineral property to insert a clause binding her lessees, where reasonably practicable, to ship a fair proportion of their output at Port Talbot dock, provided always that the facilities at Port Talbot dock are equal in character in adjoining ports.

Miss Emily Charlotte Talbot (1840–1918) photographed circa 1880. Apart from being the major financier of, and shareholder in, the PTR&D Co., Miss Talbot was noted for her philanthropy, particularly towards the church and local public and civic works.
Courtesy John Vivian Hughes

This postcard view of Mansel Tinplate Works was used by R B Byass & Co. for their 1918 Christmas card. The upper weir held back the River Avon to divert water into the dock feeder off to the right. Alleged encroachment of the reconstructed weir on the land of the Avon Vale Tinplate Works on the opposite bank resulted in the PT Co. purchasing this land in 1907. The bracket signal controlled Burrows Junction for the R&SBR's direct line to North Bank, following the route of the Cwmavon Railway, and to the PTR/R&SBR Burrows Junction Exchange Sidings nearby. The junction for the R&SBR Dock Branch was situated about 100 yards further down the line towards Swansea. *Author's collection*

6. The Purchasers and their successors to be bound by all the Statutory Provisions of the Port Talbot Company's Acts of Parliament, viz.:
   4 William Cap. XLIII,
   3 William Cap. XLVIII,
   3 Victoria Cap. LXXI
   [these three descriptors are all wrong]
   and the Port Talbot Company's Act of 1865.

7. In consideration of Miss Talbot not requiring the whole of the purchase money to be paid in cash, Miss Talbot to have in perpetuity the right to appoint a director to act with the other directors of the Port Talbot Company or of any readjustment of the same.

8. Miss Talbot and the Port Talbot Company shall concur in all the necessary Acts to give effect to these presents at the expense of the purchasers.

9. Miss Talbot will agree to these conditions on being satisfied that the Capital necessary for the extension and proper working of the dock is subscribed or guaranteed, and with the character and position of the proposed purchasers, and also subject to a binding and satisfactory contract being entered into by the 2nd August next.

Margam Estate, Port Talbot
2 July 1891
(Signed) Edward Knox, agent.

Meanwhile, on 18th July 1891 Yockney had produced his description of Port Talbot Dock and his report of proposed improvements, on which the R&SBR would presumably have acted if it had acquired the property. According to Yockney, the dock covered an area of approximately 126 acres and was entered by a lock 290 feet by 44 feet. There were three quays, which he named Cwmavon Wharf, Llewellyn's Wharf and New (North) Bank, on which were situated two "antiquated" coal drops. There were also several steam cranes for the import trade, which in copper ores was considerable, being brought in by steamer from Bilbao for the Rio Tinto works at Cwmavon. The dock was served by the GWR to the New Bank, and by the R&SBR practically throughout.

McConnochie had suggested a number of improvements, at total cost of £177,200. These included:

- erection of two modern hydraulic coal tips alongside the existing tips,
- joining the existing crane jetties by a continuous timber wharf about 450 feet in length, furnished with sheds and with two movable hydraulic cranes in addition to the two existing steam cranes,
- deepening the dock to the level of the sill for a width of 130 feet in front of the new tips and wharf,
- extending the existing breakwater,
- constructing a north breakwater,

- widening and deepening the entrance channel,
- constructing a groyne on north side of the entrance channel,
- constructing a tidal basin 500 feet long outside the present dock with an entrance of 55 feet with a single gate on the south side of the channel, and
- provision of further coal tips by extending the embankment on the east side of the dock and dredging in front, two worked by (hydraulic) engine power already available, and three requiring additional engine power.

Yockney estimated that the seven modern tips would be capable of shipping 2½–3 million tons of coal per annum, and suggested that further improvements could be contemplated:

- provision of a second tidal basin,
- further extension of the breakwater, which would be more generally useful if carried out at Mumbles, and
- provision of additional coal tips, at least thirty could easily be accommodated.

A great portion of the work of widening the entrance channel could be achieved by natural action (scouring, etc.) at minimal cost. The main objection of Port Talbot being on a lee shore would be greatly lessened by the works proposed, and was a diminishing consideration on account of steamships now being more extensively used.

If it had accepted the Margam Estate's fairly demanding terms, the R&SBR would have acquired Port Talbot Docks. However, at their directors' meeting on 5th August 1891 Sir Henry Hussey Vivian, the chairman, stated that unless colliery owners and shippers became involved in the proposed Port Talbot Dock it would not be desirable for the company to move in the matter. Knox later claimed that the scheme was ended by the opposition of Sir Henry Hussey Vivian as it would favour Port Talbot over Swansea.[56]

The only one of the ideas put forward by McConnochie that seems to have been considered further was the provision of one new coal tip. The R&SBR directors noted at their meeting on 2nd November 1891 that this subject was to be discussed further with him. On 1st December 1891 they noted that a plan was to be made showing siding accommodation for 100 wagons. Nineteen feet of water was to be maintained up to and at the tip. Miss Talbot had asked for a guarantee of £400 per annum for use of the new tip, and was to be offered £300. The terms of use of the proposed hydraulic tip were approved at their meeting on 16th March 1892, subject to Miss Talbot agreeing to maintain a sufficient depth of water. The draft agreement was ready on 24th March and provided for a hydraulic tip on New Bank adjoining an existing balance tip, plus full and empty sidings. The guaranteed average for the first three years was to be not less than £300 per annum. There is no evidence that this agreement was ever put into effect.

On 27th August 1892 the R&SBR directors met Messrs W Leatham Bright, Howard Brunlees, civil engineer, and S Morse, solicitor, representatives of a syndicate formed to acquire Port Talbot Docks, and resolved to give every facility to the new undertaking. News of this proposal had already reached the press. *The Cambrian* had reported on 12th August:

Cwmavon, Colliery Enterprise. We have the best authority for stating that on the surrender of the Oakwood Colliery in September next, by Messrs Wright, Butler & Co., that they and the Bryn, Bryngurnos, and other workings will be acquired by a powerful syndicate, who intend, not only reopening the collieries which have been idle for some years, but will sink fresh pits on the south side of the R Avon, at Cwmavon. This, together with the enlargement and improvement of Port Talbot Docks, portends a brilliant future for the Cwm [*sic*] Valley.

The Times reported on 8th September that an agreement had just been completed between Edward Knox, agent for the Margam Estate, acting for Miss Talbot of Margam Abbey, the owner of the Port Talbot Docks, and a powerful London syndicate for the sale of that undertaking. The syndicate styled itself The Port Talbot Dock & Railway Co. Ltd, not to be confused with the later Port Talbot Railway & Dock Company. A proof prospectus was prepared[57] which contained the following provisions:

1 proposed works including a half-tide basin of 10 acres, a dock of 45 acres, 25 coal tips, at an estimated cost £980,000;
2 an estimated revenue £146,000 per annum;
3 the company to acquire the existing and additional freehold land from Miss Talbot at a rental of £4,000 per annum and royalty of one farthing per ton, and redeemable for £100,000;
4 contracts had been entered into between Miss Talbot and James Renwick acting as a trustee for the limited company, and between Wright, Butler & Co. Ltd and James Renwick acting as trustee for the limited company;
5 engineers: Messrs J & H Brunlees,
6 solicitor: S Morse.

No directors were listed and there was no mention of a railway.

A draft agreement between this new company and the R&SBR was sent by Morse to Yockney on 3rd October 1892. It contained a clause stating that the R&SBR was to do everything necessary to obtain Parliamentary powers to connect their Briton Ferry Extension (then in the course of construction) to the Neath & Brecon Railway so as to bring anthracite to Port Talbot, to make the Tylorstown Loop between the Rhondda Fach and the Rhondda Fawr, and to connect their existing line with the Tondu, Garw and other valleys in the district. It was also to encourage its shareholders to subscribe to shares and debentures of the new company. In return the new company would not construct a competitive line from the Rhondda to Port Talbot.

These proposals, which would have radically altered the railway map of the area if they had been put into effect, were considered by the R&SBR directors on 14th October and again on 8th November. They resolved that they needed the following information before proceeding:

1 names and description of the promoters of the proposed company,
2 the amount for which they had agreed to be liable,
3 amount of capital proposed,
4 whether negotiations had been concluded for the purchase of the dock, and on what terms,

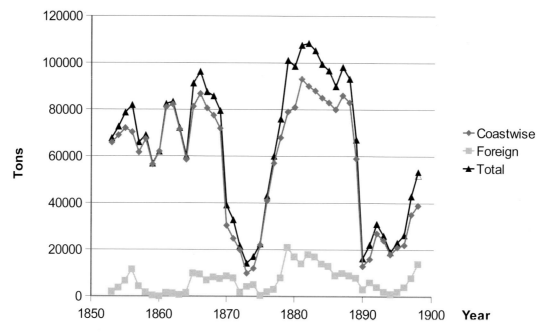

FIGURE 2.1: PORT TALBOT COAL EXPORTS, 1853–98

5 whether they had considered if they could legally acquire the PT Co. without Parliamentary sanction,

6 to what extent they intended to increase the dock accommodation.

Ludlow, the company secretary, wrote to Morse to this effect the same day. It seems no satisfactory reply was received, and the matter was dropped.

This was the last attempt to further the development of Port Talbot without recourse to Parliament. The R&SBR restricted itself to a clause in its 1893 Act[58] authorising it to subscribe to or lend the PT Co. a sum not exceeding £25,000. Subsequent events precluded the company from taking advantage of this opportunity.

Nevertheless, some of the improvements suggested by McConnochie were put into effect. At the first Board meeting of the new Port Talbot Railway & Docks Co. on 26th September 1894, he reported that five contracts with a total value of about £13,500 were in progress.[59] The work included a new hydraulic house and coal hoist on North Bank, which was being lowered to quay level. The entrance channel and the area known as The Float were being dredged to improve access, and new inner lock gates were being constructed. The weir across the River Avon built by the first PT Co. to divert water into its new dock had fallen into a state of disrepair and was being reconstructed. The northern end of the new weir was later claimed to encroach on land occupied by the Port Talbot Tinplate Co.'s Avon Vale works, and although these had closed by 1899,[60] the PT Co. agreed in 1907 to purchase the

disputed land above the high water mark for £20 to obviate any expensive litigation.[61] McConnochie also reported that one of the existing coal tips on the North Bank was obsolete and unworkable, and the other, a balance tip, was nearly worn out and too low to bunker even small steamers. The old dock was closed for the month of May 1895 for the new lock gates to be fitted.

TRADE OF THE PORT

Figure 2.1 shows the exports of coal from Port Talbot from 1853 to 1898, the year before the new dock opened (prior to 1853 Port Talbot's exports were combined with those of Swansea). During this period the trade was mostly coastwise and rarely exceeded 100,000 tons per year. The recession in the coal trade either side of 1870 is particularly evident, as is the slump in the 1890s, partly due to the unsatisfactory state the dock facilities had fallen into. The other exports were iron, tinplates, copper and modest amounts of coke. The principal imports were iron ore, copper ore and timber. Data is elusive, but Table 2.1 is illustrative.[62]

TUGS

The company's first steam tug, the *Prometheus*, arrived in March 1839, to be replaced in 1842 by the *Don*, which lasted until November 1851. The *Donna* was purchased from Mr Talbot in January 1856, and seized by the Sheriff of Glamorgan in July 1857, presumably in lieu of an unpaid debt. By September 1860 the *Donna* was owned by the English Copper Company.

TABLE 2.1: FREIGHT THROUGH PORT TALBOT

YEAR ENDING 30TH APRIL	NUMBER OF VESSELS ENTERING PORT TALBOT	REGISTERED TONNAGE	TOTAL RECEIPTS OF PORT DUES	IMPORTS (TONS)	EXPORTS (TONS)
1876	450	36,151	£ 675 8s 10d		
1881	811	82,133	£1308 7s 10d	106,000	107,000
1882	789	82,907	£1270 19s 10d	106,100	108,300
1883	716	87,663	£1403 12s 11d	113,000	115,100
1884	691	91,032	£1501 10s 0d	118,200	119,000
1885	695	92,897	£1538 11s 7d	120,100	122,000

NOTES

1. Hughes, *Wealthiest Commoner*, p. 11.
2. See Chapter 1.
3. Rees, *CRM Talbot*, p. 4.
4. Ibid., p. 3.
5. TM Campbell, 'CRM Talbot (1803–1890): A Welsh Landowner in Politics and Industry', Morgannwg 44 (2000), pp. 86–100.
6. Ince, *Neath Abbey* (Tempus 2001), pp. 74–5.
7. PA HL/PO/PB/3/plan98.
8. *House of Commons Journal*, 1836.
9. 4 & 5 William 4 c.xliii.
10. The bulk of this account of the Port Talbot Company up to 1875 is taken from the company's Minute Books, TNA: PRO RAIL 573/1–3.
11. *House of Commons Journal*, 1836.
12. 6 & 7 William 4 c.xcviii.
13. D John Adams and Arthur Rees, *A Celebration of Margam Park and Gardens* (West Glamorgan County Council 1989), pp. 46–7.
14. PA HL/PO/PB/3/plan113.
15. TNA: PRO RAIL 1057/2472.
16. HR Palmer, 'Description of the Harbour of Port Talbot (Glamorganshire)', *Proc. Inst. Civil Eng.*, 2 (1842), pp. 188–9.
17. *The Times*, 17 May 1837.
18. *The Cambrian*, 4 March 1837.
19. *Industrial Rivers of the United Kingdom* (T Fisher Unwin 1888), pp. 211–4.
20. *The Cambrian*, 11 January 1840.
21. *The London Gazette*, 13 March 1840.
22. *House of Commons Journal*, 1840, and *House of Lords Journal*, 1840.
23. 3 & 4 Vict. c.lxxxv.
24. Jux, 'South Wales Snippets, Part 32', p. 101.
25. See Chapter 1.
26. *The Cambrian*, 7 and 14 March 1862.
27. TNA: PRO RAIL 640/10.
28. TNA: PRO RAIL 250/18.
29. NLW P&M 9429.
30. *The Cambrian*, 9 September 1964.
31. TNA: PRO RAIL 253/520.
32. 28 & 29 Vict. c.lxxxv.
33. TNA: PRO RAIL 253/520.
34. TNA: PRO RAIL 250/29.
35. *The Cambrian*, 20 June 1873.
36. *The Cambrian*, 27 March 1874.
37. Preamble to the Port Talbot Railway & Docks Act 1894, 57 & 58 Vict. cxli.
38. *Industrial Rivers*, pp. 211–4.
39. Phillips, *Copper*, pp. 30–31.
40. *The London Gazette*, 30 April 1872, p. 2122.
41. *The Cambrian*, 1 November 1872.
42. *The London Gazette*, 21 March 1867, p. 2044.
43. Hughes, *Wealthiest Commoner*, p. 32.
44. The remainder of this chapter is based on a file containing Mr Yockney's correspondence on the improvement of Port Talbot, TNA: PRO RAIL 1057/1551.
45. *The London Gazette*, 29 Nov 1889, p. 6656.
46. PA HL/PO/PB/3/plan1890/R2.
47. TNA: PRO RAIL 1066/2554–2555.
48. 53 & 54 Vict. c.cxlv.
49. John Vivian Hughes, 'Emily Charlotte Talbot', *Trans Port Talbot Historical Society* (1974), pp. 85–95.
50. Obituary, 'James Adair McConnochie', *Proc. Inst. Civil Eng.*, 125 (1896), pp. 406–8.
51. Adams, *Margam Life*, p. 14.
52. *The Jubilee of County Councils, 1889–1939: Fifty Years of Local Government – Glamorgan* (Evan Brothers Ltd 1939), p. 75.
53. TNA: PRO RAIL 581/3.
54. TNA: PRO RAIL 250/40.
55. Port Talbot Co. Bill 1894, House of Commons Committee, TNA: PRO RAIL 1066/1243.
56. Port Talbot Railway & Docks Co. (South Wales Mineral Railway Junction) Bill 1896, House of Commons Committee, TNA: PRO RAIL 1066/2505.
57. TNA: PRO RAIL 1057/1530.
58. 56 & 57 Vict. c.lxiv.
59. TNA: PRO RAIL 574/1; see also Chapter 3.
60. TNA: PRO BT 31/4673/30751.
61. TNA: PRO RAIL 1057/2621.
62. *Industrial Rivers*, pp. 211–4.

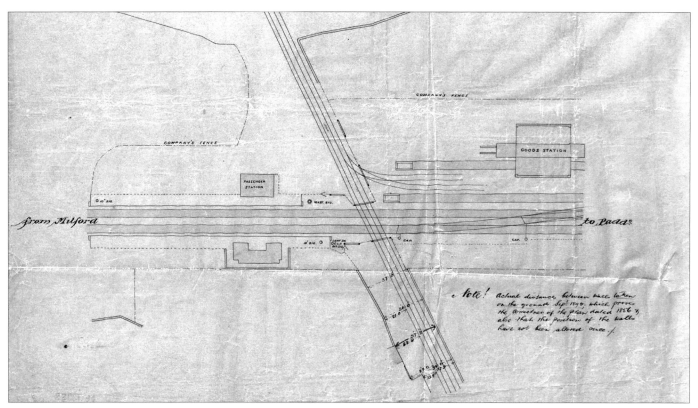

ABOVE: Survey dated 18th September 1856 showing the Oakwood Railway and a narrower gauge tramroad crossing the broad gauge SWR adjacent to Port Talbot station. What appear to be exchange sidings were laid next to the goods shed [TNA: PRO RAIL 258/421]. The Oakwood Railway Crossing was removed by 1872.

BELOW: The Oakwood Crossing surveyed on 7th September 1892, by then consisting of Byass's standard gauge line with a short connection to the SWR via the goods yard [TNA: PRO RAIL 258/421]. The dispute with the GWR originated with the Margam Estate's desire to reinstate the Oakwood Railway as a second standard gauge crossing here.

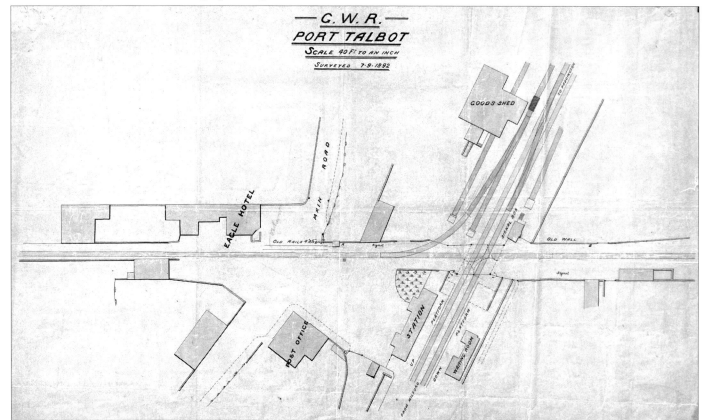

3

Formation of the Port Talbot Railway & Docks Company

By 1892 THE R&SBR and the L&OR were well established throughout the length of the Avon Valley and the Llynvi and Garw valleys respectively. These railways intersected at Cymmer in the Avon Valley and were connected towards their seaward ends by the SWR between Port Talbot and Bridgend, which thereby provided good communications with the rest of Great Britain. Apart from the coastal strip from Port Talbot to Kenfig Burrows, the Margam Estate was effectively surrounded by railways.

No acceptable proposal for the development of Port Talbot Dock had so far been put forward. The first hint that a new scheme was under consideration came when on 21st July 1892 Edward Knox, Miss Talbot's agent, wrote to A E Bolter, the GWR's assistant secretary, requesting the GWR to maintain the defunct level crossing for the railway leading from Oakwood Ironworks to Port Talbot.[1] This seemingly innocuous request was to generate much correspondence and lead eventually to litigation.[2] The existing crossing belonged to Messrs Byass & Co., connecting their tinplate works to their wharf at Port Talbot Dock, and Knox required a new line on the London side of it. Mr Lloyd, the GWR's divisional engineer, met Knox and tried without success to persuade him to connect a restored Oakwood Railway to the existing crossing, Knox maintaining that Miss Talbot had the right to two lines of rails. Knox also alleged that the GWR boundary at the crossing was in the wrong place and that if no satisfactory response was received by 25th October the matter would be put in the hands of their solicitors, Messrs Cheston & Sons. At a meeting with Messrs Lambert (GWR general manager) and Mills (GWR secretary) on 6th December, Cheston admitted that Miss Talbot was only entitled to a 4 foot 4 inch gauge tramroad which was of no practical use. He suggested that the GWR might reasonably replace it with a standard gauge tramroad, which would not be used as a public railway, but to accommodate the traffic of Miss Talbot's property, on which it was proposed to develop mining and other works.

Two days later Mills was informed that a letter had been received from John Felton, Miss Talbot's bookkeeper, stating that she had declined to settle the late Mr Talbot's account with the GWR until the Oakwood Crossing had been restored and the matter of encroachment amicably arranged. Felton had written to the Accounts Department at Paddington on 26th August 1891 asking for a statement of this account, which amounted to £7,199 6s 0d, less £5,275 4s 0d for cottages and other property rented by the GWR, giving a balance of £1,924 2s 0d. This figure was amended by agreement in August 1892 to £1,977 6s 10d. Cheston pressed in February 1893 and again in March for a decision on the crossing, as the matter was of some importance to the development of the Margam Estate. Miss Talbot was willing to pay the cost and formally demanded permission for her men to start work.

In the meantime the GWR's solicitor, Mr Nelson, had obtained counsels' opinion on the subject. In a joint opinion, Mr Cripps KC and Mr Haldane KC advised the company not to proceed on the basis that an easement no longer existed, as Miss Talbot was entitled to restore the tramroad to its original condition. The right of way was created by a lease of 14th December 1838, allowing the transport of minerals from Oakwood Ironworks, but Miss Talbot had no right to widen the gauge or to bring traffic over it other than from the ironworks. The arrangement with Messrs Byass & Co. had no bearing on the matter.

The GWR officers present at the 6th December 1892 meeting had noted that the development of the Margam Estate included the construction of a railway, and were promised a copy of the survey. In a memorandum dated 28th April 1893 summarising a meeting with his chairman, Lambert noted that Knox was proposing the construction of a new line seven and a half miles in length up the Duffryn Valley, at a cost £85,000. It was not in the interests of the GWR to support it if was intended to compete with the L&OR line, but it would be if it was merely a feeder to the GWR line. The GWR Board was to be recommended to support the scheme if the necessary mineral traffic was provided by Miss Talbot at a favourable price.

There was no mention of improving Port Talbot Dock at this time, although Knox no doubt had McConnochie's scheme in mind.[3] It seems that at first the intention was that the new railway should reach the dock via the Oakwood Crossing. However, at a meeting with Lambert on 16th May, Knox suggested it might be worthwhile to carry the lines over the SWR by means of a bridge, and that the question of the crossing could be allowed to stand over until a decision was reached regarding the proposed line.

The subject was brought before the GWR Board on 10th August 1893 when the possibility of a GWR-inspired alternative was first mooted.[4] The directors authorised the continuance of negotiations, and the engineer was instructed to prepare a scheme generally along the lines indicated by Knox's plan, but with a more convenient arrangement for crossing the SWR main line at Port Talbot than was already proposed, whilst also allowing a convenient approach to the proposed new docks. The matter came before the GWR Board again on 26th October, when Lambert submitted a letter from Knox intimating that Miss Talbot considered it absolutely essential that the construction of the Duffryn Llynvi Valley Railway and the improvement of Port Talbot Dock should be one scheme, and asking whether the company was prepared to take an interest in the scheme as a whole. Miss Talbot would have been well aware of the success of the nearby combined dock and railway system that comprised the Barry Railway Company, and which opened from 1889 onwards.[5] Lambert had informed Knox that no proposal that the GWR should contribute to the improvement of the dock had

A 1920s aerial view of Port Talbot showing the relative positions of the GWR station at the bottom left and the site of the contentious Oakwood Crossing alongside. The Oakwood Crossing was by the date of this photograph a private road into the docks and to Baldwins offices. The PTR's Central station is at the lower centre, above and to the right of the white painted building, with the line running round the rugby ground to Tonygroes Junction at the upper right. The PTR&D's offices on the corner of Eagle Street and Talbot Road can be clearly seen.

Author's collection

ever been discussed, and while the company did not see its way to subscribe to the dock undertaking, it proposed to include in the notice for its Bill for the 1894 Session of Parliament an application for power to construct a line to serve the Duffryn Valley and thus give a further opportunity for discussing the matter. It is not known if the Margam Estate was at this time actively preparing a Bill for this Session, but the GWR's stated intention would have convinced it of the need to do so.

Sidney Yockney, the R&SBR's engineer, reported the proposed scheme to that Board on 22nd September.[6] The directors recorded that while they were glad to hear of the proposed improvements to Port Talbot Dock they could not look favourably on the proposed line to Maesteg as it would compete for the traffic which their line was constructed to carry.

Miss Talbot was of course the sole shareholder of the PT Co.,[7] and no public meetings were necessary to consider any proposals. Any major improvements to the dock, however, required Parliamentary sanction, and consequently when the Parliamentary Notice appeared it was in the name of the PT Co.[8] The GWR's proposal was included as a relatively small part of its No. 1 Bill for the 1894 Session, the Notice for which appeared three days later despite being dated earlier, 9th November compared to 16th November.

CONTEST IN PARLIAMENT

The PT Co.'s notice announced the intention to introduce a Bill in the next Session of Parliament, the most significant parts of which were to be to empower it to:

- dissolve and reincorporate the company,
- rearrange the share and loan capital,
- raise further money by the issue of shares or by borrowing,
- define the limits of the port and harbour,
- constitute the company as a Pilotage Authority,
- empower the company to make breakwaters, a dock and an entrance lock, with associated works,
- construct a railway from the dock area, up the Duffryn Valley, through to Maesteg in the Llynvi Valley and on to a junction with the GWR at Pontyrhyl in the Garw Valley, together with three other short railways in Aberavon,
- exercise running powers over the GWR to the head of the Garw Valley, and over the GWR and R&SBR routes to Swansea Docks.

The GWR would have been somewhat surprised by the extension of the proposed railway beyond Maesteg, no mention of this having been made of this earlier, and by the running powers sought over its line to Swansea. Its own more modest proposals were for a railway from a junction with its main line at Port Talbot, up the Duffryn Valley and through to a junction with its Llynvi Valley line at Tywith, and also for two short railways in Aberavon. The stage was now set for a contest in Parliament between the two companies, made more pointed by the fact that Miss Talbot was a major shareholder in the GWR.

The details were clarified by the Deposited Plans. Those for the Port Talbot scheme named James Adair McConnochie, Patrick Walter Meik and Thomas Forster Brown as the engineers.[9] The proposed main line was made up of three single line railways.

Railway No. 1, eight and seven-eighths miles in length, commenced at a point about 400 yards south of the proposed new dock, headed approximately east to pass over the GWR main line near Margam Copper Works, and proceeded up the Duffryn Valley with a maximum gradient of 1 in 40 into the head of Cwm Varteg where it passed through a 975 yard long tunnel, still climbing at 1 in 300, to reach the Llynvi Valley. It then headed north up this valley on a falling gradient to reach the site of the disused Llynvi Ironworks. Here it was proposed that the new line use the broad embankment which formerly carried the tramroads connecting the Llynvi and Maesteg Ironworks over the River Llynvi and the L&OR. Railway No. 1 terminated just east of where this embankment crossed the river. Railway No. 2, which was to be three miles long, continued over the embankment and proceeded down the opposite side of the valley more or less on the level to reach Cwm Du, which was to be crossed on a 100 yard long viaduct. Railway No. 3 continued the main line for a further three and a quarter miles heading east and then turning north and dropping down to terminate at a junction with the GWR Garw Branch south of Pontyrhyll station, a total distance of about fifteen and a quarter miles. The total cost of these three railways was estimated to be £181,139 18s 6d. Two railways, Nos 4 and 6, made up a one mile connection between what later became known as Duffryn Junction on the main line and the R&SBR at Aberavon, and included an 80 yard long viaduct over the outer corner of a bend in the River Avon close to the site of the now disused Margam Tinplate works at Lower Forge. Railway No. 5 provided a half mile connection between a point later known as Tonygroes South Junction and the moribund Oakwood Railway, and commenced just north of where the latter crossed Station Road in Port Talbot. Finally, Railway No. 7 was a half mile long east to south connection between the proposed main line and the GWR at Margam. The combined estimated cost of these four short railways was £30,639 12s 0d, making the total estimate for all the railways £211,779 10s 6d. No provision was made at this stage for a passenger terminus at Port Talbot.

As originally conceived, a proposed new dock with dimensions of 1,000 feet by 600 feet, approximately 13.75 acres, was to be built immediately west of the existing lock and entered directly from the River Avon by a new double lock with a chamber 650 feet long. These works were estimated to cost £285,697. Entrance to the port had always been difficult in bad weather, and it was proposed to further protect the entrance channel by extending the existing south pier by 1,000 feet and providing a new north 1,600 foot pier/breakwater at an estimated cost of £66,200. The grand total for the whole scheme therefore came to £563,676 10s 6d. All the land required for the new dock and associated works belonged to Miss Talbot and was readily available. The Deposited Plans specifically show that all the land on Talbot Wharf was to be acquired except that occupied by the R&SBR, which was shown as having no wharf.

The engineers for the GWR scheme were Sir John Fowler, consulting engineer, and James C Inglis, the company's chief engineer.[10] The proposed main line consisted of two railways. Railway No. 4 on the Deposited Plans commenced on the seaward side of the SWR just south of the Oakwood Crossing at Port Talbot, passed under the main line and then headed up the Duffryn Valley at a constant 1 in 56 gradient to terminate at Varteg Fach near the

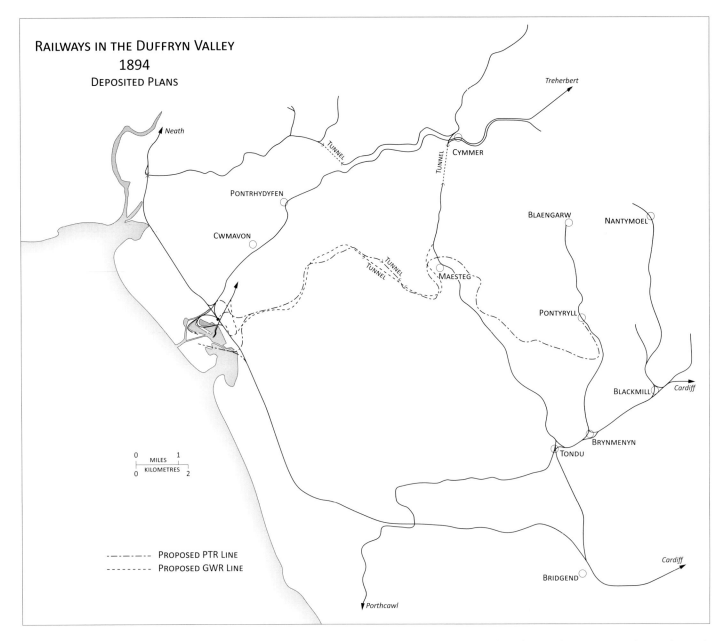

RAILWAYS IN THE DUFFRYN VALLEY
1894
DEPOSITED PLANS

PROPOSED PTR LINE
PROPOSED GWR LINE

head of the valley. It continued as Railway No. 5 through a 2,076 yard long tunnel, still climbing at 1 in 56, before descending into the Llynvi Valley and terminating by a junction with the Llynvi Valley line south of Tywith station. The estimated cost of this eight mile double track line was £338,705 11s 4d. A short single line branch, Railway No. 6, was planned to connect the new line to the existing Port Talbot Dock Branch, and another, Railway No. 7, connected it to Messrs Byass' railway,[11] these two estimated to cost a further £17,766 1s 0d. The longer tunnel and double track railway resulted in the GWR line being estimated to cost about three and a half times more to build per mile than the Port Talbot line.

The R&SBR Board tried every means available to it to frustrate the PT Co.'s Bill. On 12th December it decided to oppose the Bill on Standing Orders if the notices did not disclose all the property to be taken. This matter was settled on 15th January 1894.[12] Another issue was the ownership of Talbot Wharf at the old dock. Negotiations on this, and on mileage rates to Swansea, were terminated without agreement on 6th February.

Both Bills were introduced to Parliament on 3rd March 1894, when it was decided that they would originate in the House of Lords, as was the normal practice with conflicting or opposed Bills. Both passed the preliminary stages without any issues arising.[13]

Not surprisingly, petitions from the GWR and the R&SBR were among the five which were lodged against the PT Co.'s Bill.[14] The GWR contended that the proposed railways were unnecessary for local or through traffic and would establish unnecessary competition with its Llynvi & Ogmore and Garw branch railways. The GWR's proposed railways would provide greater accommodation for the district than one constructed by a local dock company for their own purposes. There was no reason why the PT Co. should not improve its dock, but there was also no reason for it being authorised to construct new railways, which were quite beyond its province, as the dock was already provided with railway accommodation, which would be augmented by the railways being promoted by the GWR. The GWR strongly objected to the proposed running powers over part of the Garw Branch, the SWR to Landore, the branch to

Swansea High Street station, the Swansea & Neath Railway and the Swansea Harbour Railway, a total of about twenty-seven miles. These lines were heavily used and the proposed running powers would do serious injury to the GWR.

The R&SBR claimed it was the owner of land and a quay at the dock. Also, the company was exempt from the rates levied under the Acts relating to the PT Co., and was empowered under its own Acts to levy rates at the quays belonging to it at Port Talbot. Repeal of the existing Acts would deprive the company of this exemption, and the reconstituted PT Co. would have such wide powers over the harbour area as to materially prejudice the R&SBR's position. The lack of any improvement at Port Talbot had resulted in the company not deriving any benefit from the expenditure it had incurred in accommodating traffic to Port Talbot, and it submitted that its position should not be made worse by the powers proposed by the Bill. It also claimed that the junction of the R&SBR with the L&OR at Cymmer was made to handle traffic for Port Talbot from the upper Llynvi Valley, and that the proposed new railway was unnecessary competition. The company also objected to running powers to Swansea being granted over its line, which was still being built, or those of the GWR.

The Neath Harbour Commissioners complained that the intended port included portions of the Neath port and harbour as authorised by its 1874 Act, and traffic would be diverted causing serious loss. The Earl of Jersey owned about eight acres, mainly sand hills, near the intended new dock, these were a source of revenue and formed a barrier against the sea, and he sought suitable restrictions. Charles Evan-Thomas and Henry Jeffrys Bushby owned the foreshore under grants from the Crown and complained that the Bill, if enacted, would injure their interests.

Sixteen petitions were submitted against the GWR's Bill, of which seven were relevant to its proposed Port Talbot to Maesteg line.[15] The PT Co.'s petition pointed out that it was physically impossible for both lines to be constructed as laid out. Its own line was superior, as it included the improvement of the port and harbour of Port Talbot. The GWR scheme was projected with knowledge of the PT Co. scheme, and was being promoted in direct hostility to it and to prevent its construction. A double line was not required for the traffic to be accommodated. The petition was signed by John Felton (1830–1906), who, for this purpose at least, was designated the chairman of the PT Co.

The R&SBR was particularly vehement in its petition. This company claimed that since incorporation in 1882 it had been exposed to the strongest opposition from the GWR, and the development of its business had been seriously retarded. It had withdrawn a proposed line from Cymmer to the upper Llynvi Valley from its 1893 Bill on the understanding that an arrangement would made to with the GWR regarding traffic to Swansea.[16] It was unfair that the railways now proposed would divert such traffic entirely to the GWR, as the existing railways were adequate for the available traffic.

The joint petition of the owners of seven collieries and works in the Llynvi, Garw and Avon valleys claimed that the proposed railways would interfere unnecessarily with their works and private railways, whereas those of the PT Co. were laid out to suit their requirements, and were of much greater value as they served a much wider area. Port Talbot Dock was of no value as an export dock

at the present time, and building the GWR's railways without the dock would be of no benefit to the export of minerals. The GWR monopoly in the Llynvi and Garw valleys would be confirmed if the Port Talbot scheme was rejected. There was also a risk that the GWR would build Railway No. 4 only, terminating at Bryn, to avoid the expense of building a tunnel.

Emily Charlotte Talbot, John Hopkin Traherne and Henry Lewis were the owners of estates through which the proposed railways would pass. Their joint petition submitted that the railways were laid out to occupy the more valuable parts of their estates so as to prevent any future development. Port Talbot should be improved for the export of the valuable minerals which the estates contained. The proposed railways did not do this, would prevent future development of the port, were not laid out to enable development of the minerals of the district, nor were they suitable for passenger traffic.

Margam Local Board petitioned that the proposed railways would be of little use to the district, and were laid out in such a way as to cause the greatest inconvenience, unlike those of the PT Co.'s scheme. Glamorgan County Council independently raised similar objections, and added that it appeared not to be intended to provide accommodation for passengers or to run passenger trains.

The PT Co.'s Bill also received nine petitions against changes being made to it, in effect votes of support.[17] These came from the owners of collieries and works in the Llynvi, Garw and Avon valleys, the Corporation of Swansea, Swansea, Briton Ferry, Bettws and Maesteg Chambers of Commerce, Blaengarw Chamber of Trade, Margam Local Board, and the inhabitants of Aberavon. No such petitions were submitted in favour of the GWR's Bill.

The House of Lords Select Committee appointed to scrutinise the two Bills first convened on Tuesday 17th April under the chairmanship of the Earl of Camperdown.[18] The other members of the committee were the Earl of Stamford, Lord Teynham, Lord Sudley (the Earl of Arran) and Lord Stanmore.

The Port Talbot Bill was considered first. The chairman opened the proceedings by remarking that he understood that the R&SBR wished to keep things very much as they were, and that the colliery owners, who would appear and had petitioned against the GWR Bill, preferred the Port Talbot scheme. In reply, Mr Littler KC, The PT Co.'s counsel, stated that the dock was unopposed, but the getting to it was opposed, as were running powers to Swansea via the GWR and the R&SBR. Plans for the railway and dock were submitted to the GWR, who had not been not interested in the dock as they had their own, Porthcawl and Briton Ferry, on either side. The GWR only deposited the plans for their line after the PT Co. had deposited theirs. The GWR's argument was inconsistent as it claimed the line as unnecessary, but said they were surprised it had not been made before. The R&SBRs petition claimed they would lose the benefit of a small piece of land at the dock; however, this benefit had never been realised as no wharf had been built.

The Committee then heard evidence from witnesses in favour of the Bill. Those appearing were:

- R Jones, Ocean Coal Co.
- T E Watson, managing director of Pyman & Watson Co. and manager of Ffaldau Colliery.
- E L Evan-Thomas, North's Navigation Collieries.

- O H Thomas, Llynvi Valley Colliery, International Colliery, Windsor Engineering Works.
- T Forster Brown, consulting engineer, who commented that the Vale of Glamorgan line, then about to start construction,[19] would have the effect of reducing rates eastwards, but would have no effects westwards, and that competition was needed.
- M Tutton, Alderman of Swansea and a Swansea Harbour trustee.
- G Thomas, Swansea Harbour trustee.
- E Knox, Miss Talbot's agent, who stated that he lent the plans for the proposed dock and railways to GWR in February 1893. The GWR was not interested in the dock, only the railway. The original plan showed the railway crossing the GWR main line on the level, but the GWR suggested going either over or under. The PT Co. was willing that the GWR make the line if they subscribed £150,000 towards the cost of the dock. The original plan showed a line terminating at Maesteg, the scheme being a line from Maesteg to Port Talbot and the development of Port Talbot Docks, which would have suited the development of Miss Talbot's estate quite well. Continuing the line to the Garw was the idea of the colliery owners. All the wharf owners at Port Talbot except the R&SBR, whose ownership was disputed, strongly supported the Bill.
- Col J R Wright, chairman of Wright, Butler & Co., who informed the Committee that his company had a wharf at Port Talbot which could take two vessels of 1,200 tons each. The R&SBR had no wharf. His company had agreed so sell its wharf to the PT Co. for shares in the new company, to permit its development. This wharf, which had been owned for nine years, was purchased from J Shaw, successor to the English Copper Company, no part of it being available to the R&SBR.[20]
- W Low, superintendent of Swansea Harbour Trust, who opined that giving running powers to the PT Co. would make competition more effective.
- J Hurman, formerly traffic manager, Taff Vale Railway.
- D R David, of Taibach Tinplate Works, Port Talbot, who pointed out the high cost of traffic from his works to the dock. The GWR charged 9d per ton for the half mile journey, and he also had to pay 3d per ton to Miss Talbot.
- C V Pegge, Briton Ferry Chamber of Commerce.
- J H Jones, Maesteg Chamber of Trade.
- P W Meik, a partner in the firm of PW & CS Meik, civil engineers, who informed the Committee that he and McConnochie designed the docks, and that he and Alexander Simpson designed the railway scheme, which was planned chiefly as a mineral line. He noted that the GWR scheme passed under the main line, and would need to climb to get to quay level.
- Sir Douglas Fox, civil engineer, who stated that in his opinion the lines were well laid out, and the estimates reasonable. He could not understand why the GWR wanted to build a double line.

The evidence against the Port Talbot Bill mainly concerned the proposed running powers. The R&SBR's case was given by Yockney. The railway from Port Talbot to Swansea was being constructed as a single line except for the section over Neath bridge. The introduction of compulsory running powers over the line would hinder its development and inconvenience the public using it. The R&SBR desired to carry any traffic there may be between Port Talbot and Swansea. The objection to running powers over the old Cwmavon Railway was based largely on the fact that the line had been bought from the PT Co., and the R&SBR was looking for some reciprocal arrangement regarding access to the new dock. Henry Tennant, formerly general manager of the North Eastern Railway, argued that the Garw Branch railway was not suitable for running powers because of a lack of colliery sidings, and it was not in the GWR's interests to grant them. Running powers over the GWR line from Port Talbot to Swansea were unnecessary.

Vice-Admiral Sir George Nares, Harbour Department, Board of Trade, informed the Committee that the limit beyond which tolls could be levied should be restricted to a semicircle of 1,000 yards radius from the tower on Port Talbot pier. Beyond that, shipping would receive no benefit from the new dock.

Consideration of the GWR's Bill began on 18th April, following the conclusion of the arguments for and against the PT Co.'s Bill. Henry Lambert, general manager of the GWR, stated that he was approached by Miss Talbot's agent in February 1893, she being desirous of developing her coal property in the Duffryn Valley, and asked if the GWR would assist; he was authorised to tell Knox that they was prepared to construct a railway in the Duffryn Valley. Subsequently he was asked if the GWR would take an interest in the dock, but was obliged to say it could not. He then found that the promoters of the PT Co.'s Bill had extended their line to the Garw, with proposals for running powers up the Garw and to Swansea. The GWR's Bill was deposited after Knox told them of the PT Co.'s intention. Physical conditions made running powers up the Garw inconvenient, and running powers over the GWR to Swansea offered no advantage to the PT Co. and would cause great inconvenience to everyone. Port Talbot was the best interchange point. James Charles Inglis, engineer of the GWR, seemed to confirm the colliery owners fears when he suggested under cross-examination that the GWR might drop their railway No. 2 (Bryn–Maesteg) on the grounds of expense. The Great Western Line at Port Talbot was designed to fit in with the PT Co.'s first plans for approaching the dock via the Oakwood Railway. James Thompson, general manager of the Caledonian Railway, and Herbert Yate Adye, district superintendent, GWR, also gave evidence supporting the GWR's position on running powers.

The case in favour of the GWR's Bill ended on 19th April. The Committee had evidently heard enough, because the chairman announced that it was not necessary to call the opponents of that line; they had decided that it was not expedient that the GWR lines should proceed.[21] The PT Co.'s Bill would be allowed to proceed, despite some concerns regarding access to the new dock by the GWR and R&SBR. The Committee would not grant running powers to a line between Port Talbot and Swansea, either over the GWR or the R&SBR, but such powers over the Garw line would be given.

The Committee and interested parties then proceeded to consider in detail the preamble and the 131 clauses which made up the original Bill. As a result of their deliberations the preamble and seven clauses were modified, and twelve new clauses and two new schedules were added.[22] On 23rd April the chairman declared that it was not desirable to insert a special clause regarding the rates or facilities over R&SBR or the GWR between Port Talbot and Swansea. The alterations were agreed on 24th April, and the amended Bill passed to the House of Commons on 8th May.

Nelson, solicitor for the GWR, reported the position of the two Bills to the GWR's Law & Parliamentary Committee on 26th April, and was authorised to communicate with the promoters of the Port Talbot Bill to see if a satisfactory arrangement could be come to for the construction of a railway in the district without prejudicing the GWRs interests,[23] seemingly to no avail.

In the House of Commons the examiners discovered that Standing Orders of the House not previously enquired into had not been complied with. It was agreed that these could be dispensed with, and the parties could proceed, provided powers proposed to be conferred on the GWR and SWMR companies regarding working agreements were struck out of the Bill.

Two petitions against the amended Bill were lodged. The GWR repeated its contention that the line was unnecessary and would provide unnecessary competition, and that running powers over the Garw Branch would seriously impede its own traffic there.[24] Glamorgan County Council claimed that the Bill would injuriously affect them and the interests of the county and its inhabitants.

The House of Commons Select Committee convened on 26th June with Sir Theodore Fry MP in the chair.[25] The arguments in favour the proposed scheme were repeated, with Knox adding that about three years ago (that is, circa 1891) he had discovered that the GWR was using the connection from their line to the dock as a siding for their own convenience, and hindering traffic to Port Talbot. The traffic could have been worked by the R&SBR, but the GWR had threatened that if that had occurred there would have been no more traffic from the GWR to Port Talbot.

An insight into how mineral traffic in the upper Garw valley was handled at the time emerged from the evidence. Meik informed the Committee that Ffaldau Colliery would have one siding for Port Talbot traffic, unsorted, to be marshalled at Port Talbot, whereas the GWR had separate sidings for several destinations. F Paxton, district superintendent of the GWR, appearing as a witness against the scheme, noted that the Ocean Colliery sorted its traffic well and used its own locomotives to bring coal to the exchange sidings. Nant-hir, Darran and Ffaldau collieries had limited sidings and their traffic was therefore mixed. Traffic from International Colliery was brought down by wire rope to the exchange sidings. The traffic from Braichycymmer, Garw and Llest collieries was all mixed.

It turned out that Glamorgan County Council's objections were to the lack of a double line above Pontycymmer and a station at Blaengarw. Lambert, general manager of the GWR, appearing as a witness against the Bill, opposed running powers in the Garw valley, but that if they were granted the GWR would prefer to double the line themselves rather than the PT Co. doing it.

On 28th June the chairman announced that the preamble to the Bill was provisionally proved, subject to the insertion of a clause stating that the PT Co. would bear the cost of doubling the Garw line if the GWR decided it was to be done. This clause was struck out on the following day at the request of the GWR. Glamorgan County Council withdrew its provisional clause regarding passenger traffic over the Garw Branch, having reached agreement with the PT Co. that if the line from Pontycymmer to Blaengarw was adapted for passenger traffic and if they obtained running powers thereon, those running powers would be exercised for passenger traffic.

The following day the GWR asked for running powers over Railways Nos 1 and 7 so as to develop traffic in the district and as a *quid pro quo* for the PT Co. gaining running powers over the upper section of the Garw Branch. The Committee decided they would grant such powers over Railway No. 7, the proposed connection at Margam, but not over Railway No. 1. After further discussion, the preamble, four new clauses, two amended clauses and 141 other clauses were agreed to. There were no further changes and the Port Talbot Railway & Docks Act, 1894, entitled "An Act to dissolve and re-incorporate and to confer powers upon the Port Talbot Company and to authorise them to construct an additional dock and railways and for other purposes", gained the Royal Assent on 31st July 1894.[26]

The Great Western chairman, F G Saunders, referred to his company's failure to get its Port Talbot to Maesteg railway at the half-yearly meeting held on 9th August.[27] In particular, he described the running powers granted to new company as offensive, and the existing docks as a white elephant, and he thought they would continue to be so. Time was to prove him wrong.

THE 1894 ACT

The lengthy Port Talbot Railway & Docks (PTR&D) Act 1894 was divided into eleven sections. The first part dealt with preliminary matters and defined the limits of the new port and harbour of Port Talbot. The dissolution of the PT Co. and its re-incorporation as defined by the Act was covered by the second section. The existing property was transferred to the new company along with all rights, liabilities, debts, agreements and contracts. All officers and staff employed by the PT Co. became employees of the new company on the same terms and conditions as hitherto. The mortgage of £23,500 held by Miss Talbot was to be surrendered and cancelled. The capital of the PTR&D was set at £600,000 in shares of £10 each. Miss Talbot was to be allotted 7,500 shares in the new company and required to pay the calls on them as they arose. In addition she was granted 5,000 fully paid up shares in settlement of all debts owing to her and as compensation for the shares she held in the old company. Thus Miss Talbot almost immediately become the owner of nearly 21 per cent of the authorised capital of the new company. Furthermore, any land purchased from Miss Talbot was to be paid for in shares. All other shareholders in the old company were granted five shares for every £100 of capital held. The new company was also authorised to borrow on mortgage up to £174,000. The minimum number of directors was set at five and the maximum nine, with a quorum of three. The qualification for a director was the possession of not less than fifty shares. The Act named the first directors as John Roper Wright, Charles Richard Franklen and Sidney Hutchinson Byass, and allowed two more to be nominated by them.

The power to construct the railways, piers, dock and lock shown on the deposited plans was contained in the third section of the Act. All the railways except the line from what became known as Duffryn Junction to the dock area and the connection with the GWR at Margam were to be built and equipped as passenger lines. The new company was authorised to construct within the limits of the harbour all railways, appliances and subsidiary works necessary for the general purposes of its undertaking. The water of the River Avon could be diverted into the intended dock through the existing sluices under the R&SBR near to its Burrows Junction signal box, and the new company was empowered to purchase plant and vessels suitable for dredging the dock and entrance channel. The railway works were to be completed within three years and the other works within seven years.

The agreed running powers made up section four of the Act. In addition to its power to run over the Garw Branch from the junction at Pontyrhyll to its northern termination, and the GWR's power to run over the connection at Margam, the company was required to provide junctions with the GWR suitable for the efficient exchange of traffic. An agreement with the R&SBR dated 20th April 1894 was incorporated as the sixth schedule to the Act. Compulsory running powers were substituted by agreed powers to run over the R&SBR from the junction at Aberavon to the dock. In exchange, the R&SBR was to be allowed to run over the new railways to the south side of the dock. In addition, the R&SBR was to be allowed to run over the new lines to be laid down to the north side of the dock to do shipping business, and to have access to the existing works situated along its eastern edge, provided that company paid for any additional works required. The new company was also given power to enter into working agreements with the R&SBR.

Rates for passengers and merchandise, and ships' dues and wharfage rates comprised sections five and six, and the third, fourth and fifth schedules of the Act. Section seven allowed the company to provide, with the agreement of the Commissioners of Customs, warehouses and transit sheds, and section eight named the company as the pilotage authority for the port with the power to appoint pilots. The remaining sections allowed the company to use or license the use of steam tugs, and to make byelaws.

THE PORT TALBOT RAILWAY & DOCKS COMPANY UNDERWAY

Having obtained their Act, the directors of the new company seemed to be in no hurry to begin implementing it. Their first meeting was held on 26th September 1894 at Margam, presumably in the estate office.[28] Present were the three gentlemen appointed by the Act, Col J R Wright, chairman of Messrs Wright, Butler & Co. Ltd., Col C R Franklen, representing Miss Talbot, and S H Byass, Esq., chairman of RB Byass & Co. In the absence of the Earl of Dunraven, who had evidently been expected to attend, Col Wright was elected chairman. Also present was Edward Knox, Miss Talbot's agent, who was appointed secretary.

The two nominee directors were elected at the second meeting, held on 11th December, in the persons of T E Watson Esq., chairman of Messrs Pyman, Watson & Co. and a director of Ffaldau Collieries Co. Ltd, and Llewellyn Wood, JP, of Penarth. The latter gentleman was a well known supporter of the developments at Barry but apparently took the directorship as Port Talbot was not considered to be a serious rival to either Cardiff or Barry.[29] The Earl of Dunraven and Col John North, chairman of North's Navigation Collieries (1889) Ltd were elected directors at the first shareholders meeting on 27th December 1894.[30] The earl subsequently became chairman of the company, although he rarely attended Board meetings, and Col Wright took the unofficial position of deputy chairman.

NORTH'S NAVIGATION COLLIERIES (1899) CO. LTD

The election of Col North (1842–96) as a director of the PTR&D was particularly significant, although he never attended a Board meeting. He had made a fortune from the nitrate trade in Peru between 1871 and 1882, such that he became known as "The Nitrate King".[31] Col North acquired the Llynvi & Tondu Co.[32] in June 1888 for £150,000 from the receiver, John Smith, who happened to be his neighbour, following a chance meeting at a garden party. The property was immediately transferred to the hastily formed Western Navigation Collieries Syndicate Ltd, soon renamed North's Navigation Collieries Syndicate Ltd, and then sold in January 1889 for £350,000 to North's Navigation Collieries (1889) Co. Ltd, a newly formed company capitalised at £450,000, with Col North as the major shareholder and chairman.[33] The new company became owner of six collieries in the Bridgend area: Park Slip near Tondu, Wyndham, Tynewydd, Maesteg No. 9, Maesteg Deep and Coegnant, together with the ironworks at Maesteg and Tondu. The Maesteg Ironworks were immediately dismantled and sold, but those at Tondu continued in operation until 1895. Park Slip was closed in 1904, and Wyndham and Tynewydd collieries in the Ogmore Valley were sold off as going concerns in 1906, leaving North's to concentrate on working the coal in the upper Llynvi Valley. This process had started in 1890 with the sinking of Caerau Colliery.[34]

North's of course needed an outlet for their coal. Porthcawl Docks were totally inadequate and in any case were in decline.[35] The Ogmore Dock & Railway (OD&R) scheme of 1883[36] had failed to get off the ground, leaving the company at the mercy of the GWR for access to the docks at Cardiff, Penarth and Barry, the latter then under construction. North's did show some interest in revitalising the Ogmore project, but another scheme for a railway from Bridgend through the Vale of Glamorgan to Barry showed much more promise. This route was developed following the GWR's refusal to grant concessions in rates for coal traffic to those three ports.[37] As originally planned, the route ran from Barry through Llantwit Major and to the west of Bridgend to terminate at Tondu Ironworks. There were also to be connections to the SWR main line at Bridgend and to the L&OR north of that town.[38] Running powers were sought over the L&OR up the Llynvi, Garw, Ogmore and Avon valleys, into Bridgend station and over the lines of the Barry Dock & Railway (BD&R) to Cogan. Although this scheme would obviously have been of great benefit to North's, Col North hedged his bets and accepted the chairmanship of the OD&R until the viability of the Vale of Glamorgan (VoGR) was assured. This was forthcoming in an agreement dated 8th July 1889 between the promoters of the VoGR, who included North's, and the BD&R, whereby the former would build the line and the latter would work and staff the railway once completed for 60 per cent of the gross receipts. The only significant changes to the Bill as it affected the western end of the line were brought about by the House of Commons Select Committee which, as a concession to the GWR, rejected the railway from Bridgend to Tondu and running powers over the L&OR. The VoGR Act received the Royal Assent on 26th August 1889,[39] whereas the OD&R was eventually abandoned in 1891.[40] The influence of North's was evidenced by the fact that two of its directors as well as a business associate of Col North were named in the VoGR Act as being among its first directors. The new company had great difficulty in raising the necessary capital and was forced to return to Parliament in 1892 for an extension of time.[41] Hitherto, the directors of the Barry Railway (ByR), as it had by then become, had given little assistance to the promoters of the VoGR, but the threat of further intervention in South Glamorgan by the Taff Vale Railway prompted them to become more involved. The Parliamentary Notice for the Barry Company's 1893 Bill included transfer to and vesting of the powers of the VoGR Co. in the ByR Co., and the lease of and powers to subscribe to that undertaking.[42] A clause was inserted in the Bill permitting the ByR to pay interest and dividends to the VoGR out of its share of the gross receipts and the Act received the Royal Assent on 24th August 1893.[43]

Although these guarantees improved the prospects for the VoGR considerably, they were temporarily dimmed by the revelation in February 1894 that North's and some of the other VoGR promoters, including its engineer Thomas Forster Brown, were associated with the rival scheme at Port Talbot, and indeed were to be witnesses before Parliament in favour of it, as already noted. No doubt impatience over the lack of progress with the VoGR influenced this action. However Col North remained committed to both projects and in May 1894 his company made an agreement to send 360,000 tons of coal per year for twenty years to Barry Docks via the VoGR. With this difficulty resolved, the VoGR could move on. Although problems arose during the construction of the line, the railway was opened throughout on 1st December 1897, and remained nominally independent until the grouping.[44]

Returning to the first meeting of the new Port Talbot Railway & Docks Company: it was decided that the principal office of the company was to be at Margam. Three months later it was transferred to Bank Chambers, Port Talbot, which sufficed until 1897. In January that year the directors resolved to seek from Miss Talbot a site for the company's office near the GWR station. They were offered the Port Talbot Coffee Tavern but could not justify the cost of conversion to offices. New plans were prepared, and in May 1897 the directors accepted the tender of J Davies to build the offices for £2,080 on a site on Talbot Road adjacent to the Central station. Increases in the numbers of clerical staff rendered this building inadequate, and in December 1915 additional office space in the adjacent Royal Buildings was leased, an arrangement which lasted until June 1922 when the staff remaining were transferred to the Central Office. In 1948 the building became the docks manager's office.

Some of the financial actions required by the Act were dealt with a the first meeting. The first 5,000 shares in the new company were allotted to Miss Talbot. John Felton, Miss Talbot's bookkeeper, was awarded ten shares and Knox fifty shares, in exchange for their holdings in the old company, the latter thereby becoming qualified to be elected a director. Miss Talbot surrendered her mortgages and at the same time applied for a further tranche of shares to the value of £23,000. The five existing contracts for improvements at Port Talbot[45] were approved and adopted.

Reliable sources of mineral traffic were essential to the success of the undertaking and guarantees of traffic had been sought from Ffaldau, Ocean, International and Lluest collieries in the

The PTR&D's offices as built in 1897, with the 1905 extension to the rear which was leased as the Customs House. This building was scheduled for demolition in 2010.

Author's collection

Garw Valley, and Garth Merthyr, Maesteg Merthyr, Llynvi Valley, and North's Navigation collieries in the Llynvi Valley. The Board meeting of 23rd January 1895 heard that all guarantees except with International Colliery had been exchanged. The agreement with North's was particularly important bearing in mind its recent commitment to send coal to Barry via the VoGR. These agreements were of a common form, by which the colliery company agreed to send over the Port Talbot Railway (PTR) all coal for shipment at Port Talbot or Swansea for a period of ten years from the opening of the railway, at a rate not exceeding 8d per ton to Port Talbot, or 1s 2d per ton to Swansea. These rates did not including shipping charges. Also included was coal for destinations north or west of Port Talbot which could be reached via the PTR, provided the rate was not greater than that charged by any other railway company for the same route.[46] A second agreement with O H Thomas, the proprietor of Llynvi Valley Colliery, was made on 4th July 1896 concerning a new pit to be sunk at Lletty Brongu with a siding connection to the PTR.[47] The directors decided at their meeting on 21st December 1898 that the traffic agreement with North's Navigation Collieries[48] would be deemed to have taken effect as from 1st September 1898, despite the docks not having been completed.

The meeting of 23rd January also finally approved the company's prospectus inviting the public to subscribe to £500,000 in £10 shares of the authorised capital of £600,000. Six directors were named: the Earl of Dunraven, chairman, Cols North, Wright and Franklen, the latter representing Miss Talbot, and Messrs Byass and Watson.[49] The prospectus noted that one special advantage possessed by the company was that no great expenditure on new docks was required as the new dock would be connected by the existing lock to the old dock, which could be improved as trade developed. Together these provided sites for eighteen coal tips, capable of shipping four million tons per annum. The potential for increased coal production in the Llynvi Valley, as well as the existing output of the Garw, Corrwg, Avon and Ogmore valleys and the undeveloped coal reserves in the Duffryn Valley and the Margam Estate were emphasised. Miss Talbot had inserted in her leases, and would insert in future leases, covenants compelling lessees to ship at Port Talbot 50 per cent of all coal destined for shipment. The best guarantee for the success of the undertaking lay in the fact that Port Talbot was the natural and most economical outlet for one of the richest portions of the South Wales coalfield, to which it was eleven to sixteen miles nearer than Barry or Cardiff, and fifteen to twenty miles nearer than Swansea. The company had acquired from Miss Talbot 154 acres of freehold land adjoining the docks in consideration of ½d per ton on all minerals and goods shipped or imported. The company had unlimited rights of use of this land which would afford ample space for the erection of works and warehouses. £50,600 of the authorised share capital had been issued for the purchase of the existing dock and £49,400 was reserved for the purchase of land of the erection of additional coal tips. Furthermore, the directors had received undertakings from Miss Talbot and other persons of undoubted financial stability to take £480,000 of the present issue in the event of insufficient public subscription. Forster Brown estimated that on completion of the dock and railways 1.25 million tons of coal would be shipped per annum which, together with import and passenger traffic, might be expected to yield a dividend of 6½ per cent.

The lists opened on 29th January and closed on 31st January for London and 1st February for country applicants. Miss Talbot transferred 100 shares each to Cols Wright and Franklen, thereby qualifying them to act as directors. The only initial applicants were the other four directors who between them subscribed to a total of 800 shares.

SPECIFICATION AND CONTRACT

Meanwhile, the engineers had produced a 27-page specification of the work to be done, and the conditions to be observed, in the construction of Railways Nos 1–4, 6 and 7 from Port Talbot and Aberavon to the Garw Valley, and a wet dock, entrance lock, piers and associated works at Port Talbot.[50] Eighty-three drawings accompanied the specification. The specification called for three stations, at Bryn, Maesteg and Lletty Brongu, all with timber goods sheds 40 feet long by 22 feet wide. The construction of the railway was based on the latest GWR practice: 75 lb/yd bullhead rail, chairs, fishplates, points and crossings, gradient boards and buffers stops were all to be of the most recent GWR pattern. Likewise, signal boxes were to be in keeping with the station buildings and similar in other respects to those built most recently on GWR branches in the neighbourhood. Signal posts were to be light iron lattice uprights with semaphore arms, similar to those made by Saxby & Farmer or other approved makers. A very detailed specification was given for the new lock gates, these being crucial for the proper operation of the new dock, which was to be provided with four coal jetties. The dock railways were to be constructed in a similar manner to the main line railway, with self-acting approaches to and from the coal hoists. The contractor was required to provide offices for the engineers near the dock works and at Maesteg.

No provision was made for the construction of Railway No. 5, the connection to the Oakwood Railway, which was intended to provide a route to the north side of the dock area. The question of reinstating the Oakwood Crossing had still not been resolved. This issue generated a series of internal memos during October to December 1894 between Messrs Mills and Inglis at Paddington, which culminated in Mills suggesting on 11th January 1895 that as it was not in the GWR's interest to have two level crossings, it would be worth the company's while to contribute to some alternative scheme for crossing the GWR main line by a bridge similar to that in its 1894 Bill.[51]

The specification was unusual in that it named one particular contractor, Messrs S Pearson & Son. This firm was formed in 1856 by Samuel Pearson and had by 1894 completed a number of major contracts in the UK and abroad. Samuel Pearson retired in 1879 and the partnership then consisted of his son George and grandson Weetman. Weetman Pearson became the sole partner in 1894, and was created a baronet in December that year, becoming president when the business was re-formed as a limited company in 1897.[52]

Sir Weetman wrote at length to Cheston, the PTR&D's solicitor, on 3rd January 1895 about the basis of his offer and the means of financing it.[53] One fifth of the contract price, which had been provisionally agreed with Meik, was to be paid in shares at par. He proposed that Miss Talbot should purchase Wright, Butler & Co.'s wharf for £30,000 and lease it to the company for £1,000 per annum, and that Wright, Butler should take the £30,000 as shares. The capital released could then to be used to install three extra coal lifts. Sir Weetman's principal concern was that all the share capital should be subscribed to, presumably to get a good return on his investment.

It appears that it had always been the engineers' intention to award the contract to Pearson's. This issue was of major concern to the Board of the PTR&D. A discussion took place at its meeting held on 19th January 1895, at which all five directors were present, as to the desirability of entering into a contract of any kind without having first asked for competitive tenders. Messrs Wood and Watson both expressed their dissent from such a course being adopted, which was favoured by the majority. Wood withdrew and Watson informed the Board that he wished to further consider the question. A statement from McConnochie was read at the meeting on 23rd January, to the effect that while he still preferred the competitive system, he had carefully examined Messrs Pearson's prices and was of the opinion that they were fair and reasonable and that it was unlikely that better terms could have been obtained from any other firm of equal standing under like circumstances and conditions. Watson, having considered the full explanation he had received from the secretary and his assurance that the opinion of the minority of the Board with regard to contracting without obtaining competitive tenders had been fully explained to Miss Talbot and that Miss Talbot was nevertheless prepared to subscribe for £300,000 of ordinary shares in addition to the £75,000 she was required to subscribe to under the company's Act, considered that

his objections had been overcome and that consequently he would be pleased to remain on the Board. Wood, who did not attend, resigned from the Board over this matter. Ivor Bertie Guest, Lord Wimborne, was elected to replace him on 18th June 1895.

Pearson's contract price of £527,000 for the works as specified was accepted at the 23rd January meeting and the contract was signed. The matter had evidently already been decided as the printed contract bore this date.[54] The contractors were allowed free use of the existing dock railways and works and to pass over the new works whether open for traffic or not, provided the working arrangements of the company and trade of the existing dock were not interfered with. The railway was to be completed within two years and the dock works within three years of notice being given to commence work. The engineers were to deduct 10 per cent of value of work done and 25 per cent of value of materials used from the monthly certificates and this money would be invested to create a guarantee fund, up to a total of 10 per cent of the contract price. The fund would be repaid in stages from the completion of each part of the contract up to the end of one year maintenance periods. The contractor was liable to a penalty of £200 per week each for non-completion of the railway or dock works by the specified dates. Sir Benjamin Baker, or failing him, Sir Douglas Fox, was appointed arbitrator in case of any dispute arising, and as things turned out the latter's services were sorely needed.

NOTES

1. See Chapter 1.
2. TNA: PRO RAIL 258/421.
3. See Chapter 2.
4. TNA: PRO RAIL 250/41.
5. D S M Barrie, *The Barry Railway* (Oakwood Press 1978).
6. TNA: PRO RAIL 581/4.
7. See Chapter 2.
8. *The London Gazette*, 21 November 1893.
9. PA HL/PO/PB/3/plan1894/P11.
10. PA HL/PO/PB/3/plan1894/G6, GRO Q/DP 582.
11. See Chapter 1.
12. TNA: PRO RAIL 581/4.
13. *House of Lords Journal*, 1894.
14. TNA: PRO RAIL 1066/2504.
15. TNA: PRO RAIL 1066/1237.
16. See Chapter 1.
17. *House of Lords Journal*, 1894.
18. TNA: PRO RAIL 1066/1242.
19. Colin Chapman, *The Vale of Glamorgan Railway* (Oakwood 1998).
20. See Chapter 2.
21. All references to the Port Talbot to Maesteg line were deleted from GWR's Bill. After further amendment by both Houses of Parliament it passed into law as the GWR (No. 1) Act 1894, 57 & 58 Vict. c.cxliii.
22. TNA: PRO RAIL 1055/2504.
23. TNA: PRO RAIL 250/254, RAIL 258/421.
24. TNA: PRO RAIL 1066/2504.
25. TNA: PRO RAIL 1066/1243.
26. 57 & 58 Vict. c.cxli.
27. *The Railway Times*, 11 August 1894.
28. TNA: PRO RAIL 574/1.
29. *The Railway Times*, 10 November 1894.
30. TNA: PRO RAIL 574/6.
31. William Edmundson, *The Nitrate King: A Biography of "Colonel" John Thomas North* (Palgrave Macmillan 2011).
32. See Chapter 1.
33. David Lewis, *The Coal Industry in the Llynfi Valley* (Tempus 2006) pp. 37–41.
34. Joseph Davies (ed.), 'North's Navigation Collieries (1889) Ltd.: A Historical Retrospect', *The South Wales Coal Annual for 1917* (Joseph Davies 1917), pp. 2–42; A P Barnett & D Wilson-Lloyd, 'North's Navigation Collieries (1889) Ltd.', *The South Wales Coalfield* (The Business Statistics Co. 1921), pp. 72–7.
35. See Chapter 1.
36. 46 & 47 Vict. c.cxcvii.
37. Chapman, *Vale of Glamorgan Railway*, pp. 13–16.
38. *The London Gazette*, 23 November 1888.
39. 52 & 53 Vict. c. clxxxviii.
40. 54 & 55 Vict. c.xvii.
41. 55 & 56 Vict. c.cxxv.
42. *The London Gazette*, 22 November 1892.
43. 56 & 57 Vict. c.ccvi.
44. Chapman, *Vale of Glamorgan Railway*, p. 67.
45. See Chapter 2.
46. TNA: PRO RAIL 574/77, 78, 104, 105.
47. TNA: PRO RAIL 574/98.
48. TNA: PRO RAIL 574/104.
49. TNA: PRO RAIL 1075/89/50.
50. SML PEA/Box 4.
51. TNA: PRO RAIL 258/421.
52. J A Spender, *Weetman Pearson, First Viscount Cowdray, 1856–1927* (Cassell & Co. 1930).
53. TNA: PRO RAIL 1057/1530/2.
54. TNA: PRO RAIL 1057/1531.

Duffryn engine shed and junction nearing completion, circa May 1897. The shed roof was of northlight construction, although perversely the windows faced southwest. Only five out of a possible six roads were laid into the engine shed. The turntable is in place but the coaling stage has yet to be erected. Duffryn No. 1 signal box is to the far right of the view, with the cabin controlling Chapel of Ease Crossing behind it. A newly delivered, but partly obscured, PTR&D goods bake van is to be seen next to the junction signals, as are a variety of PO wagons, including Duffryn Rhondda, North's Navigation and Bryn Navigation. It appears that Pearson's were coming to the end of the railway part of their contract judging by the number of their side-tipping wagons assembled here.
SML

4

Construction of the 1894 Railway

THE MAIN LINE FROM Duffryn Junction to Pontyrhyll Junction was very simple, and was constructed as a single track railway with stations at Bryn, Maesteg and Lletty Brongu. These three stations were of similar layout, consisting of a passing loop with two platform faces and two goods sidings, and, as originally planned, possessed the only signal boxes between the two junctions, a distance of about thirteen miles.

Messrs Pearson were given three week's notice on 21st February 1895 to start work on the railway, which fixed the completion date as defined by the contract as 14th March 1897. Pearson's based their operations at Maesteg, their engineer was George Hay.[1] Work began on the new railway almost immediately, there being no cutting-the-first-sod ceremony. To facilitate construction, Pearson's were allowed to make a temporary connection with one of the GWR's sidings at Pontyrhyll, the agreement being dated 27th July 1895.[2]

The only problem that arose during the construction of the tunnel was that it was found necessary to insert inverts at intervals towards the Maesteg end in order to arrest the downward and inward movement of the side walls, which were lined with kiln-burnt bricks.[3] No particular problems seem to have arisen with the construction of Lletty Brongu Viaduct. During the construction of

the railway it was found necessary to deviate from the authorised line for about 1,200 yards near Bryn and 385 yards across the site of Maesteg Ironworks. These deviations were sanctioned retrospectively by the company's 1899 Act. The only other change was that the rails to be laid in the tunnel were to be 90lb per yard instead of the 75lb specified, this was regarded as an extra and agreed in August 1896.

Pearson's did experience some difficulties near Garth. In June 1896, Knox was informed that Mr Boyd Harvey of North's Navigation Collieries had threatened to cut off water, and was also preventing the contractor from getting material from the GWR to the new line and disputing their use of the old tramroad bridge over the GWR, road and river at Maesteg.[4] The real cause of the dispute was the new railway crossing a disused section of the Cwmdu tramroad. This tramroad was built in the 1860s,[5] but by 1896 only a short section remained in use connecting Garth Merthyr Colliery to the GWR. The agreement with the landowner was that he could construct an accommodation bridge for the tramroad when needed, the PTR&D contributing £1,000 towards the cost. As a less expensive alternative, Meik recommended putting in an on/off junction[6] and North's were informed in December 1896 that the company was prepared to do this forthwith, although in the event

Pearson's staff engaged on construction of the PTR outside their office, believed to be at Maesteg. The gentleman seated in the centre is thought to be George Hay, Pearson's manager for this part of their contract.

Author's collection

ABOVE: The rear of the new engine shed circa May 1897, showing the gasholder, which was supplied from Margam UDC's gasworks, water tank and offices. *SML*

BELOW: The newly-constructed PTR in the Duffryn Valley near Cwm Gwineu, with what looks like a contractor's locomotive in the distance. The Board of Trade inspector commented on the apparently light construction of the railway bearing in mind the type of traffic it was intended to carry. *WGAS*

The newly completed station at Bryn, looking down the line towards Port Talbot. Despite the main part of the village being off to the right of this view, the station building and goods yard were to the left and accessed via the level crossing. *Author's collection*

nothing was done. This issue arose again in January 1899, with the same outcome,[7] but again nothing was done.

No doubt with a mind to improving the working of the line, on 17th February 1897 the directors authorised the construction of a passing loop at the Maesteg end of the tunnel, the location becoming known as East End. The construction of a short mileage siding at East End was approved in November 1897, provided that the landowners who would benefit from it made the necessary approaches. On 28th January 1898 the directors noted that Miss Talbot had agreed to make the necessary road, and resolved to seek tenders for a siding holding twelve wagons. The siding was made by extending the trailing dead-end off the Down loop, and in the event held only ten wagons.[8] The works earned the approbation of the Board of Trade as they were carried without their authorisation and without proper provision for runaways.[9] In February 1897 the directors also approved the construction of two sidings at Pontyrhyll to facilitate interchange with the GWR.

The main line had been planned without any colliery siding connections. Two were put in while the line was being built. North's Navigation Collieries at Maesteg were potentially the largest source of revenue and in December 1896 the directors proposed that the company should construct and maintain the sidings, North's paying 2d per ton up to 100,000 tons and 1d per ton above this. The general manager reported in January 1897 that North's had agreed to this, and that the contractors had put in a junction with North's private line at the position where it was intended to lay the sidings.[10] North's though had second thoughts, and in April 1897 proposed a modified scheme.[11] This was agreed by the PTR&D Board, which resolved that the company would pay half the estimated cost of £1,375, the work was to be done to the satisfaction of its engineer,

and the sidings were to be conveyed to the company. The PTR&D required the land so as to be able to maintain the bridge over the GWR and to have room for doubling the line at some time in the future. The sidings held forty-five full wagons and forty-two empties, deemed to be sufficient until the dock was completed. North's, however, considered it better if they constructed the sidings on their own land, although the engineer reported on 12th July 1897 that nothing much had yet been done by North's towards making them.[12] In October 1897 the directors noted that a turnout was to be put in for the accommodation of North's traffic, possibly replacing the one put in earlier by Pearson's.

Although the main line was constructed according to the deposited plans, North's were not happy about conveying the requisite land at Maesteg to the PTR&D as it included ground on which their own railway across the GWR was laid. In January 1899 North's suggested that the PTR&D should widen the three bridges in question (over the road, the river and the GWR), double their line and move North's line to the north, with a fence separating the two.[13] However, the directors agreed with Meik's view that it would be cheaper to employ a man to look after the existing gate at the entrance to North's railway than to go to the expense of widening the embankment over the three bridges. An agreement dated 7th June 1894 required North's to convey as much of the freehold land as required for the construction of the railway at £40 per acre and as much of the leasehold land at £20 per acre; it also granted the PTR&D an easement to maintain their railway over the three bridges belonging to North's, and gave them the power to strengthen, widen or alter them. The directors insisted on the agreement being carried out as originally proposed, and it was sealed on 21st June 1899.

CONNECTION TO THE R&SBR AT ABERAVON

The connection between Duffryn Junction and the R&SBR at Aberavon, made up of Railways Nos 4 and 6, was part of an important route to the north side of the existing dock, at least until all the works associated with the new dock were completed. Although the necessary land through Margam Tinplate Works had been purchased from Messrs Byass & Co. in June 1895, in July 1896 the directors instructed Meik to report on an alternative route for Railway No. 4, presumably before work had started on the authorised viaduct. In a report dated 19th August 1896, Meik proposed to do away with the viaduct through Byass' works, and instead cross the Oakwood Railway on the level. This scheme would have needed the consent of all parties and the closure of the Oakwood Railway; it also would have led to complications for traffic using the upper part of the Oakwood Railway and any development of it. The main advantage of the scheme would have been an easier junction with the R&SBR at Aberavon. In the event, the original plan was adhered to and the directors of the R&SBR approved the plans for the junction on 28th September 1896.[14]

An agreement for running powers over the R&SBR from Aberavon to North Bank Junction, as allowed by the 1894 Act, was accepted on 15th July 1897 and finalised in September. The PTR&D agreed to pay ¾d per ton for coal, coke and pitwood, with a minimum of 4 tons per wagon. The new double junction, which was inspected in August 1897, was controlled from the R&SBR's Aberavon station signal box.[15] Confusingly, the PTR also had a signal box nearly, called Aberavon Junction, situated at the start of the short double line section to the junction. This too was inspected in August 1897.[16] Col Yorke's report noted that although the railway was not sufficiently complete for passenger traffic, the company desired to bring it into use for goods and minerals. He recommended the box be sanctioned for goods and mineral traffic provided some minor matters were attended to.

RAILWAY NO. 5

A further meeting to resolve the question of the Oakwood Crossing was held at Paddington in October 1895 between Cheston, representing the PTR&D, and Messrs Lambert, Nelson and Mills of the GWR.[17] Cheston had a new objective, to obtain the traffic from the Rio Tinto works at Cwmavon. He had been advised by eminent counsel (Sir Horace Davey) that Miss Talbot was entitled to lay the tramway as an ordinary narrow (standard) gauge line and to use it for all purposes. The GWR was advised that Miss Talbot's rights, if any, were confined to the restoration of the original line and for use for Oakwood Colliery traffic only. Their view was that it would be better if the crossing was not doubled and that a bridge was constructed to carry both tramroads, and a proposal to this effect was made to Knox on 13th November 1895.

A follow-up meeting was held at Paddington on 18th February 1896, this time attended by Messrs Knox, Meik, Watson and Col Wright, with Messrs Inglis and Wilkinson of the GWR, when the full extent of the proposal became apparent. In essence, the GWR was to construct an overhead station, to be treated as a joint station and to which the PTR&D would bring all its passenger traffic. Knox suggested that the GWR should contribute £10,000 plus £4,000, being one half of the cost of a new public road bridge, this being necessary to totally eliminate the Oakwood Crossing. Wilkinson's

response was that he could not see what inducement there was for the GWR to make so large a payment, and there the matter rested again.

Cheston wrote to Nelson again on 19th August 1896, suggesting that some adjustments should be made in the interests of all concerned. Although Miss Talbot was advised that she had a right to lay a second line of rails across the GWR line, she was aware this would cause an increase in difficulty in working. She might be disposed to forego the right if the company admitted her right to maintain and use the crossing for all purposes. If an arrangement could be come to, he was prepared to advise Miss Talbot to settle.

The arrangements which might have satisfied Miss Talbot appeared in two proposals dated December 1896, seemingly written by Knox.[18] Under the first proposal the company was to make Railway No. 5 as shown on the deposited plan, but, with the permission of the Board of Trade, raised to an elevation of 18 feet above the main road, and to raise the Oakwood Railway alongside to the same height. A temporary station north of the main road was to be made also. Subject to satisfactory arrangements with the GWR and Glamorgan County Council, Miss Talbot was to carry the Oakwood Railway over the main road and the GWR line, and to make suitable connections on her land south of the GWR with the dock railways. Miss Talbot was prepared to grant the PTR&D a perpetual easement over Oakwood Railway from near Upper Forge to the junction with its dock railways and any railways and works it communicated with. The wayleaves were to be used for maintaining and improving the Oakwood Railway, paying Miss Talbot interest on the capital she expended, and rebates on charges for use of the Morfa Railway, with the company retaining the balance. The second proposal envisaged that the GWR would allow Miss Talbot a sum, £5,000 being suggested, for eliminating the Oakwood Crossing and that she would pay the PTR&D this amount in return for being granted free running powers over their lines connecting the Morfa Railway with all works and other railways accessible from it. Neither scheme found favour, although aspects of the first reappeared when wayleaves over the dock railways were settled in 1900, as described later.

LITIGATION

Eventually, in 1901, the GWR took the dispute over the Oakwood Crossing to the Chancery Division of the High Court. However, Mr Justice Kekewich found for Miss Talbot, holding that the indentures dated 13th March 1868 whereby the GWR legally acquired the land needed for the SWR and Mr Talbot acquired the rights of crossing for two tramroads and a public road, meant that Mr Talbot and his successors could use the Oakwood Crossing for all time without limitation, provided the traffic of the GWR was not interfered with.[19] The question of gauge was not mentioned. Nelson, the GWR's solicitor, advised against accepting this decision without appealing. The appeal was heard in July 1902 before Lord Justices Vaughan Williams, Romer and Stirling who, in a reserved judgement, found largely in favour of the GWR. Although Miss Talbot was entitled by the covenant to bring traffic to Port Talbot from existing works served by the Oakwood Railway (at the time of the covenant only Tewgoed Colliery was working), this did not include the whole traffic of the recently constructed Port Talbot Railway, this being far beyond anything contemplated when the crossings were made.[20] Miss Talbot was ordered to pay the costs of the appeal.

ABOVE: The cutting and mouth at the east end of Cwm Cerwyn Tunnel during construction. *SML*

RIGHT: The completed cutting and mouth at the east end of Cwm Cerwyn Tunnel. The keystone was inscribed PTR 1897. *SML*

Excavation of the approach to the west end of Cwm Cerwyn Tunnel. Note the massive excavator employed for the purpose. The locomotive is unidentifiable, but is one of seventeen standard gauge engine used on Pearson's combined railway and dock contract. Three 3 foot gauge engines were also employed, presumably in the dock area. See Potts, M & GW Green, *Industrial Locomotives of West Glamorgan*, Industrial Railway Society 1996.

SML

Such a decision might have been thought to have killed off any idea of taking traffic from the PTR to the docks via the Oakwood Crossing. Although the PTR&D had by now acquired the right to use what it referred to as Miss Talbot's private railway, in effect the extant section of the Oakwood Railway from Llewellyn's Quay to Upper Forge, it had developed the docks railways in such way that the crossing was not needed. Indeed, the directors had decided at their meeting on 19th October 1898 not to apply for powers in their 1899 Act to carry Railway No. 5 of the 1894 Act over the GWR and on to the docks. However, Miss Talbot's advisors thought otherwise, and in November 1902 her agent, Godfrey Lipscomb, informed the GWR that she was considering an appeal to the House of Lords. This was repeated in July 1903, but in December 1903 Cheston, her solicitor, informed Nelson that she had abandoned her appeal, not wishing to continue the litigation.

There remained the settlement of the costs awarded and the long-outstanding amount owed by the late Mr Talbot. Mills, the GWR secretary, opined that his directors would probably forego the payment of costs if the outstanding account of £1,874 2s 1d was paid. Eventually a meeting was held in December 1904 between Mills, Lipscomb and Frederick Page, the PTR&D's accountant, at which it was revealed that the costs incurred by Miss Talbot totalled £880. Not surprisingly, Lipscomb's request that these be deducted from the amount owing to the GWR was refused, but Mills offered to deduct Miss Talbot's costs of £263 for the appeal. As a further compromise, and to settle the matter, he agreed to recommend to his Board Lipscomb's intimation that Miss Talbot would be advised

to pay £1,500. Miss Talbot accepted this arrangement, which was approved by the GWR Board on 15th December 1904, thereby bringing to an end a dispute which had endured for twelve years.

PORT TALBOT CENTRAL STATION

The need for a passenger station at Port Talbot was now pressing. At their meeting on 16th December 1896, the directors resolved that Railway No. 5 of the 1894 Act, linking Tonygroes to the Oakwood Railway, was to be made as originally conceived, together with the temporary station near the Port Talbot Coffee Tavern, and that tenders were to be sought. At their next meeting on 28th January 1897 the tender of £6,000 4s 0d submitted by T W Davies was accepted. The new station was built parallel to, and close to, Oakwood Lane, down which the Oakwood Railway ran. The original design must have been extremely simple as at their March meeting the directors approved plans for increased coal sidings at a cost not exceeding £350. The final layout consisted of a single platform road with run-round loop and two parallel goods sidings. The railway into the terminus effectively became the main line, as the connection to the Oakwood Railway was constructed as a short spur running behind the station. The station building was of wooden construction and was apparently of the same design as those built by Pearson's at Bryn, Maesteg and Lletty Brongu. Unlike these stations, there was no goods shed, merely a lock-up and cattle pens on a loading bank alongside the outermost siding, which were accessed from Eagle Street. The directors decided at their meeting on 19th May 1897 that the station was to be called Port Talbot (Central).

The newly constructed bridge over the main line near milepost 6¾. This bridge carried the existing road from Maesteg to Bryn, which was superseded in the 1920s by a new road leading on from Neath Road, Maesteg, the present day B4282.   *SML*

ABOVE: Lletty Brongu or Pontrhydycyff Viaduct under construction circa 1896. The necessary bricks were delivered via the sidings for O H Thomas' Llynvi Valley Colliery nearby. These sidings made a connection to the LVR about a quarter of a mile below Llangynwyd station. *SML*

BELOW: The finished Lletty Brongu Viaduct about circa September 1897. PTR&D 0-6-0ST No. 2 and goods brake van No. 65, which probably conveyed the photographer, are paused on the viaduct. Some of the colliery surface workings have gone and the industrial locomotive has an abandoned air about it. *SML*

Gwyn Briwnant Jones used this scene near milepost 11½ as the setting for his painting of PTR&D No. 20 that is reproduced on the dust jacket of this volume. Connections for Celtic Lower Colliery were installed in 1919 just off the right of this photograph. *SML*

RAILWAY PROGRESS

Construction of the railway initially progressed satisfactorily. In their report for the half-year ending 30th June 1895 the directors noted that six miles of temporary line had been laid and that eleven bridges and viaducts were in hand.[21] At the half-yearly meeting held on 13th February 1896 Lord Dunraven, the chairman, remarked that the work would no doubt be completed by the guaranteed time, and that the company was fortunate in having a contractor able to put so much plant on the ground.[22] Six month's later the cuttings were two-thirds completed, twenty-two of the forty bridges were approaching completion, the tunnel headings had been driven through and the lining was progressing, and four miles of permanent way had been laid and ballasted.[23] At a special general meeting held on 21st October, the deputy chairman, Col Wright, said he hoped the railway would be open by April 1897.[24] By the end of 1896 the earthworks were 92 per cent finished, the bridges and viaducts were five-sixths finished and 90 per cent of the tunnel had been lined;[25] however it was now clear that the railway would not be competed within the specified time. The director's report for the half-year ending 30th June 1897 noted that the railways authorised by the 1894 Act were practically complete except for the junction with the GWR at Pontyrhyll and the construction of private sidings, which were in hand, and regretted that the opening of these line would be delayed beyond the time stated in the prospectus.[26]

OPEN FOR MINERALS

At the half-yearly meeting held on 18th August 1897, Col Wright was able to state that the sidings had been completed and that the line would be opened on Wednesday 1st September for mineral traffic as far as Lletty Brongu. It would depend on connections with the GWR when mineral traffic and passengers would be carried from the Garw Valley. Apart from that, the line was ready and they could now run round to their own tips on the north bank of the dock. They did not intend to open for passenger traffic until it was possible to get through to Pontyrhyll.[27]

In fact, the line was first used for revenue traffic on Monday 30th August 1897 when 400 tons of coal were carried from Garth Merthyr Colliery, Maesteg, for shipment at Port Talbot, going via Aberavon Junction and the R&SBR to the north side of the dock. This remained the route to the docks until the Dock Branch to Copper Works Junction opened in August 1898. The line was formally opened the following day,[28] six months after the date specified in the contract. Sir John Jones Jenkins, chairman of the R&SBR, speaking at the luncheon which followed the opening and no doubt thinking of his own company, remarked that bringing Port Talbot into prominence would call attention to all the Bristol Channel ports. George Sims, Swansea district goods manager, said the GWR desired friendly relations with all companies, a marked change from its earlier attitude.

Maesteg station shortly after opening for passenger service in February 1898, with a train of empty PO wagons heading under Neath Road bridge towards North's junction. The design of the station buildings and goods shed was common to Bryn, Maesteg and Lletty Brongu. All the woodwork appears to be painted in the GWR's light and dark stone colours. The Railway Signal Co.'s distinctive signal box is in its original, platform level, position. Note the ornate gas lamps. *SML*

Garw

As already alluded to, construction of the junction with the GWR at Pontyrhyll had been delayed, possibly due to that company's antagonism towards the new line. The GWR had not agreed to the plan for the junction by May 1897, and the following month the directors contemplated asking the Board of Trade to settle what should be done. The cost of the junction was put at £4,419 and was part of Pearson's contract. It was not until 15th September 1897 that the directors noted that the GWR had started work on the junction. The Board of Trade had provisionally approved the works on 31st August 1897, provided the Port Talbot line was used for goods traffic only.[29] The junction was completed on 7th January 1898.[30]

With a view to imminent opening, the directors inspected the colliery sidings on the Garw Branch on 2nd December 1897. Mineral traffic was conveyed from the Garw over the new line from the middle of January 1898,[31] actually on the 17th according to the date of the Working Time Table. By virtue of the running powers, Ffaldau, Braich-y-Cymmer, Darren, Llest, Ocean and International collieries could all be tapped.

Initially, passenger trains would only be able to run as far as Pontycymmer, and the GWR proposed that the existing loop should be extended to stable the PTR&D's engine and coaches. Instead, Probert, the general manager, suggested that if the trains were made up of three 42-foot coaches and the timings altered, this extension was unnecessary.[32] The directors agreed and on 15th December 1897 resolved that nothing was to be done at Pontycymmer.

It remained to give substance to the running powers over the Garw Branch authorised by the 1894 Act. A draft agreement passed back and forth between the two companies in May, June and July 1897, but on 21st February 1898, after passenger services had started, the Port Talbot directors decided that they could not make any further concessions and that they were prepared to go to arbitration. It is not clear whether this occurred, but the matter was eventually finalised by an agreement dated 11th August 1898.[33] The principal clauses of the agreement stated that:

1. The PTR&D could run a reasonable number of passenger, goods and mineral trains between Pontyrhyll and Blaengarw.
2. The GWR would accommodate the trains and perform the usual and necessary terminal services.
3. The trains were to be run at mutually convenient times.
4. The passenger trains were to have a brake van at each end.
5. The drivers and guards were to be subject to the regulations and requirements of the GWR.
6. The PTR&D would clean and examine its own trains, but the GWR would provide water on terms to be agreed.
7. The rates and fares would be fixed by the PTR&D after consultation with the GWR.
8. The liability of the PTR&D to pay all the expenses of maintaining, working and signalling Pontyrhyll Junction was not affected.

Inspection and Full Opening

The directors had minuted in July 1897 that they intended to open and equip for passenger traffic all their lines authorised by the 1894 Act except for part of No. 1, but proposed to run passenger trains to Port Talbot Central only. The necessary construction work being virtually complete, the particulars of this part of the undertaking

There is nothing remarkable about this newly finished girder bridge at the 12 milepost, except to note that in 1900 a siding connection was put in just beyond the bridge at this isolated spot for Moelgilau Colliery.

SML

This rather dramatic view was taken near the 13¼ milepost where the line curved north to enter the Garw Valley. Note the check rail. The photographer's train adds interest to the scene. *SML*

were submitted to the Board of Trade in December 1897 with a request that the railway be sanctioned for passenger traffic.[34]

The line was inspected by Lt Col H A Yorke, RE, in January 1898. His report, dated 22nd January 1898, dealt with the line from Port Talbot Central to Pontyrhyll and from Port Talbot to Aberavon, comprising Railways Nos 1–6 authorised by the 1894 Act.[35] The description of the line included the comment that having regard to the heavy gradients and the nature of the traffic to be conducted

over the railway, the permanent way appeared to be light. The inspector observed that there was only one turntable, at Duffryn Junction engine shed, but submitted that as all the locomotives were to be tank engines, the provision of turntables need not be insisted on. The interlocking at all nine signal boxes and three ground frames inspected was found to be correct apart from a small change required at Aberavon Junction, but owing to the gradients certain precautions were to be taken in working the traffic:

Reconstruction of Pontyrhyll station circa 1897, in preparation for the opening of the PTR in January 1898. 0-6-0ST No. 959 of the '1076' Class was built at Swindon in July 1874. The open veranda brake van No. 17598 dates from 1871. The view is looking up the valley towards Blaengarw.

Courtesy Richard Keen

- No mineral train was to be brought to a stand on the single line at the east end of the loop at East End signal box unless there was an engine at the lower end of the train.
- No Down mineral train was to be allowed to leave East End box for Bryn station while an Up train (passenger or mineral) was approaching Bryn from Duffryn Junction.
- No Up train other than a passenger train was to be brought to a stand on the gradient at the west end of Bryn station unless it had an engine or 20-ton brake van in rear.
- Any train working traffic in or out of Bryn Colliery siding was to have an engine at the Port Talbot end.

Subject to these conditions and to the usual undertaking that the line would be worked on the electric train staff system, Lt Col Yorke recommended that the Board of Trade sanction the opening of the PTR for passenger traffic, and this was given on 27th January 1898.

The Port Talbot directors considered the report at a specially convened meeting on 3rd February 1898. The conditions were agreed to and the decision was made to open the line throughout for passenger traffic on 14th February. The secretary replied to the Board of Trade to this effect, but pointed out that the second condition would seriously inconvenience the working of the traffic and cause delays to trains between Duffryn Yard and Bryn. A modified method of working Bryn station was suggested so as to allow a train to be accepted from Duffryn Yard whilst another was in section from East End:[36]

- That all Down goods and mineral trains were to be brought to a dead stop at Bryn Down home signal and the Down facing points were to be kept in their normal position, i.e. for the sidings, until such trains had stopped. The loading bank siding was to kept for use as runaway siding only.

This modification was accepted, and the undertaking required by the Board of Trade was signed and sealed on 12th March 1898.[37]

Col Yorke also inspected Pontyrhyll Junction in January 1898. His report noted that both lines were single but that a double junction had been formed, new loops having been put in for the purpose. A new signal box, with correct interlocking, was erected about 175 yards south of the junction, alongside the GWR line. Col Yorke also observed that alterations were in progress at Pontyrhyll station signal box in connection with the opening of the PTR, and these would be inspected later. He recommended the Board of Trade to sanction the use of the junction and signalling. The works at Pontyrhyll station were re-inspected in April 1898. Col Yorke reported that the junction and signals were worked from the station signal box, leading to the unusual situation that the new junction signal box down the line did not actually work the junction, but functioned as a block post and worked the loop points.[38]

The railway was duly opened for passenger traffic on Monday 14th February 1898. There was no formal ceremony, but two directors, Col Franklen and Mr Byass, and the secretary, Knox,

A view circa September 1897 at the 13½ milepost of the newly finished approach to the junction of the PTR with the GWR at Pontyrhyll. Double lines of both railways commenced near the further river bridge, the short-lived junction signal box being just out of sight. This single line section of the Garw Valley Branch was doubled in 1904. *SML*

The newly constructed bridge carrying the Dock Branch over the GWR main line at Taibach. The view is looking north towards Vivian's Taibach Copper Works. The span was sufficient to allow future quadrupling of the GWR. The Morfa Railway was carried through the left hand embankment and the abandoned Margam Copper Works just beyond, and then under the GWR to reach the Taibach works. *SML*

made the first journey.[39] The journey time from Pontycymmer to Port Talbot had been reduced from 2 hours via Bridgend to 39 minutes, with corresponding improvements from Pontyrhyll and Maesteg. Pearson's manager for the construction of the railway throughout had been George Hay, who went on to manage the construction of the GWR's South Wales and Bristol Direct Line.[40] The general manager, Probert, reported on 15th February that it had been necessary to slacken the couplings of trains at Tonygroes and Duffryn Junctions and at the east end of the tunnel due to the curves of loops being so acute, and also to reduce speed between Lletty Brongu and Pontyrhyll due to the wrong super-elevation. All of these defects were being put right by Pearson's.[41]

Pearson's estimated in February 1898 that by measurement of the quantities of materials used the railway had cost £209,910, but as expenditure and interest on the capital employed had amounted to £212,781 their loss was £2,961.[42]

The milestones of the completion of the railways authorised by the 1894 Act and of opening the railway for passenger traffic were of course mentioned at the seventh half-yearly meeting held on 16th February.[43] The chairman's report noted that the train service was run in connection with GWR system at Port Talbot to the benefit of the public. In fact not all the railways had been completed. Work on the line to Margam Junction with the GWR (Railway No. 7) did not begin until September 1897, and this railway and the portion of Railway No. 1 between Duffryn Junction and Copper Works Junction in the new dock area were not opened for mineral traffic until 10th August 1898.[44] The latter line enabled the company to get directly to the docks without passing over the R&SBR, resulting in a considerable saving.

In September 1897 the R&SBR had sought the PTR&D's view on reopening their Docks station, which had been closed since March 1895 following the opening of the line to Swansea. The reply is not

recorded, but in March 1898 the PTR&D was offered the use of Aberavon and Docks stations at an annual rental of £150 for the first year and £200 thereafter.[45] This was declined, and instead £50 was offered for the use of Aberavon station, this being somewhat closer to the centre of Aberavon than the Central station. This offer was accepted by the R&SBR directors at their meeting 15th April, and on 25th May Meik informed the Board of Trade that the PTR&D desired to start working passenger traffic to and from Aberavon on 1st June 1898. Provisional sanction was given, although the alterations at Tonygroes were not inspected until May 1899.[46]

PENALTIES

The railway had only been opened for one month when one of the directors, Mr Byass, called attention to the unsatisfactory state of the permanent way. Shortcomings included loose keys and insufficient spikes, and dangerous points and crossings, matters which the company's engineers should have noticed. At their meeting on 18th May 1898 the directors resolved that unless Pearson's dealt with the matters requiring attention within one week the company would do the work themselves and debit the contractor with the cost. At their August meeting the directors decided that the resident engineer, Albert Havelock Case, would take over the maintenance of the line, which by now included the railway south of the bridge over the GWR, as from 1st September. Any work which should have been done by the contractor was to be done by Case and the cost deducted from the contractor's certificate. This action removed from Pearson's their contractual obligation to maintain the railway for one year after its completion. With the question of penalties looming, Pearson's wrote to the company on 15th November 1898 claiming that they had no control over the delays in making the junctions at Pontyrhyll and Aberavon; under the conditions the railway was finished well within the contract date.[47]

ABOVE: A view showing the almost completed viaduct carrying the Aberavon Branch from Tonygroes Junction to its junction with the R&SBR skirting round the disused Margam Tinplate Works and, then on lower girders, crossing the corner of a bend in the River Avon. Just visible is the home signal for the PTR's Aberavon Junction signal box. The nearest span carried the line over Ynys Road, Port Talbot. *SML*

BELOW: A slightly earlier view from a different direction of the unfinished viaduct, which is awaiting handrails on the low-girder portion. *SML*

Port Talbot Central station before train services began. The loop was just long enough to allow a train of four of the PTR&D short bogie carriages to be run round. Anything longer required a backing movement which may account for the removal of the signal box, signals and crossover pre-1920. Note that a working distant signal for Tonygroes Junction was provided from new. Also put in at the time was a short connection to the Oakwood Railway which ran parallel to the PTR about 30 yards distant. This connection joined the main line between the water tank and house. The connection to the two road goods yard off to the right was sited beyond the signal box. *Author's collection*

The secretary of the PTR&D informed the Board on 9th December 1898 that the retention money, that proportion of the contract price retained against disputes, for the railway contract was £21,080, of which £9,436 was paid on 22nd November 1897. Pearson's had applied for the balance of £11,644, saying the line had been certified as complete. The directors at their meeting on 20th December resolved to hand over to Pearson's the retention money, less the penalty claimed by the company of £4,800. They had a change of mind at their meeting on 4th January 1899, and agreed to pay without prejudice the full amount of £11,644 due for the railway section. They were no doubt influenced by the arbitrator's interim award regarding Pearson's alleged non-completion of the dock part of their contract.[48]

ENGINE AND CARRIAGE SHEDS
In December 1895 the directors authorised the secretary and engineer to obtain tenders for a shed for two locomotives for the dock railways. The following month it was confirmed that the shed would be built of galvanised iron on North Bank. The tender by J Davis for £200 was accepted, for completion in June 1896.[49] Its exact location is uncertain, and it probably closed in mid-1897 when the main shed at Duffryn Yard was ready. Presumably locomotive No. 1, which was delivered during the first half of 1896, was initially shedded there.

At their meeting on 28th March 1896 the directors instructed Meik to prepare plans and specifications for a locomotive running shed. At first this was intended to be sited at Margam Junction,

but at their meeting on 19th August this was changed to Duffryn Junction, on land to be acquired from Miss Talbot. Maesteg Chamber of Trade applied to the Board in October 1896 for the shed to be built at Maesteg, but were informed that it would be on the site already accepted. The shed was designed to house fifteen engines plus eight bogie carriages, although it was pointed out that the later construction of a separate carriage shed would give space for twenty-five engines.[50] The tender of £9,600 by Mr Palmer of Neath was accepted at the October meeting, but a month later Palmer informed the Board that he could not finish the work in five months, and on 18th November 1896 the directors decided to award the tender to Messrs Pearson for £9,752. The directors learned on 19th May 1897 that Pearson's running shed contract had not been completed on time, and decided to enforce penalties. Although no date is recorded, the shed must have been ready shortly afterwards for the new locomotives on order, and the temporary shed in the dock area was closed.

In the meantime the PTR&D had acquired the Cefn & Pyle Railway as authorised by one of its 1896 Acts.[51] Included in the purchase were three locomotives[52] and the engine shed, which in all probability was situated at Bryndu,[53] although referred to by the GWR as "Penylan". There is no mention of this shed in the PTR&D's records, but eight engines were shedded there in 1908.[54] There is no record of an allocation after August 1908 and this shed is presumed to have closed then.

The new Duffryn Yard running shed had limited facilities for repair work, and in July 1899 the locomotive superintendent

RIGHT AND BELOW: During 1897 the directors of the PTR&D made an inspection of the railway works by then nearing completion. The inspection train consisted of a contractor's locomotive and at least one GWR open wagon fitted with bench seating, and started from the unfinished Central station. Most of those present have not been identified, but the tall, standing figure is thought to be Edward Knox, Miss Talbot's agent and the first secretary of the PTR&D. *Author's collection*

reported the need for shearlegs for lifting locomotives. Progress was slow, and it was not until August 1900 that the foundations were reported to have been put in. The hoist and the shed that housed it were reported to be completed and in use in the following November.[55] Also in August 1900 Hosgood proposed an extension to the running shed to do under-cover repair work hitherto done outside. The directors agreed to this, instructing Hosgood to do only what was absolutely necessary to cover all machinery and boilers then outdoors, at a cost not exceeding £200.

By June 1899 the company's locomotives totalled eighteen, and although some of these were probably outstationed at Bryndu, Duffryn Yard shed was at capacity. At the Board meeting on 26th July 1899 Hosgood proposed the erection of a carriage shed and additional sidings for stock, at an estimated cost of £1,600. Such a shed would free up space at the running shed, and Hosgood was instructed to do only what was necessary at the lowest possible price. A two-road corrugated iron shed was built in the vee between the lines to Tonygroes and the docks at Duffryn Junction, with a trailing connection to the Up running loop. One siding alongside the shed was also provided. The new connection was brought into use on about 1st June 1900.[56] The works were found to be satisfactory when inspected by Major Pringle on 14th August, and were sanctioned for use by the Board of Trade on 22nd August 1900.[57] By now the railway was fully stocked with twenty locomotives, eight passenger carriages and 403 wagons, and Hosgood equipped the sheds with machinery for their maintenance.[58]

The R&SBR's Aberavon station circa 1905 looking up towards Cymmer with the junction of the PTR&D's Aberavon Branch at the end of the platforms and the engine shed beyond. A PTR&D 2-plank loco coal wagon is in the siding on the right. *Author's collection*

NOTES

1. *The Times*, 3 August 1896.
2. TNA: PRO RAIL 574/14.
3. W Cleaver, *Proc. Inst. Civil Engineers*, 177, 1908–9, pp. 199–208.
4. TNA: PRO RAIL 1057/2656.
5. See Chapter 1.
6. TNA: PRO RAIL 1057/1529/13.
7. TNA: PRO RAIL 1057/2550.
8. TNA: PRO RAIL 1057/2515.
9. TNA: PRO MT 6/997/8.
10. TNA: PRO RAIL 1057/1528/3.
11. TNA: PRO RAIL 1057/2534.
12. TNA: PRO RAIL 1057/1529/20.
13. TNA: PRO RAIL 1057/2552.
14. TNA: PRO RAIL 581/4.
15. TNA: PRO MT 6/799/6.
16. TNA: PRO MT 6/880/2.
17. TNA: PRO RAIL 258/421.
18. TNA: PRO RAIL 1057/2514.
19. *The Times*, 23 June 1901.
20. TNA: PRO RAIL 258/421; *The Times*, 29 July 1902.
21. *Railway Times*, 20 July 1895.
22. *Railway Times*, 15 February 1896.
23. *Railway Times*, 22 August 1896.
24. *Railway News*, 24 October 1896.
25. *Railway Times*, 20 February 1897.
26. *Railway Times*, 7 August 1897.
27. *Railway Times*, 21 August 1897.
28. *Railway News*, 4 September 1897.
29. TNA: PRO MT 6/825/5.
30. TNA: PRO RAIL 1057/1531.
31. *Railway News*, 19 February 1898.
32. TNA: PRO RAIL 1057/1528/10.
33. TNA: PRO RAIL 574/16, RAIL 252/1206.
34. TNA: PRO MT 6/821/4.
35. TNA: PRO MT 29/60, RAIL 1057/2624.
36. TNA: PRO MT 6/821/4.
37. TNA: PRO RAIL 1057/2624.
38. TNA: PRO MT 6/825/5, MT 29/60.
39. *Railway News*, 19 February 1898.
40. Spender, *Weetman Pearson*, pp. 140–41.
41. TNA: PRO RAIL 1057/1528/13.
42. SML PEA 4/9.
43. *Railway News*, 19 February 1898.
44. *Railway News*, 20 August 1898; TNA: PRO RAIL 1057/1528/24.
45. TNA: PRO RAIL 581/5.
46. See Chapter 5.
47. TNA: PRO RAIL 1057/1531.
48. See Chapter 11.
49. TNA: PRO RAIL 1057/1530.
50. TNA: PRO RAIL 1057/1529/11.
51. See Chapter 5.
52. See Chapter 9.
53. See Chapter 1.
54. TNA: PRO RAIL 254/66.
55. TNA: PRO RAIL 1057/1529/44.
56. TNA: PRO RAIL 1057/1529/38.
57. TNA: PRO MT 6/961/8.
58. TNA: PRO RAIL 1057/1529/34

5

Expanding the Network

THE 1894 ACT SATISFIED the Margam Estate's expressed desire for a modern dock at Port Talbot and a railway through the Duffryn Valley. The Port Talbot Railway & Docks Company as re-formed by this Act never, publicly at least, evinced any intentions to expand its undertaking. However, events which occurred in 1895, and which had the potential to affect its interests, caused the company to promote two Bills in Parliament. The first was a response to GWR disinterest in Port Talbot, and to a proposal to build a railway within three-quarters of a mile of Margam Castle which was itself part of a much larger scheme. The PTR&D's initial, elaborate, alternative was to become much simplified and eventually reached the Statue Book without opposition. The second Bill arose because coal owners in the upper Pelenna Valley could not reach agreement with the R&SBR over a short railway to Port Talbot, and was to generate almost as much Parliamentary heat as had the company's 1894 Bill.

THE OGMORE VALLEYS EXTENSION RAILWAY (OVER)

The Port Talbot directors at their meeting on 4th October 1895 authorised Col Wright and/or Mr Watson to take whatever steps might be necessary to protect the company's interests in regard to Bills submitted to the 1896 Session of Parliament. The Board had not met for two months and in the meantime much had happened which had the potential to change the railway map of South Wales and southern England. In particular, dissatisfaction over the GWR's monopoly of the traffic between South Wales and London came to a head. In order to challenge this position, South Wales interests, most prominently the Barry Railway, promoted the London & South Wales Railway to run from a junction with the ByR at Cogan via Oxford to junctions with the Midland Railway at Hendon and the Metropolitan Railway at Great Missenden, with numerous connections en route.[1] The engineers of this grandiose scheme were J Wolf Barry, Sir James W Szlumper, T Forster Brown & Rees, and William W Szlumper, who estimated the cost of the line to be nearly £5.7 million.[2] This line did not directly affect the Port Talbot Company, of course, but as it connected with the VoGR at Barry the proposed westward extension of it most certainly did. The VoGR, by now under strong Barry influence,[3] proposed to extend its railway from Ewenny south of Bridgend to a junction at Aberavon with the R&SBR, the line of which was envisaged to complete the new route from London to Swansea.

It is not clear when the PTR&D directors became aware of these schemes, but they had at most two months to prepare a response. Although not a director, Thomas Mansel Franklen, Miss Talbot's cousin and business advisor, had learned of them and produced for her information a document summarising, with reasons, the actions the directors proposed to take,[4] which is quoted in full here.

<u>Observations as to New Railways on the Margam Estate</u>
The Great Western Company are not willing to give fair play to the interests of Port Talbot. They say that they have a dock themselves on each side, viz. at Porthcawl and Briton Ferry, and cannot feel any interest in the development of Port Talbot, in fact they are charging 2d per ton less for carrying coal to Porthcawl and 1d per ton less to Briton Ferry than they charge to Port Talbot, though the latter is four miles further. For the protection of the Port Talbot Company's shareholders, the directors of the Port Talbot Company feel it necessary to obtain access to the sources of traffic independently of the Great Western Company. For this purpose they desire to connect the Morfa Tramway with the Pyle & Cefn private railway and to extend the latter to the Tondu Ironworks. It is estimated that these extensions will not cost more than £60000 and the traffic already available is estimated to be sufficient to pay 5% on the outlay. Of course, this would also be very beneficial to the Margam Estate, both as ensuring the keeping open of the Cefn brickworks and also for developing the coal on the south side of the estate about Cwm Kenfig, Smith's Cwm, etc. There can be no doubt that this line is desirable both for the Margam Estate and the Port Talbot Company independently of any proposed action on the part of other companies, and the directors of the Port Talbot Company have decided to introduce a Bill to Parliament next session for the construction of this line and also for the extension of it to the Ogmore Valley.

Quite independently of this, and without any notice to either the Port Talbot Company or the representatives of the Margam Estate, the Vale of Glamorgan Company have been surveying a line which would pass through the best sporting part of the Margam Estate and right through the building ground at Port Talbot, their object being to complete a connection from Cardiff to Swansea to be used in conjunction with the scheme for a through line from Cardiff to London which is being promoted by powerful interests in England and is understood to have the support of Lord Bute, Lord Tredegar, the Duke of Beaufort and others. If a case is made out for this line before the Parliamentary Committee it would be on the ground that the interests of the South Wales Mineral District are insufficiently supported by the Great Western Company, who of course will strongly contend that they can and do give all the needful accommodation. I believe that all the public bodies in the district will join in supporting a competitive through route, and I think that if the public need is established to the satisfaction of the Parliamentary Committee, no private opposition would be of any avail to stop the grant of this line. Under the circumstances, the safest way to protect the interests of the Margam Estate seems to be to offer the promoters of

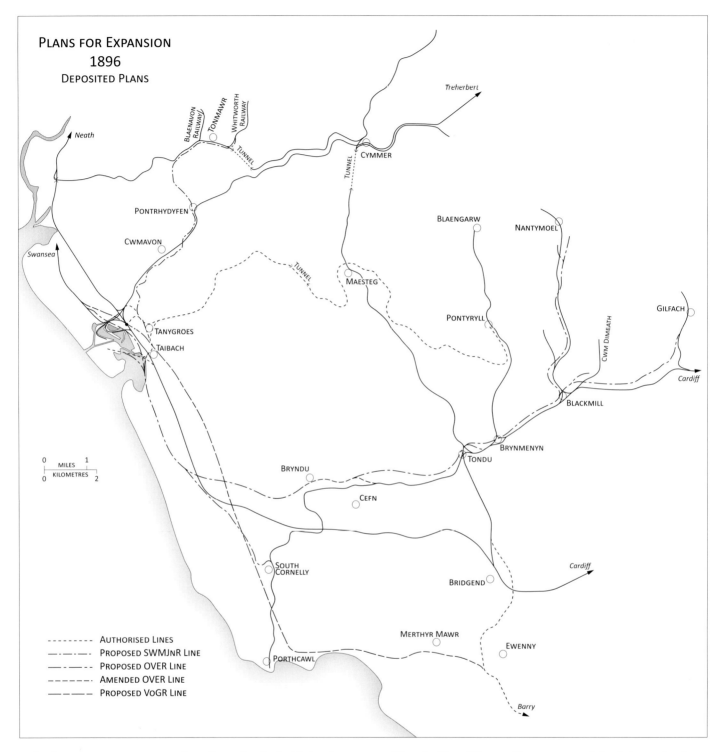

PLANS FOR EXPANSION
1896
DEPOSITED PLANS

Neath

BLAENAVON RAILWAY
TONMAWR
WHITWORTH RAILWAY
TUNNEL

Treherbert

CYMMER
TUNNEL

PONTRHYDYFEN

Swansea

CWMAVON

BLAENGARW

NANTYMOEL

TUNNEL

MAESTEG

GILFACH

TANYGROES

PONTYRYLL

CWM DIMEATH

TAIBACH

Cardiff

BLACKMILL

0   MILES   1
0   KILOMETRES   2

BRYNMENYN

TONDU

BRYNDU

CEFN

Cardiff

SOUTH CORNELLY

BRIDGEND

MERTHYR MAWR

EWENNY

- - - - - - - AUTHORISED LINES
- · - · - PROPOSED SWMJnR LINE
- · · - · · PROPOSED OVER LINE
- - - - - AMENDED OVER LINE
- - - - - - PROPOSED VoGR LINE

PORTHCAWL

Barry

this line running powers over the railway already decided to be constructed by the Port Talbot Company, which railway will run along any route which best suits the interest of the Margam Estate. Of course, if the through line is thrown out no harm can arise from this offer, while if it is granted the Estate will not suffer and the shareholders of the Port Talbot Company will be greatly benefited by the additional traffic the through line will bring upon their extension. The Port Talbot directors have agreed to offer these running powers and the promoters of this scheme are willing to accept them and abandon their line through the Margam Estate.

Thus the Great Western Company may fight their own battles with the promoters of the through line without the interests of the Margam Estate being affected injuriously in any event, and the Port Talbot Company would be gainers in either case. It would not be necessary for you to take any part adverse to the Great Western Company in respect of the through scheme, and I know no other way than this which would protect your Estate from being forcibly being cut through by a hostile Company which would carry off all the profits that would otherwise fall to the Port Talbot shareholders, and, further, would not give the accommodation to your collieries and other interests which can be insisted upon if the Port Talbot Company have the only line beside the Great Western Railway.

The Parliamentary Notices for the London & South Wales Railway, the VoGR, and the PTR&D (OVER) Bills intended for the 1896 Session were all published on the same date.[5] Apart from authority to build railways, amongst numerous other provisions the proposed London & South Wales Railway sought running powers over the ByR, the R&SBR, the VoGR and the PTR; for the latter two these included any railways that might be authorised in 1896. The VoGR sought similar running powers over the PTR and the R&SBR; their proposed extension commenced at a junction with VoGR then under construction near Ewenny, crossed the River Ogmore south of Merthyr Mawr, and proceeded via Newton Nottage near Porthcawl to a short tunnel at Taibach, through Miss Talbot's land at Port Talbot Docks and on to the junction with the R&SBR on Aberavon Burrows, having crossed the GWR twice and the PTR and R&SBR once each in a total distance of about seven and a half miles. Also planned was a short connection to the PTR Railway No. 1 of 1894, then under construction, at Taibach. The engineers were Thomas Forster Brown and Sir James Szlumper, who estimated the total cost to be £285,446.[6]

Having become aware of these schemes, the PTR&D promoted its own extensions, principally to the Ogmore Valleys as envisioned by Mr Franklen, made up of thirteen railways with a total length of nearly twenty-eight and a half miles. Railways No. 1 – which commenced at a junction with the Railway No. 1 authorised by the 1894 Act near Margam Copper Works – and No. 2 made use of the Morfa Railway and Cefn & Pyle Railway respectively[7] to create the main line from Port Talbot to Tondu. Railway No. 4 continued the line eastwards to Blackmill from where Railway No. 7 ran

northwards to terminate at the Ocean Colliery, Nantymoel, in the Ogmore Valley, seventeen miles from Port Talbot. A short branch here, Railway No. 8, led to Wyndham Colliery. Railway No. 5 was intended to make a connection to the moribund Dimbath Branch, and from it Railway No. 6 connected with the GWR just south of Gilfach station in the Little Ogmore Valley. Finally, as part of these eastward extensions, Railway No. 3 made a short connection from the proposed main line at Tondu to the GWR's Blackmill Branch near Brynmenyn. Railway No. 9, which branched southwards from the main line on Margam Moors, was intended to line up with the proposed VoGR extension at South Cornelly and thus provided the promised alternative route through the Margam Estate. A short branch, Railway No. 10, provided a connection to the tramway which ran from Pant Mawr Quarries to the Porthcawl Branch at Cornelly. Railway No. 11 extended the main line northwards through Port Talbot Docks on a line that suited the owners rather than that of the VoGR extension and connected to the R&SBR at Aberavon near the site of the future Seaside station. Lastly, Railways Nos 12 and 13 provided short connections at Taibach to the PTR&D's 1894 railway. No additional direct connections to the GWR were planned at Port Talbot. The estimated total cost was put at £557,876.[8] The engineers were Patrick Meik and Thomas Forster Brown, the latter gentleman rather remarkably being associated with all three schemes referred to here, whether they were complementary to or in competition with one another.

Among other provisions, the PTR&D sought powers to acquire the Morfa Railway and the C&PR, and to complete the Dimbath Branch in default of the GWR doing so.[9] At the time the Bill for the OVER was deposited, Miss Talbot offered to give the lands required and the C&PR free of charge, subject to certain conditions regarding running powers and level crossings. The PTR&D directors

Vivian & Sons' Morfa Colliery was connected to Taibach Copper Works by the Morfa Railway which crossed the Ogmore Valleys Extension Railway on the level near Copper Works Junction. This view looking south might well have been different if the PTR&D had purchased the railway and constructed the OVER along its route. Morfa Colliery closed in 1913. Postcard, postally used 2nd September 1908. *Author's collection*

eventually decided they could not entertain these conditions, and the lands and railway were later sold to the company at valuations made by Miss Talbot's agent, Edward Knox, and agreed by Mr Franklen on Miss Talbot's behalf.[10] Railways Nos 9, 11 and part of No. 1 made up a line about seven miles long connecting the R&SBR and the proposed VoGR extension and would have comprised the most westerly of the new works associated with the proposed London & South Wales Railway. The directors of the R&SBR raised no objections to Railway No. 12 when informed of it at their meeting on 31st October 1895.[11] Not surprisingly, Messrs Vivian's sought compensation for the disturbance to their Margam Copper Works and wharf caused by the proposed new lines.

The GWR could not countenance a competing line from London to South Wales, and before long moves were made in an attempt to reach an accommodation with its promoters. Viscount Emlyn, the chairman, reported to the GWR Board on 9th January 1896 that, having received a hint that they would be prepared to withdraw their Bill, discussions had taken place which had resulted in an agreement.[12] Conceivably as a result of foreknowledge of the London & South Wales Railway proposal, the GWR had deposited plans for the South Wales & Bristol Railway from Wootton Bassett

to Patchway in November 1895,[13] and now undertook to use its best endeavours to obtain Parliamentary authority and to expedite its construction.[14] This so-called Badminton Cut-off shortened the distance from South Wales to London by about ten miles and gave the GWR the opportunity to reduce its rates for the conveyance of coal. The GWR also agreed to pay £15,000 towards the costs incurred by the promoters of the London & South Wales Railway Bill. Other clauses addressed specific concerns of South Wales coal owners and the ByR, and included powers for the VoGR to run directly into Bridgend station.[15] Consequently, the London & South Wales Railway Bill was withdrawn and all thoughts of a second main line from London to South Wales vanished. The VoGR Bill was much amended before it was considered by Parliament, being restricted to an extension of time for its authorised railways.[16] In consequence, Railways Nos 9–11 and 13 of the Port Talbot Bill became superfluous and were withdrawn.

The PTR&D was not immune from these machinations. The justification for a new trunk route had disappeared and the emphasis had shifted to local matters. The GWR directors noted at their meeting on 19th December that certain of the lines proposed by the Port Talbot Bill were in competition with their own railway,

Above: A steam navvy at work on the OVER alongside the GWR main line, circa 1897. The spoil wagon is lettered TJ&R for Topham, Jones & Railton. A stack of sleepers ready for laying the track can be seen at the centre left. *WGAS*

FACING PAGE: The same location, this time showing the labour force. The crude nature of the temporary track and pointwork is apparent. *WGAS*

and approved of the steps taken by the chairman to address the matter.[17] At this point Miss Talbot became personally involved and wrote to Lord Emlyn through her solicitor, Charles Cheston, that as the proposed VoGR extension passed right in front of her house she was bound to propose an alternative line which she was advised the PTR&D would afford.[18] Nevertheless, she was anxious to establish cordial relations between the GWR and herself. This seemed to concentrate the minds of those involved and on 13th February 1896 Knox reported to the directors on meetings held with Viscount Emlyn to consider certain proposals suggested by the GWR. Five days later, Col Wright and Messrs Watson and Knox met Viscount Emlyn, Joseph Wilkinson and R Cope, the general manager and accountant respectively, to conclude an agreement between the two companies. This agreement[19] marked a noticeable change in attitude of the larger company towards the smaller and presaged similar agreements in the future. The preamble noted that its object was to fairly develop Port Talbot Docks having regard to the districts the railway served. Most significantly, the PTR&D was to withdraw from its OVER Bill all the railways proposed other than Railways Nos 1, 2 and 12. Moreover, Railway No. 2 was to be shortened and altered to follow the line of the C&PR and to form a junction with the GWR at Cefn, thus providing railway accommodation for Bryndu and Cefn Collieries and for the Pyle & Blaina Works. The total length of this line was about seven and a half miles, for which the estimated cost was £177,045. It

was emphasised that the new line was intended for mineral and merchandise traffic only. This amendment required a new plan for Railway No. 2 to be deposited at Parliament.[20] The GWR undertook to double its line between Tondu and the new junction. In exchange for the withdrawal of Railways Nos 3 to 8, the GWR agreed to convey, in through trains as far as was practicable, all coal traffic destined for shipment at Port Talbot from the Llynvi, Garw, Ogmore, Dimbath and Little Ogmore valleys via Tondu and the OVER. Rates were agreed for the conveyance of coal to Port Talbot from these valleys and from the Aberdare and Brynamman districts, and for carrying iron ore from Port Talbot to Tondu. As for other railways, the PTR&D agreed to provide sufficient sidings at the docks for loaded and empty wagons, and the GWR undertook, upon request, to complete the Dimbath Branch in the event of any reasonable area of coal being let there. The PTR&D was made responsible for converting the C&PR into a proper locomotive worked line, but the GWR was to work over it traffic intended for shipment eastwards, a provision reversed in October 1896 when GWR directors agreed to the PTR&D doing this work.[21] Finally, the GWR agreed to support the Bill in Parliament provided it was amended to reflect the terms of the agreement. This agreement was sealed on 24th February 1896.

The PTR&D introduced further amendments to the OVER Bill on its own accord so as to give it powers to sell or lease land for a graving dock, warehouses and other works,[22] as already related.[23]

There was no opposition to the amended Bill, any earlier objections having been withdrawn, and it passed through Parliament with only minor amendments being made.[24] The PTR&D (Ogmore Valleys Extension) Act received the Royal Assent on 20th July 1896.[25]

The Act authorised the PTR&D to make Railways Nos 1, 12 and the modified No. 2, and to acquire the Morfa Railway and the C&PR. Special clauses for the protection of Messrs Vivian prevented the company from interfering with the traffic from Morfa Colliery to their works at Port Talbot or to Margam Sidings. Protection was also afforded the Pyle & Blaina Works Ltd, through whose works the revised route of Railway No. 2 passed. This company now owned the Cefn Ironworks[26] and specialised in a ferromanganese alloy.[27] The PTR&D was required to not interfere with the iron company's property unless absolutely necessary, to only take land sufficient for two lines of rails, and to make provision for the removal of slag and rubbish. In a separate agreement dated 19th June 1896 the PTR&D undertook to facilitate all traffic to and from the works and to do the necessary shunting.[28] Also on that date the company agreed with Miss Talbot to purchase and work the C&PR and to give her the right to cross the OVER at five points between Port Talbot and Cefn Junction.[29] The Act also authorised the company to raise up to £210,000 in additional capital and to borrow a further £70,000.

Within one month of obtaining the Act, Meik had produced an alternative route for the OVER.[30] This deviation of Railway No. 1 commenced at a junction with Railway No. 7 of the 1894 Act at Margam and ran alongside the GWR main line to rejoin the authorised line just short of the bridge over the GWR, a distance of about two and a half miles.[31] As well as a saving of £3,955, this new route removed the need to purchase the Morfa Railway. The deviation was sanctioned by the directors at their meeting on 19th August 1896, and was authorised retrospectively by the company's 1899 Act. This scheme necessitated the elimination of Messrs Vivian's exchange sidings with the GWR at Margam and their incorporation into the PTR&D's new Margam Exchange Sidings, Vivian's consent to this being reported to the directors on 21st October. All this work was subject to the approval of the GWR, this being granted on 26th October provided sufficient room was left for future quadrupling of its main line,[32] but not received by the Board until 16th December. At this meeting the directors resolved that the C&PR would be purchased from Miss Talbot for £14,000 as from 1st January 1897, payment to be in shares issued under the 1896 Act, although the agreement was not sealed until 15th March 1899. James Probert, the general manager, reported on 7th January 1897 that the transaction had taken place, and that the line would now be worked by one engine. The recent closure of Cefn Ironworks was expected to result in a loss in revenue of £2,000 per annum and consequently six C&PR employees were given notice.

A specification of the work to be done in constructing the OVER was issued by the engineers on 1st January 1897.[33] It was generally similar in nature to that produced for the 1894 railway.[34] Specific to the OVER contract were clauses that the work was to be completed within twelve months of the date of acceptance of a tender, and

A view looking north from the new Margam East signal box circa 1898 showing Margam Exchange Sidings. The OVER is on the left, the two tracks merging and heading south for Waterhall Junction; the track in the centre foreground is a short headshunt; the bridge carrying the PTR&D Dock Branch over the GWR mainline can just be made out in the distance. The signalling appears to be incomplete as there is none controlling movements from some of the sidings onto the OVER.

Halcrow Group Ltd

LEFT: The newly-completed bridge carrying the OVER across the GWR main line at Margam Moors looking towards Port Talbot, with the eponymous signal box in the distance. By 1903 a connection for Margam Moors sand siding had been laid in on the left of the main line.
From Port Talbot and its Progress *(PTR&D Co. 1919), Author's collection*

BELOW: The same bridge under construction circa 1897 looking towards Cardiff. *Courtesy Arthur Rees*

that relaying of the C&PR was to be commenced immediately, but without inconveniencing the traffic on it. The most substantial work was the bridge over the GWR main line. In contrast to the 1894 works, competitive tenders were sought for the OVER contract. The identity of the firms submitting tenders is not known, but on 28th January the directors resolved to accept that of Messrs Topham, Jones & Railton for £64,010, although the contract was not sealed until 19th May. The directors agreed in June 1897 that Topham, Jones & Railton should work the Cefn & Pyle Branch for the duration of their contract. Relaying the sidings at Pyle was not necessary as this had been done within the last two years by Knox, then the general manager of the C&PR.[35]

Railway No. 1 of the OVER encountered the C&PR five and a half miles from its commencement. It then ran parallel with this line for about half a mile before crossing over it between Bryndu Colliery and Bryndu Coke Ovens and turning eastwards to eventually pick up the route of the C&PR at the 6¼ mile point, which it then followed for the final one and a quarter miles to Cefn Junction. A scissors crossing connection with the C&PR

was provided at the 5½ mile point, this location becoming known as Waterhall Junction, where a slight deviation was made to the C&PR to improve the alignment. The name seemingly comes from a nearby feature called Waterhall on the Ordnance Survey of 1875. Subsequently it is called Wetral. A crossover connection was provided about 280 yards further on, thereby creating a passing loop for the OVER. The only other connection to the C&PR was a trailing junction at the 6¼ mile point. A signal cabin was provided at Waterhall Junction to control the crossovers and connections to Bryndu Colliery. This box was evidently built too low, and in 1903 the directors approved the general manager's application for it to be raised to the necessary height, the task being completed in June 1903.[36] The one mile section of the C&PR from Waterhall Junction to Pyle became known as the Pyle Branch. The engineer reported in September 1900 that this branch had been completely renewed.[37]

A signal cabin was also provided about one mile east of Waterhall Junction to control the connection to Cefn Ironworks.[38] These works had ceased operations in December 1896,[39] although the lessee, Pyle & Blaina Works Ltd, was not wound up until 1918.[40]

By February 1899 the lease had been taken over by a new company, Cefn Ironworks Ltd,[41] and resumed operations in April 1899.[42] Two of its three directors were also PTR&D directors, Messrs Byass and Knox, and Miss Talbot was the principal shareholder.[43] The resumption proved short-lived, the works closing for good in September 1900, depriving the PTR&D of the import and transport of 27,000 tons of iron ore annually.[44] The disused signal cabin at Cefn Ironworks was moved in 1907 to Blaenavon Junction to form the staff station there.[45]

The rerouting of the OVER necessitated the modification of the plans for the junction of Railway No. 7 of the 1894 Act with the GWR at Margam. Meik reported on 18th May 1897 that the work there had been transferred from Topham, Jones & Railton to Messrs Pearson who were building the earlier railway.[46] The directors agreed to the additional costs involved at their meeting on 19th May. The position of the new route of the OVER also precluded the construction of the authorised Railway No. 12, a north to east connection with the 1894 railway, and powers to do so were abandoned by the company's 1899 Act. Probert reported in December 1897 that an extra line was required at Margam to form a loop for crossing trains, and that the total additional cost including signalling and telegraphs was estimated to be £2,486.[47]

ABOVE: The almost completed bridge carrying the OVER over Water Street, Margam, circa 1898.
Courtesy Arthur Rees

LEFT: The newly completed bridge carrying the OVER over the erstwhile Bridgend to Aberavon turnpike, at a point about 600 yards north of Pyle crossroads, circa 1898. This road is nowadays the A48.
Halcrow Group Ltd

A second loop which became the down main line was added by January 1899.[48] The PTR&D was responsible for the whole of the expense at, and in connection with, the GWR's new Margam West signal box, and the signalmen were regarded as the servants of the PTR&D when dealing with their trains and traffic. On 17th August 1898 the directors noted that Margam Junction had been opened for traffic, along with the short single line to Copper Works Junction.[49] The necessary alterations to the GWR main line at Margam had been provisionally sanctioned by the Board of Trade on 9th May 1898.[50] The works there, which consisted of six loop sidings for exchange traffic, the two bypass loops, Up and Down trailing connections to the GWR and new East and West signal boxes, were reported on 3rd January 1899 to be ready for inspection, which was carried by Col Yorke on 17th January. In March 1899 the general manager reported that trains were being delayed at Margam Junction and that additional sidings and a neck were required to enable them to shunt clear of the main line.[51] The directors declined this request, pointing out that the GWR had not provided sufficient accommodation for their own traffic.

In April 1897 the directors had resolved to remind the GWR that under the agreement of 18th February 1896 the line from Tondu to Cefn Junction was to be doubled, and ask it to do this in time for the opening of the OVER. Probert reported on 13th June 1898 that the GWR had found it necessary, until the line was doubled between Cefn and Tondu, to erect two new signal boxes (Cefn Junction and Ffos Bank), but they would bear the cost and maintenance of one of them. In the event, this doubling was delayed indefinitely. The directors noted on 15th June that nothing had been done at Cefn Junction, the estimated cost due to the PTR&D being £1,972. In fact the GWR did not seek the sanction of the Board of Trade to commence the works until 27th June.[52] These delays by the GWR meant that it was impossible for Topham, Jones & Railton to complete their contract by the due date, 1st February 1898, and although the directors resolved to claim penalties of £100 per week, it is not certain that they did so. Topham, Jones & Railton continued to maintain the OVER until 7th August 1899. The shareholders were informed at the half-yearly meeting held on 17th August 1898 that the OVER was approaching completion and that

Cefn Ironworks shortly after closing for good in 1900. The OVER is the line nearer the camera. The further track led to Cefn Slip Colliery; in 1930 this track became the Up line to Cefn Junction.
NM&GW

traffic was being worked on it and delivered to the GWR at Margam Junction.[53] Probert reported to his directors on 17th December that the OVER and Cefn Junction with the GWR would be opened throughout on 19th December 1898.[54] The report for the half-year ending 31st December 1898 noted that the GWR was working traffic over the OVER with satisfactory results[55] as a consequence of an agreement made in November 1898. Although the GWR had reported on 10th January 1899 that the works at Cefn Junction had been completed they were not inspected until 6th May.[56]

The OVER was intended to be a mineral line only, but a clause in the Act provided for it to be converted to a passenger line if Glamorgan County Council made out the case for such an alteration. The council had enquired of the directors to this effect in September 1898, but was advised that this railway could not be made fit for passenger traffic for want of sites for stations at Port Talbot or elsewhere.

THE SOUTH WALES MINERAL JUNCTION RAILWAY

In 1893 the first steps were taken to connect the collieries in the upper Pelenna Valley to Port Talbot. The first of the two colliery proprietors involved, R P Williams, was the lessee of Nantybar Colliery, which, until it closed in 1893, had a tramway connection with the SWMR about one mile east of Gyfylchi Tunnel, delays at Ynysmaerdy Incline being stated as one of the reasons for closure.[57] Prior to the closure Williams had approached the R&SBR to get an improved connection, and even suggested that he could build a viaduct across to the other aide of the Avon Valley to reach the R&SBR main line. Sidney Yockney, the R&SBR's engineer, more realistically proposed the use of the as yet unbuilt Railway No. 8,[58] but that idea was rejected because it would have involved the payment to the SWMR of a short distance toll of 8d per ton. Meanwhile Williams had acquired Fforchdwm Colliery in the Pelenna Valley and this led him to suggest to Yockney that a railway should be built to join the Whitworth Railway with the R&SBR at Pontrhydyfen.

The other colliery proprietor involved was W C Shout, managing director of the South Wales Whitworth Mineral Estates Ltd and of Whitworth Colliery. These two gentlemen, together with Yockney, who had agreed to act as engineer for the scheme independently of his connection with the R&SBR, met on the ground on 10th April 1893 to finalise the line of the new railway. The route branched off the Whitworth Railway just north of its junction with the SWMR, passed under that line and then ran parallel to it before heading down the Pelenna Valley to make an end-on connection with Lord Jersey's tramroad to Tewgoed Colliery, and thence down to a junction with the R&SBR at Tymaen. Initially it had been intended to join the this line directly at Oakwood, but in an exchange of letters between Knox and Yockney in March 1893 the Margam Estate refused to sell a small but essential piece of land unless the new line joined the Oakwood Railway.

At first the proposed railway was referred to as the New Whitworth Railway. The name was changed to the Western Rhondda Railway in February 1894 when a limited company was registered in this name with a capital of £50,000, with Shout one of the directors.[59] This company never carried on any business or allotted any shares and was dissolved and removed from the register of joint

stock companies in October 1897.[60] Also registered at this time was the New Railway Works Construction Co. Ltd with a capital of £10,000[61] for the purpose of constructing the line without Parliamentary powers. Williams was one of its shareholders. This company lasted somewhat longer, being dissolved in July 1901, never having carried out any business.[62]

The R&SBR viewed the proposed railway as an opportunity to gain influence in the area,[63] and by June 1893 a draft working agreement was under consideration.[64] Although the daily tonnage requirement was reduced from 700 to 500 tons per day, the promoters of the new line were not satisfied with the terms offered, which they considered favoured the R&SBR and overlooked the fact that it was not going to make the railway. Yockney, aware that the proposed PTR was shortly to become a reality, reported to the R&SBR directors in September 1893 that Williams had been in discussion with Knox, and urged them to come up with an acceptable system of rates. Recognising that this was unlikely, Williams in January 1894 asked if it would be preferable for the new railway company to work the railway themselves, the R&SBR carrying all traffic onwards at a through rate. Rather ominously, he requested a prompt reply as he had other propositions before him. In spite of this, the R&SBR directors took two months to reply that they were willing to entertain the proposal regarding rates and were prepared to abandon their Railway No. 8 of 1892 provided they were placed in a similar position in respect of the exchange of traffic with the SWMR by the construction of the proposed railway. Negotiations seem to have broken down at this point. Nevertheless, between March 1893 and November 1895 the New Whitworth and Western Rhondda railways were engaged in making arrangements for the construction of their line.[65]

A complication arose with the proposed bridge under the SWMR at Tonmawr.[66] The application of Sir William Lewis, the owner of the land on the north side of the line, for permission to construct this bridge was considered by the SWMR directors in June 1894.[67] Permission was evidently withheld as in April 1895 Sir William issued a summons to force the issue before the Aberavon magistrates at the next Petty Sessions. An order was made on 6th May 1895 for a bridge to be used for accommodation works only, and the SWMR directors resolved on 14th June that Sir William was to be held strictly to the rights the order gave. This of course precluded the use of any railway through the bridge as a new mineral railway. To get round this problem Sir William suggested two compromises: either 1) an on/off junction at the point of the Whitworth Branch junction, the SWMR receiving 1d per ton, together with a binding agreement that no sale or lease of the proposed railway would be made to the R&SBR without first giving the SWMR the option to acquire the line on equal terms; or 2) the works authorised by the justices be carried out, the SWMR receiving ½d per ton,

Neither was accepted by the SWMR directors. Nevertheless, they were informed on 1st November 1895 that Sir William had decided to proceed with the bridge.

Ever hopeful of some kind of arrangement with the Western Rhondda Railway, the R&SBR had included in its Bill for the 1895 Session of Parliament a clause empowering it to enter into an agreement to work, use, manage and maintain any railway which may be constructed by South Wales Whitworth Mineral Estates Ltd between its existing railway and the railway of the R&SBR

ABOVE: Cefn Ironworks on the left, Cefn Slip Colliery in the distance, and the OVER on the right, circa 1905. The left-hand track at the points gave access to the ironworks via a shunt-back beyond the gate, the colliery was accessed via the right-hand track. *NM&GW*

BELOW: Despite the caption, this circa 1908 postcard view is of Cefn Slip Colliery, sunk in 1860, closed in 1912. The double track approach of the OVER to Cefn Junction runs across the foreground, with mainly wagons belonging to the coal exporter William Perch in the near siding. *NM&GW*

Pontrhydyfen Viaduct on the SWMJnR under construction by Topham, Jones & Railton in 1896–97. Bricks and other materials were brought in by a temporary railway which crossed the River Avon by a makeshift trestle. There is no record of this track being connected to R&SBR nearby; an alternative route could have been via the Oakwood Railway which by then was owned by the PTR&D. *WGAS*

at Oakwood.[68] This clause was dropped from the R&SBR's 1895 Act[69] because the Whitworth company objected to it being put in without their consent.[70]

Notwithstanding Sir William Lewis' decision to proceed with the bridge under the SWMR and Yockney receiving instructions to peg out the route of the new line, the promoters of the Western Rhondda Railway, Messrs Shout and Williams, abandoned attempts to get an agreement regarding rates with the R&SBR. In early November 1895 they approached the PTR&D which agreed to take over the scheme. There were thus about two weeks in which to prepare the necessary documentation, and Meik later acknowledged that he had benefit of the plans prepared by Yockney for Williams.[71] The Parliamentary Notice was dated 19th November 1895 and published three days later.[72] The R&SBR's directors forthwith resolved to initiate the construction of Railway No. 8 of 1892[73] and to oppose the PTR&D's Bill in Parliament,[74] and Yockney declined to act any more for the promoters of the Western Rhondda Railway.[75]

The PTR&D's engineers were again Messrs Meik and T Forster Brown, and with Yockney's plan and that of the Oakwood Railway

ABOVE: Pontrhydyfen Viaduct under construction circa 1897. Topham, Jones & Railton and R&SBR wagons are on the temporary track bringing in materials. In the distance is the aqueduct built in 1827 by John Reynolds to supply water to his Oakwood Ironworks.

Courtesy Arthur Rees

RIGHT: The completed viaduct carrying the SWMJnR over the River Avon at Pontrhydyfen.
From Port Talbot and its Progress *(PTR&D Co. 1919), Author's collection*

The newly-completed earthworks at Efail Fach on the SWMJnR circa 1898. The right-hand span carries the railway over the old road to Neath.

Author's collection

to hand a new scheme was quickly arrived at.[76] Railway No. 1, just over five miles in length, commenced at a junction with the 1894 railway – a point later known as Tonygroes North Junction – and then picked up the course of the Oakwood Railway which it followed for two and a quarter miles before crossing over the R&SBR near Cwmavon and continuing up the valley, still on the left bank of the river, to Oakwood. Here the River Avon was crossed on a viaduct to reach the right bank of the Pelenna River. From hereon the route presumably pegged out by Yockney was followed up the Pelenna Valley to terminate just beyond where it crossed the River Gwenffrwd at Tonmawr. Railway No. 2 made a short connection from this point to the SWMR, and Railway No. 3 ran parallel to this line for about half a mile before passing under it through Sir William Lewis' proposed bridge to reach the Whitworth Railway. Railway No. 4 was intended to provide a direct route for traffic from the Tonmawr area towards Port Talbot Docks, and ran from Tonygroes to Doctors Crossing on the 1894 main line, thereby creating a triangle of lines. The total cost of these works was estimated to be £115,421. The company also sought powers to acquire the Whitworth Railway and other railways of the South Wales Whitworth Mineral Estates Ltd, powers to make agreements with the mineral company and with the SWMR, running powers over part of the SWMR, and authority for the SWMR to be transferred to and vested in its own undertaking provided it was freed of debts and liabilities, on terms to be agreed.

In anticipation of the Bill being passed by Parliament the directors of the PTR&D entered into three agreements with the companies that would be principally affected by it. The first was made with the

New Railway Works Construction Co. in December 1895, whereby the traffic arrangements it made with the Whitworth Mineral Estates were transferred to the PTR&D, £1,000 in fully paid up shares were to be transferred to Williams to cover expenses incurred by the New Railway Works and Western Rhondda companies, and the New Railway Works Construction Co. was indemnified against any claims made by Yockney.[77] The second agreement was made on 13th January 1896 with South Wales Whitworth Mineral Estates Ltd, the principal provision of which was the purchase of the Whitworth Railway for £9,000 within three months of obtaining the Act.

The last of these agreements was made with the SWMR and the Glyncorrwg Colliery Co. Ltd, the lessees of the SWMR,[78] on 14th January 1896[79] and in effect made the scheme possible. The principal clauses stipulated that:

1   the SWMR would support the Bill in Parliament and agree to a junction of the new railway with the SWMR near Tonmawr,

2   the SWMR would work the traffic between the junctions of the Whitworth Railway and the new railway, and also allow the PTR&D to work the traffic between these points,

3   the PTR&D would pay the cost of forming the new junction and one half of the cost of maintaining and working the section between the two junctions,

4   the Bill would contain clauses giving effect to these provisions, and

5   the PTR&D would not proceed with Railway No. 3 shown on the deposited plans.

Three petitions were lodged against the Bill, most notably by the R&SBR.[80] The R&SBR claimed that as the traffic on its line between Cwmavon and Port Talbot had not come up to expectations, the proposed line would deprive it of future traffic and would be unnecessary and unduly competitive. The proposed conversion of the moribund Oakwood Railway into a public railway was objected to as it was inconsistent with the arrangement made with the late Mr Talbot when the Cwmavon Railway was acquired. Furthermore the company was constructing a junction at Briton Ferry for SWMR traffic and was preparing to construct another junction to expedite traffic to Port Talbot (Railway No. 8). It was unfair to sanction railways designed to compete for SWMR traffic when it was amply provided for by the R&SBR. Similarly, running powers by the PTR&D over the SWMR were objected to, as was the purchase of the Whitworth Railway.

Petitions against the Bill were also presented by the traders and inhabitants of Pontrhydyfen on the grounds that the R&SBR satisfied their needs, and by Arthur Richard King Farlow, the receiver appointed on behalf of the debenture holders of the SWMR.[81] This latter petition was instigated by Sir John Jones Jenkins, chairman of the R&SBR, and Sidney William Hockney, that company's engineer, who between them held about 10 per cent of debentures, on the grounds that the Bill would deprive the SWMR of much of its traffic and revenue, to their detriment. Somewhat bizarrely, the principal debenture holders of the SWMR petitioned against changes to the Bill as their objections had been removed by the agreement made in January 1896. The SWMR and the Glyncorrwg Colliery Co. also petitioned against alterations to the Bill, their objections likewise having been overcome.

The Bill originated in the House of Lords. The Select Committee appointed to examine the Bill first met on 8th May 1896 under the chairmanship of Lord Kensington. The other members were Viscount Powercourt, and Lords Saltoun, Calthorpe and Addington.[82] As with its 1894 Bill, the PTR&D assembled an impressive list of witnesses in support of its case. The genesis of the proposed railway was recounted by Shout and Williams, the latter pointing out that the R&SBR's Railway No. 8 was of no use to the Whitworth district.

The objections raised in the R&SBR's petition were addressed by Mr Franklen, Miss Talbot's cousin and business advisor. In particular he expressed a wish to defend her against an allegation of bad faith in that Mr Talbot compelled the R&SBR to purchase the Cwmavon Railway and that it was inconsistent that the Oakwood Railway should now be made a public railway. Mr Talbot neither opposed nor promoted the R&SBR's 1882 Bill. The construction of the R&SBR severed the Oakwood Railway near the top and a right was reserved to Mr Talbot to make an 18 foot bridge under their line. In spite of several allegations that the R&SBR was thwarted in its efforts to improve Port Talbot Dock, they could have had it all to themselves.[83] There had been three opportunities: first, the R&SBR were offered the port on acceptable terms; second, Miss Talbot offered to give up her Oakwood Railway Crossing if they would treat the port on equal terms with Swansea, which was refused, and third, they could have come to terms with Messrs Shout & Co. The line now proposed was not in Miss Talbot's interests, which were in the tramway so that she would have had a wayleave on all coal passing over it. Because the R&SBR had refused the second proposal, she could not resist the PTR&D's scheme to get the traffic for themselves.

Mr Franken's remarks were amplified by Knox and Meik. During 1893–95 several attempts had been made to get the R&SBR to agree to the bridge under their line for the purpose of relaying the Oakwood Railway, the first meeting being held on 10th April 1893. Yockney had refused to approve the plan as it did not follow the line of the Oakwood Railway throughout, and to follow exactly would have been expensive. Hence the proposed new line was planned to go on a viaduct over the R&SBR and over sidings on Miss Talbot's land leased to the Cwmavon Steel Works. These sidings also served Oakwood Colliery. Miss Talbot would not have objected if the Western Rhondda Railway had wished to make use of the proposed bridge under the R&SBR to connect with the Oakwood Railway.

William Perch & Co. had been established in 1860 and owned, or were sole agents for, several collieries in the area. According to W M Lewis, the managing director, 60 to 70 per cent of their total output was currently shipped at Briton Ferry, accounting for about 75 per cent of the shipments there. As this dock was limited to ships of 1,100 tons, he needed an outlet at Port Talbot and also to be able to supply the tinplate works there, which the proposed railway would permit. Further support came from the consulting engineer, Thomas Forster Brown, who estimated that there were 600 million tons of coal in the area north of the SWMR. In addition, A Lawrence, the mining engineer, M Tennant, Town Clerk of the Borough of Aberavon, and Alderman I Evans of Glamorgan County Council all supported the Bill. Thomas Smith, the present owner of Neath Merthyr Colliery,[84] currently stopped because of high rates, stated his willingness to construct a tramway to connect with the proposed line and replace the existing tramway to the Vale of Neath Railway. F Thomas of Powley Thomas & Co., which had acquired Fforchdwm Colliery from Williams in 1894 and established Mercantile Colliery on the same site, stated that work was currently stopped because of the high rates to Briton Ferry and that the lower rate to Port Talbot would be of great benefit.

The first witness against the Bill was W Thomas, a mining engineer, who suggested there was little coal and of poor quality in the area to be served by the proposed railway, although it was immediately pointed out that the R&SBR had hoped to exploit just that. Yockney claimed that Knox had originally suggested the desirability of connecting the SWMR with the R&SBR (Railway No. 8). The proposed railway was well laid out above Oakwood, below there it was a duplication of the Cwmavon Railway. The line he laid out in 1893 for the New Whitworth Railway was very similar to that now proposed, except it was of a cheaper character. There was no objection to the present Bill from an engineering point of view, apart from details which would be agreed on the ground. The R&SBR's Railway No. 8 was being delayed until Port Talbot Dock was ready. Yockney attempted to make an issue out of the cost incurred by the R&SBR in purchasing the Cwmavon Railway, about £60,000 plus the same again to convert it to a public railway. It was suggested to Yockney that this was no more than it was worth, that it was the cheapest part of their line and it was the cheapest way to get to Port Talbot.

During cross-examination of some of the witnesses, the R&SBR's counsel referred to the ongoing improvements to Port Talbot Docks.

It was claimed that the one shipping place on the north side of the dock was not very convenient to his client. To this Meik replied that if the traffic developed by the R&SBR required three berths, the PTR&D would be happy to put them there. The issue of the line being built from the north to the south side of the dock under the general powers of the PTR&D's 1894 Act arose several times. It was eventually accepted that this was a dock line only, and not a main line. The R&SBR also claimed that as it had a prior interest in the Whitworth area it should have the opportunity to build the new line. This was rejected by the chairman of the Select Committee as being a new scheme as far as Parliament was concerned.

After four days of hearings, the chairman announced on 13th May that the committee had found the preamble to the Bill proved. There was no further discussion of the clauses, which were agreed as amended, and the Bill passed to the House of Commons on 19th May. There the R&SBR reiterated its petition against the amended Bill, as did the Glyncorrwg Colliery in its favour.[85] A new petitioner now appeared in the form of Glamorgan County Council, also in favour of the amended Bill. Its arguments against changes were based on the fact the PTR&D line crossed main roads and the GWR main line by bridges, whereas the R&SBR line between Cwmavon and Port Talbot Dock had eight level crossings of roads and one of the GWR main line. The problems with the latter line had been exacerbated by its new use as part of the main line to Swansea, and by the running powers granted to the PTR&D in 1894. The proposed new railway would mitigate the perceived increase of the inconvenience suffered by the public.

The arguments for and against the Bill were repeated before a Select Committee of the House of Commons which commenced its hearings under the chairmanship of Sir John Kennaway on 13th July. Four days later Sir John announced that the preamble to the Bill had been proved. In addition, the R&SBR was to be granted running powers over the proposed Railway No. 4, which if put into effect would have addressed some of Glamorgan County Council's concerns. However, the insertion of a clause suggested by the R&SBR for a junction at Ynysdavid for taking traffic from the new line to their line, for onward transmission to Swansea, was rejected. Following further minor amendments in the chambers of both Houses of Parliament the Port Talbot Railway & Docks (South Wales Mineral Railway Junction) Act received the Royal Assent on 7th August 1896.[86]

This Act authorised the PTR&D to construct within five years Railways Nos 1, 2 and 4 as shown on the deposited plans. It was also authorised to purchase from South Wales Whitworth Mineral Estates Ltd the Whitworth Railway and another railway owned by this company known as the Blaenavon Railway. This line, which ran the length of Cwm Gwenffrwd, made a facing connection with the SWMR in the Up direction half a mile to the west of the intended trailing junction of the The South Wales Mineral Railway Junction Railway (SWMJnR) to the SWMR. It is not so named on the first edition 25-inch Ordnance Survey map published in 1884, the name being given instead to another railway up Cwm Gwenffrwd to Tonmawr or Blaenavon Colliery which made a trailing connection with the SWMR and which had been dismantled by 1890. The dates of building these two Blaenavon Railways are not known, although they were almost certainly after 1872 when the SWMR was converted to standard gauge. The directors of the SWMR

noted that Tonmawr Colliery opened in November 1870 and was shipping a considerable quantity of coal by September 1871,[87] presumably via a tramroad to a transshipment point on the SWMR. This colliery company owned sixty broad gauge wagons in 1871.[88] In 1884 the Whitworth Railway was named by the Ordnance Survey as the Fforchdwm Railway.

The running powers granted to the R&SBR by the 1894 Act were extended to Railway No. 4 of the new Act. A lengthy clause also protected their railways against interference due to the construction or working of the new line. The interests of the SWMR and the Glyncorrwg Colliery Co. Ltd were protected by a special clause which embodied the agreement made in January 1896, particularly with regard to the junction between the two lines. Also, Miss Talbot's Oakwood Railway was afforded protection against obstruction by the new railways. The company was also empowered to enter into agreements to maintain and use or work the SWMR and the Whitworth Railway. The Act also authorised the company to raise up to £120,000 in additional capital and to borrow a further £40,000.

Questions over the purchase of the Blaenavon Railway arose almost immediately.[89] Traffic between the Blaenavon Railway and the SWMJnR would have entailed a back-shunt, a movement much disliked by railway companies. Charles Cheston, the PTR&D's solicitor, advised on 20th August that it was not in the company's interests to buy the Blaenavon Railway and unwise to seek running powers between the two junctions. Nevertheless, the company offered the SWMR 1d per ton for coal passing between these points, but this was rejected, 2d per ton being the minimum acceptable. Furthermore, if an agreement were to be reached regarding rates, the SWMR required an undertaking that the PTR&D would not construct a line under the SWMR to join the Blaenavon Railway. These terms were of course unacceptable to the PTR&D directors, and on 16th December they resolved to reject them and to make arrangements for a branch connection from their authorised line. The solicitor again urged caution, pointing out that the case for using the existing accommodation bridge under the SWMR for the connection was legally very weak. He suggested that the purchase of the Blaenavon Railway should be deferred and that the landowner, South Wales Whitworth Mineral Estates Ltd, should construct the connection, even if it be with a guarantee from the PTR&D to pay the costs.

Meanwhile, at the joint meeting of PTR&D and R&SBR company directors held on 2nd December, it had been suggested that either the new line should be abandoned between Port Talbot and Cwmavon and that the R&SBR should take the traffic onwards, or that the connection between the two railways should be put in at Oakwood if the R&SBR abandoned its Railway No. 8 above Pontrhydyfen, but both proposals were rejected as unworkable.

The specification for the construction of the railway from Port Talbot to Tonmawr which was issued on 1st January 1897 included the relaying of the Whitworth and Blaenavon railways and the construction of a new junction with the latter.[90] The most substantial works were the bridge over the R&SBR at Pontrhydyfen and the 167 yard long viaduct over the River Avon at Pontrhydyfen. The work also involved widening the embankment and bridge which had replaced the viaduct over the Gwenffrwd River.[91] Otherwise, the specification was generally similar to that produced for the

OVER, the date for completion likewise being twelve months from the acceptance of a tender. Messrs Topham, Jones & Railton were again successful, their tender of £83,449 being accepted on 28th January. The SWMJnR made a junction with the SWMR at a point 5 miles 31 chains from Briton Ferry. At their meeting on 2nd November 1897 the SWMR directors approved the PTR&D's plan for a passing loop with capacity for forty-six wagons and two double-ended sidings between the junctions with the SWMJnR and the Whitworth Branch, which became known as Tonmawr West and East junctions respectively.

The railways of the South Wales Whitworth Mineral Estates Ltd were duly purchased for £9,000, the agreement being sealed at a meeting of the directors on 20th February 1897. The conveyance, which was dated 5th April 1897, included the Whitworth Railway and the land over which it ran, and the land above Efail Fach for Railway No. 1 of the Act and for the intended new connection to the Blaenavon Railway.[92] Whitworth Mineral Estates also undertook to convey the Blaenavon Railway to the PTR&D within three months of this date without any further payment and also any land that might be required for forming a junction between the Blaenavon and Whitworth railways. By a supplemental agreement dated 23rd July 1897, Whitworth Mineral Estates undertook to extend the Blaenavon Railway southwards to a junction with Railway No. 1 authorised by the 1896 Act and was to be reimbursed all the monies it paid to the contractors for making this line, which eventually cost £7,866.[93] Thus by the questionable ruse of paying another company to make the extension and then buying it, the PTR&D acquired a short length of railway constructed without Parliamentary authority. The extension followed the course of an accommodation road and, by the time it was completed, passed through three bridges in quick succession, under the Blaenavon Railway, the SWMR and the new SWMJnR to join the SWMJnR at Blaenavon Junction, five miles from Tonygroes Junction. The points at Blaenavon Junction and those on the branch were opened by the key on the electric train staff for the Tonygroes, later Ynysdavid, to Tonmawr section. The directors of the SWMR queried the use of an accommodation bridge in such a way when they first heard of it on 24th November 1896 and as late as May 1907 resolved to seek counsel's opinion on the railway's right to do so.[94] The PTR&D directors left the matter in the hands of the company's solicitor. Nothing was done about the issue, as other events in 1907 made the matter academic.[95] Despite the wording of the first conveyance, the extended Blaenavon Railway was not conveyed to the Port Talbot Co. until 30th June 1901.[96]

Advantage was taken of the terms of the conveyance to realign the Whitworth Railway over a distance of about half a mile so as to eliminate two bridges over the Pelenna River. One consequence was that the original siding connection to Mercantile Colliery was lost,

The Blaenavon Branch passing under the PTR&D line to Tonmawr, then the SWMR, and finally the loop line from the SWMR to the branch, photographed in 1899 shortly after completion. At the time of writing, the bridge under the SWMR remained and the other earthworks were substantially unaltered.

Author's collection

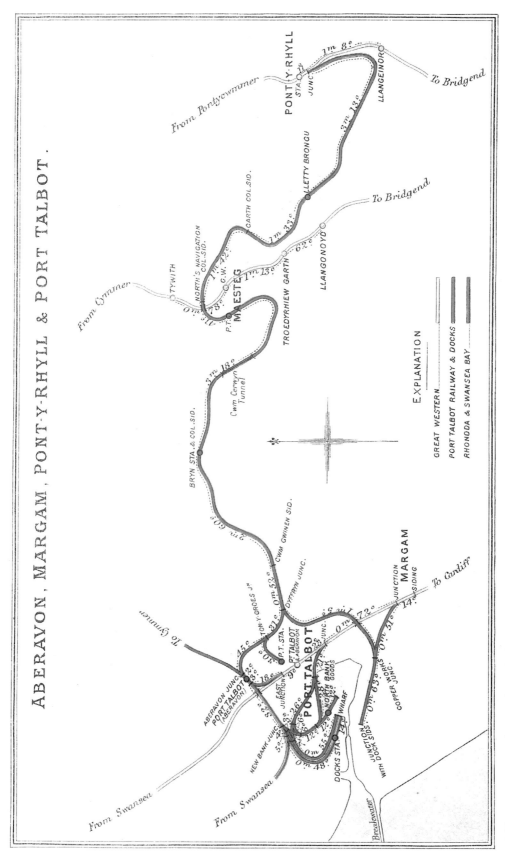

ABERAVON, MARGAM, PONT-Y-RHYLL & PORT TALBOT.

The 1898 junction diagram shows the full extent of the PTR&D's railways constructed as authorised by the 1894 Act, and those developed in the new dock area up to 1898.
Author's collection

Tonmawr photographed early in 1899 just after opening. The running line was the second track from the right. The signals were for the junction of the PTR with the SWMR which is out of sight to the bottom right. The cutting above the western portal of Gyfylchi Tunnel may be seen to the right of centre. The two 4-wheel coaches are believed to be those bought from the L&NWR for the workmen's service to Mercantile Colliery on the Whitworth Branch.

Courtesy Arthur Rees

for which Williams of the New Railway Works Construction Co. was paid compensation of £660. All the points on the Whitworth Branch were padlocked, the keys being kept in the signal box. Two deviations from the authorised line were made during the construction of Railway No. 1.[97] The most significant was the rerouting of the railway around the site of Margam Tinplate Works at Upper Forge rather than follow the course of the Oakwood Railway alongside the River Avon, which was first joined further on. Consequently these works, although out of use, remained connected to Port Talbot Dock via an unimpeded Oakwood Railway. A second, short, deviation was found to be necessary just beyond the bridge over the R&SBR at Ynysdavid where sidings were constructed for the exchange of traffic with the R&SBR and with local industry. Both were authorised retrospectively by the company's 1899 Act. The general manager suggested in December 1897 that it would be advantageous to lay in a goods siding and coal yard at milepost 2 on the new line opposite Cwmavon,[98] and the directors agreed on 26th January 1898 that this work should be carried out forthwith by Topham, Jones & Railton.

As with the OVER, Topham, Jones & Railton failed to complete their SWMJnR contract by 1st February 1898. However on 25th May Meik was able to inform the Board of Trade that the new line was connected to the 1894 railway at Tonygroes North

Junction and requested provisional sanction for its use pending inspection.[99] This was granted provided the junction was trapped and the new line was to be used for mineral traffic only. Although Col Yorke was appointed in December 1898, the new junction was not inspected until 9th May 1899. The delay in completing the contract may have been caused by the Railway Signalling Company, who had the subcontract for the signalling work at Tonmawr as required by the agreement with the SWMR. Probert reported to his directors on 15th November 1898 that this was now finished, that the SWMJnR had been opened on the previous day and that coal had been worked from Mercantile Colliery on the Whitworth Branch via Port Talbot to Cardiff.[100]

Encouraged by this achievement an advertisement was published in several south of England and South Wales newspapers describing the facilities offered by the new railway.[101] These included Cwmavon goods yard; access to Rio Tinto Copper Works and Messrs Wright, Butler & Co.'s works from Ynysdavid Sidings; New Forest, Llantwit Merthyr and Marine Collieries, and Gwenffrwd and Tynycwm Quarries on the Blaenavon Branch; Mercantile Colliery on the Whitworth Railway; and exchange with the SWMR at Tonmawr of traffic from Glyncorrwg. It was also announced that the siding connections for Craigavon and Ynys Avon collieries would be ready for opening in a few weeks.

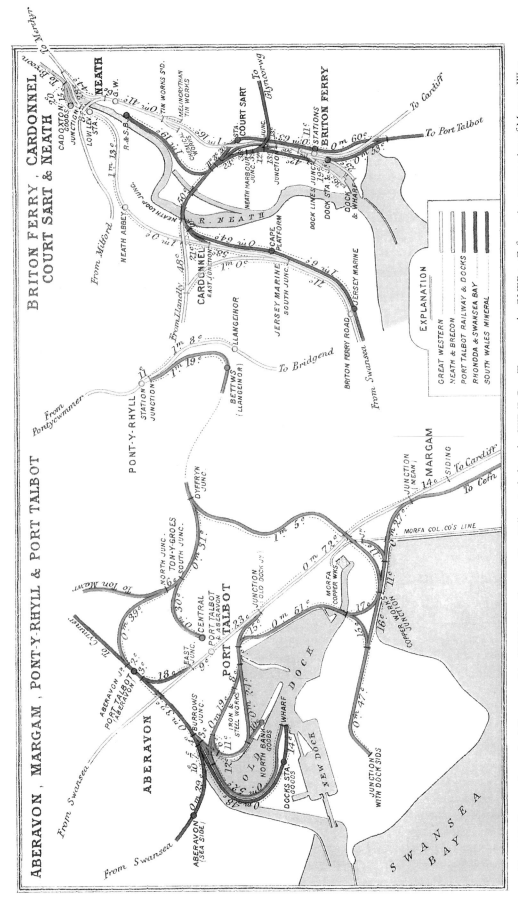

The 1920 diagram shows the full extent of the PTR&D's railways at Port Talbot, including the SWMJnR to Tonmawr, the OVER to Cefn, a misrepresentation of Margam West Curve, and the O&SSR running down the east side of the dock to Copper Works Junction. Also shown are the SWMR's railways at Briton Ferry including the short Dock Branch and Ynysmaerdy Incline, although this route to Glyncorrwg had closed in 1910.

Author's collection

NOTES

1. Chapman, *The Vale of Glamorgan Railway*, p. 47.
2. PA HL/PO/PB/3/plan1896/L13.
3. See Chapter 3.
4. TNA: PRO RAIL 1057/1532.
5. *The London Gazette*, 22 November 1895.
6. PA HL/PO/PB/3/plan1896/V1.
7. See Chapter 1.
8. PA HL/PO/PB/3/plan1896/P8.
9. The 1½ mile Dimbath Branch was authorised by the OVR Act 1866 29 & 30 Vict. c.cclii, but although construction eventually commenced it was never completed as such. A tramway or siding connection to the GWR's Blackmill to Hendreforgan line existed at the junction point in 1895: A Warrington, 'The Dimbath Branch', *Welsh Railways Archive*, 4/4 (November 2006), pp. 92–3.
10. TNA: PRO RAIL 574/2, 20 November 1900.
11. TNA: PRO RAIL 581/4.
12. TNA: PRO RAIL 250/42.
13. *The London Gazette*, 22 October 1895; PA HC/CL/PB/6/plan1896/26.
14. GWR (South Wales & Bristol Direct Railway) Act 1896, 59 & 60 Vict. c.ccxviii. Line opened throughout 1 July 1903.
15. TNA: PRO RAIL 252/1132.
16. *The London Gazette*, 1 May 1896; VoGR Act 1896, 59 & 60 Vict. c.ccx.
17. TNA: PRO RAIL 250/42.
18. TNA: PRO RAIL 1057/2952.
19. TNA: PRO RAIL 574/15.
20. *The London Gazette*, 17 April 1896; PA HL/PO/PB/3/plan1896/P8.
21. TNA: PRO RAIL 250/43.
22. *The London Gazette*, 14 April 1896.
23. See Chapter 3.
24. *House of Lords Journal*, 1896, *House of Commons Journal*, 1896.
25. 59 & 60 Vict. c.cxlv.
26. See Chapter 1.
27. Neville Granville, *Cefn Cribwr: Chronicle of a Village* (Stewart Williams 1980), pp. 138–9, 159–61.
28. TNA: PRO RAIL 574/28.
29. TNA: PRO RAIL 1057/1532.
30. TNA: PRO RAIL 1057/1529/5.
31. PA HL/PO/PB/3/plan1899/P7.
32. TNA: PRO RAIL 250/43.
33. TNA: PRO RAIL 574/7.
34. Chapter 3.
35. TNA: PRO RAIL 1057/2517; see also Chapter 1.
36. TNA: PRO RAIL 1057/1528/71.
37. TNA: PRO RAIL 1057/1529/42.
38. TNA: PRO RAIL 1057/1528/35.
39. TNA: PRO RAIL 1057/1528/2.
40. TNA: PRO BT 31/15008/29580.
41. *Railway News*, 18 February 1899.
42. *Railway Times*, 17 August 1899.
43. TNA: PRO BT 31/8337/60601.
44. *Railway Times*, 24 August 1901.
45. TNA: PRO RAIL 1057/1528/114.
46. TNA: PRO RAIL 1057/1529/19.
47. TNA: PRO RAIL 1057/1528/11.
48. PTR&D Co. Working Time Table, January 1899.
49. TNA: PRO RAIL 1057/1528/24.
50. TNA: PRO RAIL MT 6/862/5.
51. TNA: PRO RAIL 1057/1528/33.
52. TNA: PRO MT 6/878/5.
53. *Railway News*, 20 August 1898.
54. TNA: PRO RAIL 1057/1528/31.
55. *Railway News*, 4 February 1899.
56. TNA: PRO MT 6/878/5.
57. TNA: PRO RAIL 1066/2506.
58. See Chapter 1.
59. TNA: PRO BT 31/5771/40443.
60. *The London Gazette*, 22 October 1897.
61. TNA: PRO BT 31/5771/40447.
62. *The London Gazette*, 23 July 1901.
63. TNA: PRO RAIL 581/4.
64. TNA: PRO RAIL 1057/1864.
65. TNA: PRO 1066/2505.
66. TNA: PRO RAIL 1057/1539.
67. TNA: PRO RAIL 639/2.
68. *The London Gazette*, 23 November 1894.
69. 58 & 59 Vict. c.cix.
70. TNA: PRO RAIL 1066/2506.
71. TNA: PRO RAIL 1066/2505.
72. *The London Gazette*, 22 November 1895.
73. See Chapter 1.
74. TNA: PRO RAIL 581/4.
75. TNA: PRO RAIL 1066/2505.
76. PA HL/PO/PB/3/plan1896/P9.
77. TNA: PRO RAIL 574/112.
78. See Chapter 7.
79. TNA: PRO RAIL 574/72.
80. TNA: PRO RAIL 1066/2506.
81. See Chapter 7.
82. *House of Lords Journal*, 1896.
83. See Chapter 2.
84. See Chapter 1.
85. TNA: PRO RAIL 1066/2505.
86. 59 & 60 Vict. c.ccxii.
87. TNA: PRO RAIL 639/1.
88. Geoff Sheppard, 'South Wales Goods Trains – May 1872', *Broad Gauge Society Broadsheet 39*, (Spring 1998) pp. 6–7.
89. TNA: PRO RAIL 1057/2648.
90. TNA: PRO RAIL 574/8.
91. See Chapter 7.
92. WGAS D/D Xra 9.
93. TNA: PRO RAIL 1057/2648.
94. TNA: PRO RAIL 639/2.
95. See Chapter 7.
96. WGAS D/D Xra 10.
97. PA HL/PO/PB/3/plan1899/P7.
98. TNA: PRO RAIL 1057/1528/12.
99. TNA: PRO MT 6/880/2.
100. TNA: PRO RAIL 1057/1528/28.
101. *Railway Times*, 26 November 1898.

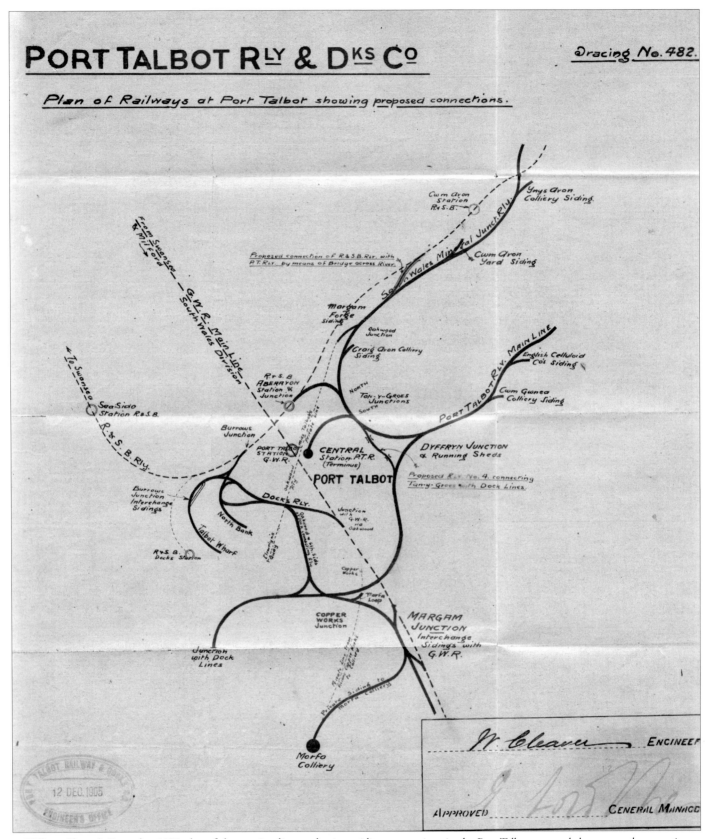

William Cleaver's December 1905 plan of the running lines and private siding connections in the Port Talbot area and the proposed connection between the R&SBR and the SWMJnR at Cwmavon and the resurrected Railway No. 4 of the SWMJnR Act 1896 which, if constructed, would have provided a direct route from the R&SBR to Port Talbot Docks. Also shown are Burrows Junction Exchange Sidings with the R&SBR and the O&SSR, neither of which are usually identified on maps. The Oakwood and Morfa Railways are marked although at the time both were moribund.

Author's collection

6

The Port Talbot Railway, 1897 to 1907

A NUMBER OF ADDITIONS and improvements were made to the railways authorised by the 1894 and 1896 Acts up to the end of 1907, at which time the working of them was taken over by the GWR.[1]

DUFFRYN JUNCTION TO PONTYRHYLL

GARTH

In December 1897, even before the line had opened for passenger traffic, the directors instructed the engineer to submit plans for a station at Garth near milepost 9½ to serve the village and the nearby Garth Merthyr Colliery. Although the plans were approved at their January 1898 meeting, the general manager then requested increased office accommodation and the revised plans were accepted in April 1898 provided the estimate could be reduced to £536. Progress was slow and in January 1899 the directors ordered that the station was to be completed as soon as possible. The Board of Trade provisionally sanctioned the use of the station on 31st January, but it was not inspected until the following May.[2]

BETTWS LLANGEINOR

In April 1899 the inhabitants of the villages of Bettws and Llangeinor in the lower Garw Valley petitioned the directors for a passenger station at Cefn Gelli, which was approximately half way between the two hamlets. The general manager reported that the station would be used mainly by colliers from the district travelling to the Garw Valley and to Lletty Brongu, and that the station master there could have responsibility for it.[3] Land was available and in September 1899 the directors approved a plan for the station at a cost of £430, towards which Miss Talbot contributed £150. The unstaffed station, named Bettws Llangeinor, was finished in December 1899[4] and brought into use on 1st January 1900,[5] but not inspected and sanctioned for use by the Board of Trade until August 1900, the only condition being that goods trains were not to stop there.

WEST END

It was becoming clear that several improvements were required for the main line to be operated more efficiently. In a report to the directors dated 14th March 1899, Probert, the general manager, pointed out that mineral trains were taking about twenty minutes to run between East End and Bryn, a distance of about one and a half miles, by having to run slowly through the tunnel owing to the change of gradient and having to stop outside to pin down brakes. A loop at West End would enable trains to cross whilst brakes were being pinned down on Down mineral trains.[6] The works at West End, which were estimated to cost £1,300, were approved at the Board meeting held on 21st June 1899. To aid the considerable

amount of excavation which was required the engineers put in a siding which would eventually become the new Up loop. Probert applied to the Board of Trade on 28th September for provisional sanction to construct the loop according to the submitted plan.[7] The Board of Trade replied that it could not sanction the works at present as there were grave objections to a loop on a gradient of 1 in 40. Although the plan included a runaway siding on the Down side and the Up loop was trapped into Bryn Brickworks siding, the matter was not resolved until 16th November when Col Yorke, one of the Board of Trade's inspectors, intimated that if the Down runaway siding was lengthened to 250 yards on a reverse 1 in 40 gradient, the objection would be removed. The works were then provisionally sanctioned on that basis, a further condition being that trap points on the new loop were to be removed when it opened for passenger traffic. Construction took some time owing to the amount of excavation required. The new loop was inspected on 14th August 1900 by Major Pringle, who found the works satisfactory apart from some minor signalling matters, and it was brought into use on 27th August 1900.[8] One condition of sanctioning the new loop for use was that the Board of Trade required an amended drawing of the works as executed. When this was supplied, the Board of Trade pointed out that there was no need to signal a Down train into the runaway siding. Lowther, Probert's replacement as traffic manger, had intended to use this siding to hold a banking engine or an engine plus brake van, but was informed by the Board in January 1901 that it must be kept clear at all times. The offending disc signal was subsequently removed.

DUFFRYN JUNCTION

Another problem was that engines and trains were being delayed at Duffryn Junction owing to the lack of additional sidings with a neck for trains to shunt clear of the main line.[9] The proposed improvements at Duffryn Junction consisted of widening the bridge over the River Ffrwdwyllt at the eastern end, extending the existing loops over the bridge by about 80 yards, and providing two shunting spurs. It was also necessary to move Duffryn No. 2 signal box back a short distance. These works were approved by the directors on 26th July 1899, the estimated cost being £1,200, and were carried out under Hosgood's direction. Major Pringle found the railway works satisfactory at his inspection on 14th August 1900.[10] The new bridge, which consisted of eight substantial steel girders each 24 feet long to carry the four tracks, was inspected by Major Druitt in October 1901. In addition to these works, a siding for local coal traffic was put in at Duffryn Junction in June 1899.

PONTYRHYLL

Probert also reported that an additional loop was required at Pontyrhyll and the existing loop needed to be extended to hold forty wagons. The new loop was approved by the directors at their June 1899 meeting, and was reported to have been completed by 14th December. It was not put into use immediately due to a delay by the GWR in rearranging their signals.[11] The extension of the existing loop was reported to be underway in March 1900. This too required signalling work by the GWR, and the secretary was instructed in April 1900 to press that company to complete the work. Although these alterations would have affected the main, passenger carrying, line, they appear not to have been inspected by the Board of Trade until August 1905 when the arrangements at the junction were simplified.

GARTH LOOP

In July 1900 Lowther reported that trains were being held up at Maesteg and Lletty Brongu due to the long section of about three and a half miles, and the work that had to be done at North's Junction and Garth.[12] By 1903 traffic patterns had changed as a result of increased mining activity in the Llynvi Valley and the diversion of Garw Valley mineral traffic for Port Talbot via the OVER, as described below. Despite this, nothing was done until November 1905 when the directors authorised a new loop be laid down at Garth at an estimated cost of £3,650 to deal with the growing traffic from Elder's Navigation Collieries at Garth more economically than hitherto. At the same time the two loops and the signal cabin at Lletty Brongu were removed, the cabin being re-erected at Garth.[13] Consequently the sections were altered to Maesteg–Garth and Garth–Pontyrhyll. The new loop at Garth, which was signalled for goods trains only, was reported to have been in use "since Easter" 1906 (15th April)[14] and Lletty Brongu was reduced to one platform

and two sidings worked from a ground frame. Due to an oversight the works were not inspected and sanctioned by the Board of Trade until March 1912.[15] The signal cabin at Garth was closed in January 1916 "owing to the existing [wartime] conditions" and the loop was probably removed a the same time.

TYNYFFRAM

While Garth Loop eased operations beyond Maesteg, the three mile section between Duffryn Yard and Bryn remained a potential bottleneck, and in April 1906 the directors requested suggestions as to how this length could be split to meet the needs of the growing traffic. The following month a plan was produced showing a proposed staff station and passing at Tynyffram, the halfway point, costing an estimated £1,820 and saving £370 per annum, the alternative being to double the line between Tynyffram and Duffryn Yard for an estimated £10,275. The loop was approved in June 1906, the company's engineering department doing the work apart from the signalling and cabin which were provided and erected by the Railway Signal Company.[16] The work included the construction of a lengthy Down runaway siding on a 1 in 40 reverse gradient. A large amount of excavation was required[17] and the loop was not ready and in use until June 1907.[18] As with Garth, the work was not inspected and sanctioned until March 1912, a restriction being that passenger trains were not to pass.[19]

DUFFRYN SIDINGS

One issue that remained unresolved was Railway No. 4 of the SWMJnR Act of 1896. The R&SBR did not exercise its right to require the PTR&D to construct this short section of railway by

Garth Loop and the upper connection to Garth Colliery, possibly photographed from the adjacent signal box. The loop was opened in 1906 and removed circa 1925.

NM&GW

The isolated signal box controlling Tynyffram Passing Loop was opened in June 1907 and closed on 31st August 1964, photographed on 17th July 1959.
Courtesy R M Casserley

7th August 1902 if asked to do so, as authorised by the PTR&D's 1899 Act.[20] In November 1902 Lowther expressed the view that the increased flexibility would not be justified by the necessary expense, and the directors resolved to abandon the line and to relieve Miss Talbot of her undertaking to sell the land. Four years later the thinking had reversed again. In June 1905 this railway was deemed in all probability to be needed, and plans were prepared for its construction and for an associated loop on the line to the docks. An application to buy the land was submitted to Miss Talbot in September 1905. However, the following June Lowther pointed out that if the Board agreed to the construction of additional sidings between Duffryn Yard and Doctors Crossing, congestion of traffic would be relieved and a saving of one engine per day would be effected between Duffryn Yard and the docks. A new plan was submitted showing accommodation for 735 wagons at an estimated cost of £6,000 excluding the required land. This scheme was deemed sufficient to render Railway No. 4 unnecessary, and the route from the SWMJnR to the docks remained via a reversal at Duffryn Junction. The directors approved this scheme in July 1906, although it deprived the PTR&D of a potentially useful turning triangle. The tender of Messrs T W Davies of £2,325 for labour was accepted in January 1907, the sidings being laid with rails recovered from relaying operations. Extensive site clearance was necessary and the grid, which initially consisted of four through and five dead-end storage sidings, was not completed until December 1907.[21] Duffryn

Nos 1 and 3 signal boxes controlled the entry to the through sidings at the north and south ends respectively. The directors were somewhat surprised that Miss Talbot required £800 per acre for the 4½ acres of land required for the sidings compared to the £500 paid in 1894–95 for land in that locality.

CWM CERWYN TUNNEL

The work done during construction to strengthen part of the tunnel walls[22] turned out to be inadequate. Two years after the tunnel had been opened for traffic, serious fractures developed in a section 70 to 100 feet further in from the Maesteg end than the previous failure.[23] During November 1899 pitch-pine longitudinal and transverse timbers, strengthened by block inserts, were placed under the wall footings and the permanent way to prevent a collapse.[24] Similar precautions had to be taken during August 1902 to strengthen the 70 foot gap between the sections already dealt with.[25] The tunnel was from then on subject to frequent inspections during which it became apparent that although movement of the side walls in the affected area had ceased, the arch was still lifting, such that crushed bricks occasionally dropped onto trains. In February 1907 a series of cross sections was taken of the defective portion, using a profile gauge fixed to one of the company's covered goods wagons for the purpose. These revealed that a 180 foot section near the centre of the tunnel, which included the two areas most recently attended to, was in a far more dangerous condition than previously suspected.

Rather than attempt further inverting, Cleaver recommended that this entire section should be relined as soon as possible.[26] This was major task and at their meeting in March 1907 the directors requested that expert opinion be obtained as to the best method of carrying it out. A system of cast iron segmental lining was adopted, similar to that used at the time on the London Underground, and at their May 1907 meeting the directors accepted the tender of Messrs Perry & Co. of Westminster for £4,709, the work to be completed within nine months of acceptance. This choice resulted in the profile of the tunnel in the relined section being almost circular, which in itself provided greater strength. Initially the segments were planned to be 3 feet wide, but the contractors advised a 20 inch width for ease of handling and the additional cost of £565 was agreed to. The Board of Trade was advised of the general nature of the work in May 1907 and at first raised no objections.[27] However, when informed in August 1907 that the track in the tunnel was to be slewed to one side for nearly one quarter of a mile, it objected on the grounds that it was dangerous for both passengers and the workmen, and asked if the work could not be done when trains were not running. This of course was out of the question. The Board of Trade was persuaded when it was informed that all traffic would be worked under special instructions with a speed limit of 2 mph, that carriage windows would be barred, and that the workmen would be protected by a shield built to the loading gauge. The work and a temporary siding for the contractors at West End were approved on 3rd September. This siding was laid in by 12th September,[28] but the time taken to prepare the contractors plant and to assemble materials meant that the relining work did not start until 20th November. The shield referred to was a specially constructed steel canopy which straddled the slewed track and ran on its own precisely positioned rails, and on which the segments could be manoeuvred into position. A 15 inch gauge tramway was laid alongside the railway from the contractors yard outside the tunnel to the work site to take segments in and rubbish out. Progress averaged five rings per week, the work under the track being done at weekends and the remainder on weekdays, working day and night shifts. In all 105 rings were installed, with tarred yarn jointing between them. There was no undue delay to trains or any serious mishap, and the relining work was completed on 14th May 1908.[29] Normal service through the tunnel was resumed at the end of May.[30]

Main Line

Between March 1905 and October 1907 the main line between Duffryn Yard and Maesteg was gradually relaid with 92 lb rails, the old 75 lb rails being taken to the docks for new sidings, grids and tip roads.[31] At the same time the curves at the siding connections to the Celluloid Works and Varteg Colliery were realigned to eliminate rough riding.[32] Material excavated at Tynyffram was used to widen the bank at Bryn so that the loop could be lengthened to take thirty-eight wagons rather than the thirty-two hitherto.[33] Cleaver notified the Board of Trade in March 1906 that owing to the increased length of trains causing the fouling of points, it had been necessary to move the Up starter at Bryn and the Down starter at Maesteg, and was informed that these works would not need inspection. A runaway siding was laid in at the lower end of the Up loop at West End in November 1906 so that trains could be drawn in on the wrong line if necessary.[34]

Llynvi Valley Colliery

O H Thomas, the proprietor of Llynvi Valley Colliery, was one of those who in January 1895 provided a guarantee of traffic for the newly authorised PTR. This was an ill-judged move by Thomas; this colliery was situated in Cwm Du with a tramway connection which passed under the PTR&D's Lletty Brongu Viaduct to reach the LVR just below Llangynwyd station. There was thus no real need for an outlet via the PTR, which resulted in a breach of the agreements made. The directors waived compliance with these agreements in July 1899 provided a date was given for sinking new pits and that the whole of the coal obtained was sent over the PTR. Probert was instructed to try and induce Thomas to make the necessary connection. Nothing was done, although the colliery continued to operate, such that the PTR&D found it necessary in June 1902 to purchase the minerals under the viaduct for £2,000. In March 1905 the directors resolved to sue Thomas for breach of agreement. The case was heard at Cardiff Assizes in March 1906, damages of £2,750 being awarded to the company, which agreed to quarterly payments over two years provided adequate security was given. In June 1906 the directors noted that Thomas had agreed to pay the company's costs and £750 forthwith, and the balance quarterly over eighteen months from 1st July, and had offered the leases on his Lletty Brongu Colliery as security. Lowther reported in August 1907 that the sum of £333 6s 6d due 5th July was unpaid and that consequently he had arranged to hire 100 of Thomas' coal wagons at 3s 6d per truck per week, retaining the money as it accumulated as security for the two remaining payments.

Temporary Siding at East End

Up until April 1905 all siding agreements had required the approval of the Board of directors. At their meeting that month the directors authorised the secretary, Knott, to enter into agreements for the construction of siding connections with his own signature on behalf of the company, in lieu of them being entered into under the company's seal, using a standard form of agreement approved by the company's solicitors, Messrs Cheston & Sons. The first siding to be approved under this arrangement was laid in as a temporary connection off the existing mileage siding at East End,[35] for William Jones & Sons who had a contract to build a reservoir in the vicinity for Margam Urban District Council. Also approved was a short workmen's platform alongside the main line. The siding was completed by May 1905,[36] and inspected by Major Druitt in August.[37] The works were sanctioned for use provided the platform, which was 60 feet long, was not advertised or used as a station for the general public. The siding, the agreement for which was dated 3rd January 1906, was out of use by about 1910.[38] The GWR purchased the rails from Jones in 1927, but left the connection in place as catch points.

The Ogmore Valleys Extension Railway

It soon became clear that the half mile long single line between Margam and Copper Works junctions was an impediment to the movement of traffic. In October 1899 the directors approved a plan to double this section at a cost of not more than £600, the work being carried out by Messrs Pearson's. This double line, which fed into the existing double line leading to the dock railways, was brought into use on 18th June 1900.[39] The most significant engineering feature on the OVER was the bridge over the GWR main line at Margam Moors. Cleaver, in his report to the directors as engineer in April 1905, noted that this bridge had been sinking slowly ever since construction, with the result that the clearance over the GWR rail level was now five inches less than their requirement.[40] The necessary clearance was achieved by depositing ballast to raise the rails on the approaches and lifting the steel superstructure twelve inches and resting it on new bed stones under the girders. The work was reported to be completed in February 1906.[41] Hosgood reported in December 1899 that the C&PR watering place was badly situated.[42] The site has not been identified but a location near the colliery or the coke ovens at Bryndu seems likely. In February 1900 the directors approved a new standpipe at Waterhall Junction, but this must have proved unsatisfactory as it was reported in September 1905 that a new supply was now in use, watering of engines now taking five minutes compared to thirty minutes previously.[43]

THE 1903 AGREEMENT

The opening of the 1894 railway from Port Talbot to the Llynvi and Garw valleys, and the OVER from Margam to Cefn Junction put the PTR&D in a position where it could seriously compete with the GWR for traffic from those valleys to Port Talbot and places westward. Recognising this, the two companies made an agreement in November 1898 whereby coal and coke traffic from the Llynvi and Garw valleys for destinations between Port Talbot and Swansea and Landore, and to Pontardawe was be forwarded via the PTR and thence by the GWR, and the rates were fixed.[44] Traffic for places west of Landore was to be forwarded by either railway as consigned. This arrangement of course allowed the GWR to chose its own route. Before entering into this agreement the directors minuted that they could not enter into any arrangement which hinted at an amalgamation with the GWR.

Ever desirous of making the fullest use of their railways, the directors in August 1901 authorised Lowther, the general manager, to attempt to induce the GWR to send all its traffic from Tondu to west of Port Talbot via the OVER instead of Pyle. In this he was unsuccessful, but further negotiations produced a more far-reaching agreement. In August 1902 Lowther reported that, subject to a satisfactory revision of the company's agreements with the Garw Valley traders, the GWR would work all the Garw Valley traffic and convey via the OVER all its traffic from the Llynvi, Garw, Ogmore, Little Ogmore and Dimbath valleys and also from South Rhondda and Raglan Collieries on its Cardiff & Ogmore line for Port Talbot Dock, places on the PTR and destinations west of Port Talbot. The conditions included the closure of Pontyrhyll signal box and the provision of additional junctions at Margam. As part of this arrangement the GWR undertook to double its Garw Valley line between Llangeinor and Pontyrhyll, the PTR&D sharing the estimated expense of £2,700. The terms were agreed by both companies in April 1903.[45]

The agreement, which was dated 5th May 1903, provided that from 1st June 1903 the GWR would work all merchandise and mineral traffic arising at those points to Port Talbot or Margam Junction via the OVER in return for 32½ per cent of the working expenses accrued over that portion of the journey.[46] The GWR was also permitted to work locomotive coal over this line. The PTR&D's signal box at Pontyrhyll Junction was to be closed at the same time as the opening of a second line from there to Llangeinor. The agreement also permitted the GWR to use the Port Talbot's sidings at Pontyrhyll, should it so desire, on payment of a nominal rent. The new junctions at Margam were estimated to cost £2,740 and, because of its increased use, the GWR agreed to pay one quarter of the working expenses of Margam West signal box. More surprisingly, the GWR had the option of temporarily employing the three sets of enginemen, three guards and one foreman made redundant by this arrangement, and of acquiring any surplus locomotives and other stock belonging to the PTR&D. This agreement, which marked an ever closer working relationship between the two companies, terminated the PTR&D's running powers between Pontyrhyll and Blaengarw for merchandise and mineral traffic, but those for passenger traffic were unaffected. All earlier agreements between the two companies remained in force except where varied by the new one.

The PTR&D simplified its arrangements at Pontyrhyll Junction by extending the single line Lletty Brongu–Pontyrhyll Junction section to Pontyrhyll station and converting the Up loop to a loop siding. Pontyrhyll Junction signal cabin was closed, and eventually sold to the GWR in 1910. The GWR took over the PTR&D's two short sidings at the junction and in due course converted them into loops.[47] Lowther submitted his plan to the Board of Trade on 8th September 1904 and received provisional sanction to carry out the work on 18th September, ready for opening on 19th September. The works were reported to be ready for inspection on 17th October,[48] but were not visited by Major Druitt until August 1905 when all was found to be satisfactory. The new arrangements at Pontyrhyll Junction, which were deemed to have come into effect on 1st March 1905, were embodied in a further agreement made between the two companies dated 11th April 1905.[49] The GWR was granted free use of the sidings for ten years and thereafter for £30 per annum, the interim presumably covering the shared cost of the signalling works, and the PTR&D was required to maintain the ground frame at the Maesteg end of the sidings. The GWR submitted its plans for doubling the Llangeinor to Pontyrhyll section to the Board of Trade in August 1904, but the work was not completed until July 1905.[50] Col Yorke, who inspected the works, reported that the arrangements for working the junction from Pontyrhyll station signal box were satisfactory.

The connection to the GWR at Margam West was converted into a full double junction by October 1903 as required by the agreement, and a new connection put in from the OVER to the GWR Down main line near Margam East signal box. These works were reported to be ready in October 1903 and were sanctioned by the Board of Trade in May 1904.[51] The points at the east end of the exchange sidings were relaid in October 1906 to remove a speed restriction.[52]

The 1903 agreement addressed the PTR&D's main operating challenge, that coal trains faced an undulating journey from Pontyrhyll to Lletty Brongu where the climb up to Maesteg and onwards to Cwm Cerwyn Tunnel really began, the ruling gradient being 1 in 75 against the load. Although the heaviest engines, the American-built 0-8-2 tank locomotives, were used on these trains, in November 1901 the GWR objected to use of these at International Colliery at the head of the Garw Valley, as they tended to derail on the sharp curve of the colliery siding.[53] Their continued use was only permitted provided the PTR&D installed an additional check rail on the outside of the siding. Subsequent to the agreement coming into effect these locomotives worked only as far as Maesteg.

The directors also hoped to divert Ely Valley traffic for Port Talbot Docks to the OVER. In February 1904 Lowther was instructed to confer with the GWR's general manager regarding the construction of a new loop line at Gellyrhaidd Junction in order to avoid the circuitous route and longer mileage via Llantrissant. This attempt to make the OVER more remunerative failed, as did a cost-saving suggestion that the GWR close its signal box at Ffos Bank and share the expenses of working the PTR&D's box at Cefn Junction.

THE SOUTH WALES MINERAL JUNCTION RAILWAY

As originally planned, the SWMJnR was a five and three-quarter mile long section from Tonygroes Junction to Tonmawr Junction. Williams, the acting traffic manager, pointed out in April 1900 that considerably delays were occurring with copper ore trains for the Rio Tinto Co. at Cwmavon as only one engine was allowed in the section, which included the Blaenavon Branch.[54] He recommended moving a staff pillar from Tonmawr cabin to the one at Ynysdavid Sidings, so that trains could safely work either side of there. The directors agreed to this proposal for crossing trains at Ynysdavid, the cost being minimal. By 1907 the SWMJnR and its branches were seeing more traffic and in April that year the directors accepted a tender from the Patent Shaft & Axletree Co. Ltd for a 3,000-gallon water tank which was erected in the vee of Blaenavon Branch Junction. This wooden structure was replaced by a standard GWR water tower in June 1918.[55]

YNYSDAVID RAILWAY

In 1889 the Copper Miners' Tinplate Co., in conjunction with Messrs RB Byass & Co., erected the Express Steel Works at Cwmavon on land reclaimed by the diversion of the River Avon and adjacent to both the tinplate works and the R&SBR.[56] Eight years later the Express Steel Co. Ltd was formed to acquire and carry on this business of steel manufacture, with the tinplate company being the majority shareholder and Byass & Co. having the right to appoint one director.[57]

These works were a potential source of traffic, and in March 1898 Meik produced a plan for a siding connection about a mile long running from Ynysdavid Sidings to the Express Tin Works and initially given the rather ungrammatical title of the Coppermines Railway.[58] The proposed route looped round the village of Cwmavon as it then was, then ran parallel to the exchange sidings behind Cwmavon station and the engineering workshops known as the Depot, to terminate at a junction with the Cwmavon Works' internal railway system just short of the tinplate works. Connections with the exchange sidings, the Depot and to the railway leading towards the Rio Tinto Works and the Cwmavon Steel Works were also proposed. Nothing was done until the scheme was considered by the directors at their March 1899 meeting. The estimated cost was £6,182 and the directors resolved to lease the line at 5 per cent of the cost for thirty-nine years, shortly thereafter increased by the solicitor to forty-eight years. Meik was instructed to invite tenders on behalf of Messrs Wright, Butler & Co., who seemingly were to

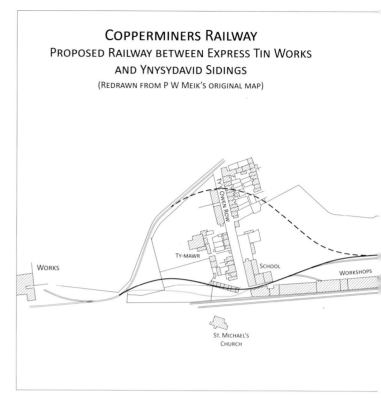

COPPERMINERS RAILWAY
PROPOSED RAILWAY BETWEEN EXPRESS TIN WORKS
AND YNYSYDAVID SIDINGS
(REDRAWN FROM P W MEIK'S ORIGINAL MAP)

be the owners of the line and were by then the owners of the tinplate and steelworks. In April 1899 a revised plan was submitted to the directors which avoided the Depot entirely but made extensive use of one of the exchange sidings and the existing internal railway to climb up to one section of the Tinplate Works, then reverse direction and run past these works and to drop down to a new terminus alongside the Express Steel Works.[59] Mr Byass promised to give this railway as much traffic as he could personally control. Probert, the general manager, pointed out several defects of this latest plan. First, the exchange sidings with the R&SBR were insufficient and continually blocked; if the company required to pass through these sidings to get to the sidings alongside the Express Steel Works it would have to provide a new siding to compensate for the one used as a running line. Second, part of the proposed route belonged to the Rio Tinto Company and the company would have to pay a proportion of the maintenance. Third, because the traffic would be worked some distance from the SWMJnR, and because of the very low rates on the R&SBR and the large number of wagons required to work the traffic, it would not be advisable to construct the line without a guarantee of traffic. The directors took these points on board at their May 1899 and resolved to defer the railway unless a sufficient guarantee of traffic was forthcoming. This was not to be, despite the chairmen of both the Express Steel Works and Cwmavon Steel Works being directors of the PTR&D. Cwmavon was not the place for large-scale steel works and both closed in 1902–3.

The proposed Ynysdavid Railway was the sole justification for the private sidings clause in the PTR&D's 1899 Bill to which the R&SBR, unsuccessfully, objected. Charles Cheston pointed out in March 1899 that this railway and the clause were essential for the Express Steel Works traffic, but not for the Rio Tinto traffic which could be worked to Ynysdavid Sidings and thence by Miss Talbot using her running powers.[60]

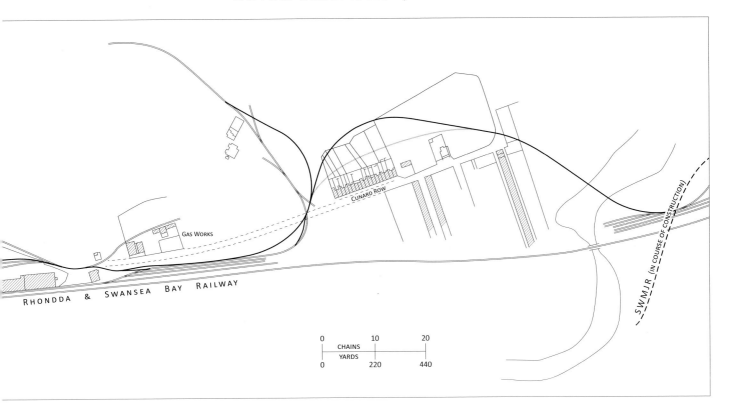

CUNARD ROW

GAS WORKS

RHONDDA & SWANSEA BAY RAILWAY

SWMJR (IN COURSE OF CONSTRUCTION)

0		10		20
	CHAINS			
	YARDS			
0		220		440

RIO TINTO

Prior to 1883, the Rio Tinto Company's mining and smelting operations were confined to Spain. In February 1883 the company realised that it would be advantageous to erect or purchase a copper smelting works in Britain, and almost immediately discovered that the Cwmavon copper works were available on attractive terms.[61] Samuel Danks, the present owner, was prepared to lease the works, then idle, for only £700 per annum, and they passed to Rio Tinto in October 1883. Copper production resumed in April 1885, the reopening of the works having a marked, although short-term, effect on the British copper smelting industry. Copper was imported at Cwmavon Wharf,[62] as it was then known, and conveyed by the R&SBR to Cwmavon over the recently converted Cwmavon Railway.

The existing agreement with Rio Tinto regarding ships' dues, which was inherited by the new PTR&D from the old PT Co., was altered in February 1895 so that the size of the ships was computed by draft rather than burthen, the copper company being satisfied with a depth in the old entrance channel of 20 feet 6 inches. The directors noted in April 1895 that the revised agreement resulted in Rio Tinto paying back-rates of £1,485 10s 4d due to the old company. Rio Tinto diverted its seaborne traffic away from Port Talbot in February 1898,[63] presumably because of its inability to berth its vessels there due to the unfinished state of the new dock.

The reacquisition of this traffic was of some importance to the PTR&D. In July 1898, with the opening of the SWMJnR imminent, Knott enquired of the general manager the value of the Rio Tinto traffic to the company when that line was open and could be worked via Ynysdavid Sidings, and also the value of this traffic when the dock could accommodate ships of the required tonnage. At the time Rio Tinto were producing 19,000 tons of refined copper and using 34,800 tons of coal per annum. The decision to quit Port Talbot affected both the PTR&D and the R&SBR, and was one of the topics discussed at a joint meeting of directors in November 1898. Pooling of receipts[64] and commutation of charges for the exchange of traffic with R&SBR were proposed.

These considerations were complicated by the terms of an agreement of 1894 arising from an injunction served on Rio Tinto by Miss Talbot as a result of the Cwmavon Copper Works smoke dispute which had arisen in 1893.[65] The damages agreed to be paid to Miss Talbot were commuted by a further agreement made in 1898, whereby, *inter alia*, the payment of £700 per annum would cease if Rio Tinto recommenced importing as much copper ore as they did in the year ending 30th June 1896, and all traffic between Port Talbot Docks and Rio Tinto's works at Cwmavon was carried over Miss Talbot's Oakwood Railway, provided this was not the most expensive route, the minimum rate payable being £2,200 per annum.

One of the terms of the acquisition from Miss Talbot of her rights over the Oakwood Railway was the grant to her of running powers over the SWMJnR from the old Oakwood Furnaces to the junction with the Oakwood Railway above Upper Forge. This agreement was on the basis that the owner of each railway would receive the mileage proportion of the rate charged after the deduction of the cost of haulage, Miss Talbot's receipts from this arrangement being limited to £350 per annum. Writing to Mr Watson, one of the directors, in January 1899, Knott remarked that nothing would be done to make it possible for Miss Talbot to compete with the PTR&D for the traffic.[66] In spite of this stance, the company eventually became reconciled to the fact that at best it could act as an agent of Miss Talbot for the Rio Tinto traffic. In March 1900 Messrs Knott and Hosgood were instructed by the directors to draft a scheme for this traffic.

A postcard view of the Express Tinplate Works, formerly part of Cwmavon Works, Postcard, postally used in 1910. The R&SBR runs across the bottom of the view past Copper Miners Junction signal box at the start of the bidirectional loop through Cwmavon. The abortive Ynysdavid Railway of 1898–99 was intended to connect these works to the SWMJnR at Ynysdavid Sidings. *Author's collection*

Knott wrote to Mr Knox on 29th January 1900 with the following observations:

1. a considerable saving would be made by working the traffic via the Oakwood Railway as almost two miles and several back-shunts would be avoided,

2. all trains proceeding to Cwmavon and back would be required to be in possession of a staff which could be obtained from the signal box at Tonygroes Junction by the guard simply jumping off the engine and slipping across to the box for it,

3. the company would sell one of their saddle tank engines to Miss Talbot,

4. Miss Talbot would be allowed running powers over the dock railways and as far as Duffryn Yard. The company would be prepared to hire Miss Talbot's engine when it is not required for her own traffic,

5. the company would provide the shed and necessary accommodation as well as the maintenance of the engine.

Knott added that if this scheme was acceptable to Miss Talbot, he would arrange transfer of the engine, have its plates removed, and repaint it if so desired.[67]

It is not clear if this arrangement was put into effect, but it would have provided a use, albeit short-term, for the Oakwood Railway – although the GWR would not have been happy with a mineral train, seemingly without a guards van, using the Oakwood Crossing. Engine No. 1 would have been the obvious candidate for transfer, and if the transfer did occur it might account for the locomotive's disappearance between 1901 and 1902.[68] In November 1900 Cheston reminded Knott that the agreement required Rio Tinto to import at Port Talbot at least two-thirds of the crude copper they required for their works and, provided the company received £2,200 per annum from Rio Tinto, there was no obligation for them to import all their ore at Port Talbot. Rio Tinto closed their works at Cwmavon and moved to a new site in Port Talbot Docks in 1906.[69]

CONNECTION TO THE R&SBR AT CWMAVON

In December 1905 Cleaver produced a plan of the company's railways in the Port Talbot area, to which was added the long-delayed Railway No. 4 and a proposed connection with the R&SBR below Cwmavon at about milepost 1¼ on the SWMJnR. These connections were considered by the directors in January 1906, and together were intended to provide a direct route to Port Talbot Docks for traffic from the newly revitalised Duffryn Rhondda Colliery situated on the R&SBR about one mile below Cymmer in the Avon Valley.[70] The proposed connection with the R&SBR, which would have required a new bridge over the River Avon, had been considered by the Rhondda officers in September 1905, apparently without any issues arising.[71] Had it been built it would have removed a fair amount of mineral traffic from the flat crossing of the R&SBR over the GWR at Aberavon. The need for Railway No. 4 finally disappeared in July 1906 when the directors approved Lowther's scheme for Duffryn Sidings in its stead, and with it went the rationale for the connection. Nevertheless, it was raised periodically at joint meetings of the respective company's officers without being revived. The Rhondda directors were content to allow the matter to stand over.[72]

WHITWORTH BRANCH

The Whitworth Branch saw little traffic in its early days under PTR&D ownership, and in February 1899 the directors ordered that only what was absolutely necessary should be done by way of maintenance. Despite this and the fact that Topham, Jones & Railton had relaid the branch, it became necessary later that year to re-sleeper the line throughout.[73]

WHITWORTH RAILWAY EXTENSION

Even while the SWMJnR was under construction a scheme for extending the Whitworth Railway was proposed. Thomas Smith, one of the petitioners in favour of the SWMJnR Bill, had stated in his evidence to the Select Committee of the House of Lords that production at his Neath Merthyr Colliery on the Whitworth Estate, normally 200 to 300 tons per day, had been stopped owing to the high rates incurred in taking the coal by a one mile-long locomotive-worked tramway to the VoNR, and that he was willing to construct a tramway to connect with the Whitworth Railway.[74]

By January 1898 Smith had changed his position somewhat and had asked the PTR&D to provide this connection, but the directors resolved on 26th January that they could not agree to such an extension of the Whitworth Railway without a guarantee of traffic. This was set in April 1898 at 150 tons per day with a penalty of 4 per cent interest on £4,000 if this amount was not reached. Meik reported in March 1898 that the estimated cost of this two and a quarter mile line, which would have involved a gradient of 1 in 25, was £4,000.[75] A shorter one mile extension up to Twynpumerw would have cost £3,000, with a tramway thence to the colliery.[76] An alternative four mile route to the colliery via the Blaenavon Valley had the advantage of a lesser gradient of 1 in 30 but was estimated to cost £8,000.

The directors modified their terms in May 1898 and offered to build the one mile extension to Twynpumerw provided the colliery company guaranteed 2,400 tons of coal per month for ten years and deposited a security of £1,500. Within one month the proposed extension was deemed to be impracticable and it was suggested that the colliery company should make a narrow gauge railway, the PTR&D being prepared to contribute £1,500 towards its construction. Although the company could not comply with Smith's suggestion that it should provide a narrow gauge locomotive, the directors resolved on 27th July 1898 that construction of the extension should be commenced forthwith. One month later, however, they learned that Smith owned only the surface and not the minerals beneath it, which belonged to the South Wales Whitworth Mineral Estates Ltd, and on 16th September deferred construction of the extension until a better security was produced.

This scheme had a brief resurgence during 1900–1901. In December 1899 the company declined W C Shout's request to subscribe £2,000 towards the light railway, and reiterated its previous offer of £1,500. In the meantime Smith had disappeared from the scene and by August 1900 had been replaced by a Mr Abbott who was offered the same terms, provided his security was approved of. Lowther, the recently appointed traffic manager, reported in October 1900 that Abbott proposed to build the extension, with curves limited to 5 chains radius and a maximum gradient of 1 in 22, and keep it in repair so long as it was used only by his colliery company.[77] The PTR&D was to provide all permanent way materials, pay nominal rental of £1 per week, and work up to the colliery levels. As this would have cost the company £3,000, Lowther recommended that until there was some likelihood of further developments other than Neath Merthyr Colliery, it was not advisable to extend the offer on the Whitworth Railway, with which the directors agreed.

Neath Merthyr Colliery Co. was registered as a limited liability company on 13th February 1901.[78] Nine days later this company signed an agreement to buy the sidings, screen and weighing machine of the old Whitworth Colliery near Blaen Pelenna Farm at the top of the Whitworth Branch, and also to acquire the right of way over Houghton's 1832 tramroad leading there.[79] Lowther reported in March 1901 that the colliery was about to restart and its owners had asked if the company was still prepared to advance £1,500 towards a light railway, subject to certain guarantees.[80] By now the company's attitude had hardened and the directors responded that no such expenditure would be considered until the proposed deep sinkings were completed. Similar applications were received in September 1902, April 1905 and January 1907, to no avail.

BLAENAVON BRANCH

From the outset the PTR&D had trouble with the SWMR working the traffic of the lessees of the Whitworth Estate over its newly acquired Blaenavon Branch. Leases granted in 1873 and subsequently allowed the use of the branch by the colliery owners upon payment of a proportion of the maintenance costs. The owners were permitted to employ SWMR engines, but this did not confer any rights on the SWMR to use the branch.[81] The directors instructed the general manager in August 1897 to attempt to arrange rates with the lessees so that only the PTR&D's engines worked over the branch. Seemingly nothing was achieved, and the matter was allowed to rest for almost three years, possibly because there was little traffic to be worked. In May 1900 Williams, the traffic manager pro tem, reported to his directors that the SWMR was working considerable traffic over the branch, but attempts to collect the maintenance charges from the lessees of Llantwit Merthyr, New Forest and Marine Collieries had been rebuffed. The SWMR was willing to pay a proportion of the maintenance of the branch, but only if it was granted a right of use.

Lowther, the newly appointed traffic manager, reported in June 1900 on interviews with the proprietors of three of the six lessees concerned, Avon Merthyr Colliery, as Marine Colliery had become, Llantwit Merthyr Colliery and Gwenffrwd Quarry.[82] These proprietors were generally sympathetic, particularly since Messrs Perch & Co., managers of Glyncorrwg Colliery,[83] were in competition with them and potentially had access to commercially sensitive information. Based on this the directors resolved that arrangements should be made to carry the bulk of the traffic over the PTR to Port Talbot. To this end two proposals were submitted to the SWMR:

1 that it should give up working the incline and hand over all traffic from the Blaenavon Branch and Glyncorrwg Colliery to the PTR&D at Tonmawr, and allowed 30 per cent of the working expenses of Blaenavon Branch and a mileage

proportion of the through rate of the distance hauled over its own railway, or

2 that it should hand over to PTR&D all traffic from the Blaenavon Branch and Glyncorrwg Colliery for Port Talbot and places eastward and pay 2d per ton on all traffic on the Blaenavon Branch.

Neither proposal was acceptable and traffic continued to be taken to Briton Ferry by the SWMR. In January 1901 the secretary informed Cheston, the solicitor, that the Board had decided that matters had to be brought to a head and asked if it was legal for two rails to be taken out of the connecting loop so as to stop the traffic. The solicitor advised the company not to take so extreme a measure but in the first instance make a claim for the cost of the maintenance. Further negotiations with the lessees in February and March 1901 failed to produce a solution.[84] The lessees even suggested that if the railway was left to them they would keep it in repair themselves. The total of maintenance charges outstanding at the end of August 1901 was over £1,567. An example of the losses arising occurred in the week ending 21st September 1901 when 800 tons of coal were hauled off the Blaenavon Railway by SWMR engines and taken to Port Talbot Docks via Briton Ferry Incline and the R&SBR.[85] Consequently, Hosgood was instructed not to make repairs of any kind to the Blaenavon Branch, no matter what happened, until a settlement was reached. The SWMR reduced its through rate from the branch to Port Talbot from 7d to 6½d per ton in November 1901 in an attempt to keep the traffic.[86]

Col Wright met a deputation from the lessees on 14th December 1901 when it was agreed that

1 the lessees were to consider whether if the PTR&D agreed to forego its maintenance charges they would give the company 50 per cent of their traffic, and

2 the company was to arrange with the SWMR to work up to the pits any empty wagons that might reach Briton Ferry whether or not the wagons had travelled that way when loaded.[87]

Lowther reported in January 1902 that he had satisfactorily arranged the second point with the SWMR, the *quid pro quo* being that any extra wagons it worked up from Briton Ferry would be made up by the PTR&D working an equivalent number of Messrs Perch & Co.'s wagons from Port Talbot to Tonmawr for the SWMR to take on to Glyncorrwg Colliery. The colliery proprietors were reluctant to commit themselves to quantities, but the threat of legal proceedings, the shorter journey time, and the fact the rate direct to Port Talbot was no higher than via the SWMR route seem to have settled the matter shortly afterwards. Under the terms of an agreement dated 16th November 1902, the SWMR was permitted to run over the branch and undertook to haul traffic for Port Talbot and east thereof from the Blaenavon Railway to Tonmawr Sidings on payment of ½d per ton towards its maintenance.[88] Hosgood noted in February 1903 that the branch required attention in various places, nothing having been done to for over a year, and was informed that maintenance was now to be done.[89] An indication that amicable relations had been restored came in November 1902 when the directors approved an extension to the New Forest Colliery siding.

Blaengarw and the 1899 Act

Pontycymmer station had opened for passengers in June 1889; since then Blaengarw Chamber of Trade, and later Glamorgan County Council, had been attempting to persuade the GWR to provide a station and extend its passenger service to Blaengarw.[90] This issue had arisen during the House of Commons' Select Committee's consideration of the PTR&D's 1894 Bill, when the county council's clause was withdrawn.[91] The GWR eventually announced its intention to apply for the necessary powers in 1896,[92] and these were granted in its Additional Powers Act of 1897.[93] The county council's Parliamentary Committee noted this development at its meeting in September 1897 and agreed with the PTR&D's request that its undertaking dated 28th June 1894 to apply for such powers should be allowed to stand over for another year, on the understanding it would be carried out if the GWR did not proceed with the necessary works in the meantime.

Knott, the company's secretary, wrote to G K Mills, the GWR's secretary, in July 1898 pointing out that nothing had been done and that the PTR&D expected to be held to its undertaking by the county council. Joseph Wilkinson, general manager of the GWR, claimed that progress was delayed by difficulties with siding arraignments for Ffaldau Colliery. On 12th September T M Talbot, the Clerk of Glamorgan County Council, and coincidently Miss Talbot's cousin and financial advisor, formally called upon the PTR&D to fulfil its undertaking in the next session of Parliament. At their meeting on 16th September the directors declared that the undertaking stood, although Cheston, their solicitor, doubted the application to Parliament would be favourably considered as the GWR's powers had not yet expired. Nevertheless, the directors decided at their meeting on 19th October that such powers would be included in the company's Bill for the 1899 Session. The Parliamentary Notice also announced the intention to confirm the deviations made in the 1894 and 1896 railways and to establish a Pilotage Board at Port Talbot.[94] The publication of the Notice surprised the GWR directors and they asked for an explanation of what they regarded as an unprecedented and hostile step.

It became apparent that the GWR was seeking financial assistance towards the cost of the work and at their November 1898 meeting the PTR&D directors resolved to pay 3 per cent on the estimated outlay of £18,000 if the GWR gave a binding undertaking to provide a station at Blaengarw. This was soon realised to be somewhat inadequate and on 5th January 1899 Cheston informed Mr Watson, standing in for Col Wright, that he had offered the GWR £2,000 to carry out the work at once, and to relieve the company of its undertaking.

The GWR counter-offered that as there was no present need to double the line between Tondu and Cefn Junction, and if the PTR&D agreed to defer this work, it would accept £3,000 to double the line to Blaengarw as soon as possible. This course of action was considered to be cheaper than defending against opposition in both Houses of Parliament. On 9th January the directors agreed to this and to withdraw the offending clauses from the Bill, provided the GWR entered into an agreement releasing the company from its undertaking with the county council and withdrew its opposition to the Bill. After further negotiations it was agreed on 20th April

that the work would be completed within two years, and the GWR sealed the tripartite agreement on 11th May 1899.[95]

The PTR&D's declared intention of seeking Parliamentary sanction to extend passenger services to Blaengarw was one of the objections the GWR raised in its petition against the Bill.[96] The other concerned the use of the new exchange sidings with the GWR at Margam for Morfa Colliery traffic. In January 1899 they pointed out that the Bill did not contain a clause for their protection regarding access to Morfa Colliery, because the OVER as constructed severed the connection from the GWR.[97] This matter was easily dealt with, the PTR&D agreeing on 9th January not to seek any tolls on traffic passing between the GWR and Morfa Colliery at Margam Junction. Agreement having been reached on both points, the GWR withdrew its petition.

The use of the new Margam Sidings was also raised by Messrs Vivian.[98] The two earlier exchange sidings, which had been eliminated by the revised route of the OVER,[99] were private ones let to Messrs Vivian by the Margam Estate. Messrs Vivian had no control over the new exchange sidings at Margam, although by an agreement dated 5th February 1895 the PTR&D had undertaken to connect the Morfa Railway to its 1894 railways near Copper Works Junction. Messrs Vivian now sought the insertion into the Bill of a clause giving them possession and control of sidings 5 and 6 at Margam, the pair furthest from the GWR main line, with connections to the GWR. The PTR&D could not agree to control and possession, but did offer Messrs Vivian sole use and benefit of these sidings and this concession was sufficient for the petition to be withdrawn. As late as March 1911, Messrs Vivian were seeking ownership of these sidings and complaining that they were unable to use them because of their being monopolised by the PTR&D and GWR. However, Morfa Colliery closed that year[100] and the Morfa Railway then saw little traffic until the Taibach end was incorporated into the internal railways of Baldwins' Margam Steelworks[101] to give access to the slag tips on Margam Burrows. The remainder of the railway reverted to the Margam Estate, the Trustees of which in September 1919 proposed that the PTR&D should take over and maintain the line. The company had no powers to do this and the matter remained in abeyance.

The R&SBR petitioned against the Bill on the grounds that a clause relating to colliery sidings was prejudicial to its interests and that, although the PTR&D was making use of the running powers to Aberavon and the north side of the dock granted by the 1894 Act, the R&SBR had not yet been able to make use of the running powers to the south side of Port Talbot Docks which were granted in exchange.[102] That would only be possible by the construction of Railway No. 4 of the SWMJnR Act of 1896,[103] and although the time limit would not be reached until 1901, the R&SBR petitioned for this line to be made by then.[104] Knott noted that the R&SBR had sent practically nothing over the PTR and that ample powers had been granted to it for shipping traffic at tip No. 6 on North Bank. Nevertheless, the Port Talbot directors agreed on 15th March to build Railway No. 4 by 7th August 1902 if called upon to do so by 1st January 1902. This and a modified sidings clause satisfied the R&SBR and its petition was withdrawn.

Objections by Aberavon Corporation, Swansea Harbour Trust and the Neath Harbour Commissioners to the composition of the proposed Pilotage Board and the modified harbour limits were easily dealt with, thereby removing the remaining opposition to the Bill. In the meantime the House of Lords had appointed a Select Committee to examine the Bill but this was discharged and the Bill was passed by both Houses of Parliament unopposed,[105] receiving the Royal Assent on 1st August 1899.[106]

The Act confirmed the construction of the deviation railways,[107] and the arrangements made with Messrs Vivian & Co. and the GWR regarding Margam Sidings. The company was authorised to enter into agreements with colliery companies to construct, maintain and use colliery sidings in communication with any of its railways. The time for the completion of Railway No. 4 of the SWMJnR Act 1896 was extended as agreed with the R&SBR, and Railway No. 12 of the OVER Act 1896 was allowed to be abandoned, the Board of Trade having raised no objections.[108] A Pilotage Board was established, consisting of three directors on the PTR&D and up to eleven additional members appointed from local authorities, owners of vessels using the dock, the pilots, the R&SBR and the Board of Trade. Finally, the company was authorised to raise additional capital up to £300,000 in stocks and shares and to borrow an additional £100,000. The company lost no time in forming the Pilotage Board, Knott, the company's secretary, being appointed to the additional responsibility as secretary of the new body on 16th August.

At its meeting on 8th June 1899 the GWR Board approved the expenditure of £24,654 to adapt the Blaengarw line for passenger traffic, the PTR&D contributing £3,000.[109] Preliminary work on doubling the line from Pontycymmer to Blaengarw and providing a new passenger station started in October 1899, and the PTR&D handed over the £3,000 it had agreed to contribute towards the cost.[110] The tender from Messrs Mackay & Davies of Cardiff of £13,168 8s 2d for completion of the work within one year was accepted in March 1900.[111] Despite what may have been agreed, progress was slow and it was not until October 1901 that the GWR informed the Board of Trade that the work was nearing completion.[112] Bad weather and a shortage of labour then intervened and the GWR did not apply for provisional sanction to open the line for passenger traffic on 5th May 1902 until 25th April that year. This was at first declined as Board of Trade regulations required double lines to be provided with two platforms, and only one had been constructed. Once the reasons for the layout, which gave an unimpeded route to the collieries at the head of the valley, had been explained, provisional sanction was granted subject to special instructions for passenger trains at Blaengarw. These stated that there was to be no delay in running round to get the engine to the lower end, no passenger train was to approach while the platform was occupied, and any train stabled overnight was to be placed on the loop so as to have the protection of the catch point. The station was opened on 26th May 1902,[113] although a short stretch of double line remained to be made. Col Yorke inspected the work on 28th August when all was found to be satisfactory. Glamorgan County Council's reaction to the delay in completing the works is not recorded; it was probably grateful that its objective had at last been met.

THE NEATH, PONTARDAWE & BRYNAMAN RAILWAY

As well as improving their railways and providing siding connections for new coal mines and other businesses, the directors also looked further afield for additional sources of traffic. Of particular interest was the untapped anthracite coalfield north of Neath. The Neath, Pontardawe & Brynaman Railway (NP&BR) Co. had obtained its Act of Incorporation in 1895[114] with the intention of opening up this area, and reciprocal running powers were granted to the GWR and Midland Railway companies with which it made connections at either end. A second Act of 1896[115] empowered the NP&BR to enter into working agreements with the GWR, whilst a third of 1898[116] authorised the construction of two branch lines at Pontardawe and granted an extension of time to complete the 1895 railways. This was a period of short money supply, however, and nothing could be done at the time to progress the NP&BR.

The promoters did not give up, and in December 1901 the directors of the PTR&D resolved to support the next NP&BR Bill to the extent of £500, subject to agreement to give the PTR&D running powers over the NP&BR and R&SBR lines to permit access to the new traffic. The R&SBR and PTD&R at this stage appeared to be in agreement regarding the new railway; at meetings held in February and March 1902 between the three companies, Col Wright undertook to provide any assistance his company could, although it was by now being asked to guarantee the deposit money.[117] Col Wright became a director of the NP&BR around this time,[118] and an agreement with the promoters for the protection of the PTR&D's interests in the next bill was signed in January 1902.

In the event the Bill was delayed until the 1903 Session of Parliament. In the Parliamentary Notice[119] the NP&BR *inter alia* sought powers to revive and extend its authorised railways, and to construct new railways in the form of connections to the R&SBR at Neath. It also sought running powers over parts of the R&SBR, the whole of the PTR&D including the dock railways, and the GWR between Neath and Port Talbot. By now the GWR's support of the NP&BR had waned and it put forward its own line in the area as part of its 1903 Additional Powers Bill.[120]

In March 1903 the PTR&D directors decided to petition against both of these Bills.[121] They also discovered that its proffered support of the NP&BR was unlikely to be beneficial, and Col Wright resigned his directorship because his views as a director were being ignored.[122] Having recently concluded an agreement with the GWR concerning traffic over the OVER at the eastern end of their system the directors now made one for the western end.[123] This agreement dated 4th May 1903 provided that:

- The PTR&D's proportion of the rate for coal from collieries on the VoNR and the N&BR was increased to 1½d per ton.
- The PTR&D was to withdraw its petition against the GWR's Garnant, Neath & Swansea Junction Railway, not to assist the NP&BR's Bill, and to oppose the running powers sought over the PTR.
- Should the GWR's proposed line be opened for traffic the rate for coal carried over it for Port Talbot was to be ½d per ton in excess over the rate for Swansea, and this would be the PTR&D's proportion.
- Should the GWR's railway not be passed and should the NP&BR's line be authorised the GWR agreed to carry all traffic from the NP&BR junction with the GWR to Margam Junction with the PTR at the same rate as to Swansea.

A postcard view of Blaengarw station taken not long after it was opened on 26th May 1902. Ocean Colliery is visible in the distance on the right; International Colliery is off to the left. Like the other stations in the Garw Valley, Blaengarw closed on 9th February 1953. *Author's collection*

The PTR&D's principal objection to the NP&BR Bill concerned the granting of compulsory running powers over the dock lines from Margam Junction and Burrows Junction. The company's position was stated forcefully to the House of Commons Select Committee by Lowther.[124] He pointed out that no company had compulsory running powers over the dock railways, such powers being granted only by agreement, and that neither the GWR nor the R&SBR had sought to run over the dock railways with traffic from the west. He also noted that this subject had not been raised when his company had supported the promoters of the NP&BR in 1902. The Committee decided that compulsory running powers would not be granted, but apart from that found the preamble to the Bill proved; the NP&BR won this particular Parliamentary struggle with the GWR, its 1903 Act gaining the Royal Assent on 11th August.[125] All reference to the PTR&D was dropped, as were running powers over the R&SBR, and running over the GWR main line was restricted to a short stretch to Neath station. The GWR returned to Parliament in 1904 to promote what became the Swansea District Railways.[126] The provisions agreed with the PTR&D in 1903 were applied to the 1904 Bill. An agreement was signed in January 1905 supplemental to that made in 1903, whereby the rates agreed for the Garnant, Neath & Swansea Junction line were deemed to be applicable to the Swansea District Railways.[127] The *coup de grâce* for the NP&BR came in 1911 when the GWR obtained powers to construct the Clydach, Pontardawe & Cwmgorse line,[128] although this was only ever partly completed. Despite modifying the authorised railways in its 1904 Act,[129] obtaining an extension of time to complete these railways in its 1907 Act,[130] and further encouragement from the Barry Railway, the powers expired in August 1912 and the NP&BR faded into history.

The proposed NP&BR had been considered to be a promising source of traffic for Barry Docks since 1897, and two of the ByR directors became directors of the NP&BR.[131] By 1906 any thoughts of a stronger link between the ByR and the NP&BR were shaken by the conclusion of an agreement, dated 2nd July 1906 but backdated to 1st January, whereby the GWR undertook to work the R&SBR.[132] Related agreements covered the hire of the R&SBR's rolling stock and the repair of its railways.[133] Fearing this step presaged full amalgamation, the general manager of the ByR, Edward Lake, reported on 20th July 1906 that he had been in communication with Lowther, and that it was desirable that the PTR&D and ByR directors should if possible confer on this subject.[134] This meeting seemingly did not take place, and discussions continued at the managerial level. In October 1906 Lake was instructed to endeavour

to obtain the PTR&D's opposition should such an application for amalgamation be made to Parliament. There is no mention of such discussions in the PTR&D directors' minutes[135] or the general manager's reports to the Board.[136]

1907 Act

Whatever may have been agreed between the PTR&D and the ByR, the directors resolved at their meeting on 2nd November 1906 to seek in the next Parliamentary Session *inter alia* powers to construct a short railway joining the dock railways to the R&SBR and compulsory running powers over the whole of that company's lines. A Parliamentary Notice to this effect was published later that month.[137] Cleaver, the PTR&D's engineer, estimated the cost of the proposed railway, which commenced near Burrows Junction, crossed the River Avon and joined the R&SBR near Aberavon Gas Works, a distance of just over a quarter of a mile, to be £8,687.[138] If built it would have provided a direct line into the docks from the R&SBR and further west, and avoided the circuitous route via Aberavon, Tonygroes and Duffryn junctions. Inglis, the general manager of the GWR, wrote to the PTR&D on 19th December 1906, stating that there was no need for the proposed running powers over the R&SBR, possibly alluding to the ongoing but unpublicised negotiations for his company to work the PTR on the same basis as it was then working the R&SBR.

Nevertheless, the deposited Bill contained all the powers sought in the Notice, and consequently attracted petitions against some of the thirty sections it contained from the GWR, the R&SBR and the Swansea Harbour Trust. The negotiations with the GWR proceeded slowly but satisfactorily, and in April 1907 Mr Broad, the company's solicitor following the death of Charles Cheston in May 1906, was instructed to withdraw from the Bill all provisions regarding running powers over the R&SBR and the construction of the related railway. This was done at the Committee stage in the House of Commons, and reduced the Bill to a Finance Bill. The Committee amended the preamble to make it consistent with the remaining provisions in the Bill, and amended the title to "An Act to enable the PTR&D Co. to raise additional capital." The Bill completed its passage through both Houses of Parliament without further amendment[139] and received the Royal Assent on 4th July 1907.[140] The Act authorised the company to raise additional capital as stocks or shares not exceeding £120,000 and to borrow in respect of this capital not more than £40,000 on mortgage.

Notes

1. See Chapter 8.
2. TNA: PRO MT 6/978/7.
3. TNA: PRO RAIL 1057/1528/39.
4. TNA: PRO RAIL 1057/1529/34.
5. TNA: PRO MT 6/978/7.
6. TNA: PRO RAIL 1057/1528/33.
7. TNA: PRO MT 6/997/8.
8. TNA: PRO RAIL 1057/1529/39.
9. TNA: PRO RAIL 1057/1528/33.
10. TNA: PRO MT 6/1036/3.
11. TNA: PRO RAIL 1057/1529/34.
12. TNA: PRO RAIL 1057/1528/58.
13. TNA: PRO RAIL 1057/1528/97.
14. TNA: PRO RAIL 1057/1528/99.
15. TNA: PRO MT 6/2074/13.
16. TNA: PRO RAIL 1057/1528/105, 111.
17. TNA: PRO RAIL 1057/1528/102, 106.
18. TNA: PRO RAIL 1057/1528/112.
19. TNA: PRO MT 6/2074/11.
20. See Chapter 5.
21. TNA: PRO RAIL 1057/1528/118.
22. See Chapter 4.

23. William Cleaver, 'The Relining of a Portion of Cwm Cerwyn Tunnel on the Port Talbot Railway', *Proc. Inst. Civil Engineers*, 177 (1908–9), pp. 199–208.
24. TNA: PRO RAIL 1057/1529/32.
25. TNA: PRO RAIL 1057/1529/58.
26. TNA: PRO RAIL 1057/1528/109.
27. TNA: PRO RAIL MT 6/1628/1.
28. TNA: PRO RAIL 1057/1528/115.
29. TNA: PRO RAIL 1057/1528/123.
30. TNA: PRO RAIL 1057/1528/124.
31. TNA: PRO RAIL 1057/1528/84, 85, 103, 116.
32. TNA: PRO RAIL 1057/1528/86, 103.
33. TNA: PRO RAIL 1057/1528/102, 103.
34. TNA: PRO RAIL 1057/1528/105.
35. See Chapter 4.
36. TNA: PRO RAIL 1057/1528/86.
37. TNA: PRO MT 6/1388/1.
38. TNA: PRO RAIL 574/32.
39. TNA: PRO RAIL 1057/1529/38, 39.
40. TNA: PRO RAIL 1057/1528/85.
41. TNA: PRO RAIL 1057/1528/96.
42. TNA: PRO RAIL 1057/1529/34.
43. TNA: PRO RAIL 1057/1528/91.
44. TNA: PRO RAIL 574/99.
45. TNA: PRO RAIL 250/46.
46. TNA: PRO RAIL 574/19.
47. TNA: PRO MT 6/1388/2.
48. TNA: PRO RAIL 1057/1528/79.
49. TNA: PRO RAIL 574/19.
50. MT 6/1383/4.
51. TNA: PRO MT 6/1247/9.
52. TNA: PRO RAIL 1057/1528/104.
53. TNA: PRO RAIL 1057/1529/56.
54. TNA: PRO RAIL 1057/1528/56.
55. TNA: PRO RAIL 1057/1058/227.
56. See Chapter 1.
57. TNA: PRO BT 31/7430/52789.
58. TNA: PRO RAIL 1057/2558.
59. TNA: PRO RAIL 1057/1528/40.
60. TNA: PRO RAIL 1057/2558.
61. Charles E Harvey, *The Rio Tinto Company: An Economic History of a Leading International Mining Concern 1873–1954* (Alison Hodge 1981); see also Chapter 5.
62. See Chapter 2.
63. TNA: PRO RAIL 1057/2527.
64. TNA: PRO RAIL 581/12.
65. Ronald Rees, *King Copper: South Wales and the Copper Trade 1584–1895* (University of Wales Press 2000), pp. 133–6.
66. TNA: PRO RAIL 1057/2655.
67. TNA: PRO RAIL 1057/2527.
68. See Chapter 9.
69. See Volume 2, Chapter 14.
70. Roger L Brown and Paul Reynolds, 'Coal Mining in the Upper Afan, Part 6: The Collieries below Cymmer, Section B', *Afan Uchaf*, 10 (1987), pp. 34–46.
71. TNA: PRO RAIL 581/15.
72. TNA: PRO RAIL 581/5.
73. TNA: PRO RAIL 1057/1529/32, 36.
74. TNA: PRO RAIL 1066/2506.
75. TNA: PRO RAIL 1057/2648.
76. TNA: PRO RAIL 1057/1528/15.
77. TNA: PRO RAIL 1057/1528/60.
78. TNA: PRO BT 31/9337/69374.
79. See Chapter 1.
80. TNA: PRO RAIL 1057/1528/62.
81. TNA: PRO RAIL 1057/2648.
82. TNA: PRO RAIL 1057/1528/57.
83. See Chapter 7.
84. TNA: PRO RAIL 1057/1528/64.
85. TNA: PRO RAIL 1057/2648.
86. TNA: PRO RAIL 639/2.
87. TNA: PRO RAIL 1057/2510.
88. TNA: PRO RAIL 574/3 minute 4236.
89. TNA: PRO RAIL 1057/2648.
90. TNA: PRO RAIL 1057/2655.
91. See Chapter 3.
92. *The London Gazette*, 24 November 1896.
93. 60 & 61 Vict. c.ccxlviii.
94. *The London Gazette*, 25 November 1898.
95. TNA: PRO RAIL 250/44.
96. TNA: PRO RAIL 1057/2549.
97. TNA: PRO RAIL 1057/2655.
98. TNA: PRO RAIL 1057/2537.
99. See Chapter 5.
100. Toomey, *Vivian*, p. 132.
101. See Volume 2, Chapter 14.
102. See Chapter 3.
103. See Chapter 5.
104. TNA: PRO RAIL 581/11, RAIL 1057/2549.
105. *House of Lords Journal*, 1899; *House of Commons Journal*, 1899.
106. 62 & 63 Vict. c.cxcix.
107. See Chapters 4 and 5.
108. TNA: PRO MT 6/869/3.
109. TNA: PRO RAIL 250/44.
110. TNA: PRO RAIL 1057/2655.
111. TNA: PRO RAIL 252/1243.
112. TNA: PRO MT 6/1105/11.
113. TNA: PRO RAIL 1005/280.
114. 58 & 59 Vict. c.cxlv.
115. 59 & 60 Vict. c.ccxliv.
116. 61 & 62 Vict. c.clxix.
117. TNA: PRO RAIL 581/5.
118. TNA: PRO RAIL 1066/2252.
119. *The London Gazette*, 25 November 1902.
120. *The London Gazette*, 21 November 1902.
121. TNA: PRO RAIL 1066/1267, RAIL 1057/2252.
122. TNA: PRO RAIL 1066/2252.
123. TNA: PRO RAIL 574/18.
124. TNA: PRO RAIL 1066/2252.
125. 3 Edw. 7 c.cxcviii.
126. 4 Edw. 7 c.cxcvii.
127. TNA: PRO RAIL 574/18.
128. 1 & 2 Geo. 5 c.lxxxv.
129. 4 Edw. 7 c.ccxxx.
130. 4 Edw. 7 c.cxxxix.
131. Chapman, *Vale of Glamorgan Railway*, pp. 48–50.
132. TNA: PRO RAIL 581/48.
133. TNA: PRO RAIL 581/49, 50.
134. TNA: PRO RAIL 23/11.
135. TNA: PRO RAIL 574/3.
136. TNA: PRO RAIL 1057/1528.
137. *The London Gazette*, 23 November 1906.
138. PA HL/PO/PB/3/plan1907/P9.
139. *House of Commons Journal*, 1907; *House of Lords Journal*, 1907.
140. 7 Edw. 7 c.xxix.

Until Port Talbot new docks opened, Brunel's Briton Ferry Dock was the nearest shipping port for coal from Glyncorrwg. Traffic was worked by the SWMR from the bottom of the incline via its 1861 Dock Branch to the Briton Ferry Floating Dock Co.'s railways and thence to the tips. The dock was opened in 1861 and taken over by the GWR 1873. This tidal dock was entered via the single massive lock gate seen here. Postcard, postally used 2nd September 1906, by which date only three tips were in use.

Author's collection

7

The South Wales Mineral Railway Company, 1853 to 1907

A T THE HALF-YEARLY MEETING of the proprietors of the PTR&D held on 20th February 1907, Col Wright announced that "the directors consider it expedient to adopt a policy which they may find useful to facilitate any possible arrangement in developing the traffics of the SWMR Co., and for exchanging the same, with a view to your railway and docks benefiting".[1] The shareholders then approved the SWMR's 1907 Bill empowering that company "to construct a deviation railway, to abandon part of their existing railway, to raise further money, to enter into working agreements with the GW, the R&SB, the TV and the PTR&D Cos., to enable those companies to subscribe for shares or stock, and for other purposes." The SWMR had been leased to or worked by the Glyncorrwg Coal Company and its successors for fifty-two years and the company had been in receivership for the last thirty years, conditions which suggested that some form of outside involvement would be desirable.

Col Wright's statement was the only public announcement that such a move was under consideration. Messrs Cleaver, Hertz and Dipper of the PTR&D accompanied by Henry Heath, the secretary of the SWMR, had inspected the railway on 14th November 1906, following which Cleaver produced a generally favourable report as to the condition of the permanent way and works. One year later, at a meeting of the directors of the PTR&D held on 20th November 1907, the drafts of the following were submitted:

1   a proposed working agreement between the PTR&D and the SWMR for the maintenance, working and use of the SWMR,
2   a proposed agreement between the Glyncorrwg Colliery Co. and the PTR&D as to rates and other matters, and
3   a proposed agreement between the GWR and the PTR&D as to indemnity.

These drafts were approved and arrangements were made to seal the documents as soon as they were ready (13th December 1907). Col Wright, Mr Byass and Mr Watson were appointed as the company's three nominees on the Board of the SWMR, Col Wright being named chairman. Correspondingly, Sir Henry Mather Jackson Bart., the chairman of the SWMR, reported to a meeting of his Board held on 29th November 1907 that the PTR&D had approached the company with a view to a working agreement being come to, and that negotiations had taken place. Following consideration of the drafts Sir Henry was authorised to conclude negotiations for an agreement.

The preceding fifty-four years had been a period of mostly unmet expectations. The promoters of the SWMR issued a prospectus dated 15th July 1853 in anticipation of obtaining their Act of incorporation, stating that responsible contractors had offered to construct the railway for £80,000 ready for opening on 1st May 1855, taking one-third of the price in shares.[2] Capital amounting to £40,000 had been subscribed by the promoters, and applications for the remaining £13,000 were invited. The Act, which was gained on 15th August 1853,[3] authorised the construction of a broad gauge railway from a junction with the SWR at Briton Ferry to Glyncorrwg and a branch from Tonmawr to Fforchdwm, all to be completed within five years. The major works were the three-quarters of a mile-long Ynysmaerdy Incline, a crossing of the River Gwenffrwd at a height of 72 feet above the river bed, and the 1,100 yard long Gyfylchi Tunnel connecting the Pelenna and Avon valleys. The capital was set at £85,000 in £10 shares, with a borrowing limit of £28,000. The company was further empowered to enter into working agreements with the SWR, the VoNR and Briton Ferry Floating Dock Co. (BFFD Co.) for their use of the authorised railways and the exchange of traffic.

At their first meeting held on 25th August 1853 the directors instructed Brunel to lay out the line, a task not completed until February 1854 for the main line, and March 1854 for the Fforchdwm Branch.[4] Viscount Villiers was appointed chairman and Robert Parsons confirmed as secretary at the next meeting held on 16th September. At the first general meeting held the same day, the shareholders were informed that most of the land required for the railway was to be given free of charge, and that Briton Ferry Dock, when completed, would be the nearest and most important outlet for its traffic.[5] Most important was the prospective opening of virgin coalfields at Glyncorrwg. Ten highly responsible gentlemen, lessees of one portion of the Glyncorrwg coal, together with some interested landowners, had offered to work the railway for thirty years, paying a dividend rising to 6 per cent, although this was deemed to be inadequate.[6]

It was soon to become clear that the early promises were unattainable. Gyfylchi Tunnel was the major engineering work on the line and tenders for its construction were not sought until March 1854. The general meeting held on 16th September 1854 was informed that the contract had been conditionally let to Messrs Dickson, McKenzie & Co. of Wellington, their price being £25,500, not too far short of Brunel's estimate of £27,500. The meeting also heard that the directors had failed to induce owners of property along the line to take the remaining shares. A proposal had been received from the Glyncorrwg Coal Co. to take up the unallotted capital provided it was granted a lease at a rental which would ensure a dividend of 5 per cent. Parliamentary sanction would be required, but completion of this arrangement required the colliery company to lease certain lands at the head of the valley. The meeting authorised the directors to effect this arrangement.

A brief Parliamentary Notice duly appeared,[7] the solicitors being Baxter, Rose & Norton of Westminster, names that were to feature prominently in the affairs of the SWMR and the Glyncorrwg Coal

Glyncorrwg circa 1905 showing the rather undeveloped station and the Glyncorrwg Colliery Co.'s offices behind the engine shed left of centre. Note the R&SBR van in the goods siding. *Courtesy Peter Sims*

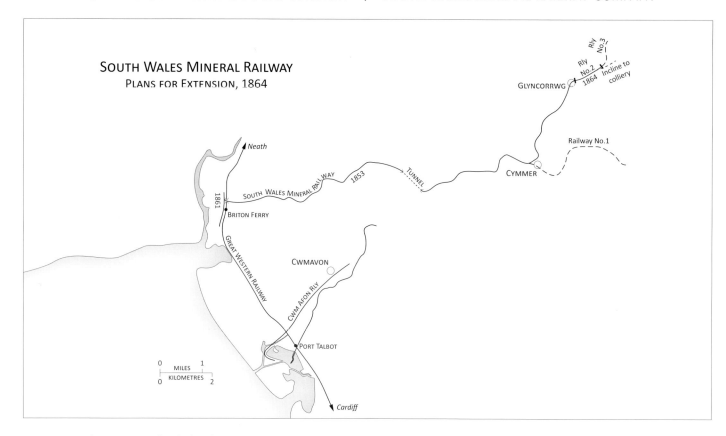

SOUTH WALES MINERAL RAILWAY
PLANS FOR EXTENSION, 1864

companies. The correspondingly brief Act gained the Royal Assent on 25th May 1855.[8] The principal clause of the Act authorised the company to lease its undertaking for up to ninety-nine years to ten gentlemen – William Henry Dawes, Thomas Jefferys Badger, Thomas Walker, Acton S Ayrton, John Forster, Robert Baxter, Dugdale Houghton, Philip Rose, George Knox and Henry Elland Norton – trading under the name of the Glyncorrwg Coal Co.

In the interim, the directors minuted the receipt of "further" loans of £4,000 from the Glyncorrwg Coal Co. The general meeting held on 20th April 1855 was informed that the lessees were prepared to guarantee 5½ per cent on the paid up capital. Having gained the Act, pending works were suspended until all the necessary land had been acquired. The Act's preamble mentioned that the Glyncorrwg Coal Co. had secured ninety-nine-year mineral leases, although one of these was not finalised until early in 1856.[9] The Glyncorrwg Coal Co. was re-formed on 3rd January 1856 as a co-partnership consisting of seven of the above gentlemen – Messrs Dawes, Badger, Walker, Ayrton, Baxter, Rose and Norton, plus Thomas Walker junior and Scarlett Lloyd Parry.[10] The lease of the SWMR by the Glyncorrwg Coal Co. was finalised the following day.

With financial backing secure, the SWMR could now return to making the railway. It was intended to let the whole line at once, but Messrs Dickson & Co.'s offer of £75,000 for the main line and £2,500 for the Fforchdwm Branch was considered excessive. The directors decided on 17th January 1856 to hold Dickson's to their original contract for the tunnel, to which they agreed to add about one and a quarter miles of railway at its western end so as to meet the Neath Road above Efail Fach in the Avon Valley, a convenient point at which to bring in materials. In the absence of Viscount Villiers the first sod was cut at Tonmawr by Mrs Parsons, the wife of the SWMR's secretary, on 25th March.[11] In July 1856 Dickson's

requested that the contract be transferred to a Mr Shield, and this was granted, but as no reply was received, Brunel was instructed to stop the contract and prepare another specification for letting the whole line. In November 1856 Shield requested payment of £2,700 for the work done, which amounted to driving a heading for the tunnel and other preparatory work, and providing materials for the completion of the contract. The directors resolved that all movable plant except centres of bridges should be given up to Dickson's. Brunel's estimate for making the whole line excluding the permanent way came to £75,000, and a Mr Tredwell's tender of £79,500 was accepted, provided he took one-quarter as shares. Tredwell declined these terms, not surprisingly as there was little prospect of any return on the shares. Likewise he seemingly declined to take one-eighth (£10,000) as shares. The directors decided in January 1857 that the engineer should proceed with the works as he saw fit until a contractor could be found. Thomas Brassey (1805–70), or one of his associates, inspected the route of the line in May 1857 but did not take on the work.[12] However, Messrs Dickson were back in contention in July 1857 when the Glyncorrwg Coal Co. authorised the SWMR through its solicitors to settle the contract in conjunction with the engineers. This proved to be a very short-lived arrangement, the general meeting held on 29th September being informed that Messrs Dickson had failed. A new contract was made with Messrs Morris & Toole who tendered £74,000 for completion of the railway ready for the permanent way. These contractors were reported to making good progress in November 1857 and the line was expected to open to Briton Ferry early next summer,[13] another extremely optimistic prediction.

Hitherto work had been concentrated on Gyfylchi Tunnel. At the general meeting held on 30th March 1858 the shareholders were informed that the tunnel had been driven a considerable distance

Glyncorrwg 1906. A variety of rolling stock is visible: a 5-compartment 4-wheeled carriage, two PTR&D wagons, one lettered PTRD, the other PT, several Glyncorrwg wagons, two of which are lettered on the top plank only, three Redgrave wagons, and one belonging to Mid Glamorganshire Coal & Coke Co., Maesteg.

Courtesy Peter Sims

at both ends and the line commenced by Messrs Dickson had been brought up to formation level. The contractors were given notice in March 1858 to proceed with the lower part of the railway between the tunnel and Briton Ferry. Construction proceeded steadily rather than spectacularly, not helped by the remoteness of some of the route. At the March 1859 general meeting Brunel reported that the earthworks of the first three miles from the junction with the SWR, which included Ynysmaerdy Incline, were progressing steadily and the remaining portion was being completed. About half the tunnel length was driven and some of the cuttings between the tunnel and Glyncorrwg were being opened out. The western section from the tunnel to Briton Ferry was expected, again optimistically, to be opened for traffic in the autumn.

The consortium leasing the railway was registered as the Glyncorrwg Coal Co. Ltd on 17th February 1859 with a capital of £100,000.[14] Its stated aims were to lease and work mines at or near Glyncorrwg, to hold shares in and advance money to the SWMR, to lease or work the SWMR, to use Briton Ferry Docks, and to take shares in or advance money to the BFFD Co. According to the prospectus issued in July 1859, the partners had so far spent £40,000 in building the railway and opening up their collieries, and proposed to stand credited with £50,000 in shares in compensation,

the balance being offered to the public.[15] Probably due to an oversight, the lease was not transferred to the limited company until January 1869.

Brunel died on 15th September 1859 following a stroke, and his chief assistant, Robert Pearson Brereton (1818–94), was asked on what terms he would undertake to complete the engineering of the line. Brereton's offer of £200 per annum for professional services was eventually accepted in August 1860. The earthworks for the western end of the railway were at last approaching completion and in November 1859 the tender of Messrs Morris & Toole for laying the permanent way for £163 per mile was accepted. Brereton was able to report significant progress to the August 1860 general meeting. The line from the junction with the SWR to the tunnel had been completed and ballasted. Permanent way had been laid for about three miles and the machinery for working the incline was being fixed in place. The tunnel was more than 80 per cent complete although it was not expected to be finished for another year. Furthermore, one and a half miles of the upper part of the line was nearly completed. Although Briton Ferry Dock was not yet completed, shipping places could be reached by means of a branch off the SWR to a wharf on the River Neath at Briton Ferry, opened circa March 1852.[16] With the opening of at least part of the line in

Glyncorrwg South Pit. In the foreground is one of the ex-GWR saddle tanks belonging to the Glyncorrwg Colliery Co. with a bespoke cab. The pit was still being sunk judging by the small winding wheel in the headgear. Most of the wagons appear to be new, purchased to serve this new colliery, but there are at least two older dumb-buffered wagons present, one lettered in an earlier Glyncorrwg style and one belonging to William Perch & Co. Note the fireman for the Lancashire-type boilers standing in the gap in the retaining wall. Postcard, postally used 20th April 1905. *Author's collection*

ABOVE: Another view of Glyncorrwg South Pits, again during sinking, with a larger winding wheel on the ground awaiting installation. Note the variety of ways in which the wagons were lettered and the rather primitive coal loading arrangements with no screens. *Courtesy Peter Sims*

BELOW: A later view of Glyncorrwg South Pit, with what looks like a new boiler house alongside the winding house. *Courtesy Peter Sims*

Glyncorrwg Colliery Co. No. 2 alongside Glyncorrwg engine shed circa 1890. The engine dates from 1873 and apart from the bespoke cab is seemingly in its original condition. Note the lining on the engine and the William Perch wagons with their distinctive marking.

Courtesy Peter Sims

sight, the directors urged potential traders in the district to be ready with their traffic.

The SWMR as far as the tunnel opened without fanfare during the summer of 1861. Brereton reported to the general meeting held on 30th September that the incline machinery and permanent way were complete on this part of the line which had been open for several months for coal traffic from collieries connected to it. Rather surprisingly, "the locomotive engine" was worked regularly over the incline, although whether this was with trains or because it was the only connection with the outside world was not stated. As for the remainder of the railway, the tunnel had been completed and the line up to the junction with the Glyncorrwg Coal Co.'s line was ready for the permanent way. Messrs Morris and Toole's total expenditure in getting the SWMR to this condition was £77,815. Brereton predicted that the whole of the works would be finished by the time the collieries at the upper part end of the line were ready to send their traffic. Coincidently, and fortuitously, Briton Ferry Dock, construction of which started in August 1853,[17] opened on 22nd August 1861, having been built at a cost of £140,000.[18]

In anticipation of this significant step, the SWMR promoted in the 1861 Session of Parliament a Bill which among other provisions was intended to authorise the construction of two railways to connect its 1853 railway to the new dock.[19] Railway No. 1 commenced at a junction with the authorised line near its junction with the SWR and ran parallel to the SWR as far as the southern end of Briton Ferry station, where it veered away to run along the east side of the

dock and terminated near the lock gate.[20] Railway No. 2 branched from Railway No. 1 and ran parallel to the west side of the dock and terminated on the bank of the River Neath near the northern entrance to the dock's outer basin. Brereton estimated the cost of these works to be £9,000. The Bill was amended by both Houses of Parliament, principally by the modification of Railway No. 1 to terminate at a junction with the railways constructed by the BFFD Co. near Briton Ferry goods shed and by the deletion of Railway No. 2. The resulting Act received the Royal Assent on 1st August 1861.[21] The Act stipulated that the new line was to be completed within three years, but surprisingly made no explicit provision for extending the time for the completion of the 1853 railway for which powers had expired in 1858. The Act also authorised the company to raise a further £30,000 of capital and to borrow on mortgage not more than £10,000.

Also in 1861, the prospect of a direct connection from the SWMR to Swansea was looming. Apart from a mixed gauge main line extending the VoNR to Swansea and a short connection to the Swansea Vale Railway, the Swansea & Neath Railway (S&NR) 1861 Bill proposed two end-on connections with the western terminus of the SWMR.[22] The first of these joined the VoNR near its goods shed at Neath, while the second crossed the River Neath to join the proposed main line on Crumlin Burrows.[23] The whole would have made a useful triangle of lines. The Neath Harbour Trustees opposed the branch over the River Neath[24] and an alternative route was introduced as an amendment to the Bill.[25] Despite the support of Mr Talbot before the House of Commons Committee, the branches to the SWMR were rejected by Parliament and the much amended Bill received the Royal Assent on 6th August 1861.[26] The Act named A P Barlow, a director of both the SWMR and the Glyncorrwg Coal Co., as one of the first directors of the S&NR. The SWMR and BFFD Co. were authorised to lay down mixed gauge track, of little immediate value as there were no narrow gauge tracks to connect to. Had the branches been included, the heads of an agreement between the various companies involved dated 28th March 1861 would have granted the SWMR powers to work to Swansea and use the staithes of the SWR, and to nominate two of the five directors of the S&NR.[27]

However, the SWMR had not yet reached its principal source of traffic. Brereton reported in January 1862 that a Messrs Flavell had estimated that the expenditure of a further £16,430 was necessary to complete the line. This included six and a quarter miles of permanent way and a platform, engine shed, and pointwork for a station at Glyncorrwg. Also included was a figure £1,865 for construction of the line to Briton Ferry Dock, much less than Brereton's estimate. The contract for the work was eventually let in August 1862 to Edwin Bray of Harrogate, the delay was presumably due to the need to raise funds. The March 1863 general meeting was informed that the railway was completed up to the incline leading to the collieries at Glyncorrwg, as was the extension to Briton Ferry Dock. The incline and line to the coal tip at the colliery remained to

be completed, although the line was reported to be open for traffic in April 1863.[28] The Glyncorrwg Coal Co. later stated the railway was not fully opened until October 1863.

The one mile of railway from Glyncorrwg to the foot of the incline to Glyncorrwg Colliery had been built without Parliamentary authority. The SWMR sought powers in 1864 to rectify this situation (Railway No. 2) and, at the request of the Glyncorrwg Coal Co., to extend the line further up the valley (Railway No. 3). The company also applied for powers to build a tramway to the head of the Avon Valley (Railway No. 1).[29] The planned route for this tramway commenced at a junction with the SWMR just below the confluence of the rivers Avon and Corrwg near Cymmer, crossed the former on an 86 foot high viaduct and continued up the Avon Valley to terminate near Blaenavon Farm, a distance of almost three miles, the final three-quarters of a mile being at a gradient of 1 in 28.[30] Railway No. 3 was planned as a half mile extension of the SWMR to Blaencorrwg, where mineral leases had recently been granted.[31] The engineer for these railways was Samuel Dobson, who estimated the total cost to be £7,000. The Bill passed through Parliament with minor amendments, the resulting Act gaining the Royal Assent on 29th July 1864.[32] In addition to being empowered to make these three railways, the company was authorised to raise a further £30,000 of capital and to increase its borrowing by a further £10,000.

An early view of Abercregan with the loading platform and level crossing clearly visible. The line to Corrwg Vale Colliery can just be made out along the bottom edge of the photograph.

Courtesy Peter Sims

In December 1863, shortly after the plans had been deposited, the SWMR entered into an agreement with Thomas Joseph that should the Act be obtained and the land acquired, the latter was to make the tramway at his own expense and rent the land for five years at 5 per cent of its cost, the company having the power to convert it to a railway at any time.[33] Various delays led the company to apply to the Board of Trade in July 1868 for an extension of time for the purchase of lands and the completion of the tramway and railways authorised by its 1864 Act.[34] The resulting warrant granted an extension until 29th July 1870 for the completion of the tramway to Blaenavon and the railway up to Blaencorrwg.[35] The tramway was never built, although it was still under active consideration in 1873 and was mentioned in the L&OR Act of that year.[36] It was not until 1886 that the GWR reached the upper Avon valley.

In July 1865 the Glyncorrwg Coal Co. produced a statement pointing out that if all the necessary capital had been raised by the SWMR, the line would have been fully opened by 1st January 1860. As a consequence of the delay in opening until October 1863, they had suffered a loss, estimated as shown in Table 7.1.

An extraordinary general meeting of the SWMR held on 30th October 1865 resolved to offer the Glyncorrwg Coal Co. £15,888 5s 10d (that is, loss of interest and loss on working the railway once opened) without prejudice, in partial settlement of the claim. The company also undertook to pay for the rolling stock and for railway construction once the costs had been confirmed. The Glyncorrwg Coal Co. accepted this offer, and requested it be allotted 3,000 preference shares (£30,000), this being the whole of the new capital authorised by the 1864 Act, the balance of £14,111 14s 2d to be repaid to the SWMR. The loans authorised by this Act were provided by W H Dawes and Robert Baxter, acting as trustees of the Glyncorrwg Coal Co., who were issued with Debentures to the value of £10,000. These manoeuvres enabled the SWMR to raise cash without going to outside investors. The rolling stock was confirmed in March 1866 to have cost £7,000 13s 9d.

In addition to using the SWMR for its own traffic, the Glyncorrwg Coal Co. was keen that others should use the railway. The 1859 prospectus noted that contracts had been entered into with lessees of minerals in the Gwenffrwd Valley to use the lower five miles of railway for £2,000 per annum. It is not clear if or how this was achieved, although collieries were active there by 1861.

Also in 1859 Dugdale Houghton requested the SWMR to make the authorised branch up to his colliery at Fforchdwm. The

TABLE 7.1: FINANCIAL STATEMENT BY GLYNCORRWG COAL CO., JULY 1865

	£	s	d
Interest on share capital and unproductive expenditure 1856–63	13,489	1	4
Construction of railways authorised by 1861 and 1864 Acts	15,132	18	9
Loss on working railway once opened	2,399	4	6
Rolling stock	7,000	0	0
	38,021	4	7
Less cash raised on Debentures	6,200	0	0
	32,021	4	7

BELOW: A rake of four empties wagons ascending Ynysmaerdy Incline, Briton Ferry, drawn by four loads coming down. Travel as depicted was not condoned. *Author's collection*

company's response was that it would only do so if Houghton or his lessees subscribed to shares to the value of the cost of the work, although they were offered use of the branch and the main line for a minimum of £1,500 per annum for ten years. This offer was declined and Houghton built his own tramroad to a transshipment point adjacent to the SWMR near the west end of the tunnel. By April 1864 three levels were putting coal onto the SWMR.[37] A further source of traffic was Avon Vale Colliery, later known as Corrwg Vale Colliery, in Cwm Cregan which commenced working in April 1864 and was sending considerable quantities of coal to Briton Ferry.[38] The siding connection was at Abercregan about one mile west of Cymmer, from where a tramway ran up to the colliery, apparently worked by two old broad gauge locomotives in use as stationary engines.[39] Circa 1885 the tramway was replaced by the Avan Vale Mineral Railway, which ran for about half a mile up Cwm Cregan to the colliery and remained in use until 1926. In February 1870 five collieries were putting coal onto the SWMR: Welsh Main or Hendregarreg at Glyncorrwg, Glyncorrwg further up the valley, Avon Vale, Fforchdwm, and Tonygregos in Cwm Gwenffrwd. Tonmawr Colliery, also in Cwm Gwenffrwd, opened in November 1870.[40] In 1886 a siding connection was put in about one mile east of the tunnel for the short-lived (1885–95) Nantybar Colliery.

The years 1869 to 1872 proved to be difficult times for the SWMR. On 31st July 1869 the Glyncorrwg Coal Co. Ltd was ordered to be wound up on the petition of Caroline, Dowager Countess of Dunraven, for non-payment of rents.[41] Robert Smith, the company's manager, was appointed liquidator, with powers to sell the business as a going concern. In August 1869 Baxter resigned as chairman of the SWMR, and A P Barlow, no longer a director of the Glyncorrwg Coal Co., was appointed in his place. A new company, the Glyncorrwg Colliery Co. Ltd, was quickly formed and registered on 4th November with a capital of £50,000 and with similar objects to its predecessor, except that it took no interest in the BFFD Co.[42] Smith became secretary of the new company, which immediately put into effect an agreement with the liquidator to purchase the collieries and associated property at Glyncorrwg. Although initially preferring to concentrate on its collieries, the Glyncorrwg Colliery Co. was induced to make an offer to work the SWMR, which was considered by a special general meeting of the railway company held on 10th December 1869. The terms included:

- maintenance and renewal of the engines, rope and permanent way and payment of rates and taxes, management costs and other working expenses for twenty-one years,
- payment of all receipts to the SWMR after deducting 9d per ton on up to 120,000 tons of coal in the first year and 8d per ton in subsequent years, and over 120,000 tons per year to be fixed by arbitration but not more than 4d per ton, and
- payment by the Glyncorrwg Colliery Co. of a nominal rent of 1s per ton on its own coal.

A second special general meeting held on 21st December agreed to enter into this arrangement provided no other responsible contractor came forward. None was forthcoming, and on 14th January 1870 the directors resolved to proceed as authorised by the general meeting, the agreement being signed on 23rd March 1870. Steps were taken to reclaim the railway from the liquidator and Smith agreed to manage the railway in a individual capacity. The March 1871 general meeting heard that Messrs Barlow and Smith had inspected the railway, which was found to be in good order with the engines being well taken care of. At the end of that year the company's working stock amounted to three engines and one goods brake van,[43] the same as in March 1869.

The next issue to confront the directors of the SWMR came in February 1871 when the GWR at last decided to convert the SWR to narrow (standard) gauge.[44] This decision evidently took some months to become public, as it was not until October 1871 that a general meeting was held to consider what course of action to take to obtain compensation for the injury and loss that would be sustained. Robert Baxter of the Glyncorrwg Colliery Co. represented the SWMR as a member of the deputation which met Daniel Gooch that month to press the matter, to no avail. Consequently the directors resolved to join in any action to compel the GWR to pay compensation to branch railways and broad gauge wagon owners for their change of gauge. As a first step the company, together with the affected wagon owners, promoted in Parliament a Bill requiring the GWR to make such compensation.[45] The ensuing negotiations with the GWR failed, and in April 1872 it became necessary for the company's counsel to argue the case before the House of Commons committee considering the Bill. However the committee found the preamble not proved and the Bill failed.[46]

General powers to convert its broad gauge railways to the narrow gauge were contained in the GWR (Further Powers) Act 1866.[47] As part of its omnibus 1872 Bill the GWR included powers to make arrangements with six South Wales railway companies affected by the change of gauge.[48] The Bill contained a clause authorising "the Company on the one hand and … the SWMR Co. … [and] the BFFD Co. … on the other hand to enter into and carry into effect contracts, agreements or arrangements as to the alteration of the gauge of the railways belonging to those companies from the broad to the narrow gauge …". The directors of the SWMR in February 1872 filed a petition against the Bill presumably because it did not offer adequate compensation. The outcome was that there was no mention of the SWMR in the GWR 1872 Act.[49]

The directors anticipated these failures in April 1872 when they recognised that the cost of the change of gauge would have to be borne by the SWMR, the Glyncorrwg Colliery Co. having to find new engines, and the expense to be charged to the capital account. The line was closed from 1st May to 4th June 1872 for the gauge conversion.[50] The first narrow gauge engine, presumably belonging to the contractor, arrived at Glyncorrwg on 28th May 1872.[51] In response to Mr Baxter's application, in June 1872 the GWR Board authorised its Wolverhampton works to construct three tank engines for the Glyncorrwg Colliery Co., and the following month approved the sale of an old narrow gauge coach which evidently replaced the goods brake van.[52] The directors at first decided to sell the four broad gauge engines leased to the Glyncorrwg Colliery Co., but in the event one was retained and converted to narrow gauge. The Glyncorrwg Colliery Co. spent £14,599 12s 11d on the new locomotives and converting the SWMR in order to maintain continuous communication with Briton Ferry Dock.[53] SWMR capital expenditure on gauge conversion amounted to £4,585.[54]

Pointsmen at the bottom of Ynysmaerdy Incline.

Author's collection

Mr Barlow of the SWMR and T Walker Jr of the Glyncorrwg Colliery Co. inspected the railway in March 1874 and presented a generally positive report. Considerable improvements had been made at the bottom of the incline where a total of four lines had been provided for sorting empty and loaded wagons. The permanent way was in a far better state than it had been left by the contractor who altered the gauge, and only a few more weeks of remedial work remained. Four colliery companies had either laid in, or applied to lay in, sidings on the company's land in anticipation of new workings being productive, these being Welsh Freehold, Avon Vale, Hendregarreg and Corrwg Fechan at Blaencorrwg.

Although the railway was deemed to be in reasonably good condition, the same could not be said of the SWMR finances. By November 1873 considerable arrears of dividends had accrued, and debts and liabilities incurred by or on behalf of the company amounted to £35,000. Consequently application was made to Parliament to bring in a Bill raise additional capital by shares and borrowing, and to capitalise the arrears of dividends.[55] The desired powers were contained in the SWMR Act 1874[56] which gained the Royal Assent on 16th July 1874. At an extraordinary general meeting of shareholders held later that month the directors were authorised to create £22,210 of preference shares for the conversion of the arrears of dividends and to issue £35,000 of debentures. The conversion was reported as capital expenditure in December 1876.

The first branch line into the Pelenna valley had been opened in 1873. Tenders for making the one and three-quarter mile-long railway were invited in February 1873,[57] and the line was reported to be almost complete on 27th August.[58] The Welsh Freehold Coal & Iron Co. expected to ship 100 tons of coal per day, but by March 1873 a large quantity of stock, unsold due to its poor quality, was being held on the railway's sidings. This colliery ceased working in 1875 and the branch was lifted.

This turned out to be a foretaste of what was to come. The September 1876 general meeting was informed that three more collieries on the line had closed due to the state of the coal trade in South Wales. By the following March only two collieries were working, Glyncorrwg and Corrwg Fechan. The Glyncorrwg Colliery Co. was not now in a financial position to continue the working agreement, and in June 1877 Mr Baxter asked the directors of the SWMR to make a special agreement, to be renewed every six or even three months, failing which the company would go into liquidation. The directors had no powers to alter the terms of the lease and consequently on 21st July 1877 the Glyncorrwg Colliery Co. was, on the petition of Thomas Andrew, an ironmonger of Neath, ordered by the High Court to be wound up.[59] Robert Smith, manager of the Glyncorrwg Colliery Co. was appointed liquidator and continued to work the colliery and the railway. It was reported at the general meeting held in September 1877 that the quantity of

The loops at the bottom of the incline at the time when the SWMR was worked by the Glyncorrwg Colliery Co., which may account for the crude state of the track. The crossover connection between the running lines was about 200 yards behind the photographer. Postcard, postally used 30th May 1906. *Author's collection*

coal carried was so small it would not cover the working expenses, and some new arrangement had to be made.

Matters came to a head the following month when, on 23rd August 1877, Mr Woods, the secretary, informed the directors that he had been appointed receiver of the SWMR on the application of a debenture holder named Mrs A A Hall. The SWMR remained in receivership until 1907, one consequence of which was that all future agreements and financial arrangements concerning the company had to be approved by the Court of Chancery. The directors also considered the effects of a notice dated 17th October 1877 from the liquidator of the Glyncorrwg Colliery Co. Ltd to terminate the agreement of 23rd March 1870 between the Glyncorrwg Colliery Co. and the SWMR. The solicitor was instructed to communicate with the GWR to see whether it would be disposed to insert a clause into its next omnibus Bill to purchase, lease or make a working arrangement with the SWMR. This request was considered by the GWR directors at their meeting on 8th November, but in the absence of any proposed terms of arrangement they were unable to comply.[60] In the meantime, Smith continued to manage the railway under a temporary agreement terminable on three month's notice. Such notice was given on 8th July 1879 and it appears that for few months the railway was without a manager.

A new Glyncorrwg Colliery Co. Ltd was registered on 13th March 1880 with the same objects as the 1869 company, but this time with a capital of £78,000.[61] The assets of the previous company were taken over by an agreement dated 19th March. On the same

day an agreement was signed with the SWMR permitting the new Glyncorrwg Colliery Co. to haul as much coal as it pleased from its colliery to Briton Ferry using its own locomotives whist not being responsible for the repair or maintenance of the railway.[62] This agreement, which had been approved by the Court on 17th March 1880, was soon realised to be inadequate. A further agreement, made on 27th November 1880, allowed the Glyncorrwg Colliery Co. to haul other colliery company's coal and merchandise over the SWMR at approved rates. More importantly, the Glyncorrwg Colliery Co. acquired responsibility for the repair and maintenance of the whole of the railway and sidings, as well as all the fixed assets, to be charged to the SWMR's account at cost price plus 10 per cent. The assets included the engine sheds at Briton Ferry, Incline Top, and Glyncorrwg, and the workshops attached to the engine shed at Briton Ferry. The railway company became liable for the costs of an accountant's services, a superintendent and an engineer, and to contribute towards the salaries of a consultant engineer and a secretary. Particularly relevant to the remoteness of Glyncorrwg, officers, colliers, workmen and their families were to be carried without charge, even though such carriage had not been sanctioned by the Board of Trade.

These arrangements came into effect not before time. Back in July 1873 the condition of the viaduct carrying the SWMR over the River Gwenffrwd was giving cause for concern. It was estimated that the cost of altering this wooden structure into a culvert across the river and a bridge over the adjacent farm track

A later view of the loops at the bottom of the incline with eight empty wagons waiting to be taken up. *Author's collection*

amounted to £4,000. Tenders of approximately £2,000 were obtained for carrying out the masonry part of this work, and that of a Mr George of £1,972 for the construction of the culvert was accepted. Two years later, the subject was revisited, modified this time to include widening the embankment that would be created to take a double track which was planned to extend for distance of about two and three-quarter miles to the west of the tunnel. The cost had now escalated to between £4,100 and £5,700, which was considered by the Glyncorrwg Colliery Co. to be excessive in the straightened financial circumstances of the time, and the matter was shelved for five years. In April 1880 Messrs Thomas and Perch of the Glyncorrwg Colliery Co reported that the line was in need of urgent repairs which were estimated to cost £4,000, money which their company was believed to be willing to advance.

Once the November 1880 agreement had been approved by the Court it became possible to make progress. Messrs Brown & Adams of Cardiff were confirmed in January 1881 as engineers to the SWMR for the repairs of the viaduct and the line generally. Within one month Messrs Brown & Adams had obtained six tenders for the formation of the embankment, and that of Messrs Jones & Jepson of Neath, for the construction of an embankment wide enough for two lines of rails for £2,550, was accepted on 14th February 1881. It was not until July 1881 that the Court of Chancery ordered that the SWMR and its receiver were free to enter into a contract with the Glyncorrwg Colliery Co. for the embankment and other works and to borrow a sum not exceeding £4,000 for the purpose. The contract with Messrs Jones & Jepson for filling in the viaduct was signed on 15th October 1881. The work was planned to be done without interfering with the traffic of the railway, and the earth

had to be carefully deposited so as not to run any risk of damaging the viaduct. Nevertheless, the engineers reported on 5th November that 15,000 out of a total of 52,700 cubic yards had been filled, and that the condition of the viaduct showed that the work had not been started too soon. Fifty per cent of this work was reported to be completed by 3rd December, a rate of progress suggesting that the embankment was completed by March 1882. Other work could now be carried out, and on 21st January 1882 the Court of Chancery amended the previous order and agreed that of the £4,000, £2,550 could be applied to the filling in of the viaduct, £730 to relaying the line and £720 to general repairs sworn as being necessary by the engineers. The loan of £4,000 at 7 per cent per annum by the Glyncorrwg Colliery Co. was formalised in an agreement dated 26th January 1883, by which date £3,600 had already been advanced.[63] One of the terms of this agreement stipulated that the SWMR was not to terminate either of the two earlier agreements regarding haulage by the Glyncorrwg Colliery Co. until all the monies owing had been paid.

Towards the end of 1880 a possible means of extracting the SWMR from its financial difficulties presented itself. The promoters of the first R&SBR scheme proposed *inter alia* to take over all or part of the SWMR between Briton Ferry and Cymmer and to eliminate Ynysmaerdy Incline.[64] Although seen to be of great advantage to the SWMR, in January 1881 the directors decided to petition against the Bill in the hope of getting the best possible terms. Agreement was soon reached with the promoters, but the Bill was withdrawn early in March 1881 because of a technical objection, and the opportunity was lost. The R&SBR promoters returned to Parliament in 1882 with a much modified route from Swansea to Treherbert via Briton

Looking down the incline from near the top. Postcard, postally used 12th October 1905. *Author's collection*

Ferry and the Avon Valley which made no connection with the SWMR. This time there was a competing scheme in the form of the Glyncorrwg, Rhondda & Swansea Junction Railway (GR&SJR), which was proposed to reach Glyncorrwg through a tunnel from the Rhondda Valley and make use of the SWMR as far as Efail Fach, whence it was to swing north then west towards Neath, Briton Ferry and Swansea. The directors of the SWMR were heavily involved in the planning of this scheme and the shareholders provided 15 per cent of the funds necessary for obtaining an Act.

As first mooted, the GR&SJR proposed to take over all or part of the SWMR's undertaking, but by the time the Bill was printed an agreement had been reached concerning running powers over and repairs to its railway. Additionally, the new company was prevented from using the SWMR or exercising any powers conferred on it by the Act until a sum not exceeding £20,000 had been spent on adapting the railway for such use and repaying the loan obtained from the Glyncorrwg Colliery Co. This agreement was appended as the second schedule of the Bill,[65] which was approved by the directors on 28th January 1882. Unsurprisingly, the SWMR petitioned the House of Lords in favour of the GR&SJR Bill and against the R&SBR Bill. The GR&SJR scheme, if enacted, could well have been the salvation of the SWMR, but on 30th March the Lords found the preamble not proved and the following day rejected an application to allow the incline-avoiding line to be built. On the other hand, the R&SBR Bill was approved. The SWMR directors, in the hope of gaining some concessions to their advantage, approached the Earl of Jersey, the future chairman of the R&SBR, with a view to making a junction with his line at Cymmer and being granted running powers from there to Treherbert. Although Lord Jersey was prepared to offer only the junction, both applications were rejected by the House of Commons Committee which examined the R&SBR Bill. Consequently, the only connection of the SWMR to the outside world at its eastern end remained the bridge over the River Avon to the GWR at Cymmer opened in 1878.

By October 1887, Edward Phillips, who had been elected chairman in March 1881, had become dissatisfied with the working arrangements. In particular, the expense of maintaining the line for £1,600 per annum was considered too high. The working agreement had notionally expired on 31st July 1885, but could not be terminated and renegotiated as the loan had not been repaid, an issue which also precluded some form of arrangement with the R&SBR, which had also been mooted.

In July 1889 Messrs Forster Brown & Rees, consulting engineers, reported to the directors on the terms desirable in any future working agreement. These included a fixed-term agreement of ten years, and the Glyncorrwg Colliery Co. raising £50,000, of which not more than £10,000 would be spent on putting the existing rolling stock in order and purchasing sufficient new locomotives and rolling stock to work the line. The balance was to be spent on sinking and developing a large colliery to the steam coals between Cymmer and Glyncorrwg, the coal being conveyed over the SWMR. The Glyncorrwg Colliery Co. was to work the railway, the net profit of carrying coal between Glyncorrwg and Briton Ferry being divided equally between the two companies. At this time £3,350 was still owing to the Glyncorrwg Colliery Co.[66]

The Glyncorrwg Colliery Co. was also beginning to struggle as the existing mineral rights were approaching the point of exhaustion. A

proposal to enlarge the company's capital to work the lower coal measures, and to extend the arrangement with the SWMR for a period of ten years was explained to the directors in June 1889. Before anything could be done it was necessary for the Glyncorrwg Colliery Co. to be reorganised; the 1880 company was put into liquidation in December 1889, although not wound up until April 1928. Another third Glyncorrwg Colliery Co., again with same objects as its predecessors, was registered on 9th January 1890 with a capital of £200,000.[67] Under the terms of an agreement dated 11th January 1890, Charles Lock and William Perch, the liquidator and trustee respectively, sold the assets and interests of the old company to the new for £71,409, and Perch became its managing director. Also in January 1890 the firm of William Perch & Co., which had been established in 1860 as colliery proprietors and coal shippers, acquired the mineral rights under Mynydd Ynyscorrwg between the Corrwg and Avon valleys. Perch died in 1891 and these leases were taken over by the Glyncorrwg Colliery Co. Three deep mines were eventually sunk to work this coal. The first, in 1890, were the Scatton pits, more correctly but confusingly described as the Glyncorrwg pits, near Blaengwynfi station and served by the R&SBR. The North and South pits at Glyncorrwg were sunk in 1902 and 1904 respectively, and Ynyscorrwg Colliery just south of Glyncorrwg was sunk in 1911–12. According to a prospectus issued in July 1903 offering £30,000 of debenture stock, the new pits at Glyncorrwg were expected to produce 1,000 tons of coal per week, providing much needed traffic for the SWMR. At this date the Glyncorrwg Colliery Co. owned abut 75 per cent of the shares and debentures of the SWMR, giving it a controlling interest through nominees on the Board, and had loaned the railway company nearly £5,600.

Meanwhile, the 1880 working agreement continued to be in force. In 1891 the GWR was again approached to enquire if it would be prepared to work the line, but to no avail, the subject not even being brought before its directors. In January 1892 the Glyncorrwg Colliery Co. came up with proposals for a new working agreement, which, although agreed in principle, generated a prolonged correspondence between the secretaries of the two companies.[68] Henry Heath of the Glyncorrwg Colliery Co. contended that the SWMR needed their traffic for Briton Ferry at a realistic rate or it was doomed, as it could not exist by itself. The R&SBR's proposed Railway No. 8[69] would make most of the SWMR useless, but the Glyncorrwg Colliery Co. threatened to support it unless a satisfactory arrangement was reached. Herbert Allen, who had been appointed secretary of the SWMR in November 1889, held out for the terms outlined in Messrs Forster Brown & Rees' report, which were for the most part acceptable except that the Glyncorrwg Colliery Co. desired a permanent interest in working the railway.

Matters became complicated in March 1892 when the directors received an offer from the R&SBR to work the line for 70 per cent of the present traffic receipts, find the money to put the line in order, and to pay off the loan, both at 5 per cent interest, and to make allowance for the traffic diverted by their proposed Railway No. 8. The Glyncorrwg Colliery Co.'s view was that this was a ploy to discourage opposition to Railway No. 8., which if constructed would leave the SWMR with just five miles of usable railway, from which it would derive far less profit than if the Glyncorrwg Colliery

The stretch of GWR main line between Briton Ferry station on the left and Court Sart on the right. The nearest track is the R&SBR main line, and the furthest is the SWMR line authorised by the 1861 Act to connect the bottom of the incline off to the right of the view to Briton Ferry Dock off to the left. The long buildings this side of the far road bridge were by now wagon repair works.

Author's collection

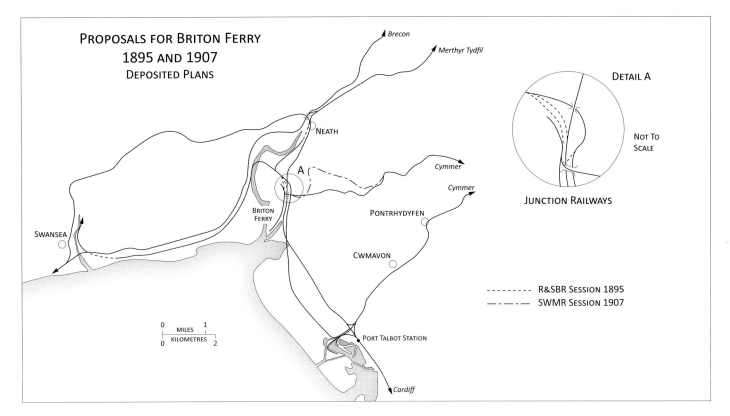

Co. worked the whole line. Nevertheless, the directors were inclined to accept the offer, but decided to ask the R&SBR if it would give a minimum of £2,500 and mileages of nine and six miles for traffic coming from east and west respectively to the junction with the proposed Railway No. 8. These terms must have been too onerous for the R&SBR and the offer was withdrawn in May 1892. The Glyncorrwg Colliery Co. then softened its position slightly and agreed to continue to maintain the line and rolling stock, such that in May 1892 a draft agreement was prepared. It was not until December 1892, however, and after much revision of the details, that a printed draft was made[70] and submitted to the Court of Chancery. On 7th March 1893 the judge declined to make any order or express any opinion on the merits of the agreement as he considered it would have to be sanctioned by Parliament. The Glyncorrwg Colliery Co. agreed, on conditions, to find the funds necessary to promote a Bill in Parliament, but nothing was done and the 1880 agreement remained in force until December 1907.

The directors of the SWMR made no comment on the scheme announced in November 1893 to reincorporate the PT Co. as a combined railway and dock undertaking,[71] although they must have realised that the new company was likely to become a major influence in the locality.

Of more immediate consequence was the proposal made by the R&SBR in 1894 to make use of a short railway partially constructed by the Neath Harbour Commissioners to connect the western end of the SWMR to its authorised main line from Briton Ferry to Swansea.[72] The R&SBR, whose acquisition of the Neath Harbour railways was confirmed by an agreement dated 1st June 1895,[73] was obliged by its 1892 Act to make this connection before opening its Railway No. 8 near Cymmer. The western end of the SWMR had been slewed in 1886 to accommodate an intended connection of the harbour railways to the GWR at Neath Harbour

Junction,[74] although the connection was not brought into use[75] until reinstated in 1903 as Court Sart Junction.[76] The Rhondda scheme envisaged the completion of the partially built railway by the construction of a 500 yard long connection from a point on the SWMR opposite the future Court Sart Junction to join its main line at Neath Junction opposite Neath engine shed.[77] This junction, which gave the SWMR a direct connection towards Swansea,[78] was inspected in March 1895, having been opened for goods traffic on 14th December 1894,[79] and was authorised retrospectively by the R&SBR Act 1895.

The PTR&D's 1895 proposals for a line from Port Talbot to Tonmawr (the SWMJnR), which were bound to affect the interests of the SWMR, were favourably received and the directors supported the Bill in Parliament.[80] Relations between the two companies were somewhat strained following the opening of the SWMJnR in November 1898, principally over working the traffic on the Blaenavon Branch. Matters were not finally resolved until an agreement was signed in November 1902.[81]

On Saturday 16th August 1902 two short mineral trains collided in Gyfylchi Tunnel, two passengers travelling in the brake van of the Down train from Glyncorrwg subsequently dying from their injuries. The enquiry conducted by Major Druitt RE of the Railway Inspectorate found the traffic clerk at Glyncorrwg to blame for the collision by failing to ensure that it was safe for the Down train to proceed beyond Cymmer, the authorised passing place, to Tonmawr.[82] Despite having a signal box, Tonmawr was not normally a passing place for SWMR trains. Major Druitt's report provides an insight into the lax way the railway was operated. No printed instructions were in effect at the time, but following the accident an improved method of working using train tickets was introduced. Surprisingly, there was telegraphic communication between Incline Top and Cymmer, Cymmer and Glyncorrwg, and Incline Top and

Tonmawr, but not between Tonmawr and Cymmer. The report recommended that this omission be rectified, but made no adverse comment on the carriage of passengers in brake vans. This practise was condoned by the November 1880 working agreement, and since 1865 newspapers had occasionally reported or implied this means of travel.[83] A survey conducted by the R&SBR when first contemplating working the SWMR found that a total of 1,053 passengers had been conveyed by the SWMR between Cymmer and Incline Top during the week-ending 31st December 1886.[84] There was a short platform and waiting room at Crythan near the top of the incline from which, for intrepid passengers, it was a two mile walk to Neath. The SWMR first reported owning passenger carriages in 1905.

Up to 1902 the SWMR had created £160,980 of capital, £55,610 as ordinary shares and £105,370 as 6 per cent preference shares, and raised mortgages totalling £48,000. Despite the capital rearrangement allowed by the 1874 Act the net revenue of its undertaking continued to be insufficient to meet the company's obligations, resulting in the appointment of the receiver in 1877. A further reorganisation was announced in 1902,[85] becoming the SWMR Act 1903[86] which received the Royal Assent on 30th June 1903. This act authorised the company to fund the improvement of the undertaking by the issue £40,000 of 3% A Debenture Stock, to substitute debentures for the existing mortgages and to fund the arrears of mortgage interest by the issue of 3% B Debenture Stock, and to consolidate the existing preference stock.

There was a wholesale change of directors at the March 1906 general meeting when four of the five resigned and were replaced by Henry Turton Norton, Henry Mather Jackson and James Philip Hurst, all also directors of the Glyncorrwg Colliery Co., and J R Baillie. Only Mr Baxter remained. Sir Henry Mather Jackson, Bart. (1855–1942), who had joined the Board of the Glyncorrwg Colliery Co. in April 1904 and who had a wealth of railway and industrial experience,[87] was elected chairman of the SWMR in April 1906. Up to this time no steps had been taken to put into effect any of the powers granted by the 1903 Act. The new Board decided in October 1906 to activate those clauses relating to the issue of the 3% B Debenture Stock and to the consolidation the existing preference stock. In due course £83,770 of the 3% B Debenture Stock was issued.

Ynysmaerdy Incline at Briton Ferry was the Achilles heel of the SWMR. A number of accidents had occurred over the years and the brake gear at the top required periodic renewal. In October 1906 the new Board resolved to go to Parliament for an Act to make a deviation railway obviating the use of the incline as announced in the Parliamentary Notice.[88] The intended route was almost identical to that proposed for the R&SBR in 1881 and the GR&SJnR in 1882.[89] The latter was no surprise, as the engineer was again Trevor F Thomas, by now a director and engineer of the Glyncorrwg Colliery Co. and a partner in William Perch & Co., their shipping agents, who estimated the three mile long deviation railway to cost £59,415.[90]

This closer view of Court Sart shows at the far right the sidings at the bottom of the incline which after its closure became known as Balls Yard. Nearby can be seen the roof of the SWMR's engine shed, and to the left of the road bridge the wagon repair works bearing the legend "Glyncorrwg Foundry, Engineering & Wagon Works", which would date the view pre-1912.

Author's collection

A pre-1914 view of the Court Sart area of Briton Ferry. The Shelone Road bridges run across the centre of the view, with the SWMR Dock Branch running under the left-hand arch, the GWR main line through the middle arch and the R&SBR under the right-hand span. Behind are the SWMR bridges over the latter two lines, with the loops at the bottom of the incline seemingly in use as a goods yard. The SWMR engine shed, possibly with a resident locomotive, is in the left background, with the Glyncorrwg Foundry, Engineering & Wagon works in the foreground.   *Author's collection*

It was at this time that the PTR&D, with the cooperation of the SWMR, inspected the railway. Cleaver noted that the line was in fairly good condition for the existing traffic, which in April 1907 amounted to three trains each way. Trains speeds were restricted to 20 mph, but if this were to be increased and engines heavier than 45 tons used, most of the line would have to be relaid. The incline and machinery were found to be in good condition, but the line was not signalled in any way. This report no doubt helped persuade Col Wright to make his announcement at the February 1907 general meeting of the PTR&D.

The deposited Bill was made up of 43 clauses, but before it received Parliamentary scrutiny a clause giving the GWR, R&SBR, PTR&D and TVR powers to subscribe to the SWMR and eleven related clauses regarding working agreements were deleted as they did not comply with the Standing Orders of the House of Commons.[91] The principal objector to the Bill was the R&SBR on the grounds that the proposed railway was a danger to its own railway on account of the steep gradient, about 1 in 30. This objection was settled by an agreement of 19th March 1907 in which the SWMR agreed to lay down safety points and runaway sidings near the junction with the R&SBR. Sir Henry Mather Jackson testified to the House of Commons Select Committee that the reasons for the deviation were threefold: the anachronistic nature of the incline, an increase in traffic due to new collieries in the Glyncorrwg area, and a desire to run passenger trains. Thomas

informed the Committee that currently carriages were put on the tail of mineral trains, and carried mainly workmen at no charge. On 9th April 1907 the chairman announced that the Committee found the preamble proved, but it was not disposed to grant the special powers asked for regarding trespass on the company's railway as this should come under common railway law. The title was amended to "A Bill to empower the SWMR Co. to construct a deviation railway; to abandon part of their existing railway; to raise further money; and for other purposes." To fund the construction of the deviation railway the creation of a further £60,000 of 3% A Debenture Stock was authorised. Further minor amendments were made to the Bill, now reduced to 30 clauses, by both Houses of Parliament and the ensuing Act received the Royal Assent on 2nd August 1907.[92]

Meanwhile, the directors had resolved on a somewhat more confrontational attitude to the PTR&D, for example deciding on 24th January 1907 to terminate, on 27th April, the agreement made on 16th November 1902 regarding working traffic on the Blaenavon Branch. Possibly they felt that the powers sought in their 1907 Bill would give them a greater independence. However, removal of the clauses giving other companies powers to subscribe to SWMR shares removed that possibility. The only parts of the 1907 Act the directors considered putting into effect were those empowering them to increase the funds that could be raised under their 1903 Act with a view to discharging the receiver.

NOTES

1. *Railway News*, 23 February 1907.
2. *Railway Times*, 16 July 1853.
3. See Chapter 1.
4. The bulk of this account is taken from the Minutes of the Board and Shareholder's Meetings 1853–1908, TNA: PRO RAIL 639/1–2.
5. Authorised by the Briton Ferry Dock & Railways Act 1851, 14 & 15 Vict. c.xlix, opened August 1861.
6. *The Cambrian*, 23 September 1853.
7. *The London Gazette*, 24 November 1854.
8. 16 & 17 Vict. c.cxcvii.
9. Roger L Brown, 'Coal Mining in the Upper Afan, Part 1', *Afan Uchaf*, 5 (1982), pp. 20–31; P Reynolds, 'Coal Mining in the Upper Afan: Some Further Notes', *Afan Uchaf*, 6 (1983), pp. 53–5.
10. TNA: PRO BT 41/258/1477.
11. *The Cambrian*, 28 March 1856.
12. *The Cambrian*, 29 May 1857.
13. *The Cambrian*, 27 November 1857.
14. TNA: PRO BT 31/387/1451.
15. *Railway Times*, 30 July 1859.
16. *The Cambrian*, 26 March 1852.
17. *The Cambrian*, 5 August 1853.
18. *The Cambrian*, 23 August 1861.
19. *The London Gazette*, 23 November 1860.
20. PA HL/PO/PB/3/plan1861/S22.
21. 24 & 25 Vict. c.ccx.
22. *The London Gazette*, 23 November 1860.
23. PA HL/PO/PB/3/plan1861/S21.
24. *The Cambrian*, 21 December 1860.
25. *The London Gazette*, 26 February 1861.
26. 24 & 25 Vict. c.ccxlii; Jones and Dunstone, *The Vale of Neath Line*, pp. 52–3.
27. TNA: PRO RAIL 678/4.
28. *The Cambrian*, 10 April 1863.
29. *The London Gazette*, 24 November 1863.
30. PA HL/PO/PB/3/plan1864/S6; GRO Q/DP 241.
31. Brown, 'Coal Mining, Part 1', pp 20–21.
32. 27 & 28 Vict c.ccxcvii.
33. TNA: PRO RAIL 639/7.
34. *London Gazette*, 31 July 1868.
35. *London Gazette*, 4 June 1869.
36. See Chapter 1.
37. *The Cambrian*, 29 April 1864.
38. *The Cambrian*, 8 April 1864.
39. Potts & Green, *Industrial Locomotives of West Glamorgan*, p. 65.
40. See Chapter 5.
41. TNA: PRO BT 31/387/1451.
42. TNA: PRO BT 31/1492/4609.
43. TNA: PRO RAIL 1110/430.
44. See Chapter 1.
45. *London Gazette*, 24 November 1871.

46. *House of Commons Journal*, 1872.
47. 29 & 30 Vict. c.cccvii.
48. *London Gazette*, 28 November 1871.
49. 35–36 Vict. c.cxxix.
50. *The Times*, 18 September 1872.
51. Jennie Light, 'Glyncorrwg Diary', *Glamorgan Family History Society Journal*, 59 (2000), p. 13.
52. TNA: PRO RAIL 250/24; see also Chapter 9.
53. TNA: PRO BT 31/1492/4609.
54. TNA: PRO RAIL 1110/430.
55. *The London Gazette*, 28 November 1873.
56. 37 & 38 Vict. c.cxv.
57. *The Cambrian*, 21 February 1873.
58. *The Cambrian*, 29 August 1873.
59. TNA: PRO BT 31/1492/4609.
60. TNA: PRO RAIL 250/29.
61. TNA: PRO BT 31/14645/13881.
62. TNA: PRO RAIL 639/9.
63. TNA: PRO RAIL 639/9.
64. See Chapter 1.
65. PA HL/PO/JO/10/9/1053.
66. TNA: PRO RAIL 1057/1546.
67. TNA: PRO BT 31/15048/30591.
68. TNA: PRO RAIL 1057/1546.
69. See Chapter 1.
70. TNA: PRO RAIL 1057/1546.
71. See Chapter 3.
72. *The London Gazette*, 23 November 1894.
73. Neath Harbour Act 1900, 63 & 64 Vict. c.lxxvii.
74. Neath Harbour Act 1878, 41 & 42 Vict. c.cxlvi.
75. TNA: PRO MT 6/673/4.
76. R&SBR Act 1895 58 & 59 Vict. c.cix; TNA: PRO MT 6/1223/11.
77. PA HL/PO/PB/3/plan1895/R4.
78. TNA: PRO RAIL 1057/1542.
79. TNA: PRO MT 6/1223/11.
80. See Chapter 5.
81. See Chapter 6.
82. TNA: PRO RAIL MT 6/2481/10.
83. Paul Reynolds, 'Unofficial Passenger Travel on the SWMR', *Railway & Canal Historical Society Journal*, 27/3 (1981), pp. 10–11.
84. TNA: PRO RAIL 1057/1545/5.
85. *The London Gazette*, 18 November 1902.
86. 3 Edw. 7 c.xxiv.
87. *The Times*, 25 March 1942.
88. *The London Gazette*, 20 November 1906.
89. See Chapter 1.
90. PA HL/PO/PB/3/plan1907/S15.
91. TNA: PRO RAIL 1057/1541.
92. 7 Edw. 7 c.cvii.

8

Running Powers of the Great Western Company

THE PORT TALBOT RAILWAY

The notion of a working arrangement between the GWR and PTR&D went back to at least 1902 when Sir Joseph Wilkinson, the then general manager of the GWR, suggested to Col Wright that his own company should work the PTR, leaving the PTR&D to concentrate on the docks.[1] Bearing in mind that most directorial and managerial effort as well as capital expenditure was focussed on that aspect of the undertaking, this was not an unreasonable suggestion. The GWR surveyed the PTR in June 1905 and, although a Mr Monkhouse reported that the line did not appear to present any features which would incline his company to obtain control over it even at a loss in working so as to safeguard its interests elsewhere, a colleague opined that there was no reason why Sir Joseph's offer should not be made again.

In a memorandum dated 12th September 1905, James Inglis (1851–1911), the new general manager of the GWR, reported on a discussion on this subject with Col Wright. The Colonel was evidently negotiating without the knowledge of his fellow directors, who were unaware of many of the impending developments at Port Talbot, including a new steel works. This was a reference to Cammell, Laird & Co. who were negotiating, ultimately unsuccessfully, for a 100-acre site able to store one million tons of ore. Inglis noted that the PTR&D's target for working expenses was 50 per cent of gross receipts, these having been reduced from 69 per cent in 1900 to 58 per cent in 1904, and that Miss Talbot would follow Col Wright's advice over any arrangement with the GWR. A six per cent return on ordinary shares was the lower limit of acceptability of any proposition. Col Wright thought that if a GWR/PTR&D deal came off it might induce a GWR/R&SBR arrangement. If not, he felt bound to attempt an amalgamation with the R&SBR. He was extremely annoyed by rumours appearing in the newspapers of both a large steelworks coming to Port Talbot and the amalgamation of the PTR&D with the GWR, and wrote to Alfred Baldwin, the chairman of the GWR, that if much more delay arose he could not be held to what had been agreed with Inglis.

Col Wright's thinking was precisely the opposite of what happened. Whether his remark provoked the GWR into action, or negotiations had already commenced, is not clear, but the outcome was the agreement dated 2nd July 1906, but backdated to 1st January, whereby the GWR undertook to work the R&SBR, as already related.[2] The directors became aware of this arrangement at their meeting in July 1906, and resolved to take whatever steps were necessary to protect the company's interests.

The Barry Railway, already concerned that the R&SBR was being worked by the GWR, was now concerned that the PTR, or indeed the whole company, would go the same way. Edward Lake, the general manager, produced a report in July 1906 on the PTR&D,

rather portentously titled "Political Position of Port Talbot".[3] After listing what were considered to be the most important agreements between the PTR&D and the GWR and/or R&SBR, the report outlined three scenarios for amalgamation with the ByR:

1. The ByR to work the PTR&D for 50 per cent of the gross receipts with a minimum guaranteed dividend of 4 per cent to take effect from the date of amalgamation. The PTR&D would be safeguarded by a clause that the ByR would fully and fairly develop Port Talbot Docks in competition with Barry Docks or any other docks in the Bristol Channel between Swansea and Cardiff inclusive.
2. The ByR to lease the PTR&D at a rental commencing at £60,000 a year from the date of amalgamation, this being equal to a dividend of 3 per cent on the Ordinary Port Talbot Stock, the rental increasing by £5,000 annually to £90,000 equivalent to nearly 8 per cent on the Port Talbot Stock.
3. Full amalgamation, with the Port Talbot shareholders receiving a minimum dividend of 4 per cent up to a maximum of 8½ per cent depending on the sliding scale adopted.

Whichever course was adopted, further capital expenditure on Port Talbot's docks and railways of £500,000 spread over five years could be expected. Lake and his managerial colleagues were unable to agree on a joint recommendation and the figures were submitted for consideration by the directors. The report added that in the event of any form of amalgamation it would be essential to build a railway to connect the respective lines, either from Coity Junction, Bridgend, to Cefn Junction, or from Ewenny to Margam, the latter being essentially a revival of the proposed VoGR extension of 1895–96.[4] Running powers over the R&SBR, especially to Neath and Swansea, would also be desirable.

Some of the wording of the report is ambiguous as it is not clear whether PTR&D officials were consulted before the report was written, although there is no mention of their being so in PTR&D records. The local press reported in November 1906 that negotiations were all but concluded with the ByR.[5] However, it is unlikely that any of the options would have appealed to the directors of the PTR&D or to Miss Talbot and her advisors, and the advisors at least would have required an uncontested Act of Parliament. Discussions with the GWR continued, but it was not until April 1907 that the basis of an agreement emerged. At their meeting that month the directors resolved that Col Wright should continue negotiating with the GWR regarding the railway portion of the undertaking, any agreement to include:

1. payment to the PTR&D of a fixed sum of at least 4 per cent on £750,000, the agreed capital outlay on the PTR, for the

present year and for 1908, rising by ½ per cent until 1912 and thereafter 6 per cent per annum, plus one half of the net profits of the railway undertaking for each year in excess of the sums needed to pay the percentages,

2 an arrangement similar to that between the GWR and the R&SBR, unless counsel advised a lease was preferable,

3 guarantees necessary for the proper development of the district served by the PTR&D and for the full protection of the dock portion of the undertaking, including maintaining the present differences in railway rates in favour of the Port Talbot Dock.

Inglis reported on the status of the discussions to the directors of the GWR on 18th April, and was authorised to continue negotiations for running powers over the PTR, his company having no interest in working the docks.[6] The sticking points were the rate of return on the capital outlay and the target figure for working expenses. News of a likely agreement reached the national press, the *Western Mail* even reporting that it had been signed on 17th April, and the matter was freely discussed in the Committee Rooms of the House of Commons.[7]

In July 1907 the PTR&D directors settled on a return of 5 per cent for 1907–10 (£37,500), increasing to 5½ per cent for 1911 (£41,250) and 6 per cent thereafter (£45,000), plus one half of the excess profits. These terms were agreed by the GWR Board in November 1907, the *quid pro quo* being an increase in the retained working expenses to 52½ per cent of the gross receipts. The news of an impending agreement reached the local press, but Inglis was able to deny, quite correctly, a rumour that the GWR was about to absorb the PTR&D. The heads of a draft running powers and working agreement were approved by the PTR&D directors on 20th November 1907, but not sealed by Col Wright until 20th January 1908 or by Inglis until 24th January. In anticipation of this step, Col Wright and Messrs Byass and Watson were appointed in November 1907 to be the company's nominees on the joint Consultation Committee of directors of the two companies. The directors of the GWR approved the agreement at their meeting on 23rd January 1908 and appointed the chairman and two deputy chairmen to be their representatives on the Consultation Committee. The proprietors of the PTR&D were formally notified of the terms by a circular dated 31st January 1908,[8] a summary of which appeared in the 8th February issue of the *Railway Times*.

The R&SBR of course became aware of these negotiations and was concerned that its interests should be protected. Only bland reassurances were forthcoming, and in January 1908 the directors concluded that it would be useless to take their objections to the Railway Commissioners, and that instead they had to rely on the GWR acting fairly.[9]

Early in February 1908 the Incorporated Swansea & District Freighters' Association, concerned about the GWRs apparent near monopoly in the Swansea area, raised with the Board of Trade the legality of that company's agreements for working the PTR&D, the R&SBR and the SWMR.[10] The Board of Trade declined to become involved, and in September 1909 the matter was raised in Parliament by George Wardle, MP for Stockport and also Editor of the *Railway Review*. The Board's President, Winston Churchill, replied that it could take no action, that no complaints had been received, but

it was enquiring into Railway Agreements and Arrangements, and would welcome evidence.[11]

The running powers and working agreement, which was dated 24th January 1908, was deemed to have commenced on 1st January 1907 and to continue until terminated by mutual consent.[12] The GWR was granted the right to run over and use for traffic of all descriptions the railways authorised by the 1894 and 1896 Acts, including the Whitworth and Blaenavon branches, and to use all associated infrastructure. These railways were to be maintained in good repair and working order by the PTR&D. The PTR&D was to employ officers, clerks and servants for the efficient management, operation and maintenance of the railways, although the GWR might also use its own staff. For its part, the GWR undertook to run a sufficient number of passenger and goods trains over these railways to accommodate and develop through traffic, and to run trains provided or requested by the PTR&D to handle its local or originating traffic. The financial arrangements previously agreed were confirmed. A Consultation Committee of six directors was created, appointed annually and consisting of three from each company including its chairman or deputy chairman; the Committee was to consider additional works including those which would require an Act of Parliament, additional rolling stock, and the raising of additional share capital or increasing borrowing powers. The remainder of the PTR&D's undertaking, including the dock and its installations and the dock railways and grids, remained under the PTR&D's control.

Following the approval of the running powers agreement, but before it was signed, two further agreements were made which added to or modified some of its terms, both also dated 24th January 1908. The first of these provided for the GWR to hire the existing rolling stock belonging to the railway portion of the PTR&D's undertaking for the sum of 5s annually.[13] An inventory of such rolling stock was to be made, with a valuation by George Jackson Churchward and Albert Holger Hertz representing the two companies. This rolling stock was to be returned at the end of the working agreement in as good a condition as at the beginning, or replaced by rolling stock of equal value. The provision of the principal agreement whereby the PTR&D was to maintain the railways was soon seen to be inappropriate; under the terms of the second agreement the GWR contracted to maintain the railway portion of the PTR&D's undertaking for a sum not exceeding the cost incurred and, upon termination of the working agreement, to return these railways in good repair and working order.[14] The GWR also agreed to purchase the PTR&D's unissued stores at valuation. Furthermore, all eligible and suitable staff were to be transferred to the GWR's service. Provision was made for carrying these three heads into formal agreements, but this was never done.

Although the first meeting of the Consultation Committee was not held until 2nd April 1908, the draft minutes were considered by the directors on 15th January, implying that by then a considerable number of decisions had been taken and arrangements made to give effect to the agreements. A particularly pressing problem was the provision of additional locomotive power; the locomotive superintendent's requests, the most recent in January 1907,[15] had been repeatedly deferred. However, the imminent prospect of the running powers agreement enabled the general manager to report to the Board in November 1907 that owing to a shortage of engine power two locomotives had been hired from the GWR. By 13th March 1908 five GWR engines were working on the PTR&D.[16]

The first meeting of the Consultation Committee was attended by Viscount Churchill and Messrs W Robinson and S E Palmer representing the GWR, and Col Wright and Messrs Byass and Watson representing the PTR&D.[17] Also present were Messrs Inglis, Nelson and Whitelaw of the GWR, and Messrs Lowther and Knott of the PTR&D. Viscount Churchill was elected chairman and Edward Knott appointed secretary; both retained their positions throughout the life of the Committee. This first meeting confirmed or approved the decisions and arrangements already made.

1   Edward Lowther, the general manager of the PTR&D was to continue to manage the railway and to consult Inglis on policy and management matters, Mr Morrison on traffic arrangements, and Mr Rendell on rates.

2   William Cleaver and his staff were appointed to act for the GWR for the railway portion of the PTR&D's undertaking, in consultation with William Grierson, its engineer.

3   Frederick Page, the PTR&D's accountant, was appointed to deal with the revenues of the railway under the direction of Mr Whitelaw, chief accountant.

4   The GWR was to take over the entire staff of the Locomotive and the Carriage & Wagon departments of the PTR&D. At this juncture the PTR&D employed thirty drivers and twenty-eight firemen under Albert Hertz, who was appointed the divisional locomotive superintendent.

5   The PTR&D undertook to apply for admission of its salaried staff to the RCH Superannuation Fund, to be financed by the two companies in proportion to wages paid by the railway and dock portions of the undertaking.

6   The GWR was to take over all the locomotives of the PTR&D except the six required for dock purposes, which were to be hired by the GWR. Dock engines were to be allowed to run to and from Duffryn Yard without charge. The company's wagon stock was to be divided 240 for the railway and 167 for the dock, the latter to be lettered "Dock Traffic Only". The steam rail motor and passenger carriages were also to be transferred to the GWR.[18]

7   Particular attention was given to working traffic between the railway and dock portions of the undertaking.
    • Railway engines were to deliver coal and coke for shipment to and remove empties from the storage sidings at Old and new docks. Traffic was to be moved on from there and returned by dock engines, except that the railway's engines could work to the tip roads directly if these were available.
    • Coal for the Crown Preserved Coal Co.'s works was to be delivered by the railway's engines.
    • Other traffic was to be worked to and from the storage sidings by dock engines.
    • Traffic detached at Old Dock Junction on the GWR main line by GWR trains was to be worked to the docks and empties returned by dock engines, and vice versa.
    • Traffic within the docks and between the Old and new docks via Copper Works Junction was to be worked by dock engines.

8   Purchase of the PTR&D's stores for £11,130 was approved.

The valuation of the rolling stock taken over by the GWR was approved at the second meeting of the Consultation Committee held on 5th May 1908 as:

Cost prices	£	s	d
Locomotive	58,461	6	5
Wagons	15,803	10	9
Coaching stock	9,404	7	5
Five extra vans	418	12	6
Total	84,087	17	1
less 35% depreciation	29,430	15	0
Agreed total value	54,657	2	1

A few minor issues arose with putting these decisions into effect. Four of the engine drivers transferred were deemed to be unsuitable for service on the GWR, and at first it was intended to discharge them. The Amalgamated Society of Railway Servants proposed to Churchward that these men could be employed on the docks traffic, but this was rejected and in October 1908 it was reported that the GWR had found inside work for them. The Consultation Committee met a further seven times, the last occasion being on 4th July 1919, principally to approve proposals made by the PTR&D and to deal with staff and financial matters. To deal with everyday matters the GWR set up a series of Conferences of its officers concerned with putting the working agreements into effect, the minutes of which were subject to approval by the general manager of the GWR. Only Messrs Lowther and Page of the PTR&D attended these meetings, the first of which took place on 27th November 1908.[19] The Conference was suspended during the First World War from 20th January 1916 until 13th March 1919; the thirty-eighth and last meeting was held on 10th May 1921.

The division of the railways of the PTR&D's undertaking into the mainline portion worked by the GWR and the dock portion worked by the PTR&D was not the most practicable of arrangements. By February 1911 the heads of a supplementary agreement had been agreed whereby the GWR also worked and had running powers over the dock railways.[20] These were approved by the directors of the GWR on 3rd March 1911, but the PTR&D delayed matters, apparently due to concerns over the GWR's 1911 Bill for the Clydach, Pontardawe & Cwmgorse line.[21] The agreement was eventually signed on 9th August 1911, although backdated to 1st January 1911.[22] The GWR gained the right to run over and use the dock railways in connection with traffic of all descriptions. The PTR&D retained control of the docks and related facilities, and was responsible for maintaining and staffing the dock lines. The dock railways were defined as all those lines in the dock area apart from those on the waterfront at the tips and on wharves, and included all grids and loaded and empty roads associated with the tips and the approaches to the several industries established there. At the date the definitive plan was prepared, 29th November 1910, the dock railways constituted 25m 18ch of the 27m 46ch of the lines in the dock area, although these figures changed as the docks were further developed.[23] The charges the PTR&D paid the GWR were based on the ratio of these two distances. Although not mentioned in the agreement, the extant docks wagons, including those for internal use, were transferred to the GWR as hired stock.[24] The GWR undertook to run a sufficient number of trains over the dock lines to accommodate and develop the traffic over them and to work all local traffic, and paid the PTR&D 40 per cent of the gross dock traffic receipts as a toll for the use of the lines. In view of Miss Talbot's large financial interest in the dock undertaking, an additional PTR&D director was appointed to the Consultation Committee, this being Mr Lipscomb, and to maintain the balance Stanley Baldwin of the GWR Board was also added. As with the earlier agreements, provision was made to legalise these heads but this was never done.

SOUTH WALES MINERAL RAILWAY

At their meeting held on 21st November 1907, the directors of the GWR noted that the PTR&D had for some time past been trying to gain control over the SWMR.[25] The preamble to one of the subsequent agreements makes it clear that this move was instigated by the Glyncorrwg Colliery Co.,[26] to which the SWMR was by then heavily indebted. Up to 1900, the expenses incurred by the Glyncorrwg Colliery Co. in running the railway under the 1880 agreements had been more or less balanced by the traffic receipts.[27] After that date the difference between rising expenses and static receipts steadily increased, such that by March 1907 the accumulated deficit was £7,163. The negotiations culminated in a draft working agreement being considered by the directors of the SWMR on 29th November 1907, the agreement having already been approved by the PTR&D directors. This agreement, which was sealed on 12th December and unanimously approved at special general meeting held on 23rd January 1908, was made under the powers of the PTR&D's SWMJnR Act of 1896 and deemed to be effective from 1st January 1908.[28] Under the agreement the PTR&D was entitled to retain as working expenses 67½ per cent of the gross receipts of the SWMR if less than £15,000 per annum, and 62½ per cent above that figure. Ordinarily this agreement would have been sufficient, but the matter was complicated by the fact that the Glyncorrwg Colliery Co. had a controlling interest in the SWMR and was working the railway. Consequently, on 31st December 1907 four more interrelated agreements were made between the various parties involved.

1   Col Wright, Mr Byass and Mr Watson, acting as trustees for the GWR, agreed to acquire from the Glyncorrwg Colliery Co. the various SWMR stocks and shares of nominal value £198,798 it held, together with five of its seven locomotives, its eleven carriages, twelve goods wagons and three brake vans, all for the sum of £125,400.
2   The GWR agreed to provide £125,400 to the trustees to effect the purchase.[29] Sufficient stock was to be retained to enable three each of the PTR&D and the remaining SWMR directors to qualify as directors of the reconstituted SWMR Board, the remainder being transferred to and held in the names of Col Wright and William Plender, of Deloitte, Plender, Griffiths & Co., in trust for the GWR. The GWR directors considered the matter at their meeting on 21st November 1907 and approved the sum on 12th December.[30] The net effect of these two agreements was that the GWR became, through trustees, the owner of nearly all the tangible assets of the SWMR.

3   The GWR and PTR&D agreed that the SWMR should be worked by the PTR&D under the management of Lowther, subject to the control of a Consultation Committee to be established under the terms of the PTR&D/GWR working agreement then being negotiated.[31] All traffic originating north of Tonmawr was to be sent via the PTR to Port Talbot Docks, other traffic by the most convenient and economical route. The level of working expenses mentioned above was confirmed, although the process for crediting the SWMR was modified by a supplemental agreement dated 19th March 1908.[32]
4   The Glyncorrwg Colliery Co. and the PTR&D agreed that all the Glyncorrwg Colliery Co. traffic for shipment at Port Talbot was to be sent via Tonmawr.[33] The Glyncorrwg Colliery Co. was to bring all coal from its collieries north of Glyncorrwg to the sidings at Glyncorrwg using its own engines, and to have free use of this portion of the SWMR. It also agreed to do everything reasonably possible to increase its shipments at Port Talbot and its traffic over the SWMR and the PTR. Engines of the Glyncorrwg Colliery Co. were to be allowed to run to Briton Ferry for repairs, or if necessary, to be hauled there by the PTR&D. The Glyncorrwg Colliery Co. was permitted to continue to occupy the workshops at Briton Ferry and to have free use of the engine shed at Glyncorrwg. A workmen's train was to be provided between there and Cymmer. Furthermore, the construction of the deviation railway authorised by the 1907 Act was not to be commenced until the Parliamentary Deposit had been repaid to the Glyncorrwg Colliery Co. Finally, the working of the SWMR by the Glyncorrwg Colliery Co. was to be terminated at once, and the approval of the Railway & Canal Commissioners of the new working agreement was to be sought by the PTR&D, this being granted on 30th January 1908.[34]

These arrangements were completed by a tripartite agreement between the three companies dated 8th October 1908, although deemed to have come into effect on 1st January, whereby the GWR was granted running powers over the SWMR.[35] The longstanding action against the SWMR in the Court of Chancery had been settled on 17th December 1907 using funds advanced by the Glyncorrwg Colliery Co., and the receiver had been discharged. By an agreement between the two companies dated 23rd January 1908, the working agreements of 1880 and 1883 were terminated absolutely.[36] Under the terms of this agreement the Glyncorrwg Colliery Co. was to be allotted SWMR "A" Debenture Stock to discharge the expenses incurred in obtained the 1903 and 1907 Acts and in settling the Court action, certified in July 1908 to total £5,023. The construction of the deviation railway authorised by the 1907 Act was not to be commenced until the Parliamentary Deposit of £3,495 1s 0d had been repaid. The deposit was eventually returned after the conclusion, in March 1911, of an agreement for the exchange of land at Glyncorrwg on which some siding connections stood.[37]

The directors of the R&SBR of course became aware of the working agreement and considered it would seriously affect their interests. Meetings with the chairman and general manager of the GWR proved fruitless, and, as with the operation of the PTR by the

GWR described above, in January 1908 they resigned themselves to relying on the GWR acting fairly.

The PTD&R shareholders approved the working agreement on 27th December 1907,[38] and the SWMR shareholders followed suit in January 1908. The agreements were quickly put into operation, and henceforth the SWMR was managed in a far more businesslike manner. The GWR/PTR&D Officers' Conference dealt with day-to-day matters. Messrs Baxter, Baillie and Lane resigned as directors of the SWMR on 16th January 1908. Col Wright, Mr Byass and Mr Watson of the PTR&D directorate were elected to replace them on 6th February and joined Sir Henry Mather Jackson, Mr Norton and Mr Hurst who had remained. At the next meeting on 13th February, Col Wright was elected chairman and Edward Knott of the PTR&D was appointed secretary replacing E E Ford, who had resigned owing the move of the company's office to Port Talbot. John Broad and Fred Page, the PTR&D's solicitor and accountant, were appointed to the same positions for the SWMR. Fourteen of the Glyncorrwg Colliery Co.'s employees were considered unsuitable for positions with the PTR&D and their services were dispensed with.

The three SWMR directors who had continued in office with the reconstituted Board resigned during 1913 and were replaced by Messrs Baldwin and Lipscomb of the PTR&D and G J Whitelaw, the GWR's accountant. Mr Whitelaw was obliged to resign in June 1916 due to ill health and was replaced by Frank Potter, representing the general manager of the GWR. Mr Baldwin was also obliged to resign in July 1917 on his appointment as Junior Lord to the Treasury. Potter died in July 1919 and his seat on the Board was taken by Mr C Aldington, his replacement at the GWR. Although Aldington relinquished this position in July 1921, he stayed on as a director of the SWMR pending its absorption into the GWR.

These appointments demonstrate the degree of interest the GWR took in the small and impecunious company it controlled. Further capital was required by the SWMR in 1912, to provide additional accommodation at Glyncorrwg for the traffic of the Glyncorrwg Colliery Co. In November 1912 the directors of the GWR agreed to provide the funds in return for SWMR "A" Debentures at £70 per cent.[39] The earlier agreements with the PTR&D and the SWMR were amended by a further agreement with the PTR&D dated 21st November 1912, such that no further SWMR "A" Debenture Stock would be issued without the GWR's consent.[40]

NOTES

1. TNA: PRO RAIL 1057/2952.
2. See Chapter 6.
3. Colin Chapman, personal communication.
4. See Chapter 5.
5. TNA: PRO RAIL 1057/1750.
6. TNA: PRO RAIL 250/48.
7. *Railway News*, 20 April 1907.
8. TNA: PRO MT 6/1846/8.
9. TNA: PRO RAIL 581/5.
10. TNA: PRO MT 6/1846/8.
11. Report of the Departmental Committee on Railway Agreements and Amalgamations (Parliamentary Papers 1911, XXIX).
12. TNA: PRO RAIL 574/20.
13. TNA: PRO RAIL 252/1523.
14. TNA: PRO RAIL 574/21.
15. TNA: PRO RAIL 1057/1528/107.
16. TNA: PRO RAIL 1057/1528/121.
17. TNA: PRO RAIL 242/1.
18. See Chapter 9.
19. TNA: PRO RAIL 242/3.
20. TNA: PRO RAIL 1057/2952.
21. See Chapter 6.
22. TNA: PRO RAIL 574/26.
23. TNA: PRO RAIL 574/100.
24. See Chapter 9.
25. TNA: PRO RAIL 250/48.
26. TNA: PRO RAIL 574/33.
27. TNA: PRO RAIL 1057/1537.
28. TNA: PRO RAIL 639/5.
29. TNA: PRO RAIL 252/1525.
30. TNA: PRO RAIL 250/48.
31. TNA: PRO RAIL 574/22.
32. TNA: PRO RAIL 574/23.
33. TNA: PRO RAIL 574/33.
34. TNA: PRO J 75/4.
35. TNA: PRO RAIL 574/24.
36. TNA: PRO RAIL 639/9.
37. TNA: PRO RAIL 574/33.
38. *Railway News*, 4 January 1908.
39. TNA: PRO RAIL 250/50.
40. TNA: PRO RAIL 574/27.

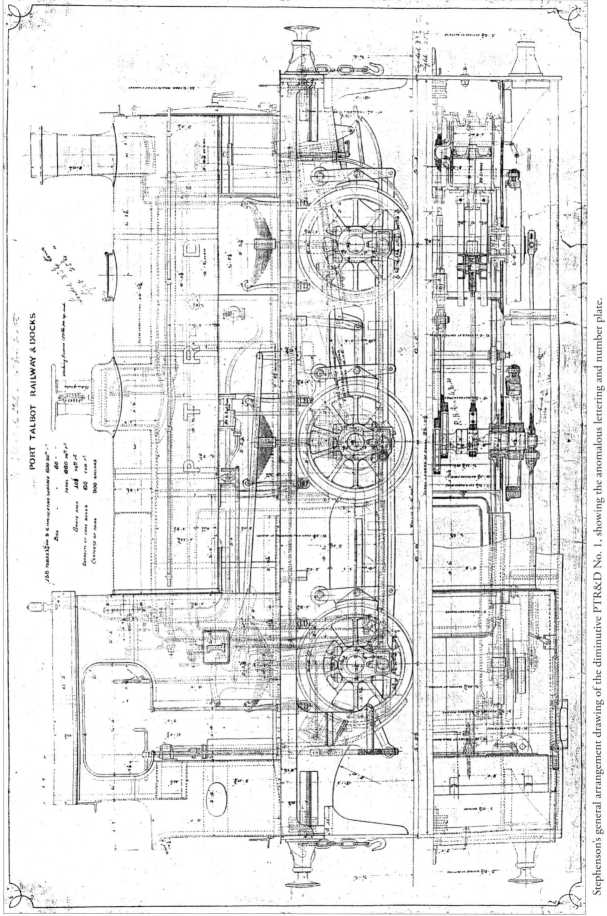

Stephenson's general arrangement drawing of the diminutive PTR&D No. 1, showing the anomalous lettering and number plate.

9

Locomotives and Rolling Stock of the Port Talbot Railway

LOCOMOTIVES

The Port Talbot Railway was conceived primarily as a mineral railway to transport coal from the mines within its reach to the company-owned docks at Port Talbot. The tasks locomotives were required to perform were mainly working loads downhill and empties back up, and shunting in the dock area. Consequently, all the locomotives were tank engines, of which the PTR&D acquired a total of thirty-one, although the maximum number in stock at any one time was twenty-six, achieved in June 1902.[1] These locomotives are dealt with here up to March 1908 by class in chronological order of their acquisition.

No. 1

In December 1895 the directors authorised Knox, the secretary, and Meik, the engineer, to obtain tenders for one locomotive for use on the docks. At that time the 1894 railway and the new dock were still under construction, but the old dock remained open throughout

and a limited trade was possible there. The tender of R Stephenson & Co. of £2,188 was successful and the order was placed in January 1896. PTR&D No. 1, Stephenson's No. 2837, arrived by February 1896,[2] suggesting it had been delivered ex-stock. The January 1898 working timetable described No. 1 as the dock pilot engine doing any necessary shunting at the docks and the adjacent industries, and making trips to and from Duffryn Junction with empty and loaded traffic. As traffic increased, this 0-6-0ST with 3 foot 6 inch wheels was of little general use and in August 1900 it was repaired[3] and seemingly transferred to Miss Talbot for the Rio Tinto traffic to Cwmavon,[4] before being sold on to the Ebbw Vale Steel, Iron & Coal Co. Ltd in February 1902, becoming its No. 22 *Stephenson*.[5] The locomotive was moved to Irthlingborough in November 1930, where it was scrapped in 1960.

BRYNDU NO. 3, DERBY AND *PENYLAN*

The next locomotives to arrive were the three purchased with the Cefn & Pyle Railway in January 1897, *Bryndu No. 3, Derby* and

PTR&D No. 1 was delivered by R Stephenson & Co. in 1896. This engine was too small to be of much general use to the PTR&D and in 1902 was sold to the Ebbw Vale Steel, Iron & Coal Co. Ltd, becoming its No. 22 *Stephenson*. The locomotive was moved to that company's ironstone works at Irthlingborough in Northamptonshire in November 1930, where it was photographed in 1953, and was scrapped in 1960. *Author's collection*

Penylan. The oldest, *Bryndu No. 3*, was built by E B Wilson of Leeds in 1853 for the Oxford, Worcester & Wolverhampton Railway, became GWR No. 222 in 1863, and was sold to Bryndu Colliery in October 1873.[6] The PTR&D directors offered the engine for sale in April 1897 but apparently found no buyers for a forty-seven-year-old locomotive. An unexplained payment in November 1897 of 12s 0d for "*Bryndu*" to Topham, Jones & Railton, who were building the OVER at the time, could have been for taking it away for scrap. This locomotive was taken out of stock during the six months to December 1897.

Derby was built by Fox, Walker of Bristol as their No. 327 of 1876 for the contractor Joseph Firbank and sold to the C&PR after 1885.[7] The directors sought to have the locomotive repaired in May 1897 and offered it for sale the following month. It was taken out of stock between July and December 1897 having been sold to Christopher Rowland who had the contract for haulage and the discharge of ships at Swansea. The engine was acquired by the Swansea Harbour Trust in August 1910, which sold it in 1911 to the dealer C D Phillips, who, finding no buyers, scrapped it.[8]

Penylan was built by Manning, Wardle as their No. 955 of 1886 for the Cardiff based contractor J E Billups and was acquired by the C&PR circa 1891. This relatively new 0-6-0ST was retained by the PTR&D, although the light duties it performed are not recorded.

Unusually, *Penylan* was occasionally hired out. The general manager reported in April 1899 that the engine had been loaned to Bryn Navigation Colliery at £10 per week, excluding stores and wages. It was at Duffryn Rhondda Colliery near Cymmer in the Avon Valley later that year, and spent most of 1905 hired to the Gwendraeth Valleys Railway.[9] It was probably not coincidental that Col Wright was closely involved with all three concerns, in particular being the chairman of the latter. *Penylan* had been overhauled in May 1904, and in October 1907 was back on the PTR&D, this time with the boiler out. The repaired engine was recorded as being shedded at "Penylan",[10] but in August 1908, after the GWR had taken over most of the locomotive stock, the locomotive was sent to Swindon where it was condemned on 1st January 1910. Although a capital replacement was required under the terms of the hire agreement,[11] none was provided. There is no evidence that *Penylan* ever carried a number although 16 was always vacant in the stock list.

0-6-0 SADDLE TANK AND 0-6-2 SIDE TANK ENGINES NOS 2–15

In the meantime the directors had, in March 1896, instructed the engineer to report as to what new locomotives were required to work the line whose opening was, according to Pearson's contract, about one year away. By July 1896 Meik had developed specifications

Ex-C&PR and PTR&D *Derby* of 1876 as Christopher Rowland's *R No. 5* working at Swansea Docks some time before January 1911 when it was sold and scrapped.

Author's collection

for five side tank engines weighing 56 tons and two saddle tank engines weighing 35 tons.[12] The directors required reassurance that these specifications were sound and resolved to obtain the opinion of William Dean at Swindon. Dean considered the design of the heavy engines to be satisfactory as it was similar to that of the 'B' and 'B1' Class 0-6-2T locomotives of the Barry Railway.[13]

Tenders were obtained and that of R Stephenson & Co. for two 0-6-0ST locomotives, Nos 2 and 3, at £1,805 each, and five 0-6-2T locomotives, Nos 4–8, at £2,212 each, being the cheapest and of earliest delivery, was accepted at the Board meeting held on 19th August 1896. The delivery deadline of 1st May 1897 was not met, Nos 2, 4, and 5 being added to stock in September 1897,[14] No. 6

RIGHT: At first all the PTR&D's 0-6-0ST engines were included on the same GWR weight diagram dated 3rd April 1908 as seen here. Subsequently Nos 2, 3 and 15 were placed into Diagram A90, and Nos 22–27 with a higher boiler pressure into Diagram A89.

BELOW: Detail from the photograph on pages 98–9, showing PTR&D 0-6-0ST No. 2 and a goods brake van shortly after delivery, circa September 1897. Note the partial use of the dot in PTR&D. No. 2 was delivered by R Stephenson & Co. in September 1897, but had a relatively short life, being condemned in January 1911 with a cracked cylinder. *SML*

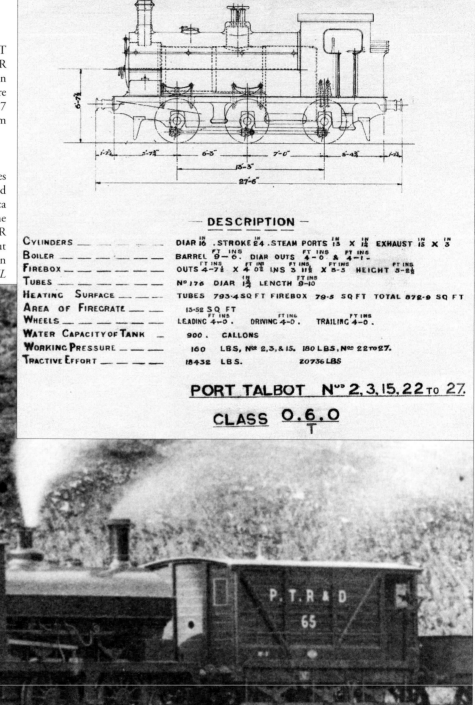

— DESCRIPTION —

CYLINDERS ___ DIAR 16 . STROKE 24 . STEAM PORTS 15 X 1½ EXHAUST 15 X 3

BOILER ___ BARREL 9—6. DIAR OUTS 4—0 & 4—1 .

FIREBOX ___ OUTS 4—7½ X 4—0½ INS 3 11½ X 5—5 HEIGHT 5—2½

TUBES ___ N° 176 DIAR 1¾ LENGTH 9—10

HEATING SURFACE ___ TUBES 793·4 SQ FT FIREBOX 79·5 SQ FT TOTAL 872·9 SQ FT

AREA OF FIRECRATE ___ 13·52 SQ FT

WHEELS ___ LEADING 4—0 . DRIVING 4—0 . TRAILING 4—0 .

WATER CAPACITY OF TANK ___ 900 . GALLONS

WORKING PRESSURE ___ 160 LBS, N°ˢ 2,3,& 15. 180 LBS, N°ˢ 22 TO 27.

TRACTIVE EFFORT ___ 18432 LBS. 20736 LBS

PORT TALBOT N°ᴰ 2, 3, 15, 22 TO 27.

CLASS 0.6.0 T

ABOVE: PTR&D Nos 14 and 15 at Duffryn Yard coaling stage circa 1922. The bunker rails of No. 15 have been filled in and the engine has been fitted with GWR boiler mountings. *Author's collection*

RIGHT: PTR&D 0-6-0ST No. 3 with a train of loaded Elders Navigation Collieries' wagons at Margam circa 1905. *NM&GW*

PTR&D locomotives, especially the smaller ones in pre-grouping days, were particularly camera shy. This is former PTR&D No. 3, which came from Stephenson's early in 1898, after modifications including GWR-style chimney, safety valve cover and enlarged bunker. It was renumbered to GWR 815 at the grouping and lasted until November 1930 when it was sold into industrial use. *Author's collection*

by December 1897, and Nos 3, 7 and 8 early in 1898, and the directors enforced the penalty clause in the contract.

Walter James Hosgood was appointed to the new position of locomotive and machinery superintendent of the PTR&D, starting 1st March 1897, and was responsible for locomotives, carriages, wagons and hydraulic machinery. Hosgood had spent the previous seven years on the Barry Railway working under his brother John

Hosgood, latterly as assistant chief engineer, and before that one year with Sharp, Stewart & Co. in Glasgow.

In June 1897, even before the first two 0-6-0ST locomotives had been delivered, Meik sought tenders for three more of this type. The directors would only countenance one more, No. 15, which was ordered from Stephenson's for £1,945 in September 1897[15] and delivered in the second half of 1898. These three engines, builder's

Four of the PTR&D's eleven 0-6-2 tank engines were sold to neighbouring companies, Nos 4 and 7 going to the R&SBR in October 1901, becoming that company's Nos 23 and 24, and Nos 5 and 6 to the Neath & Brecon Railway in June 1903, becoming Nos 10 and 9. This is former PTR&D No. 6 as N&BR No. 9, seemingly in original condition apart from the new number plate. *Author's collection*

One of the former PTR&D 0-6-2 tank engines which was sold to the R&SBR standing alongside Duffryn Rhondda Sidings, later East, signal box circa 1906.

Author's collection

GWR weight diagram for the PTR&D 0-6-2T engines dated 3rd April 1908, later Diagram W. The two engines sold to the N&BR were included in this diagram, but the two that went to the R&SBR were assigned Diagram U owing to differences in boiler heating surfaces.

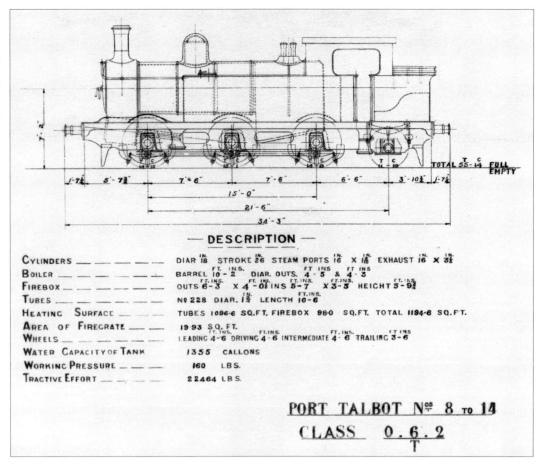

Nos 2862, 2863 and 2901, had 16 inch cylinders and 4 foot 0 inch wheels, and delivered a tractive effort of 15,230 lb.

As with the saddle tanks, Meik sought tenders in June 1897 for five additional large tank engines. At first the directors only authorised three, Nos 9–11, to be purchased from Stephenson's for £2,596 each, but in August 1897 they authorised three more, Nos 12–14, which were ordered in September 1897. Nos 9–13 were delivered during the latter half of 1898, and No. 14 early in 1899. The extended delivery times were a direct consequence of the business boom which coincided with the aftermath of a damaging strike in the engineering industry from July 1897 to January 1898.[16] These eleven 0-6-2T locomotives, builders Nos 2864–2868, 2895–2900 respectively, had 18 inch cylinders and 4 foot 6 inch coupled wheels and produced a tractive effort of 21,215 lb.

Events for these engines then took an unusual course. In May 1901 the secretary of the R&SBR was instructed to write to the GWR, ByR, PTR&D and TVR companies regarding the possibility of hiring one or two locomotives.[17] Four of these companies were unable to lend locomotives, and the PTR&D's offer to hire out two at £5 each per day was declined as being much too high. A revised offer of two locomotives at £20 each per week of six 12-hour days manned by their own crews, payable monthly in advance, was accepted in June 1901, and Nos 4 and 7 were handed over to the R&SBR on 1st July 1901.[18] In August 1901 the accountant reported a probable negative balance on the capital account of £16,049, and the directors immediately resolved that superfluous engines were to be sold. The two on hire, plus an 0-8-2T then being built by Sharp, Stewart (see page 200) were offered to the R&SBR,

the asking price for the 0-6-2Ts being £2,250 each. This was declined, with a counter-offer of £1,750 each being made, and after further bargaining the sale was settled in October 1901 at £2,000 each plus £240 each for the balance of the hire charge, the engines becoming R&SBR Nos 23 and 24 respectively. They had previously been examined by the engineers of the TVR and North's Navigation Collieries, who pronounced themselves thoroughly satisfied with them.[19] A further offer of two similar locomotives was declined by the R&SBR in August 1902, but in June 1903 Nos 5 and 6 were sold to the Neath & Brecon Railway for £4,000 plus free spare parts worth £70, becoming N&BR Nos 10 and 9 respectively.

Numbers 4–7 each had one general repair at Duffryn Yard before they were sold. The remaining seven were overhauled seemingly as necessary, but for the most part details are lacking. Rather surprisingly, No. 8 was given a new boiler during its 1902 overhaul.[20] Tyre wear was a particular problem for the 0-6-2Ts, and in February 1907 the directors considered purchasing two spare sets of wheels and axles for this class of locomotives so as to avoid the need to take them out of service for any length of time. In the event eight leading and trailing and four driving wheel tyres for each of the Stephenson-built classes and four radial wheel tyres for the larger engines were ordered from Messrs Cammell Laird in April 1907. Nos 9, 10 and 12 were re-tyred during their 1907 overhauls.[21]

PASSENGER ENGINES, NOS 36 AND 37

When the passenger services authorised by the 1894 Act commenced on 14th February 1898,[22] trains had to be worked by locomotives intended primarily for shunting or working mineral trains. In March

ABOVE: PTR&D No. 10 was fitted with GWR boiler mountings in the 1910s and renumbered GWR No. 185 at the grouping. The engine was photographed in this condition at Duffryn Yard on 1st March 1924, and was condemned in August 1929. *Author's collection*

BELOW: As well as GWR boiler mountings, PTR&D No. 12 was fitted with top feed and a larger bunker and is seen here as GWR No. 187 on the Sales List at Swindon in 1935. *Author's collection*

1898, in an attempt to address this issue, Hosgood reported on the possibility of hiring a suitable engine from the ByR, having no doubt already negotiated with his brother John, and was instructed to endeavour to obtain this engine for £2 per day with the option of purchase. The terms were apparently agreed and Barry No. 37 was hired in June 1898. This was one of the small 'C' Class of 2-4-0 tank engines built by Sharp, Stewart in 1890 for local passenger work, with 5 foot 3 inch coupled wheels and 17 inch cylinders, giving a tractive effort of 14,040 lb. The ByR's asking price for No. 37 of £1,100 was accepted and the engine was transferred to the PTR&D by August 1898. For no apparent reason the number was retained although new plates were provided. A second engine of the same class, No. 52, was offered by the ByR in August 1898, this one for £850 plus the option of fitting trailing wheels for £350.

ABOVE: PTR No. 14 at Duffryn Yard on 25th April 1910. By this date the bunker rails had been filled in and larger front sandboxes provided, to which the builders plate had been moved. *Author's collection*

BELOW: PTR No. 14 carrying GWR boiler mountings at Duffryn Yard coaling stage circa 1922. *Author's collection*

This offer was accepted and the work of extending the rear frames by 4 feet to accommodate the radial wheels and enlarged water and coal space was carried out at Barry along with similar alterations to the other two members of the class. The resulting 2-4-2T was delivered to the PTR&D in January 1899, becoming PTR No. 36. In February 1899 the directors deferred unspecified alterations to No. 37, but probably conversion to a 2-4-2T, until further notice.

It soon became apparent that these two engines were not in the best of condition and in March 1900 new cylinders for both were purchased from Sharp, Stewart. At the same time tenders for new boilers were sought, and in May 1900 that of Hudswell, Clarke & Co. for two boilers with fittings for £780 each was accepted. No. 37 was reboilered in April–May 1901 and No. 36 in June that year. These new boilers operated at the higher pressure of 160 psi, giving

ABOVE: The PTR&D purchased Barry Railway 2-4-0T No. 52 in 1898 and took up the option for conversion to a 2-4-2T by that company. The engine is seen here in its original condition on the Barry Railway.

Courtesy Brian Miller

BELOW: PTR&D 2-4-2T No. 36 circa 1900. Note the armorial device on the cabside.

The Railway Magazine

an increased tractive effort of 14,975 lb. The boiler taken off No. 36 was sold to the Port Talbot Iron & Steel Co. for £200. General overhauls were given at intervals, No. 37 being re-tyred during its visit to the workshops in 1903.[23]

0-8-2 SIDE TANK ENGINES NOS 17–21

By early 1899 the PTR&D possessed eighteen locomotives to work its lines. The January 1899 working timetable gives no information of the particular duties of these locomotives. Apart from *Penylan* and No. 1, any of the newly ordered engines could take an appropriate load through to or from Pwllcarne at the head of the Garw Valley where International and Ocean Collieries were situated. Banking and double heading of both Up and Down trains was provided for:

Thirty loads can be worked down from East End to Duffryn, provided that two engines are attached.

When the load renders it necessary for a Bank Engine to be used with Down trains, the Assistant Engine must be in front from Pontyrhyl Junction to Maesteg, in rear from Maesteg to the East end of Tunnel, and in front from the East end of Tunnel to Duffryn Junction.

When Assistant Engines are used with Up Trains from Duffryn Junction to East End of Tunnel, the Bank Engine must be attached in rear.

It appears that the existing locomotives could cope with the traffic on offer, but only with recourse to assistant engines. In October 1898 the Board declined an offer of new locomotives from Sharp, Stewart which possibly arose from Hosgood's previous association with that company. The next month the directors instructed the secretary to obtain a joint report from Probert, the traffic manager, and the locomotive superintendent regarding new engines, and that drawings be prepared as soon as convenient, so that tenders could be obtained. So began the process by which the PTR&D acquired its most distinctive locomotives, the five 0-8-2 tank engines. Voluminous correspondence was generated,[24] and much directorial and managerial effort was expended in achieving this end. Hosgood's plan was considered by the Board at its meeting in April 1899 but was not approved. Instead he was authorised to get offers from American and other builders to provide engines to their own designs, with the object of running longer trains through with only one engine. Consequently, a specification for locomotive side tank engines to handle the anticipated increase in traffic was

PTR&D No. 36 at an unidentified location. Note the non-standard numerals on the chimney and the jack on the tank top. *Author's collection*

ABOVE: No. 36 was little altered by the GWR and is seen at Swindon as GWR No. 1326 on 27th July 1923.

Author's collection

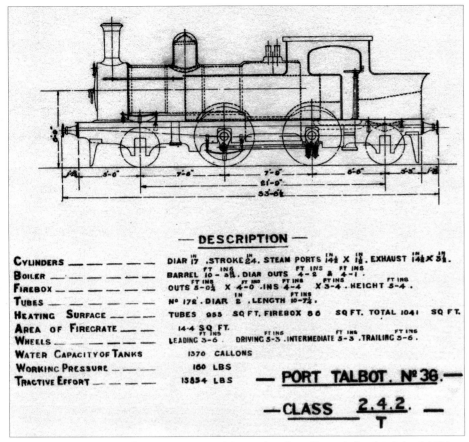

GWR weight diagrams for PTR&D Nos 36 (Above) and 37 (Below) dated 3rd April 1908, subsequently Diagrams P and M respectively, differing only in the alterations required in producing a 2-4-2T.

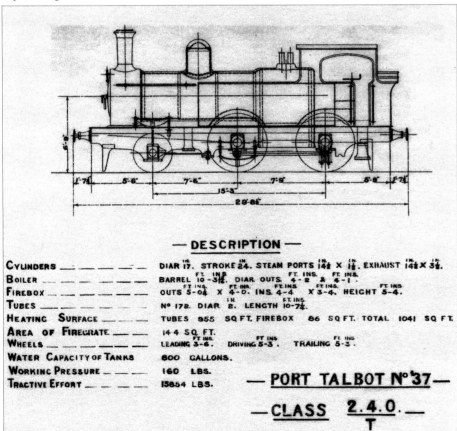

prepared. The specification ran to fourteen typed foolscap pages, and included the following clauses, some of which must have alluded to existing practise, particularly those regarding livery and driving position:

Number of Engines

The number of engines to be made under this specification is five, and the price and time of delivery shall be as given in the foregoing tender.

General & Detail Drawings

The contractor to submit a fully dimensioned drawing when tendering, showing distribution of weights on each axle (loaded and empty). Detail drawings of all parts of the engines to be submitted for approval before any of the work is put in hand.

Locomotive Engineer may give instructions, or make alterations

The Locomotive Engineer shall have full power to inspect, or appoint any other person to inspect, the engines while in progress of building. He shall also have power to reject any materials or workmanship which he may think imperfect, or to make any alterations in same which he may consider necessary, and any alterations made by the contractor shall not affect the contract, or interfere with prices, terms or penalties agreed upon.

Completion, Delivery, Mileage & Payment

The contractor must deliver the engines to the Coy at Port Talbot, carriage paid, complete and ready for work, and each engine, before payment, will be required to run 2000 miles on the Company's Railway, doing the ordinary work of the line, before being certified by the Locomotive Engineer. All repairs and alterations necessary during the time of such running to be performed by the contractor at his own cost.

Completion & Penalty

Should the Contractor fail to complete any Engine contracted for within the time specified and agreed upon, he shall forfeit to the Company the sum of Five Pounds (£5) per Engine per day for each day, by which the completion of each engine or any Engines shall exceed the time in each case appointed.

Duty on Engines

The engines will be required to haul a load of 300 tons, exclusive of weight

ABOVE: PTR&D No. 37 seems to have eluded the camera in pre-grouping days. This engine was moved from Newport to Swindon in 1917 and is seen here as GWR No. 1189 working a Swindon Junction to Swindon Town service in the 1920s. *Author's collection*

BELOW: PTR&D No. 37 as GWR No. 1189 at Swindon as in February 1927 after withdrawal. *Author's collection*

TABLE 9.1: DETAILS OF TENDERS SUBMITTED MAY 1899

MAKER	TOTAL WEIGHT	COUPLED WHEEL DIAMETER	WHEEL ARRANGEMENT	PRICE EACH
Sharp, Stewart & Co.	72 tons	4ft 3in	0-8-2	£3,350
Kitson & Co.	80 tons	4ft 4in	0-8-2	£3,900
Vulcan Foundry	74 tons	4ft 0in	0-8-2	£3,935
Neilson, Reid & Co. (1)	83 tons	4ft 3in	0-8-4	£4,375
Neilson, Reid & Co. (2)	92 tons	4ft 3in	0-10-4	£4,699
Beyer, Peacock & Co.	79 tons	4ft 3in	0-8-4	£4,475
R. Stephenson & Co.	same as present type of engine		0-6-2	£3,047
Richmond Loco Works, Richmond VA, USA	not stated	4ft 0in	0-6-0	£2,190
Cooke Loco Co., Paterson, NJ, USA	72 tons	4ft 3in	0-6-4, later amended to 0-8-2	£2,750
Baldwin Locomotive Works, Philadelphia, USA	73 tons	3ft 10in	0-8-4	£3,350

of engine, up a bank of 1 in 40 for a distance of 4 miles at a speed of 12 miles per hour. The ruling curves on this being not less than 10 chains. Also to haul a load of 800 tons, exclusive of weight of engine, up a bank of 1 in 75 for distance of 2½ miles at a speed of 12 miles per hour; the ruling curves on this being not less than 12 chains. In designing the engines, makers must arrange these to work over 7 chains. The section rail these engines have to work over is 75 lbs per yard.

Valve Motion

… The motion to be reversed by lever and quadrant fixed on the tank on the right side of the engine.

Painting

Before any paint is applied the whole surface of iron must be thoroughly cleaned from rust and scale. The boiler is to receive two coats of red oxide paint before being lagged. The whole of the boiler, lagging plates, frames, buffer beams, wheels side tanks, bunker, and cab to receive two coats of lead color [sic], and the whole of the surface to be stopped all over with hard stopping, then to receive four coats of filling up, with the exception of the lagging plates, which are to receive two coats, which is to be rubbed down and faced, then to receive one coat of lead color and two coats of brown (sample of which will be supplied by the P.T.R. & Dks. Coy) to be then picked out and lined, and finally to receive four coats of best copal engine varnish, manufactured by Messrs Docker Bros, Birmingham. The inside of the frames & cross stays to have three coats of vermillion and two coats of best engine varnish as above. Inside of cab to be painted to sample. The axles to have two coats of white lead and two coats of black paint.

Number Plates

A brass frame with letters and numbers to be fixed on each side of tank, also plain brass numbers at back of coal bunk, and front of chimney of engine.

Advertisements inviting tenders were placed in *Engineering* and *The Engineer* on 28th April and 5th May 1899 giving a deadline of 15th May 1899. Although tight, this timetable seems to have been typical for the period. Only the successful tender has survived, but a hand-written summary table of all those received was prepared, as shown in Table 9.1.

Six British makers submitted tenders, one of them with two propositions. The extended delivery times quoted by these makers, a minimum of nine months and up to two years, were a consequence of the business boom which had caused the long delivery times for of Nos 9–14. The three American makers who tendered were in a position to offer much shorter delivery times. The 0-8-2T type was proposed by three makers including Sharp, Stewart who had supplied seven to the ByR in 1896, the first examples of this wheel arrangement in the UK. The 0-8-4T (three makers) and 0-10-4T types would have been novel, and would have made an impressive sight working hard up the 1 in 40 gradient to Bryn. Fortunately, Beyer, Peacock's drawing showing the rather ungainly 0-8-4T proposed for the PTR&D has survived (see page 201). Stephenson's proposed to provide more of the 0-6-2Ts already supplied, but this offer was not considered further. Richmond Locomotive Works offered an 0-6-0T which would not meet the haulage requirement, but nevertheless was included on a shortlist of tenders drawn up by Knott for consideration at the next Board meeting, presumably on the grounds of cost and delivery time. The others included on the shortlist were those from Vulcan Foundry & Co., Sharp, Stewart & Co., Kitson & Co., Neilson, Reid & Co. and Cooke Locomotive and Machine Co.

Cooke Locomotive's tender was submitted by their London agents, Messrs Thos W Ford & Co. of Palace Chambers, 9 Bridge Street, Westminster, the accompanying letter being dated 13th May 1899. Mr Ford, who spent ten years in the Locomotive Department of the Great Eastern Railway up to 1897, played a prominent part in the events that followed. On the reverse of the tender was handwritten:

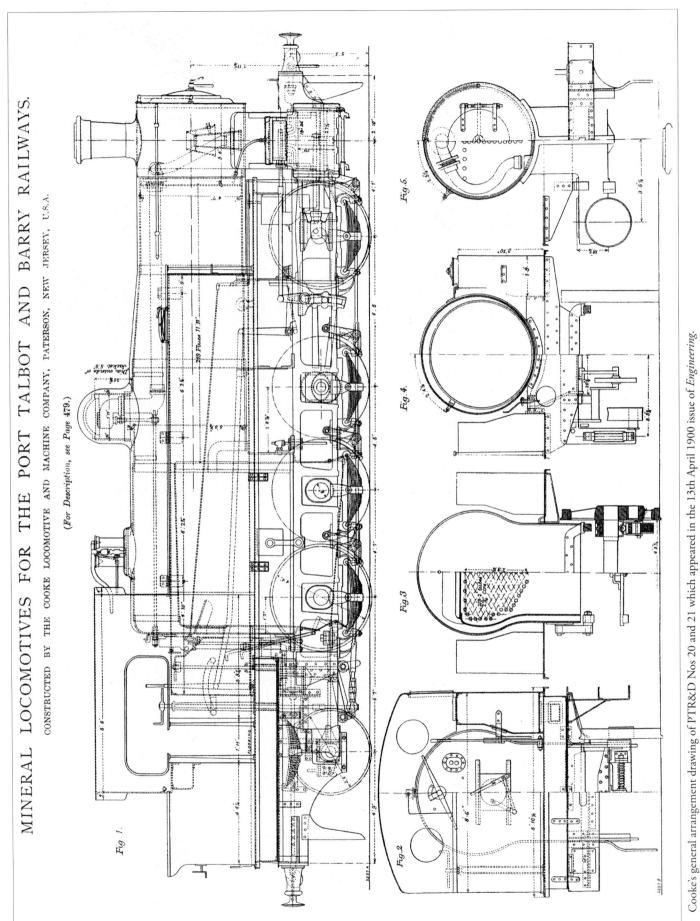

MINERAL LOCOMOTIVES FOR THE PORT TALBOT AND BARRY RAILWAYS.

CONSTRUCTED BY THE COOKE LOCOMOTIVE AND MACHINE COMPANY, PATERSON, NEW JERSEY, U.S.A.

(For Description, see Page 479.)

Fig. 1.

Fig. 2.

Fig. 3.

Fig. 4.

Fig. 5.

Cooke's general arrangement drawing of PTR&D Nos 20 and 21 which appeared in the 13th April 1900 issue of *Engineering*.

The drawing submitted is to be taken as the type of engine to be built, the dimensions are the Barry Co.'s dimensions but these will be increased so that the engine will fulfil the haulage conditions specified, thereby making them very much heavier machines.

This was a reference to the five 0-6-2 tank locomotives ordered by the ByR from Cooke Locomotive in April 1899.[25] The summary table gave the total number of wheels as ten, with six driving wheels. This figure was subsequently altered to eight, suggesting that the engines as originally proposed – enlarged 0-6-4T versions of those ordered for the ByR – were deemed unsuitable and that the design was subsequently altered to 0-8-2T.

At the Board meeting held on 17th May 1899, and on the basis of somewhat limited information, Cooke's tender was accepted, subject to the locomotive superintendent being satisfied as to all details, for two locomotives only, modified to the company's requirements, for delivery in July next, with an option for three or five more for delivery in September. The PTR&D thus joined the Midland, the Great Central, the Great Northern and the Barry companies in buying American-built engines as a result of the 1899 locomotive famine.[26]

The modifications required become clear in correspondence generated during a dispute over the performance of the engines. In February 1900 Messrs Ford & Co. wrote to Knott:

Messrs Cooke have advised us that in their original proposition to your Company for the locomotives they have recently supplied, they undertook to build six-wheels coupled engines that would fulfil the conditions of your line. Subsequently, however, Mr. Hosgood asked that an additional pair of driving wheels be should be added making the engines eight wheels coupled instead of six. This of course considerably increased the cost to Cooke's over the amount they estimated at the time they sent in their proposition. Mr. Hosgood also asked for a further addition to these engines, which was not agreed to at the time the order was taken, viz. that the engines should be fitted with Automatic Vacuum Brake. Inasmuch as our Mr. Ford at the Meeting of your Board heard the request that an eight-wheels coupled engine should be supplied and took no exception to it at the time, we feel that although Messrs Cooke look to us for payment we cannot ask your company to incur this, but as the supplying and fitting of the Automatic Vacuum Brake was additional to what was asked for, that you will agree with us that this is a proper charge for your Company to meet.

It is not clear why the vacuum brake was requested. As far as is known the engines were never used on passenger trains, and it was removed soon after they were delivered. The PTR&D's solicitor, Mr Cheston, became involved and in March 1900 expressed the opinion that:

[I]t is not wise to have a specification for an engine and for the Board to suppose that they are making a tender on it and then for the Loco Superintendent to alter the kind of engine, so as to give an opportunity the builder to evade his liability. Your letter

Builder's photograph of PTR&D No. 20 decked out as specified. Note the short-lived vacuum brake, the flangeless centre pairs of drivers – the gap between them being a mere one inch – and the brass numerals on the chimney. An obvious feature of the new engines was the valance under the cab and bunker. Neither the general arrangement drawing nor the GWR weight diagram show it, and one wonders if it was a late addition to improve their appearance.
Alco Historic Photos

ABOVE: Views of the PTR&D's American locomotives in service in their original condition are extremely rare. This is No. 20 at Duffryn Yard circa November 1900. Note the jack on the tank top.
The Railway Magazine

RIGHT: PTR&D No. 20 with an Up train of empty coal wagons on the 1 in 40 gradient near Tynyffram, circa November 1900. The train is presumably stationary as the driver appears to be on the footplate oiling the motion. *The Railway Magazine*

of 17th May to Messrs Ford & Co. [placing the order] was all in order but in their reply of 18th May they did not accept it and there was no sufficient contract.

Hosgood had expressed himself satisfied with the general dimensions and design of the engines on 24th May 1899. Thus it appears that eight-coupled engines were first proposed at the Board meeting of 17th May and confirmed on the 24th May. At the May 1899 meeting it was also agreed that a trial of working heavy trains using two locomotives and no goods brake van was not to be proceeded with, presumably because more powerful engines were imminent. A delivery time of at most two and a half months

was extremely optimistic, especially as the design was only approved by the directors on 21st June 1899.

The two locomotives were shipped on 7th October[27] and arrived at Bristol on 6th November 1899.[28] The form in which they were transported is not recorded, although one imagines they were completely dismantled and packed into crates, the largest component being the boiler/firebox. Arrangements were made for the engines to be erected at Barry, where there were "good appliances for the purpose". Hosgood's December report noted that they would be delivered "the week after next", that is, the week beginning 25th December.[29] Hosgood's report dated 19th January 1900 noted that the Cooke engines, Nos 20 and 21, maker's Nos

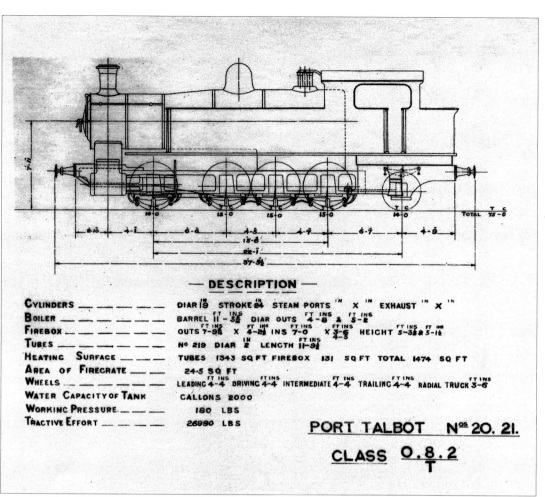

LEFT: GWR weight diagram for the Cooke-built 0-8-2T engines Nos 20 and 21 dated 3rd April 1908. These locomotives were only briefly under GWR control in this form.

DESCRIPTION

CYLINDERS	DIAR 19 IN STROKE 24 IN STEAM PORTS IN X IN EXHAUST IN X IN
BOILER	BARREL 11-5½ FT INS DIAR OUTS 4-8 FT INS & 5-2 FT INS
FIREBOX	OUTS 7-9½ FT INS X 4-2½ FT INS INS 7-0 FT INS X 3-6 FT INS / 4-5 HEIGHT 5-3½ & 5-1½
TUBES	No 219 DIAR 2 IN LENGTH 11-9½ FT INS
HEATING SURFACE	TUBES 1343 SQ FT FIREBOX 131 SQ FT TOTAL 1474 SQ FT
AREA OF FIREGRATE	24·5 SQ FT
WHEELS	LEADING 4-4 FT INS DRIVING 4-4 FT INS INTERMEDIATE 4-4 FT INS TRAILING 4-4 FT INS RADIAL TRUCK 3-6 FT INS
WATER CAPACITY OF TANK	GALLONS 2000
WORKING PRESSURE	180 LBS
TRACTIVE EFFORT	26990 LBS

PORT TALBOT Nos 20, 21.

CLASS O.8.2 / T

BELOW: PTR&D 0-8-2T No. 20 after being fitted with a GWR standard No. 4 boiler and modified firebox, circa August 1908. The locomotive is finished in the livery originally specified apart from brass numerals on the chimney, and carries the PTR&D's armorial device.

2492 and 2493, had been delivered, No. 20 arriving first.[30] They must have arrived earlier that month as the Stock Returns indicate no locomotive additions between June and December 1899.

The new engines sported a distinctly hybrid appearance, the smokebox, boiler fittings, side tanks, cab and bunker having a British look, the remainder, including the bar frames, being typically American. One noticeable feature was the coupled-wheel spacing of 6 feet 6 inches + 4 feet 5 inches + 4 feet 7 inches, which with a driving wheel diameter of 4 feet 4 inches, required the two centre pairs to be flangeless, this arrangement presumably arising from Cooke's engineers having to squeeze a fourth driving axle into their original design. Another obvious feature of the new engines was the valance under the cab and bunker. Neither the general arrangement drawing[31] nor the GWR weight diagram show it, and it may have been a late addition to improve their appearance. With 19 inch cylinders, Nos 20 and 21 had a tractive effort of 25,490 lb. The choice of these numbers is something of a mystery; 1–15 were already in use and 16 may have been allotted to, although not carried by, *Penylan*. Reserving 17–19 for future acquisitions seems somewhat idiosyncratic.

At their meeting of 24th January 1900 the directors instructed Messrs Probert and Hosgood to make a joint test of the American engines with thirty loaded wagons and a 20-ton brake van over the Duffryn line. The working arrangements were altered accordingly, the existing limit being twenty-four loaded wagons.[32] It was immediately clear that performance was far below that specified.

Initially this was due to the boiler pressure being set at 150 rather than 180 psi, which was soon rectified. Also, at Hosgood's request, they had been fitted with Jenkins' patent blastpipe which had been found to be unsatisfactory on the Barry engines. More seriously, early in March 1900, a Mr Evans, Cooke's representative who had been supervising the erection of the locomotives, found that two steam pipe joints required to be made good, a fault discovered five weeks previously. The Duffryn Yard foreman had failed to do this, causing much unnecessary delay. Once these problems had been dealt with both engines were able to take a load of thirty loaded wagons plus van, about 500 tons, up a 1 in 75 gradient. This was far short of that specified, but in Hosgood's view was the most that could be achieved.

Despite the improvements the directors were still not entirely happy with the performance of the American engines. At their meeting on 21st March it was resolved that henceforth they would be daily loaded to the utmost of their capacity, that a record be kept of their work, and that a joint report be submitted to the Board at their next meeting. Cheston was authorised to see Ford as to what allowance would be made to the company for non-compliance with the specification. Messrs Ford submitted their statement of account for two locomotives on 30th March. Following discussions with the solicitor, the PTR&D agreed to take over the engines as they then stood, provided Messrs Ford waived all claims for extras (vacuum brakes, etc.), bore the whole of the cost of erection by the ByR and repaid the whole of the sum already paid by the company

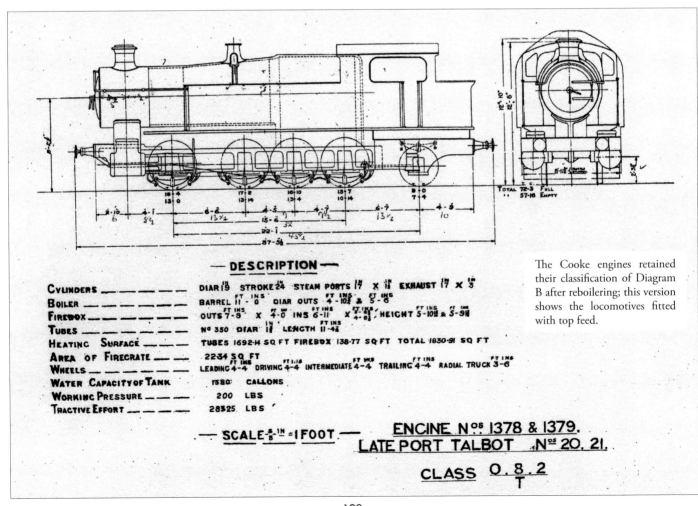

The Cooke engines retained their classification of Diagram B after reboilering; this version shows the locomotives fitted with top feed.

ABOVE: PTR&D No. 20 as GWR No. 1378 at Duffryn Yard on 26th May 1926. By this date the engine had been fitted with top feed and the bunker had been enlarged. Note the unaltered bunker of PTR&D No. 21/GWR No. 1379 on the right. *Author's collection*

BELOW: With connecting rods off, No. 20 looks a sorry sight at Danygraig on 16th October 1927, but in fact it was returned to service and not withdrawn until fourteen months later. *Author's collection*

Author's collection

PTR&D 0-8-2T No. 21 with a partial view of a Tonhir wagon, circa 1912.

PTR&D No. 21 at Duffryn Yard on 25th April 1910. To the right is a partial view of PTR&D 2-plank open wagon No. 100, one of a batch of twenty purchased secondhand in April 1898; behind that is what appears to be an S J Claye-built PTR&D open wagon No. 8 of 1896. *Author's collection*

for carriage from Bristol to Port Talbot. This was accepted and the contract sum of £5,500 was paid on 25th April 1900. The time penalty, which would have saved the company about £1,000 as the two engines were delivered at least three months late, was either overlooked or ignored. In the meantime, at their meeting on 18th April the directors noted that the American engines were working satisfactorily.

Both engines suffered failures to both pistons in late 1900/early 1901, suggesting a serious design or material fault, and one of No. 20's firebox stays broke. Both fireboxes were strengthened and the engines were reported in April 1901 to be working well.[33] The R&SBR must have been impressed by their performance, as in April 1901 its locomotive superintendent was instructed to ascertain if one could be loaned for trial, apparently to no avail.[34] Complete sets of tyres for both engines were ordered in September 1906 and fitted at their next general overhauls.

Hosgood tendered his resignation in December 1904 and left in March 1905 to take up the position of locomotive, carriage and wagon superintendent of Rhodesian Railways. He was replaced by Albert Holger Hertz as locomotive and mechanical superintendent reporting to the general manager, Lowther. Hertz, who was born in Copenhagen, had been engineer in charge of the PTR&D's hydraulic machinery and marine plant since 1894.

By February 1906 it had become clear that the boiler/fireboxes were the Achilles' heels of these locomotives. Hertz reported that No. 21 was undergoing extensive repairs to its boiler, requiring new tube plates and new tubes, which took over one month to complete. Then, in March, he reported that No. 20 was undergoing heavy

repairs to its boiler, including new tube plates and tubes, and a new smokebox and door, this work not being completed until the end of June 1906. Hertz returned to this theme in March 1907 when he noted that since the American locomotives had been under his care (and previously), considerable trouble had been experienced with their boilers.[35] Several patches had been fitted to the fireboxes and over 70 per cent of the stays had been renewed from time to time. No. 20's boiler was currently under repair and a large copper patch, 5 feet 6 inches long and 10 inches wide, was being fitted. He considered these repairs to be no more than temporary, and it would be necessary to fit new boilers in the near future. Hertz had satisfied himself that it would be advantageous to adopt the Brotan water-tube boiler for the engines, but nothing came of this proposal. Both engines required further boiler repairs later that year.

By then a solution to the boiler problem was in sight. Nos 20 and 21 were the first to benefit under the terms of the agreement for the hire of the PTR&D's locomotives and rolling stock by the GWR.[36] Hertz reported on 13th March 1908 that these two locomotives had been dispatched to Swindon,[37] travelling via the Severn & Wye Joint Railway over the Severn Bridge.[38] In July 1908 they were fitted with Standard No. 4 Belpaire boilers with fireboxes modified to be 9 inches longer and having horizontal grates which rested on the bar frames.[39] The boiler pressure was raised to 200 psi, giving an increased tractive effort of 28,325 lb. Standard GWR copper-capped chimneys and brass safety valve covers were utilised, but otherwise the engines were unmodified. Initially the boiler feed was in the same position as on the original engines, the

ABOVE AND BELOW: PTR&D No. 21 with a short train including Ton Hir wagons standing on the wrong line in the Down loop at East End of Tunnel. Note the signal box supplied by the Railway Signal Co. The Ton Hir Colliery Co.'s siding connected to the Up loop at a point opposite the goods brake van.

Courtesy John Lyons

RIGHT: A very clean-looking PTR&D No. 21 standing in the Up loop at Maesteg opposite Salisbury Road, possibly having just shunted a train of empties into North's siding about half a mile up the line. *Author's collection*

BELOW: PTR&D No. 21, this time at North's Junction, Maesteg, at a later date fitted with top feed.
Clifford Collection, courtesy C C Green

front bottom of the firebox; this was later altered to the normal top feed arrangement. Nos 20 and 21 returned to Duffryn Yard in September and August 1908 respectively. The livery remained as hitherto, with the addition of the company's crest on the cab sides.

Despite the earlier problems, the directors at their meeting held on 21st March 1900 authorised their solicitor to negotiate with Messrs Ford for the extension of the option for Cooke Locomotive to supply three or five more engines at the same price but with haulage and speed capacity definitely named in the specification. Cooke's had already foreseen the need to modify the design. The outcome was a scheme to construct a 2-8-2 tank engine with equalising beam suspension, which if built would have been the first of this type in the UK. The driving wheels remained at 4 feet

4 inches, but tractive effort was increased to 30,600 lb, presumably by increasing the cylinder diameter and raising the boiler pressure, such that it would haul 452 US tons up a gradient 1 in 40 and 799 US tons up 1 in 75. The price was given as £3,150 each for delivery in September 1900.

Further negotiations over specification, price and delivery delayed any consideration of this proposition by the directors until their June meeting. In the meantime Mr S H Byass, one of their number, produced at the end of May 1900 a report in which he compared the working costs of the American engines with those of the existing 0-6-2 tank engines. The former working singly were routinely taking thirty empties from the docks to Pontycymmer in 50 minutes and returning with thirty loads to Maesteg and twenty-five down to

PTR&D No. 21 at Duffryn Yard circa 1921.

Author's collection

ABOVE: PTR&D No. 21 as GWR No. 1379 at Duffryn Yard circa 1927. Unusually, the locomotive is facing towards the engine shed, rather than the normal Up direction. These engines were less powerful but more restricted in route than the Sharp, Stewart locomotives, and were classified Red D.

Author's collection

BELOW: PTR&D No. 21/GWR No. 1379 was condemned in April 1929 and is seen at Duffryn Yard at about that time.   *Author's collection*

the docks in 65 minutes. Two of the smaller engines required 70 minutes to take thirty empties to Pontycymmer and 90 minutes to take thirty loads to the docks. The saving in favour of the American engines was considerable: 60 lb of coal per mile as against 94, as well as in labour and journey time. Mr Byass concluded his report by stating that in his opinion there was no doubt that the American engines reduced working costs very materially, but he was not so convinced of the cheapness of the new offer and had instructed Hosgood to invite tenders from English makers for an engine of similar capacity, the tenders being returnable on the 9th June 1900.

As before, the makers were given about two weeks to return their tenders, presumably to the specification originally drawn up. The submitted tenders considered at the Board meeting on 19th June 1900 consisted of:

Kitson & Co.	£2,995
Cooke Locomotive	£3,150
Sharp, Stewart & Co.	£3,490
Beyer, Peacock & Co.	£3,580
R Stephenson & Co.	£3,769
Neilson, Reid & Co.	£3,975
Vulcan Foundry Co.	£4,165

Unfortunately, details of most of the proposed engines are unknown; the makers may well have resubmitted their previous designs with a price increase. The directors resolved that Messrs Sharp, Stewart & Co. be given an order for two large locomotives provided they agreed to carry out the necessary alterations required in their design, and that one of the principals of the firm made an inspection of the PTR to satisfy himself as to the company's exact requirements. Thus, after more than five months of fruitless negotiation with Cooke's, a rerun of the process used a year earlier produced a satisfactory result in three weeks.

At the next Board meeting on 25th July, Hosgood reported that he had arranged to his satisfaction all details of the large engines. It was resolved to increase the order with Sharp, Stewart to three engines, as per the tender, with the modifications mutually agreed upon – subject, however, to Mr Byass' approval of the form of agreement. In fact, the order had already been entered in Sharp, Stewart's books on 16th July (order no. E1179) for delivery in fourteen months, being noted as generally as order no. E1071 (that being the Barry Railway's 'H' Class 0-8-2 tank engines ordered in 1895),[40] the principal modifications being a six inches longer firebox, a six inches shorter rear tank and coal bunker, and a low blast pipe and hood. The PTR&D was evidently prepared to wait

PTR&D 0-8-2T No. 17 circa 1910, shunting at North's Junction. Driver F Walsingham, fireman S Lane.   *Author's collection*

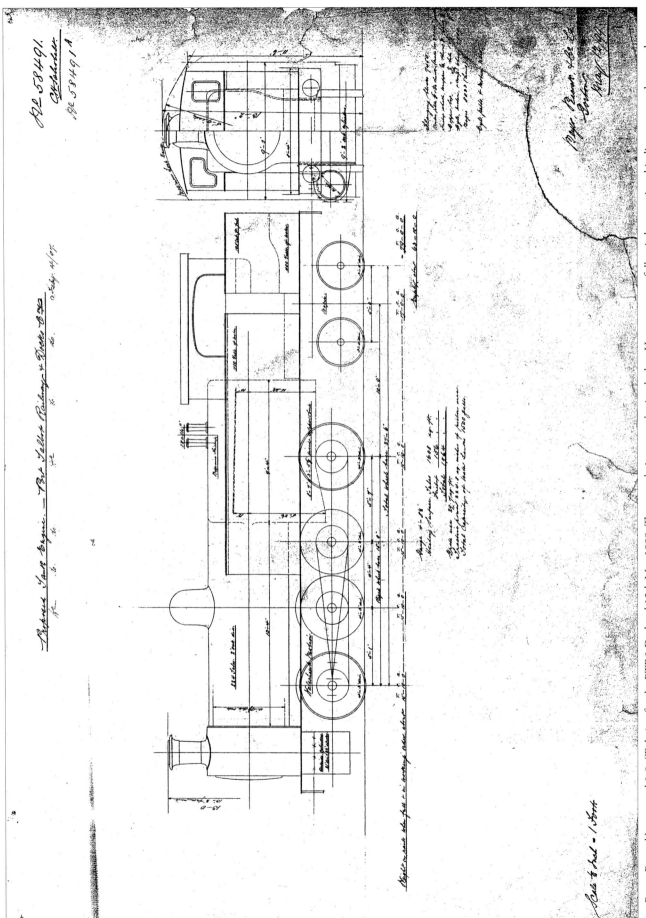

Beyer, Peacock's proposed 0-8-4T design for the PTR&D, dated 12th May 1899. The same design was submitted when Hertz unsuccessfully tried to convince his directors to order more large tank engines. Note that this too was planned with the 2nd and 3rd pairs of driving wheels flangeless.
Courtesy the Museum of Science and Industry in Manchester

for urgently needed engines rather than risk buying American again. The engines, Nos 17–19, maker's Nos 4794–6, were reported as being delivered in November 1901,[41] and the directors received a satisfactory report on No. 19 in December, although they were not added to stock until early in 1902. With 4 foot 3 inch wheels, 20 inch cylinders, and a boiler pressure of 180 psi, these 0-8-2 tank engines were the most powerful locomotives purchased by the PTR&D, with a tractive effort of 31,200 lb. To ease their passage through curves the third pair of driving wheels was flangeless.

These locomotives were far more reliable than those built by

Cooke and did not require a general overhaul until May 1904.[42] As with the smaller classes, re-tyring became necessary and was carried out in 1906/7. During this work small cracks were observed in the cylinders of Nos 18 and 19, which was attributed to the throttling of exhaust steam in the blast pipe.[43] A new type of blast pipe was fitted which considerably improved the performance of the engines,[44] such that they could haul thirty-five loaded wagons over the main line, rather than thirty which was the previous maximum.[45] The only recorded serious failure of the engines occurred at Maesteg in June 1907 when two of No. 17's coupling rods broke.

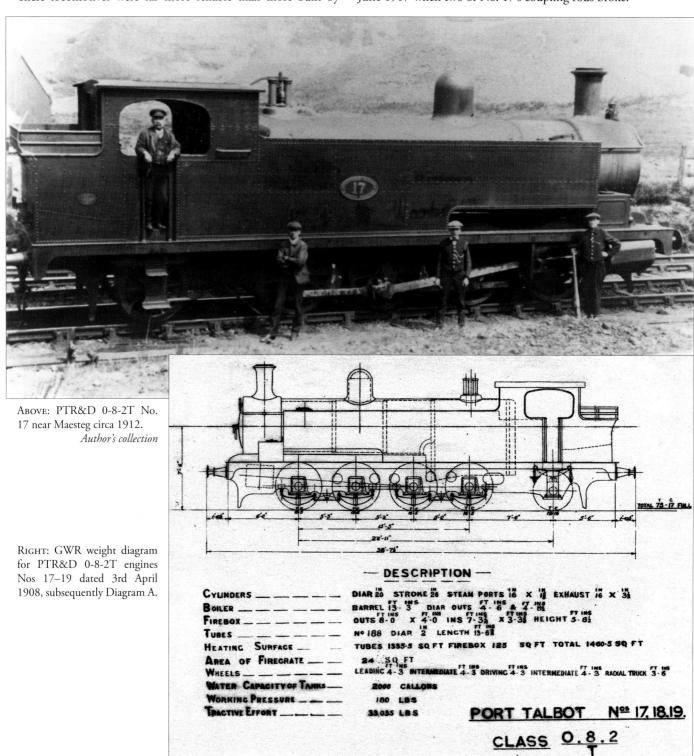

ABOVE: PTR&D 0-8-2T No. 17 near Maesteg circa 1912.
Author's collection

RIGHT: GWR weight diagram for PTR&D 0-8-2T engines Nos 17–19 dated 3rd April 1908, subsequently Diagram A.

— DESCRIPTION —

CYLINDERS	DIAR 20 IN STROKE 26 IN STEAM PORTS 16 X 1½ IN EXHAUST 16 X 3½ IN
BOILER	BARREL 13-3 FT INS DIAR OUTS 4-6 & 7-8¼ FT INS
FIREBOX	OUTS 8-0 FT INS X 4-0 FT INS INS 7-3½ FT INS X 3-3½ FT INS HEIGHT 5-8½ FT INS
TUBES	No 188 DIAR 2 IN LENGTH 13-6⅝ FT INS
HEATING SURFACE	TUBES 1335·5 SQ FT FIREBOX 125 SQ FT TOTAL 1460·5 SQ FT
AREA OF FIREGRATE	24 SQ FT
WHEELS	LEADING 4-3 FT INS INTERMEDIATE 4-3 FT INS DRIVING 4-3 FT INS INTERMEDIATE 4-3 FT INS RADIAL TRUCK 3-6 FT INS
WATER CAPACITY OF TANKS	2000 GALLONS
WORKING PRESSURE	180 LBS
TRACTIVE EFFORT	33,035 LBS

PORT TALBOT Nos 17. 18. 19.

CLASS O.8.2 / T

PTR&D 0-8-2T No. 17. Judging by the livery of the North's wagon this is a post-1912 view.

Author's collection

ABOVE: PTR&D No. 17 at North's Junction, Maesteg, in 1912. On this occasion the driver was J Griffiths, fireman R Ackland, guard J Penhale. *Author's collection*

BELOW: PTR&D No. 17 was renumbered GWR No. 1358 at the grouping and is seen at Duffryn Yard on 17th April 1933 in the 1923 livery with GWR-style boiler mountings and bunker. One of the ex-R&SBR 0-6-0 tank engines, No. 801, 802 or 806, is in the background. *Author's collection*

0-6-0 Saddle Tank Engines Nos 22–27

Hosgood and Meik jointly reported in September 1899 that, in addition to the American engines then on order, more 16-inch 0-6-0 saddle tank engines were urgently required to cope with the growing traffic on the railway. Specifications were immediately sent out to tender,[46] and in October 1899 the directors accepted that of Hudswell, Clarke & Co. for six such engines at £2,165 each, provided they were allowed to declare their option to increase the

number to eight after a trial of the first engine. Although the option was granted, the directors decided not to accept it. Two engines had been delivered by mid-January 1901[47] and all were in stock by June. Nos 22–27, maker's Nos 551–6, were very similar to the earlier three built by Stephenson – the main difference being that the boiler pressure was raised from 140 to 160 psi, giving a tractive effort of 17,410 lb. No. 23 of this group required re-tyring, which was done in 1908.

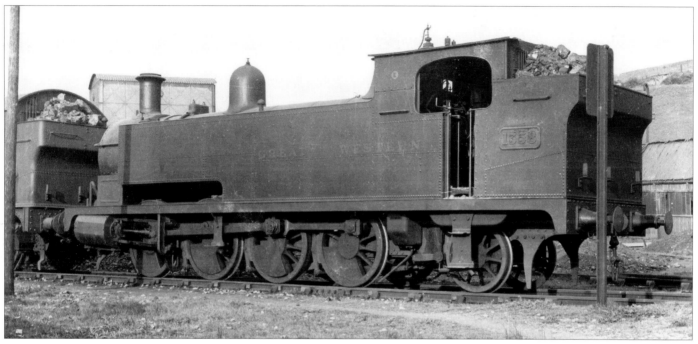

Above: PTR&D engines were not often photographed from the rear. This is former No. 17 near the new turntable at Duffryn Yard in the 1930s. Clearly visible is the route and power classification, Blue E.

Author's collection

Below: No. 1358 in due course received the GWR shirt button which had been introduced in 1934, and is seen here near Margam.

Courtesy J A Peden

ADDITIONAL LOCOMOTIVES

Hertz reported in December 1905, and again in February 1906, that the 0-8-2 tank engines were being heavily worked, and because of this and the prospects of increased traffic it would shortly be necessary to consider the question of additional large side tank locomotives.[48] In April 1906 he reported that the Sharpe, Stewart engines in particular were being very heavily worked, Sundays being the only day on which they were available for washing out boilers and attending to necessary repairs.[49] The directors responded to these requests in April 1906 by resolving that careful observations were be made of the large engines recently constructed by the GWR and other companies, and that a report was to be submitted with details of the class of locomotive most suitable for the company's requirements for heavy haulage, due regard being given to the carrying capacity of the existing bridges. This was an allusion in

(Continued on page 212)

ABOVE: Former PTR&D No. 17 ended its days at Danygraig, where it is seen on 7th July 1947, seven months before being withdrawn from service.
Courtesy H C Casserley

BELOW: PTR&D No. 18 at Duffryn Yard on 25th April 1910, little changed externally apart from the bunker rails have been filled in.
Author's collection

Engine cleaners and other shed staff pose on PTR&D No. 18 at Duffryn Yard circa 1922.

Author's collection

ABOVE: Photographs of PTR&D engines working are not common. No 18 as GWR No. 1359 is seen here shunting on the main line at Duffryn Junction on 30th July 1931. GWR goods brake van No. 56716 is a Diagram AA15 vehicle of immediate post-First World War design.

Courtesy V R Webster

BELOW: A somewhat grainy view of PTR&D No. 18/GWR No. 1359 at Duffryn Yard in April 1934, twenty months before being withdrawn.

Author's collection

Above: Builder's photograph of PTR&D No. 19, circa December 1901, in photographic grey livery. The armorial device was seemingly not applied to these locomotives when painted in their normal livery. *Mitchell Library, Glasgow*

Below: No. 19 was the first PTR&D engine to be withdrawn, as GWR No. 1360, in November 1926, and consequently was not photographed as often other members of its class. No. 19 is seen here at Cwmdu in 1912. *Author's collection*

PTR&D No. 25 at Duffryn Yard on 25th April 1910. By this date the bunker rails had been plated over and a GWR pattern injector fitted.

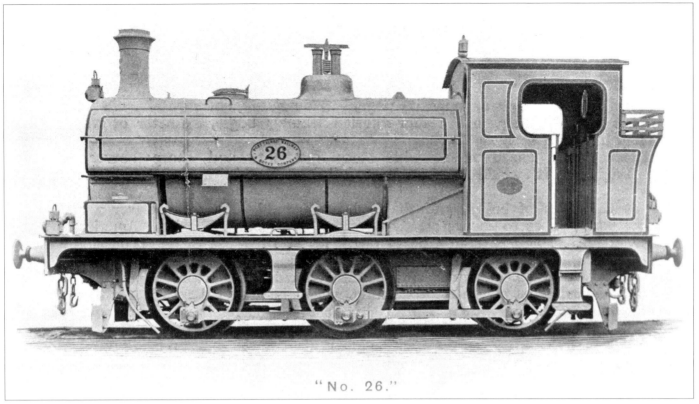

"No. 26."

ABOVE: PTR&D No. 26 in as-built condition apart from the photographic grey livery, as featured in an early 1900s Hudswell, Clarke catalogue.
Courtesy Paddy Goss

BELOW: PTR&D No. 26 shunting on North Bank. Note the engine number on the rear of the bunker.
Author's collection

(Continued from page 206)

particular to the GWR's '3100' Class of 2-6-2 tank engines, of which the first production batch of thirty-nine was approaching completion at Swindon.[50] Hertz's report in June 1906 proposed the construction of 2-8-0 side tank engines,[51] which, if built, would have been another first, as it anticipated the GWR's '4200' Class by four years and their appearance on the Port Talbot section by a further thirteen. The wheel arrangement and other features might have been inspired by the 8-coupled tank engines under consideration by Churchward at the time.[52] Hertz's specification included 19¼ by 30 inch outside cylinders, slide valves worked by Walshaert's gear, 4 foot 7½ inch driving wheels on a 16 foot 10 inch wheelbase, and a Belpaire firebox. The directors at first deferred consideration of the purchase of these large engines until the effects on operations of the planned Duffryn Sidings were known,[53] but following a further request from Hertz in January 1907[54] they resolved to obtain tenders for two locomotives to his specification, an additional criterion being that they were to be capable of handling forty loaded wagons on the main line. Consideration of the tenders received, which included Beyer, Peacock resubmitting its 0-8-4T design, was deferred in March 1907 pending enquiries about the Brotan water-tube boiler, but by then negotiations for the GWR to work the railway portion of the PTR&D's undertaking were nearing a conclusion,[55] and the matter was dropped. Instead, the general manager was able to report to the directors in November 1907 that two GWR locomotives had been hired under the terms of the proposed running powers agreement, although only one of these, 2-6-2 tank engine No. 3121, has been identified.

GWR RUNNING POWERS AND WORKING AGREEMENT

This agreement and the two subsidiary agreements for the hire of the PTR&D's rolling stock and the maintenance of its railways were all dated 24th January 1908 but deemed to have come into effect on 1st January 1907. At first it was envisaged that eighteen of the PTR&D's twenty-four engines would be hired to the GWR for traffic purposes and six would be retained (Nos 8–11, 22 and 23) for working in the docks. Instead of this arrangement, Churchward proposed in February 1908 that his company should also take over these locomotives and provide the power required for the docks at a mutually agreed rate. The directors agreed to negotiate over this and in March 1908 Lowther reported that the GWR's rate was 4s 0d per hour which included the upkeep of the company's locomotives and all necessary repairs. Alternatively, Lowther was instructed to try to sell the six engines to the GWR for their present value and to agree to pay 4s 6d per hour for the necessary power for a period of five years. A compromise was reached whereby these six locomotives were hired for five years at 5 per cent of their capital value (£14,956) per annum, and the GWR undertook to provide all suitable and proper engines for dock working at 4s 6d per hour.

Under the terms of the hire agreement Churchward and Hertz prepared inventories and valuations of all the PTR&Ds locomotives, coaching stock, wagon stock, machinery, tools and plant.[56] The total original cost the existing locomotive stock, including extras, came to £58,461 6s 5d, from which 35 per cent was deducted as agreed for depreciation, giving a current valuation of £37,999 17s 2d. Surprisingly, these figures included small sums for locomotive No. 1, which had been disposed of in 1902.

PTR&D No. 26 at Duffryn Yard, now carrying a GWR pattern short parallel chimney.   *Author's collection*

ABOVE: PTR&D No. 27 at Burrows Junction circa 1914. The chimneys of Mansel Tinplate Works are just visible in the right background.

Author's collection

BELOW: In due course all of the Hudswell, Clarke 0-6-0 saddle tank engines were given GWR-pattern safety valve covers and bunkers, which increased the coal capacity to two tons and necessitated a short extension to the rear frames. Former PTR&D No. 22 as GWR No. 808 is seen at Duffryn Yard near the new coaling stage on 2nd August 1931.

Courtesy J A Peden

ABOVE: Former PTR No. 24 as GWR No. 811 is seen in a similar condition except it has a tall safety valve cover. Note the patch where the PTR cast number plated was fixed. *Author's collection*

BELOW: By contrast GWR No. 814, former PTR No. 27, has a short safety valve cover. Photographed in the dock area circa 1930. Note the engine carries a target in front of its chimney indicating the duty it was performing. *Author's collection*

TABLE 9.2:   DIAGRAMS ASSIGNED BY GREAT WESTERN

Nos	Type	As Built	Rebuilt With GW Boiler
2, 3, 15	0-6-0T	A90	
8–14	0-6-2T	W	A35
17–19	0-8-2T	A	
20, 21	0-8-2T	B	B
22–27	0-6-0T	A89	
36	2-4-2T	P	S
37	2-4-0T	M	N

Once under GWR control the engines were assigned diagrams in the Churchward system in April 1908, as shown in Table 9.2. Also from April 1908 the engines were included in the GWR's registers of monthly shed allocations, being listed separately until they were renumbered in 1922.[57] In April 1908 Nos 9, 17 and 36 were in Swindon Works, having joined Nos 20 and 21 as noted above. Eight engines, Nos 8, 11, 18, 19, 22, 25, 27, and *Penylan*, were listed as being allocated to "Penylan". The remaining thirteen locomotives were at Duffryn Yard. The "Penylan" allocation ceased between May and August 1908, when Nos 18, 19, 22 and *Penylan* were sent to Swindon Works for repairs, and the other four moved back to Duffryn Yard. *Penylan's* visit to Swindon in August 1908 proved to be the only one. The necessary repairs were never effected

and the locomotive was condemned in January 1910. No. 2 was sent to Swindon Works for cylinder repairs in April 1910, but these were not carried out and the engine was condemned on 1st January 1911. Replacements as stipulated by the hire agreement were not provided by the GWR for these two withdrawals, but no doubt they would have been supplied if it had become necessary to do so.

During the period of GWR control the Port Talbot locomotives made periodic visits to Swindon Works for repairs and modifications. The most significant alteration was the fitting of standard boilers to Nos 20 and 21 as already noted. The 0-6-0 saddle tank engines were given GWR smokeboxes with a short chimney, and GWR-pattern safety valves in place of the original Ramsbottom type. The original bunker coal rails had been plated over by the PTR&D; the bunkers were extended by the GWR to increase the coal capacity from 1½ to 2 tons, which necessitated a short frame extension. Fewer changes were made to the 0-6-2 and Sharp, Stewart 0-8-2 tank engines, both classes receiving GWR-pattern boiler mountings. The dates these changes were made are not known, but they are apparent in photographs.

Apart from Nos 36 and 37, these engines continued to work on the PTR&D's railways and dock lines; they were in addition also occasionally hired out to local collieries, particularly to Bryn Navigation. No. 26 was there from March to April 1914 and again from November to December 1916, being followed immediately by No. 3, which left on 9th February 1917 for Swindon Works before returning to Duffryn Yard in June, and was in turn succeeded by No. 15 which stayed at Bryn Navigation until 3rd March that

Two of the 0-6-2 tank engines, former Nos 9 and 13, were rebuilt in August 1925 with Standard No. 10 superheated boilers and fitted with GWR-style cabs and bunkers, giving them a much more modern appearance. GWR No. 184, ex PTR&D No. 9, is seen here at Duffryn Yard circa 1930.

Author's collection

Without any sign of ownership but bearing a strange plaque on the smokebox door, former PTR&D No. 9 is seen alongside Duffryn Yard lifting house in May 1939.
Author's collection

year. The last visitor to Bryn Navigation Colliery was No. 24, which was there for six months from December 1918 to May 1919. Ton Phillip Colliery hired No. 23 during March 1918 and North's Navigation had No. 25 for two months in 1921. The arrival of GWR engines at Duffryn and the general nature of the work seems to have resulted in the two 4-coupled tank engines being underemployed. No. 36 left Port Talbot towards the end of 1914 and spent most of its remaining working life at Llanelly. It was given a GWR 'Metro' Class Belpaire boiler in 1925 and was condemned as GWR No. 1326 in August 1930. No. 37 had been given the same boiler treatment in November 1914,[58] after which it spent two years at Newport before being allocated to Swindon, where it was observed working a service to Swindon Town, until being condemned as GWR No. 1189 in November 1926.

Absorption

The twenty-two locomotives acquired by the GWR following the absorption of the PTR&D were assigned new numbers during September to November 1922,[59] although it is not known when they were actually applied (see Table 9.3).

Apart from Nos 36 and 37, the engines continued to be allocated to Duffryn Yard, with occasional visits to Caerphilly, Carmarthen, Danygraig, Neath or Swindon Works for repairs and overhauls. Repairs were mostly of a routine nature, but two of the 0-6-2 tank engines, Nos 9 and 13 as GWR Nos 184 and 188 respectively, were rebuilt in August 1925 with Standard No. 10 superheated

boilers[60] and fitted with GWR-style cabs, giving them a much more modern appearance. No. 184 was also given a GWR-style bunker, as were the three Sharp, Stewart 0-8-2 tank engines. Although not particularly old, the ex-PTR&D engines did not fit into the Great Western's scheme of standard classes, and nineteen of the twenty-two were withdrawn between 1926 and 1935,[61] No. 19 as GWR No. 1360 being the first to go, in November 1926. The 0-6-0 saddle tanks were still useful engines and five of these were sold, four direct from running stock, into industrial use, all surviving long enough to become part of the National Coal Board's stock (see Table 9.4).[62]

The re-boilered 0-6-2 tank engines and the remaining 0-8-2 lasted until the late 1940s, No. 13 as GWR No. 188 going in September 1947. Two survived long enough to briefly become part of the nationalised British Railways: No. 17 as BR No. 1358, having been moved to Danygraig in October 1944 and being withdrawn from there in February 1948; and No. 9 as BR No. 184, still allocated to Duffryn Yard, finally succumbing in October 1948.

No. 26 as GWR No. 813 did not suffer the fate of the other PTR&D engines. After languishing at Backworth Colliery in Northumberland, the engine was purchased by the GWR 813 Preservation Fund in 1967 and moved to the Severn Valley Railway. After a prolonged period of restoration No. 813 was steamed for the first time in August 1976, only to suffer a major mechanical failure.[63] Although back in service in 1985, further major work on the chassis and elsewhere was required,[64] and full restoration to GWR condition was only finished in July 2000.[65]

LIVERY

The only available official description of the livery of the PTR&D's locomotives occurs in the specification drawn up by Hosgood for the large tank engines, as recounted above. As far as it goes, it is very similar to that of the ByR's locomotives, not surprisingly, as

TABLE 9.3: LOCOMOTIVES ABSORBED BY THE GREAT WESTERN

PTR	GW No.	RENUMBERED 4 WEEKS ENDING	WITHDRAWN	NOTES
Penylan			1/1/10	
2			1/1/11	
3	815	10/9/22	25/11/30	sold
8	183	10/9/22	4/3/29	
9	184	10/9/22	19/10/48	
10	185	8/10/22	20/8/29	
11	186	10/9/22	7/12/34	
12	187	10/9/22	28/2/35	
13	188	10/9/22	1/9/47	
14	189	10/9/22	2/1/30	
15	816	10/9/22	–/7/29	sold
17	1358	10/9/22	23/2/48	
18	1359	10/9/22	14/12/35	
19	1360	8/10/22	15/11/26	
20	1378	10/9/22	4/12/28	
21	1379	10/9/22	11/4/29	
22	808	10/9/22	–/12/33	sold
23	809	10/9/22	15/5/28	
24	811	10/9/22	–/10/33	
25	812	10/9/22	21/6/34	sold
26	813	10/9/22	24/1/34	sold
27	814	10/9/22	11/8/30	
36	1326	10/9/22	7/8/30	
37	1189	5/11/22	19/11/26	

Hosgood came from that company in 1897. Apart from No. 1, all new engines were delivered after Hosgood took office, and it would appear that all were painted in the Barry style,[66] viz. a shade of brown known as India Red, initially at least edged in black and with white-black-white lining, each line approximately ½ inch wide. It is not clear how long these latter lasted, being either hidden by grime or removed by cleaning or later repaints. Inside frames and buffer beams were vermilion. All engines except Nos 1–3 and 15 carried centrally on the tank sides brass oval number plates with PORT TALBOT RAILWAY above the number and & DOCKS COMPANY below. The plates on Nos 2, 3 and 15 were somewhat smaller and carried on the cab side. The livery of No. 1 in its PTR&D days seems to have been anomalous. Stephenson's general arrangement drawing shows the engine lettered PTR&D on the tank side and bearing a square number plate on the cab side. The PTR&D did not use buffer beam numbers, but all those engines which Hosgood specified and ordered – that is, No. 17 onwards – were fitted with brass numbers on their bunkers. No. 20 onwards also carried numbers on their chimneys. The numerals were in the Barry style, apart from those fixed to No. 36, which were smaller and thicker, perhaps because they were made in the Duffryn workshops rather than by a locomotive manufacturer. An armorial device was introduced in 1897 for use on the passenger carriages and was also applied to the principal passenger engine No. 36, carried high up on the cab side, and to the Sharp, Stewart 0-8-2 tank engines when new, affixed to the cab sides almost in line with the number plate. How long these lasted is open to question; they are not apparent in later photographs. The device consisted of an 11 inch diameter emerald green garter edged in gilt bearing the company's full title, surrounding on a dark brown background a Welsh lion supported by a cap of dignity. Beneath this was a red rose and the company's motto, *par mare et terram* (by sea and land). The order of these words is perhaps significant and reflected where the company's priorities lay.

There is nothing to suggest that this livery did not last until the engines were repainted in the then-current GWR livery post-grouping. Interestingly, the re-boilered Nos 20 and 21 were returned to service in 1908 painted and fully lined as originally specified,[67] although without numbers on the GWR-pattern chimneys In addition, they carried the armorial device on their cab sides almost in line with the number plate, although these had vanished by about 1911.

TABLE 9.4: LOCOMOTIVES SOLD BY THE GREAT WESTERN

PTR	GW No.	SOLD	PURCHASER	SCRAPPED
3	815	1933	1) R Stephenson & Co. 2) Seaton Burn Coal Co., Northumberland 3) Hartley Main Collieries Ltd, Northumberland	1952
15	816	20/8/29	Partridge Jones & John Paton Ltd, Abersychan Colliery	1954
22	808	–/12/33	Blaendare Colliery Co., Monmouthshire	1962
25	812	21/6/34	John Vipond & Co., Varteg Colliery, Monmouthshire	1950
26	813	24/1/34	1) R Stephenson & Co. 2) Backworth Colliery Ltd, Northumberland 3) GWR 813 Preservation Fund, Severn Valley Railway	

ABOVE: Former PTR&D No. 13 was rebuilt in the same fashion as No. 9 and is seen at Duffryn Yard on 3rd October 1946. As GWR No. 188 this was the third-longest surviving PTR&D engine and was withdrawn on 1st September 1947 just before nationalisation. *Courtesy R C Riley*

BELOW: PTR&D No. 9 as GWR No. 184 just survived long enough to see nationalisation, and was the last PTR&D engine to be condemned. It is seen here at Swindon after withdrawal in October 1948. *Author's collection*

ABOVE: Former PTR&D No. 3 in Northumberland as Seaton Burn Coal Co. No. 2; it later became Hartley Main Collieries Ltd No. 32.

Author's collection

BELOW: PTR&D No. 15 became GWR No. 816 at the grouping and was sold to Partridge Jones & John Paton Ltd in 1929. It is seen as it left the GWR, with enlarged bunker, at NCB Talywain.

Author's collection

Former PTR&D 0-6-0ST No. 15 is seen here near Blaenserchan Colliery descending one of the ferocious gradients in the Talywain area in 1950.
Courtesy Desmond Coakham

PASSENGER CARRIAGES

Clause 57 of the PTR&D's 1894 Act required the company to commence a passenger service on its main line within twelve months of it being opened for goods traffic. On 28th March 1896, the company's consulting engineer, Mr Meik, was instructed by the directors to ascertain what rolling stock would be required to work the railway. The following July he reported the preparation of specifications for eight bogie carriages (two Composite, two Third Class, four Brake Third).[68] Tenders were invited, seemingly from only two makers, and considered by the directors on 19th August 1896 (see Table 9.5).[69]

Despite Meik recommending that the Lancaster RC&W Co. tender be accepted as its total price was the lower, the directors decided to order from the Midland RC&W Co. In the meantime, the designs had been submitted to William Dean at Swindon for comment, who advised in October 1896 that they were suitable, provided gas lamps were substituted for oil.[70] There was then a considerable delay, as it was not until 4th September 1897 that Meik could report that one train of four carriages had been delivered and that the other was imminent.[71] Passenger services on the Garw

TABLE 9.5: CARRIAGE TENDERS, 1896

	MIDLAND RAILWAY CARRIAGE & WAGON CO.	LANCASTER RAILWAY CARRIAGE & WAGON CO.
Two First/Third Composite	£1,626	£1,680
Two Third Class	£1,482	£1,484
Four Brake Third Class	£3,074	£2,972
Total	£6,182	£6,136

Valley line opened on 14th February 1898, well within one year of the goods service commencing to Lletty Brongu (31st August 1897) and Pontyrhyll (17th January 1898).

These carriages, at 42 feet 0 inches over end panels and 8 feet 0¾ inch over door mouldings, were among the smallest bogie passenger stock to run in the UK. The common underframe ran on 8 foot 6 inch Dean-type bogies set at 27 feet 0 inches centres and

PTR&D No. 26/GWR No. 813 was sold to Backworth Colliery in January 1934 and is seen there minus the GWR safety valve cover on 5th June 1934.
Courtesy H C Casserley

ABOVE: PTR&D No. 26/GWR No. 813 was purchased by the GWR 813 Preservation Fund in 1967 and moved to the Severn Valley Railway for restoration to GWR condition. The engine is seen here at Bewdley in April 1976 with restoration nearly complete. *Author's collection*

had full-length running boards, although these were removed in later years. Unusually, the ends were vertical with no tumble-home, and those on the Brake Third carriages had two small end windows. Third Class passenger accommodation was cramped and consisted of un-upholstered wooden seating. Each compartment was 5 feet 10¼ inches long in the all-Third and Brake Third carriages, and only 5 feet 6 inches in the Composites. First Class passengers benefited from 6 foot 8⅞ inch compartments and sprung upholstered seating.

The condition of the carriages was giving concern by 1905, but in July that year the directors only agreed to those repairs that were absolutely necessary being carried out, and these were put in hand immediately.[72] However, Hertz reported that one reason for their poor condition was the lack of steam heating, causing rotting of the frames and panelling, and recommend that this should be provided at a cost of £20–25 per coach.[73] The renovation of the carriages was well in hand by April 1906.[74]

There were three types of passenger stock originally: five-compartment Brake Third (Nos 1, 4, 5 and 8), seven-compartment all-Third (Nos 2 and 6) and First/Third Composite with five Third Class and two First Class compartments (Nos 3 and 7). In August 1903 the directors agreed with Lowther's suggestion that two Third compartments in each of Nos 1 and 8 should be re-upholstered and upgraded to Second Class, so that from 1st January 1904 First,

Second and Third Class accommodation was provided on passengers trains.[75] In anticipation of the introduction of the steam rail motor, which was to be all Third Class, the directors decided in December 1905 that First Class accommodation was to be discontinued, and by June 1907 composites Nos 3 and 7 had been downgraded. The GWR, having worked the PTR&D since 1908 and decided upon the abolition of Second Class on its own services, duly reclassified Brake Composites Nos 1 and 8 as Third Class only by the end of 1910. Thus, there were then four all-Third Class carriages, Nos 2, 3, 6 and 7, and four Brake Third carriages, Nos 1, 4, 5 and 8.

The bogie carriages were originally purchased for use on the passenger service between Aberavon or Port Talbot Central and Blaengarw. The first workmen's service, to Mercantile Colliery on the Whitworth Branch, was agreed to in January 1899,[76] and to provide for this the L&NWRs offer of two coaches for £85 and £80 was accepted in February 1899. This deal was probably arranged by Probert, the coaches coming from Swansea. They were both four-wheeled: a four-compartment Third Class carriage became No. 9, and a three-compartment Brake Third became No. 10. Both were withdrawn by the GWR in February 1916, but not replaced. The body of No. 10 was reportedly then used as a cabin at an unidentified location in Port Talbot.[77] To supplement these two, a third *(Continued on page 230)*

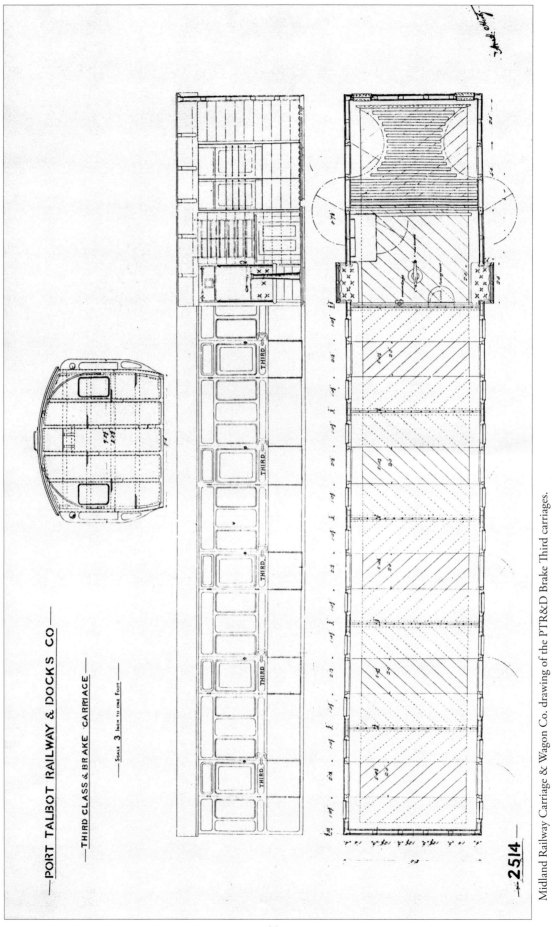

PORT TALBOT RAILWAY & DOCKS CO

THIRD CLASS & BRAKE CARRIAGE

Scale 3 Inch to one Foot

2514

Midland Railway Carriage & Wagon Co. drawing of the PTR&D Brake Third carriages.

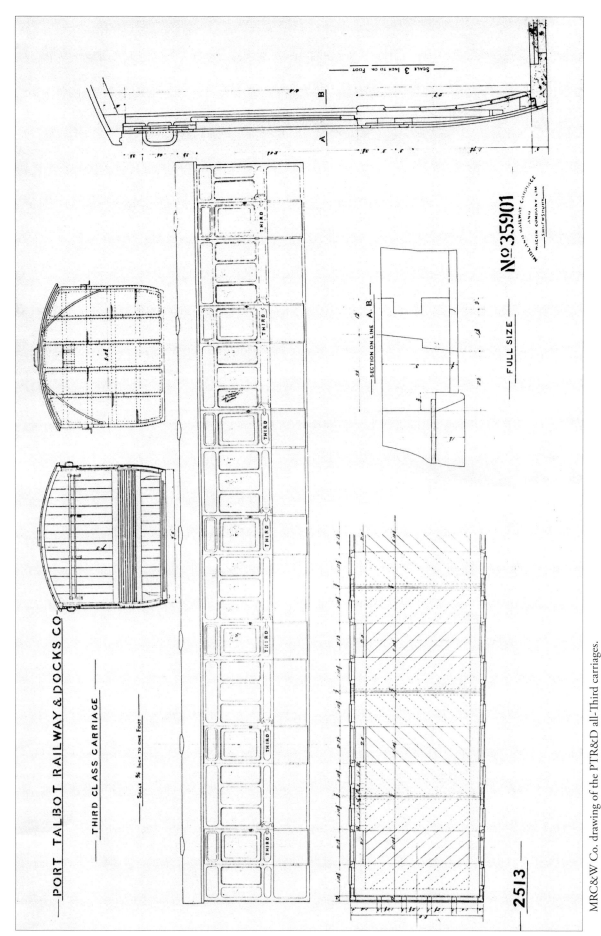

MRC&W Co. drawing of the PTR&D all-Third carriages.

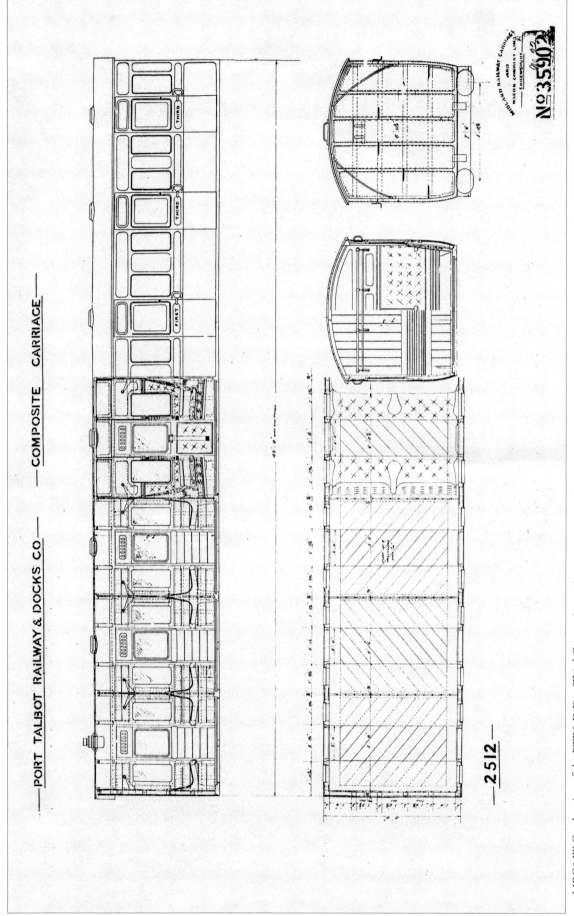

MRC&W Co. drawing of the PTR&D First/Third Composite carriages.

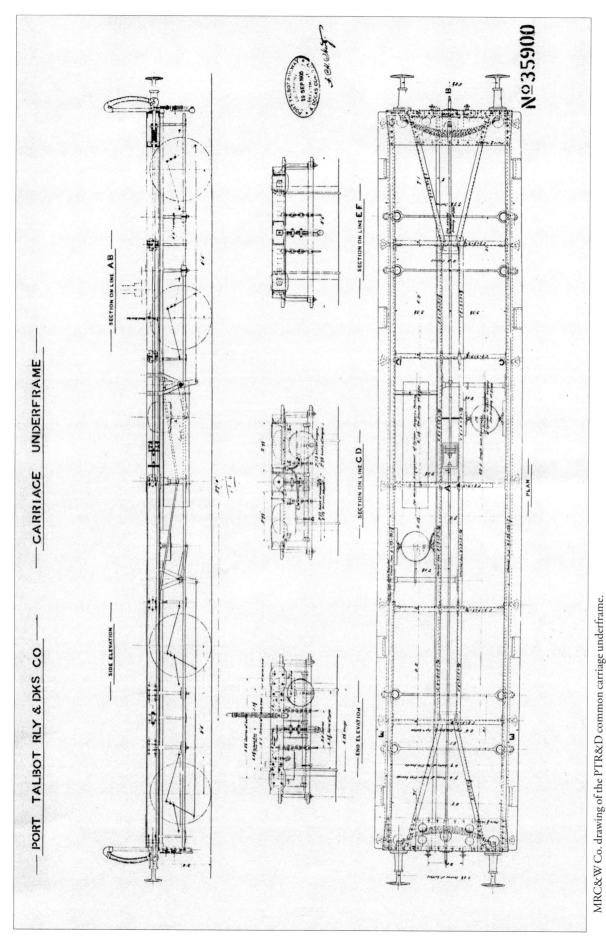

MRC&W Co. drawing of the PTR&D common carriage underframe.

PTR 0-6-2T No. 5 and a train of new bogie carriage stock at Tonygroes North Junction in September 1897. The first and fourth coaches are Brake Thirds, the second is a First/Third Composite and the third an all-Third. Note the position of the company's armorial device and the end windows. The junction signal controlled movements to Aberavon (R&SBR) (left) and Tonmawr (right).   *Author's collection*

PTR&D First/Third Composite carriage No. 3 as featured in a Midland Railway Carriage & Wagon Co. catalogue dated circa 1900, clearly showing the style of lettering. *Author's collection*

(Continued from page 223)

four-wheel four-compartment Third Class carriage was purchased from the GWR in 1900 for £55 and became PTR&D No. 11.[78] This carriage was withdrawn in October 1914, but in this instance a replacement was provided, a GWR Diagram S1 four-compartment Third built in 1872, which survived into the grouping period. A further coach for workmen's services was purchased from the GWR in 1900 for £65, this being an unidentified 4-wheel passenger brake van. This vehicle, which was also used as a breakdown van,[79] was given the number 1 in a separate series; it was withdrawn, without replacement, in March 1915 and transferred to the Inspector of Military Trains.[80] Nos 1–8 and 11 were renumbered into GWR stock following absorption in 1922 and lasted well into the post-grouping period, No. 3 even just managing to survive into nationalisation (see Table 9.6).

TABLE 9.6: CARRIAGES ABSORBED BY THE GREAT WESTERN

PTR&D	GWR No.	RENUMBERED	WITHDRAWN
1	4335	21/10/23	21/11/31
2	4336	21/10/23	6/3/34
3	4337	4/3/23	30/10/48
4	4338	21/10/23	27/10/28
5	4339	29/7/23	18/1/30
6	4340	21/10/23	3/6/33
7	4341	4/3/23	14/9/40
8	4342	4/3/23	3/6/33
11	4343	3/6/23	–/11/26

LIVERY

The livery was chocolate sides, black ends and underworks, and white roofs. The company's armorial device was carried twice on each side, and the compartment designation and running number indicated by lettering in the waist panels. There is no record of the directors being asked to sanction a change to standard GWR livery (as happened with the wagon stock) and this was probably only applied as appropriate post grouping.

STEAM RAIL MOTOR

During the early years of the twentieth century, steam rail motors, as they came to be known, were seen as an economical means of conveying passengers on lightly-used services. After their introduction on a joint service of the London & South Western and London Brighton & South Coast railways in 1902, the GWR experimented with and then developed a large fleet of these vehicles; in South Wales they were followed by the Taff Vale Railway (1903), the Alexander (Newport & South Wales) Docks & Railway (1904) and the Barry Railway (1905).[81] The contemporary arguments were discussed by T Hurry Riches, the locomotive superintendent of the TVR, in 1906.[82] Although there is no record of the directors of the PTR&D asking for a report on how these developments could be applied to their railway, on 26th July 1905 they resolved to invite tenders for a "steam motor car" suitable for the company's requirements. The contract and general description drawn up by Hertz contained the following provisions:[83]

- The six-coupled front power bogie was to carry a locomotive-type boiler and to be complete apart from the water tank of 550–600 gallons capacity which was to situated at the front end of the coach, and to be capable of pulling a 20–25 ton

ABOVE: PTR&D Brake Third and all-Third at Duffryn Yard on 1st June 1926. The coaches have been repainted in the GWR 1922 livery. Note the end windows and the provision of steam heating. *Author's collection*

BELOW: PTR&D Composite coach No. 7 as GWR No. 4341 at Birmingham Snow Hill, circa 1928. Note that some of the panelling has been sheeted over and the running boards removed. Steam heating is very much in evidence. *Clifford Collection, courtesy C C Green*

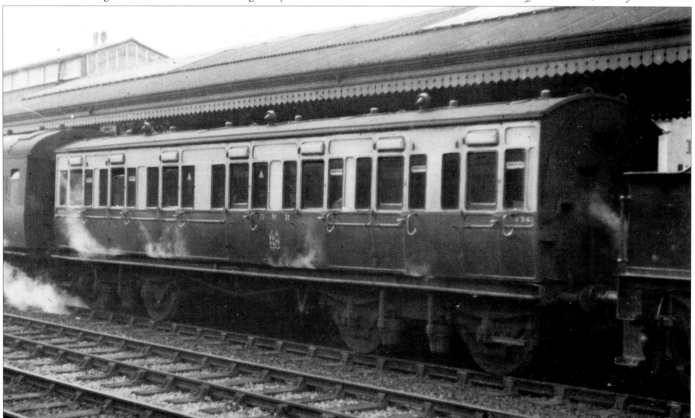

Builder's photographs of PTR&D SRM No. 1. Note the armorial devices and the lettering on the doors: DRIVER and LUGGAGE COMPT. The SRM carried its number in gilt lettering on the coach portion and on a cast plate on the power unit. The second view was used in Hawthorn, Leslie's *Brief Historical Sketch & Catalogue 1817–1921* and in its *Brief Description of Exhibits* at the 1924 British Empire Exhibition.

Author's collection

Two views of SRM No. 1 near Tonygroes Junction on 25th April 1910. It is believed that, like the locomotives, the SRM worked chimney first up the gradient to Bryn and beyond.

Author's collection

trailer in addition to the motor coach up a 1 in 40 gradient at 20 mph.

- The cylinders were to placed outside the frames and the slide valves actuated by Walshaert's motion.
- The coach was to have a guards compartment with tip-up seats, a smoking compartment seating twenty passengers, and a non-smoking compartment seating forty, all Third Class, the double seats being arranged transversely with a passage down the middle.
- Lighting was to be by electricity generated by a steam turbine-powered dynamo carried on the motor portion.
- The coach portion was to be easily detachable to enable the motor to be taken into the running shed for repairs.
- The colour of the whole vehicle was to be chocolate.
- Brass number plates were to be fitted to the front and sides of the motor portion.

Lowther reported on 16th September 1906 that fifteen tenders had been received, of which he short-listed those from Andrew Barclay, Kerr Stuart & Co. and a joint tender from Hurst, Nelson & Co. (coach portion) and Hawthorn, Leslie & Co. (motor portion).[84] At their meeting on 20th September the directors provisionally accepted the joint tender from Hurst, Nelson & Co. Ltd and R & W Hawthorn, Leslie & Co. Ltd of £2,624 for one steam rail motor, and £5,148 for two – subject to the company being granted a twelve-month option on the second vehicle, and to a slight increase in the dimensions of the boiler. These conditions were readily accepted, but then there was a slight delay while the seating arrangement was finalised. Hurst, Nelson submitted two seating plans on 6th October 1906, the first having a 7 foot 6 inch luggage compartment with eight seats, a 14 foot 8 inch smoking compartment with twenty seats crosswise in pairs, a 28 foot 8 inch non-smoking compartment with forty seats crosswise in pairs, and a 3 foot 9 inch driving compartment. The second plan had the same dimensions except the non-smoking compartment had twenty seats crosswise in pairs and nine seats each side placed lengthwise. The amendments to the design were finalised on 17th October. The second seating plan, being similar to that of the Diagram O motor coaches then being constructed by Hurst, Nelson for the GWR, was accepted, except that the internal partitions were moved slightly to provide more room in the smoking compartment, and the body width was increased from the original 8 feet to 9 feet for an extra £15. The directors accepted the modified tenders the following day, and the order was placed immediately for delivery in June 1906,[85] although in the event the rail motor was not delivered until early 1907.

The PTR&D thereby acquired the largest steam rail motor ever to run in the UK. The overall length was 76 feet 10 inches, with the coach portion carried on a conventional bogie at the rear end and pivoted on the engine unit at a point between the driving and trailing axles.[86] The bodywork was metal, that covering the engine fashioned to match the carriage; the mouldings were purely decorative. Retractable steps were fitted under each of the four recessed passenger doors; these steps were later fixed in position. Despite the specification, water was not carried on the coach but in a well tank on the locomotive, which was provided with a conventional locomotive boiler with the firebox leading.

With 3 foot 0 inch wheels, 12 inch by 16 inch cylinders and a boiler pressure of 170 psi, the tractive effort was 9,792 lbs, sufficient to maintain 40 mph on the level with a trailing load of 111 tons. The rail motor was given the number 1, displayed on standard PTR&D number plates carried centrally on the sides of the motor unit. Whether this was the start of a new series or use of the vacant number in the locomotive series is not known. The rail motor was delivered in a two-tone livery, white or cream above the waistline and a dark colour, which may have been chocolate, below, and with a white roof. Windows and doors were outlined in the dark colour. The driving and luggage compartment doors were lettered as such, with the armorial device was applied twice to each side and the number painted centrally in between. It is not certain how long this livery lasted. Old railwaymen have asserted that the upper panels were white and lower ones green.[87] The armorial devices were absent by 1910. Hawthorn, Leslie included the rail motor in their publication *Historical Sketch & Catalogue 1817–1921*, although this did not elicit any further orders.

Hertz reported in March 1907 that the point locking bars on the PTR main line, on the GWR between Pontyrhyll and Blacngarw, and on the R&SBR at Aberavon, had been lengthened to suit the rail motor, that the permanent way on Aberavon Viaduct had been raised 2 inches so that the gearing of the motor coach would clear the angle iron guards, and that trials hauling a trailer were proving satisfactory.[88] Despite the working timetable dated 1st April 1907 stating that a rail motor had been provided for running the weekday passenger service between Port Talbot and Blaengarw, Hertz reported on 19th April that it was not yet in traffic,[89] although it was so a month later.[90] The rail motor gradually took up the majority of the passenger traffic, and by July 1907 was working the ordinary passenger trains four days per week, at a daily saving of £3 6s 6d.[91]

Along with the locomotives and carriages, the steam rail motor was transferred to the GWR as hired stock in 1908 under the terms of the running powers agreement and continued to work the majority of the passenger services between Port Talbot and Blaengarw. Like the locomotives, it was assigned a diagram in the Churchward system, in this case Diagram S in the steam rail motor series.

The rail motor was involved in an accident on 24th November 1911 when, due to excessive overhang, it struck the end of a wagon standing in the Down loop at Aberavon Junction whilst being shunted into the station prior to working the 5.45 a.m. to Blaengarw. On this occasion a passenger brake was leading the rail motor, presumably being used as a trailer, and the pair were being propelled by a locomotive. A recurrence was prevented by repositioning the fouling point. The rail motor made periodic visits to Swindon Works for repairs and on these occasions GWR steam rail motors went sent to Duffryn Yard as replacements (see Table 9.7).[92]

The final journey to Swindon Works was made on 7th August 1915, where a light repair was undertaken. Instead of returning to Duffryn Yard the rail motor was moved to Swindon Stock Shed on 22nd October 1915. It remained there until July 1920 when it was sold to a Mr Graham of the Port of London Authority,[93] where it worked on the Millwall Extension Railway until 1926. It was cut up in 1928.

TABLE 9.7: RAIL MOTOR VISITS TO SWINDON

DATE	REPLACEMENT
24/6/08 to 1/12/08	20, 21
–/2/09 to 22/3/09	21
–/12/10 to 29/3/11	21, 79
24/11/11 to 3/6/12	21
10/2/13 to 7/6/13	21, 13

WAGON STOCK

All the mineral traffic on the PTR was carried in private owner wagons. For its own general traffic, to handle some of the imports and to cope with its engineering needs, the PTR&D acquired 411 vehicles, including fourteen brake vans, which sufficed for all its freight trains. PTR&D record-keeping of its wagon stock in the early days is sparse or non-existent; matters improved once the GWR running powers agreement was in effect – information is available in the 1908 inventory[94] and the GWR condemned wagon stock registers held at TNA: PRO, and the wagon stock registers held at TNA: PRO and the National Railway Museum. Unlike the locomotive stock, none of the PTR&D's wagons were given a GWR diagram.

OPEN WAGONS

To go with engine No. 1, the directors in December 1895 obtained tenders for 10-ton open wagons for use on the dock railways, and in January 1896 resolved to order thirty from S J Claye Ltd of Long Eaton, Derbyshire for £57 10s 0d each. These wagons were delivered in February 1896 and given the numbers 1–30.[95] They had steel underframes on a 9 foot wheelbase which carried a 2-plank body 15 feet by 7 feet 6 inches by 1 foot 10 inches (external dimensions).[96] In July 1896 Meik, the resident engineer, reported that twenty more similar wagons were required.[97] Messrs Claye's tender at the same price was again successful and these wagons, Nos 31–50, were ordered in August 1896, this batch being specified to be fitted with either-side brakes.[98] Fifty tarpaulins for these wagons were purchased in April 1897.

Fifty open wagons sufficed until April 1898 when twenty secondhand 10-ton wooden-underframed opens (Nos 84–103) were purchased from Andrews & Baby of Cardiff for £28 each. These appear to have been of the same general dimensions as the Claye-built wagons. No. 95 of this batch was later designated a rail wagon. The following month the directors identified a need for fifty more wagons "to be stronger than those built by Claye". The prices quoted in the initial tenders received were too high, but in August 1898 that of Harrison & Camm Ltd of Rotherham was accepted, and the wagons were ordered on redemption hire (that is, hire purchase) in September 1898. These wagons (Nos 104–153) were one foot longer but otherwise similar to the Claye-built examples, and were redeemed by April 1906.

Ballasting and re-ballasting the main lines and dock railways was an ongoing operation, and in November 1898 the directors asked for tenders for secondhand wagons for use as ballast wagons by the resident engineer. As an interim measure thirteen existing secondhand wagons were used for this purpose. In February 1899 the directors gave authority to purchase 100 secondhand wooden-underframed wagons (Nos 154–253) for £27 each from Messrs J R Nichols, who seemingly were acting as agents for Messrs Pyman, Watson & Co., coal shippers.[99] Although not individually

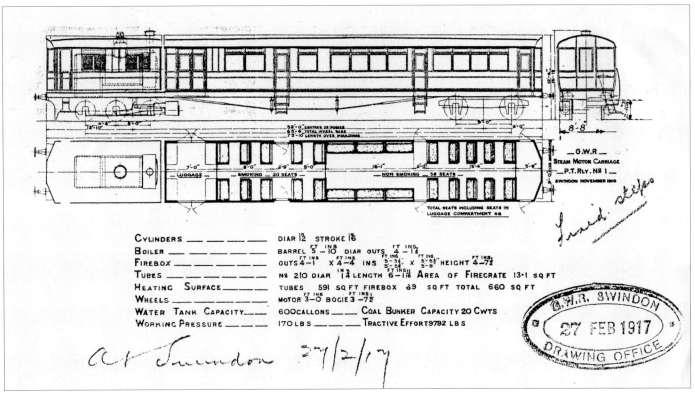

PTR&D SRM No. 1 depicted on Diagram S in the GWR's SRM series.

identified, these wagons were built by or purchased from Andrews & Baby (fifty-six), the Bristol Wagon Co. (twenty-three), and the Lincoln Wagon & Engine Co. (twenty-one).[100] Also purchased at the same time were fifty similar Harrison & Camm-built wagons from the Chorley Railway Wagon Co. Ltd for £26 each (Nos 254–303). Confusingly, GWR records indicate that most of these 150 wagons came from Andrews & Baby. Whichever was the case, they came in at least three varieties, 2- and 3-plank full-length door and 5-plank short door. Nos 155, 161 and 196 later became rail wagons, and No 283 became the match truck to the company's first travelling crane. Some of the secondhand wagons were apparently of the end-door type as the R&SBR objected to them running over its lines for conveying copper slag for the extension of a training wall.[101] Fifty more wagon tarpaulins were purchased at this time.

The last order for secondhand wagons was placed with Edmunds & Radley of Cardiff in September 1899 at a cost at £33 10s 0d each. Thirty were assigned to the Permanent Way Department (Nos 354–383) and ten to traffic use (Nos 384–393), although the last six of these later became loco coal wagons. The final order for open wagons was placed in November 1899. Fifty more new wagons of the existing type were obtained from Harrison & Camm on redemption hire for £93 2s 6d each and placed in service in 1900 as Nos 304–353. These wagons were redeemed by December 1907. Thus the railway acquired a total of 360 open wagons, although a further four secondhand wagons from an unidentified source (Nos 408–411) were added by December 1908 after the GWR had taken over the working of the railway.

In September 1905 the directors noted the bad condition of the secondhand wagons and asked for tenders for such new wagons as were absolutely necessary. The following month this policy was reversed and instead estimates for the repair of defective wagons were sought. In November 1905 the directors accepted the tender of the North Central Wagon Co. for reconstructing forty wagons, presumably at its East Moors, Cardiff, site, for £29 each, subject to the first six being rebuilt satisfactorily, with the rebuilding spread over two years. Six wagons were reported to be under repair in December 1905.[102] Twenty-three secondhand wagons were described as having been reconstructed between 1905 and 1907.[103] The state of the secondhand wagons gave concern again in August 1907, but nothing more was done pending the conclusion of the working agreement with the GWR in 1908.

The hire agreement dated 24th January 1908 required an inventory be prepared; this formed the basis of the division of the rolling stock between the railway and dock sides of the PTR&D's undertaking, and was agreed at the first meeting of the joint Consultation Committee held on 2nd April 1908. Two hundred open wagons were assigned to general railway use and were henceforth to be maintained by the GWR, appearing in the GWR accounts as hired stock. One hundred and fifty were designated for dock use only and lettered accordingly, although somewhat bizarrely the list included twenty-three wagons that had already been broken up or condemned.

Railway (200 wagons)
    1–50, 84, 85, 87–94, 96–154, 156–159, 162–170, 172–176, 178, 180, 181, 183–186, 188–194, 197, 198, 202, 206, 217, 234, 240, 241, 252, 283, 344–381, 383

Dock (150 wagons)
    86, 160, 171, 177, 179, 182, 187, 195, 199–201, 203–205, 207–216, 218–233, 235–239, 242–251, 253–282, 284–343, 382, 384–387

Nos 408–411 were added to the railway stock during 1908.

The PTR&D was responsible for maintaining the dock opens, and in May 1908 took on a handyman to carry out small repairs and to grease to them. The twenty-three defunct wagons were not written off until the half-year ending December 1910 and their scrap value of £653 was transferred to the capital account.

As a consequence of the agreement dated 9th August 1911 giving the GWR running powers over the dock lines, maintenance of the 127 extant dock open wagons was transferred to that company, bringing their total to 331. After a further evaluation of the additional wagons, sixty-nine wagons, mostly in fair condition, were deemed to be suitable for general traffic, whereas the remaining fifty-eight, almost all in bad condition, were to be kept for dock working only.

Suitable for general traffic (69 wagons)
    204, 212, 215, 216, 221–223, 230, 232, 235–237, 243–247, 250, 256, 259, 265, 270, 273, 281, 303–343, 384–387

For dock use only (58 wagons)
    171, 199, 201, 203, 208–211, 213, 214, 218–220, 224–229, 231, 242, 248, 249, 251, 253–255, 257, 258, 260, 261, 263, 266–269, 271, 272, 274, 277–280, 282, 284–286, 289, 291–300

As open wagons became beyond economical repair the GWR adopted the practise, commencing in November 1913, of providing replacement wagons from its own fleet. This was necessary under the terms of the hire agreement to maintain the stock numbers, the replacements becoming PTR&D capital assets. In a few cases the replacements were themselves replaced. The replacements were iron-framed 3-plank opens dating from the 1880s.[104] At least 125 were supplied, some even arriving in 1922 after grouping.

Following the grouping in 1922, the number range 99401–99726 within the GWR wagon series was assigned for 326 of the PTR&D's open wagons. A total of 209 wagons were renumbered into this range, a process that took some time, No. 15 not being renumbered to 99414 until May 1929. A further 107 wagons were assigned numbers in this range, but were withdrawn before being renumbered. Ten were re-assigned as ballast wagons, with nine of these being renumbered into the 80xxx series. The remaining five PTR&D general traffic wagons were withdrawn without being assigned a GWR number. Most of the survivors were withdrawn in the 1920s, but No. 32, as GWR 99406, lasted until November 1943. Despite their alleged weakness, three of the early Claye-built wagons were later transferred to the GWR Engineering Department, at least two of them lasting into nationalisation.

COVERED GOODS WAGONS

Having settled on their first order for open wagons the directors in March 1896 instructed their engineer, Meik, to report as to what other rolling stock was required. Among his recommendations were ten covered goods wagons, specifications for which were produced

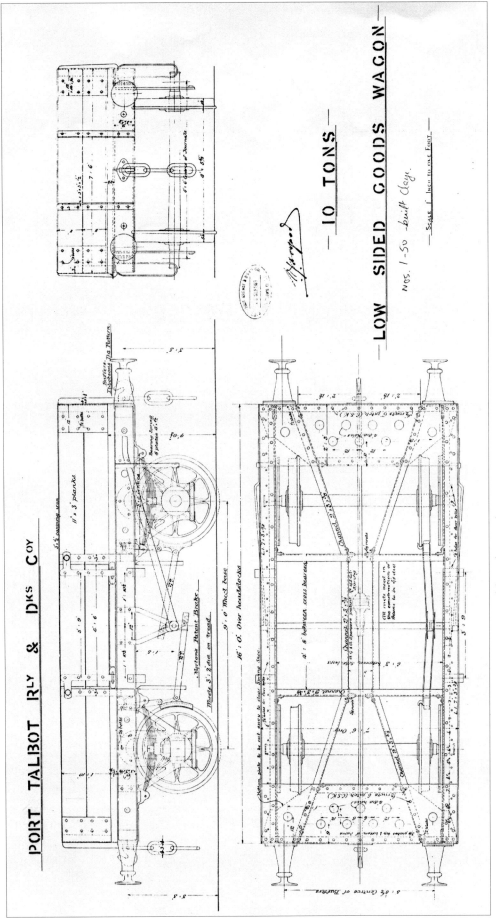

Messrs Claye drawing of PTR&D 10-ton open wagons Nos 1–50 delivered in 1896–97.

LOCO SMASH
CWMDU

In October 1909, North's 0-6-0ST *Marion* and a train of ten wagons ran out of control down the incline from St. John's Colliery to the interchange sidings with the PTR&D at Cwmdu, crashing through the stop block and killing one man. The presence of PTR&D wagons Nos 101 (secondhand 1898) and 122 (Harrison & Camm 1898) suggests that they had been used to take materials up to the colliery which was then being sunk. The almost new locomotive, Hudswell, Clark No. 881 of 1909, was repaired and put back into service. *Author's collection*

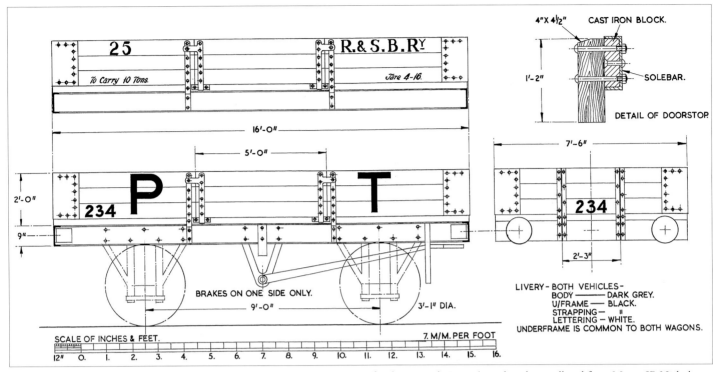

ABOVE: Drawing of PTR&D 10-ton open No. 234. This was a replacement for the original No. 234 purchased secondhand from Messrs JR Nichols in 1899 and condemned in October 1914. This replacement was built by the GWR in 1881 as No. 34246, transferred to the PTR&D in November 1914 and condemned in April 1928, having never carried its assigned grouping number 99584. *T L Jones, courtesy WRRC*

BELOW: Open wagon No. 337, photographed in Port Talbot Docks circa 1910. This Harrison & Camm-built wagon purchased in 1900 has brake levers on both sides (note the cross rod). The wagon was one of those assigned to docks use in 1908 which was deemed suitable for general traffic in 1912. It was renumbered to GWR 99673 on 4/11/23 and withdrawn on 26/9/31. The shaded lettering is noteworthy. *Author's collection*

RIGHT: PTR&D open wagon No. 23 at King's Dock, Swansea 9th February 1910. This was one of the first batch of wagons ordered by the PTR&D from SJ Claye and delivered in February 1896, and appears to be in the same livery as No. 337, grey bodywork with white lettering shaded black. This wagon was renumbered GWR 99422 on 24th December 1922 and condemned on 2nd April 1938.   *Courtesy Peter Sims*

BELOW: PTR&D wagons did not always stay on their home railway. This unidentified open wagon is at Llandebie Lime Works in Carmarthenshire.

Author's collection

BELOW: Two more travellers, PTR&D open wagons. 2-plank No. 171, secondhand 1899, and 3-plank end door No. 392, secondhand September 1899, at an unidentified location. Also present are an unidentified R&SBR wagon and Cribbwr Fawr and Glyncorrwg wagons.   *Author's collection*

in July 1896.[105] Harrison & Camm's tender to construct these ten wagons, Nos 51–60, for £77 each was accepted in August 1896 and delivery followed early in 1897. These rather squat wood-bodied wagons were 16 feet long by 7 feet 6 inches wide by 6 feet 6 inches on a 9 foot wheelbase steel underframe. The sides were cross-braced internally and had a door opening of 5 feet 1 inch high by 5 feet wide. The need for ten more such wagons specifically for tinplate traffic was identified in December 1897, and Harrison & Camm and the Midland Railway Carriage & Wagon Co. were invited to tender. The former was successful and the wagons (Nos 74–83) were ordered on 5 per cent redemption hire in March 1898 for £84 10s 0d each, and delivered later that year. These ten wagons were redeemed in April 1906. Twenty covered wagons sufficed for the PTR&D's needs, although the Board did briefly contemplate further vehicles in October 1899. In February 1907 a profile gauge was fitted to one of the vans for checking the clearances in Cwm Cerwyn Tunnel.[106]

By December 1906 only three covered goods wagons (Nos 81–83) were assigned to general railway use, and of these the GWR inventory of 1908 described No. 83 as a breakdown tool van.[107] The others were for internal docks use. Five, Nos 76–80, were re-allocated to general traffic in March 1908, and the remaining twelve wagons followed suit in the first half of 1912. Four of the covered goods wagons (Nos 52, 60, 78 and 83) were withdrawn in September 1921, and the GWR provided replacements later that year on the same basis as the open goods wagons. The replacements were

outside-framed covered goods wagons built in the 1880s. Sixteen PTR&D covered goods wagons were assigned GWR numbers in the range 101530–101545 at the grouping,[108] although only nine were actually renumbered. No. 54, as GWR 101533, was altered to a stores van in 1922 and written "To work between Carriage and Wagon Stores and Worcester" in 1927. No. 80, as GWR 101543, was the last to be withdrawn, in November 1933.

CATTLE WAGONS

The only other revenue-earning wagons acquired new were for cattle and presumably also used for other livestock. The directors were initially inclined in August 1896 to accept Harrison & Camm's tender of £79 10s 0d each for three cattle wagons built according to Meik's specification. But doubts arose, a new specification was prepared, and in October 1896 new tenders were obtained from Harrison & Camm and the Midland Railway Carriage & Wagon Co.[109] Harrison & Camm were again successful and their tender for

three cattle wagons at £87 each was accepted in November 1897,[110] the wagons, Nos 61–63, being delivered in the first half on 1897. All were renumbered into GWR stock (38055, 38060 and 38070 respectively) following the grouping and all were withdrawn by April 1927. Details of these cattle wagons are sketchy. No drawing appears to have survived and they appear only in the background of a few photographs. According to the GWR wagon register they were 18 feet in long by 7 feet 2 inches wide by 7 feet 2 inches high, presumably internally, running on a 9 foot wheelbase wood underframe.

RAIL WAGONS

As noted above, four of the open wagons, Nos 95, 155, 161 and 196, were at some stage classified as rail wagons. All four were condemned in September 1912, and were replaced in early 1913 by four newly-built GWR 14-ton rail wagons of Diagram J12 built to Lot 730.[111] Being service stock, renumbering took even longer

Although this postcard shows a funeral procession heading for Chapel of Ease Crossing near Duffryn Yard, the interesting feature is the partial view of PTR&D rail wagon No. 161 in Duffryn Sidings. The painted instructions probably refer to the wagon not being close-coupled on curves less than 3 chains radius, as applied to the GWR wagons. This wagon was assigned GWR 32395 at the grouping but not renumbered until July 1932, and lasted well into the BR period.

Author's collection

Views of wagons in the first version of the PTR&D livery are very elusive, but this postcard enlargement shows a covered goods wagon lettered PTR&D [door] No. 76, and a secondhand open wagon lettered PT No. 99 RD.

Author's collection

than revenue wagons, No. 95 not becoming GWR 32393 until November 1933. On renumbering, PTR&D 196 became a match truck for a 5-ton crane as GWR 14417. PTR&D 161 as GWR 32395 was transferred to the Engineering Department in April 1944. Three of these wagons were still in the BR fleet in 1961.

LOCO COAL WAGONS

The order of secondhand open wagons from Edmunds & Radley in September 1899 included ten specifically for use as loco coal wagons, Nos 394–403, which were added to stock later that year. These were not always sufficient, and in August 1900 the Board agreed that colliery wagons could be used as loco coal wagons provided the hire charge was not greater than 3d per ton. This situation was ameliorated by the reclassification of six unidentified open wagons, Nos 388–393, as loco coal wagons, five in 1906 and one in 1908. The 1908 inventory described all sixteen coal wagons as high-sided, the heights ranging from 3 feet 8 inches to 4 feet 1 inch. Twelve were converted from dumb to sprung buffers between 1902 and 1906, the other four being recorded as ordinary wagons. No. 402 was withdrawn in 1912 and was replaced by an unidentified wagon, although this did not survive the grouping. Fourteen were renumbered into GWR stock, and the last one was withdrawn in 1939.

GOODS BRAKE VANS

The engineer reported in July 1896 that five 10-ton goods brake vans would satisfy initial requirements,[112] and Harrison & Camm tendered to construct these for £137 10s 0d each.[113] Probert, the newly-appointed general manager, considered these to be too light and advised ordering 20-ton vans. A new specification was prepared and tenders obtained from Harrison & Camm and the Midland Railway Carriage & Wagon Co.[114] Communication between the two officers was evidently lacking because Probert objected to the new design on the grounds that the vans were open at both ends, and being an ex-L&NWR man suggested that company's 20-ton type be adopted.[115] The engineer claimed that the GWR worked its Welsh valleys with 14-ton vans and that an extra 6 tons would have to be hauled five miles up a gradient of 1 in 40. Nevertheless, the directors decided in October 1896 that Harrison & Camm should be offered the contract provided the L&NWR type was adopted. This was agreed and a revised tender of £220 each was accepted in December 1896.[116] The five brake vans were delivered during 1897 and given numbers 64–68. Nos 65–68 were six-wheeled and appeared to be indistinguishable from their L&NWR Diagram 17 counterparts, with wood underframes on a 5 foot plus 5 foot wheelbase and a van body 18 feet long by 7 feet 7 inches wide by 6 feet 3 inches high (external dimensions). Clasp brakes acting

ABOVE: The only rolling stock supplied new by the GWR under the terms of the hire agreement were four 14-ton rail wagons. These were built in 1913 to Diagram J12 to replace wagons Nos 95, 155, 161 and 196 which had been condemned in 1912. Apart from the lettering these were identical to GWR wagon No. 14451. The italic lettering on the wagon shown here reads "This vehicle must not be close coupled on any curve less than 3 chains radius. Return empty to Hayes Creosoting Works". *Author's collection*

RIGHT: Loco coal wagon No. 401 at Cardiff Cathays circa 1920. This wagon was acquired secondhand from Edmunds & Radley in 1900, renumbered to GWR 9865 on 4/11/23 and withdrawn on 23/1/29. It is believed to be in the final PTR&D livery. *Author's collection*

on all the wheels were operated by a hand-wheel fitted to the bulkhead in the veranda portion. A stove was mounted centrally in the van portion. According to the 1908 inventory No. 64 was four-wheeled,[117] but nothing more is known. Five more goods brake vans were ordered from Harrison & Camm in March 1898 at £205 each and delivered later that year, Nos 69–73. Of this batch, No. 72 was four-wheeled and designated the Engineering Department brake van. The directors agreed to the purchase of a ballast engine and a secondhand 10-ton brake van for the engineer's use in January 1899, but these requests were not proceeded with. Tenders for five additional 20-ton goods brake vans were submitted to the directors in September 1899, but were deferred pending a report on how the TVR and ByR worked mineral traffic under conditions similar to those of the PTR&D from Duffryn yard to the docks. In the meantime Harrison & Camm had increased the price from £230 to £255 each, and in December 1899 a final order for four brake vans was placed at this price. These 6-wheeled vans, Nos 404–407, were delivered in late 1900/early 1901. None of the brake vans

were equipped with sandboxes but, perhaps as a consequence to a runaway at Bryn which occurred on 15th August 1899, these were ordered to be fitted in February 1900.

No. 404 was badly damaged in December 1909 when an out-of-control Down coal train ran into it whilst standing with an engine at Ynysdavid. The van was withdrawn by the GWR on 1st January 1910, but was subsequently repaired and reinstated. Four vans, Nos 66, 68, 70 and 405, were withdrawn in November 1921 and immediately replaced by standard GWR 20-ton vans of Diagrams AA13 and 15, these becoming PTR&D capital stock. Thirteen brake vans were assigned GWR numbers in the range 68939–68951 at the grouping, although only eight were renumbered. At some stage, possibly post grouping, at least one of the vans was fitted with side windows. The former Nos 69, 71 and 407 were written "MACHYNLLETH", "SEVERN TUNNEL JCN" and "MACHYNLLETH" respectively in 1925–27. No. 69 as GWR 68944 was the last PTR&D goods brake van to be withdrawn, in September 1931, but the GWR replacements lasted well into BR days.

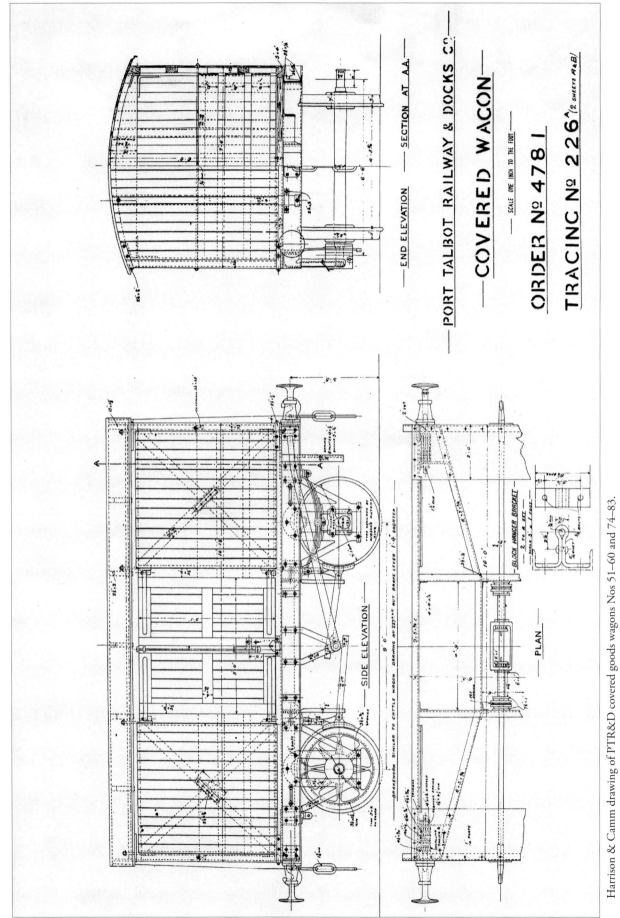

Harrison & Camm drawing of PTR&D covered goods wagons Nos 51–60 and 74–83.

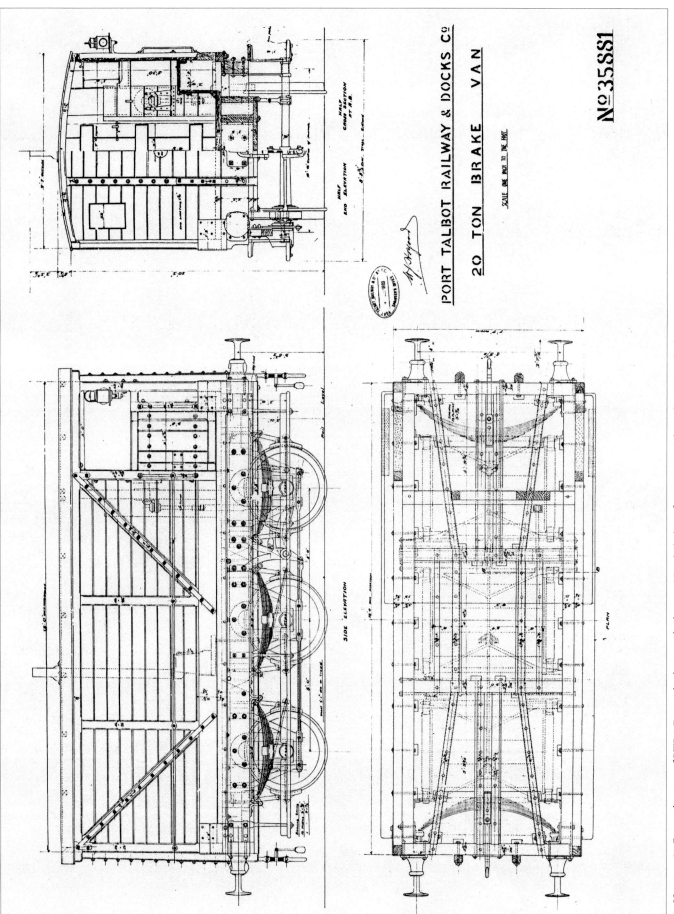

PORT TALBOT RAILWAY & DOCKS Cᵒ

20 TON BRAKE VAN

SCALE ONE INCH TO THE FOOT

№ 35881

Harrison & Camm drawing of PTR&D six-wheel 20-ton brake vans Nos 404–407 of 1899–1900. The earlier 20-ton brake vans were presumably similar.

TRAVELLING CRANES

In May 1897 the directors accepted a tender from Jessop & Appleby Bros (Leicester & London) Ltd of £535 to supply a 10-ton travelling hand crane. Although not specifically stated, a crane of this capacity would be useful for track laying and engineering work around the railways and docks, dealing with accidents, and handling loads in the docks beyond the reach of the fixed cranes. As noted above, open wagon No. 283 was used as the match truck. Nothing further is known about this crane, which was listed in the 1908 valuation as machinery at Duffryn Yard. The GWR Officer's Conference noted in July 1912 that this crane was beyond repair and that a new crane and match truck were to be provided for an estimated £950 plus £155, to be paid for by the PTR&D less the value of the old crane and match truck.[118] This course of action was changed in December 1912 when it was decided that a secondhand GWR crane would be provided at an agreed valuation of £700. Consequently GWR 12-ton six-wheel travelling hand crane No. 206 was transferred to the PTR&D on 29th January 1913, given the number 1, and became one of its capitals assets. There is some confusion over the date this crane was built. According to the GWR Crane Register held at the National Railway Museum it was built to order H2813 of 1894, whereas the Register of Travelling Hand Cranes made at Swindon[119] it was to order H2827 of 1892 – which also included Nos 205, 207, 403, 404 and 405.[120] The crane was accompanied by match truck No. 206 of Diagram L3 built in 1894 to lot 43, which suggests that the crane was also built in 1894. The old match truck was returned to revenue service. At the grouping the crane was given the GWR No. 213 and renumbered in 1922, a new No. 206 having been built in 1913.[121] No. 213 was still at Duffryn Yard in August 1936,[122] having been repaired in March 1933 at an estimated cost of £400,[123] and survived well into the BR era.

WAGON LIVERY

No official specification for PTR&D wagon livery has been found. Study of what photographs are available suggests that the wagon stock was initially painted a dark chocolate brown with metalwork in black and roofs white. Fifteen wagons condemned in 1908 were painted black.[124] By about 1910 some open wagons at least were seemingly painted light grey with black ironwork. In May 1914 the directors agreed to the GWR's application to paint the wagon stock in their standard colours, this was presumably carried out as required and continued after the grouping.

A variety of lettering styles have been noted At first the full company initials, 9 inches high, were used. On open wagons this took the form of PT to the left of the door and RD on the right, with No. XX on the door. Covered goods wagons had PTR&D just below the body centre line to the left of the doors with No. XX to

Builder's photograph of PTR&D goods brake van No. 66, as constructed by Harrison & Camm in 1897. Note the screw couplings and the opening in the end for the tail lamp. This van displays the first version of the PTR&D wagon livery. It was withdrawn on 6th November 1921 and replaced by GWR 20-ton van No. 17853.

Author's collection

the right. Goods brake vans when new had PTR&D centrally on the sides with a plain number below. Some, probably all, wagons carried cast iron number plates; this feature can be noted on the Claye-built opens and on the brake vans. The plates measured 16¾ inches by 8 inches and took the form:

PORT TALBOT RAILWAY
BUILT XXX YEAR
AND DOCKS COMPANY

At some stage the initials were simplified to P and T, 18 inches high, arranged conventionally. Numbers were applied in a variety of positions on the opens, as 9 inch numerals in the form of XX or No.

XX on the door, or as 6 inch numerals on the lower left-hand side. At least two wagons had the letters and numbers in white shaded black. Docks opens were so lettered on the door. Covered goods wagons with the simplified lettering had 6 inch numerals on the lower left side. In contrast, the cattle wagons had their numbers as XX low and centrally on the doors. All wagons provided pre-grouping by the GWR took the numbers of the PTR&D wagons they replaced, and most were renumbered again post grouping. It seems reasonable to assume that the wagons concerned carried the appropriate PTR&D livery in this period, although only one example of this has been observed. Replacement rail wagon No. 161 was lettered in the same fashion as its GWR counterparts with 12 inch P and T in place of G and W.

PTR&D goods brake van No. 407 as GWR 68951. This Harrison & Camm-built vehicle was purchased in 1900, renumbered on 10th January 1925 and withdrawn on 15th February 1930. It was branded "MACHYNLLETH" in September 1925, presumably for working on the Cambrian section. Note the provision of sanding equipment and the side window. *Clifford Collection, courtesy C C Green*

NOTES

1. *The Locomotives of the Great Western Railway, Part 10 Absorbed Engines 1922–1947* (Railway Correspondence & Travel Society 1966), pp. K242–K247.
2. TNA: PRO RAIL 1057/1529/1.
3. TNA: PRO RAIL 1057/1529/39.
4. See Chapter 6.
5. Frank Jux, 'South Wales Snippets, Part 31: Ebbw Vale Works', *The Industrial Locomotive* 12/1 (2006), p. 22.
6. See Chapter 1.
7. David Cole, *Contractor's Locomotives Part I* (Union Publications 1964).
8. Potts and Green, *Industrial Locomotives of West Glamorgan*, p. 109.
9. MRC Price, *The Gwendraeth Valleys Railway* (Oakwood Press 1997), p. 83.
10. TNA: PRO RAIL 254/66.
11. See Chapter 8.
12. TNA: PRO RAIL 1057/1529/2.
13. TNA: PRO RAIL 1057/1529/6.

14. TNA: PRO RAIL 1057/1529/23.
15. Ibid.
16. Philip Atkins, *The Golden Age of Steam Locomotive Building* (Atlantic Transport Publishers 1999).
17. TNA: PRO RAIL 581/5.
18. TNA: PRO RAIL 1057/1529/52.
19. TNA: PRO RAIL 1057/1529/55.
20. TNA: PRO RAIL 1057/1528/65.
21. TNA: PRO RAIL 1057/1528/111, 114, 116.
22. See Chapter 4.
23. TNA: PRO RAIL 1057/1528/72.
24. TNA: PRO RAIL 1057/2654; Robin Simmonds, 'The American Locomotives of the Port Talbot Railway', *Railway Archive*, 4 (2003), pp. 71–87.
25. *Locomotives of the Great Western, Absorbed Engines*, pp. K46–K47.
26. Atkins, *Golden Age of Steam Locomotive Building*.
27. TNA: PRO RAIL 1057/1529/32.
28. TNA: PRO RAIL 1057/1529/33.
29. TNA: PRO RAIL 1057/1529/34.
30. TNA: PRO RAIL 1057/1529/36.
31. *Engineering*, 13 April 1900.
32. TNA: PRO RAIL 1057/1528/53.
33. TNA: PRO RAIL 1057/1529/49.
34. TNA: PRO RAIL 581/13.
35. TNA: PRO RAIL 1057/1528/109.
36. See Chapter 8.
37. TNA: PRO RAIL 1057/1528/121.
38. H Holcroft, *An Outline of Great Western Locomotive Practice 1837–1947* (Ian Allan 1957), p. 119.
39. TNA: PRO RAIL 254/259.
40. *Locomotives of the Great Western, Absorbed Engines*, pp. K43–K44.
41. TNA: PRO RAIL 1057/1529/56.
42. TNA: PRO RAIL 105/1528/77.
43. TNA: PRO RAIL 105/1528/105.
44. TNA: PRO RAIL 105/1528/109.
45. TNA: PRO RAIL 105/1528/110.
46. TNA: PRO RAIL 1057/1529/32.
47. TNA: PRO RAIL 1057/1529/45.
48. TNA: PRO RAIL 1057/1528/94, 96.
49. TNA: PRO RAIL 1057/1528/98.
50. *The Locomotives of the Great Western Railway, Part 9 Standard Two-Cylinder Classes* (Railway Correspondence & Travel Society 1962), pp. J28–J30.
51. TNA: PRO RAIL 1057/1528/100.
52. *Locomotives of the Great Western, Standard Two-Cylinder Classes*, p. J38.
53. See Chapter 6.
54. TNA: PRO RAIL 1057/1528/107.
55. See Chapter 8.
56. TNA: PRO RAIL 254/58.
57. TNA: PRO RAIL 254/66–80.
58. TNA: PRO RAIL 254/259.
59. TNA: PRO RAIL 254/80.
60. TNA: PRO RAIL 254/259.
61. TNA: PRO RAIL 254/84–93.
62. Frank Jones, *Mainline to Industry* (Lightmoor Press 1998), p. 19.
63. Simon Marshall, '813: An Unfortunate Case of how not to Restore a Loco', *Severn Valley Railway News* (Summer 1992), pp. 34–40.
64. Paddy Goss, 'GWR 0-6-0ST No. 813 – An Historical Note and Update', *Severn Valley Railway News* (Summer 1997) pp. 46–51; Dave Reynolds, 'An Essay on a Locomotive Repair', ibid., pp. 52–4; Dave Reynolds, '813 – An Update', ibid., p. 72.
65. Hugh Madgin, 'Brighter days ahead for sole Port Talbot Survivor', *Heritage Railway* (June 2000) pp. 74–5.
66. Barry, *Barry Railway*, p. 196.
67. *The Locomotive Magazine and Railway Carriage and Wagon Review* (1908), p. 205.
68. TNA: PRO RAIL 1057/1529/2.
69. TNA: PRO RAIL 1057/1529/6.
70. TNA: PRO RAIL 1057/1529/10.
71. TNA: PRO RAIL 1057/1529/23.
72. TNA: PRO RAIL 1057/1528/89.
73. TNA: PRO RAIL 1057/1528/91.
74. TNA: PRO RAIL 1057/1528/98.
75. TNA: PRO RAIL 1057/1528/76.
76. See Volume 2, Chapter 16.
77. TNA: PRO RAIL 254/349.
78. ER Mountford, *A Register of GWR Absorbed Coaching Stock 1922/3* (Oakwood Press 1978), pp. 74–5.
79. TNA: PRO RAIL 254/58.
80. TNA: PRO RAIL 254/349.
81. *The Locomotives of the Great Western Railway, Part 11 The Rail Motor Vehicles and Internal Combustion Locomotives* (Railway Correspondence & Travel Society 1956); John Lewis, *Great Western Steam Rail Motors and Their Services* (Wild Swan Publications 2004).
82. T Hurry Riches and Sidney B Haslam, 'Railway-Motor-Traffic', *Proc. Inst. Mech. Eng.* (1906), pp. 651–878.
83. TNA: PRO RAIL 1057/1530/17.
84. TNA: PRO RAIL 1057/1528/90.
85. TNA: PRO RAIL 1057/1528/94.
86. *Railway Magazine*, November 1907, pp. 414–5.
87. Harold Morgan, personal communication.
88. TNA: PRO RAIL 1057/1528/109.
89. TNA: PRO RAIL 1057/1528/110.
90. TNA: PRO RAIL 1057/1528/111.
91. TNA: PRO RAIL 1057/1528/113.
92. TNA: PRO RAIL 254/66–71.
93. TNA: PRO RAIL 254/210.
94. TNA: PRO RAIL 254/58.
95. TNA: PRO RAIL 1057/1529/1.
96. KA Werret, *Model Railway News* (July 1960), p. 249.
97. TNA: PRO RAIL 1057/1529/2.
98. TNA: PRO RAIL 1057/1529/10.
99. TNA: PRO RAIL 1057/2655.
100. TNA: PRO RAIL 254/58.
101. TNA: PRO RAIL 1057/1529/48; see also Volume 2, Chapter 12.
102. TNA: PRO RAIL 1057/1528/94.
103. TNA: PRO RAIL 254/58.
104. AG Atkins, W Beard and R Tourret, *GWR Goods Wagons* (Tourret Publishing 1998), pp. 270 *et seq.*
105. TNA: PRO RAIL 1057/1529/2.
106. See Chapter 6.
107. TNA: PRO RAIL 254/58.
108. TNA: PRO RAIL 254/384.
109. TNA: PRO RAIL 1057/1529/10.
110. TNA: PRO RAIL 1057/1529/12.
111. Atkins et al, *GWR Goods Wagons*, p. 194.
112. TNA: PRO RAIL 1057/1529/2.
113. TNA: PRO RAIL 1057/1529/6.
114. TNA: PRO RAIL 1057/1529/10.
115. TNA: PRO RAIL 1057/1529/10.
116. TNA: PRO RAIL 1057/1529/12.
117. TNA: PRO RAIL 254/58.
118. TNA: PRO RAIL 242/3.
119. TNA: PRO RAIL 253/500.
120. No. 205 is preserved by the Great Western Society at Didcot.
121. TNA: PRO RAIL 250/274.
122. TNA: PRO RAIL 253/500.
123. TNA: PRO RAIL 250/278.
124. TNA: PRO RAIL 254/58.

10

Locomotives and Rolling Stock of the South Wales Mineral Railway

THE MINUTES OF THE meetings of the Board and shareholders of the SWMR contain very little information on the railway's rolling stock, presumably because up to 1907 it was provided by the Glyncorrwg Coal Co. Ltd and its successor companies, and latterly maintained by the GWR, as already described. What information there is refers to what was running on the railway. "The locomotive engine" reported to the general meeting held on 30th September 1961 to be running on the line probably belonged to a contractor. The next references in 1865/6 show that the Glyncorrwg Coal Co. had expended £7,000 13s 9d in providing rolling stock, a realistic figure in view of what is known of the locomotives at the time. The working agreement made in March 1870 with the re-formed Glyncorrwg Colliery Co. included provision for the maintenance and renewal of the locomotives. Two years later the Glyncorrwg Colliery Co. felt the full effect of this agreement when the change of gauge forced it to purchase three standard gauge tank engine from the GWR, as described below. The fate of the sole broad gauge brake van mentioned in the SWMR stock returns for 1868 to 1876 is unknown; possibly it was replaced by the old narrow gauge carriage sold to the Glyncorrwg Colliery

Co. by the GWR in July 1872 for £35.[1] Further restructuring of the Glyncorrwg Colliery Co. in 1880 was followed by an agreement permitting the new company to haul as much coal as it pleased from its colliery to Briton Ferry using its own locomotives whilst not being responsible for the repair or maintenance of the railway.[2] Despite occasional negotiations as to revising the 1880 agreement, the Glyncorrwg Colliery Co. continued to provide the rolling stock until December 1907.

From 1868 some insight is provided by the returns of working stock included in the new form of accounts required by the Board of Trade. The data provided by the SWMR[3] is incomplete and confused, possibly brought about by uncertainty as to whether it should have been providing the information at all. None was provided during the first twelve years the company was in the hands of a receiver, being reported as included in the lease to Glyncorrwg Colliery Co. The information was provided again following the reconstitution of the Glyncorrwg Colliery Co. in 1889, but stopped again after the wholesale change of directors in 1906. The rolling stock to be provided by the operator, according to a schedule attached to a draft revision made in 1892 of the 1880 working agreement, comprised

Builder's photograph of Glyncorrwg Colliery Co. No. 5. Built by Black, Hawthorn & Co. of Gateshead, works No. 1028 of 1891, this locomotive was scrapped in September 1911.   *Courtesy Frank Jones*

Above and Below: Two of the four GWR '645' Class engines sold to the Glyncorrwg Colliery Co. in 1872–75 and photographed at Glyncorrwg circa 1905. The cab modifications are believed to have been carried out locally. These engines are not readily identifiable, but feint lettering on the saddle tank of the view above suggests this could be No. 1. *Author's collection*

the following: five six-wheeled coupled goods engines Nos 1–5, a four-wheeled coupled shunting engine *Princess* "used as a reserve in case of breakdowns", three brake vans Nos 1–3, three goods vans Nos 4–6, two ballast trucks Nos 7 and 8, and two goods trucks Nos 9 and 10.[4] Information is available for June 1908 when the stock, five locomotives, eleven workmen's carriages, eleven goods wagons and three brake vans, was shown in the GWR's accounts as hired to that company,[5] but thereafter is subsumed into the total GWR figures. One further open wagon subsequently came to light and was included in the GWR Register of Actual Stock as at June 1909.[6] It is probable that goods brake vans were combined with other freight stock in the returns for 1891 to 1900.

LOCOMOTIVES

Two ex-contractor's locomotives are thought to have worked on the SWMR from circa 1861, one of them named *Brigand*,[7] and these became the first of the broad gauge stock. Three saddle tanks were purchased from Manning, Wardle & Co. in 1863, 1864 and 1866,[8] increasing the apparent stock to five locomotives, although the 1868 return notes only three, presumably these new engines. What seems to be certain is that Manning, Wardle No. 136 was sold to William West & Sons of Par in 1869 (see Table 10.1).

With the imminent change from broad to narrow (standard) gauge in May 1872, the directors noted in April that year that the Glyncorrwg Colliery Co. would have to find new engines, and that the four (*sic*) broad gauge engines would have to be sold and the proceeds divided by an actuary between the two companies. In

TABLE 10.1: SWMR BROAD GAUGE ENGINES

WORKS NOS	ORDERED	NAME	TYPE	DISPOSAL
74	1863	*Princess*	0-4-0, rebuilt to 0-4-2	Rebuilt standard gauge 0-6-0
116	1864	*Glyncorrwg*	0-4-2	sold 1872
136	1866		0-4-2	sold 1869

the event the two ex-contractor's engines were sold for scrap, and *Glyncorrwg* was sold to Brotherhood of Chippenham and thence to the Bristol & Exeter Railway in 1874. *Princess* lasted until circa 1901 when it too was sold for scrap. Possibly as a reaction to its refusal to assist the SWMR in its gauge conversation, Robert Baxter of the Glyncorrwg Colliery Co. applied to the GWR for new engines. In June 1872 the GWR directors authorised George Armstrong at Wolverhampton to construct three six-wheel tank engines for the Glyncorrwg Colliery Co. for £2,200 each.[9] It is conceivable that the fourth engine alluded to, presumably *Princess*, was used at least until 1877 for shunting the colliery sidings and never ventured onto the SWMR. The new locomotives were of the '645' Class, Wolverhampton Works Nos 190, 193 and 195, and became engines Nos 1–3. Another of the same class, GWR No. 767 built in 1873, was sold to the Glyncorrwg Colliery Co. in June 1875, becoming engine No. 4. This addition was not recorded in the stock return, a situation only properly rectified in the 1889 return. These four

One of the GWR '645' Class engines at the top of Ynysmaerdy Incline circa 1905. *Author's collection*

Two former South Devon Railway locomotives were purchased by the Glyncorrwg Colliery Co. from the GWR in April 1905. The one-time SDR *Emperor* became No. 6 and is seen here at Duffryn Yard in the 1920s as GWR No. 817; it was condemned in October 1926. The fireman standing next to the engine is Walter Watkins. *Author's collection*

engines were built with open cabs. At some stage, some, probably all, were fitted with enclosed cabs to protect the enginemen from the elements encountered on the upper sections of the line. These cabs were each of subtly different design and were presumably the products of the Glyncorrwg Colliery Co.'s workshops. Another 0-6-0 saddle tank locomotive was purchased in 1891, becoming engine No. 5; this was from Black Hawthorn & Co. of Gateshead, Co. Durham, No. 1028. The last two locomotives bought by the Glyncorrwg Colliery Co. for use on the SWMR also came from the GWR. These were six-coupled tank engines, originally built to broad gauge for the South Devon Railway as *Emperor* and *Achilles*, which eventually became GWR Nos 1317 and 1324 after conversion. The Glyncorrwg Colliery Co. purchased them for £775 each in April 1905[10] and gave them the numbers 6 and 7.

As noted earlier,[11] five of these seven locomotives were purchased from the Glyncorrwg Colliery Co. by Col Wright and others acting as trustees for the GWR, according to the terms of an agreement dated 31st December 1907. This transaction seemingly was not completed until early in 1910, as the five locomotives did not appear in GWR Register of Shed Allocations until January that year,[12] and only in its annual accounts to March 1910 did the Glyncorrwg Colliery Co. record the sale of its interest in the SWMR.[13] Nos 2 and 4 were retained, and remained in industrial service until 1921 and 1924 respectively.[14]

The five locomotives transferred to the SWMR were all shedded at Briton Ferry in August 1909.[15] No. 3 was evidently in a bad condition and was given a value of only £250 by Hertz. It was in Swindon Works by January 1910[16] and was cut up on 10th March 1910, having been replaced on 21st February by GWR engine No. 1806 which was then allocated to Duffryn Yard. No. 1 suffered the

same fate in April 1910, being replaced at Briton Ferry by GWR No. 1811 on 16th April. No. 5 was moved to Duffryn Yard in May 1910 and lasted until August 1911 when it too was condemned and replaced on 18th September by GWR No. 1546. These replacements were all 0-6-0 saddle tank engines of the '1501' Class built in 1880/81.[17] Nos 6 and 7, being recent ex-GWR locomotives, were evidently in much better condition and lasted well into the post-grouping period. SWMR No. 1 was moved to the nearby Neath engine shed in July 1910,[18] following the closure of Ynysmaerdy Incline, and thereafter one or two SWMR engines were usually shedded there until 1932, with balance at Duffryn Yard.[19]

The five SWMR engines were renumbered following absorption by the GWR, Nos 1, 3 and 5 regaining their earlier numbers whereas Nos 6 and 7 were put in a series that included the PTR&D saddle tank engines. Unlike most locomotives absorbed in 1922/3, those of the SWMR had GWR ancestry; nevertheless they were becoming outdated, and No. 6 as GWR No. 817 was the first to be withdrawn in October 1926, although No. 3 as GWR No. 1806 lasted until November 1938 (see Table 10.2).

PASSENGER CARRIAGES

The SWMR first admitted to using passenger carriages in September 1905, although it is possible to interpret the working stock returns as if they first appeared circa 1890. The conveyance of passengers in brake vans has already been referred to; it is likely that in earlier times open wagons and/or goods brake vans were utilised.[20] According to a summary prepared by Hertz in August 1907, the total was then eleven vehicles, and brief details of these, on which a value of £370 was placed, were tabulated by

RIGHT: Former SDR *Achilles* became No. 7 in April 1905 and is seen here at Glyncorrwg. The outline of its previous number plate, 1324, is just discernible. The driver is said to be Thomas Antony. This engine moved from Duffryn Yard to Neath in 1911 and did not return until 1917.
Courtesy Neath Railway Historical Society

BELOW: SWMR No. 7 was renumbered GWR No. 818 at the grouping and is seen here at Duffryn Yard after being fitted with pannier tanks in March 1924. This engine was condemned in May 1932.
Author's collection

TABLE 10.2: SWMR STANDARD GAUGE LOCOMOTIVES

SWMR No.	FORMER GW No.	To SWMR	RENUMBERED 4 WEEKS ENDING	POST-GROUPING GW No.	WITHDRAWN 4 WEEKS ENDING
1	1811	16/4/10	3/12/22	1811	31/5/28
3	1806	21/2/10	5/11/22	1806	–/11/38
5	1546	18/9/11	31/12/22	1546	–/12/35
6	1317	–/–/05	10/9/22	817	30/10/26
7	1324	–/–/05	10/9/22	818	26/5/32

Glyncorrwg Colliery Co. No. 7 at Glyncorrwg with the first coal raised at the new South Pit, 5th July 1906.

Courtesy Arthur Rees

GWR '1501' Class saddle tank No. 1811 was transferred to the SWMR as its No. 1 in April 1910 and regained its original number at the grouping. This engine was photographed at Duffryn Yard, having been fitted with pannier tanks in March 1925, and was condemned in May 1928.

Author's collection

Hertz in March 1909.[21] Six, Nos 1–4, 560 and 633, had been built by the Great Eastern Railway and presumably came from that source. Nos 21, 22, 24 and 26 were built by the Ashbury Railway Carriage & Iron Co. circa 1885. All ten were described as being in bad condition and were seemingly withdrawn by the PTR&D without any involvement of the GWR. No. 29, also built by Ashbury, lasted somewhat longer and was withdrawn by the GWR in November 1913.[22] This carriage was replaced by a GWR vehicle originally built as six-wheeled in 1873 and later converted to four-wheeled.[23] Although assigned a post-grouping number, 4344, this was never carried and the carriage was condemned in 1922. The GWR Register of Condemned Carriage Stock contains brief details of four further vehicles condemned in 1914–20. Three were GWR carriages which were written SWMR but retained their GWR numbers, 288, 680 and 897. The fourth, No 639, could be another of these but might also be 633 written in error. It is not known what use was made of these carriages between 1st January 1908 when the PTR&D began working the railway and 5th March 1917 when the first, official, workmen's service commenced.[24]

WAGON STOCK

In January 1908 Hertz produced a valuation of the SWMR wagons that the PTR&D had recently acquired, noting their generally bad condition.[25] From the running numbers given it appears that they were in one sequence and that a total of twenty wagons had at some stage been used on the SWMR, the gaps representing wagons that had fallen by the wayside.

OPEN WAGONS

The nine open wagons Nos 8–11, 14, 16–18 and 20 – described in the Condemned Wagon Registers as 10-ton ballast wagons – were wood-bodied on wood underframes.[26] Three were condemned in 1910, as were three more before the grouping. No. 9 was replaced by an old GWR three-plank wagon, but, more surprisingly, Nos 8, 10, 11 and 18 were replaced by GWR iron-bodied ballast wagons of Diagrams P4 and P5. Nos 14, 17 and 20, survived long enough to be assigned GWR numbers at the grouping, although only one, SWMR 14 / GWR 80829, was actually renumbered and it survived until 1926. The replacements faired better; all were renumbered at the grouping and three of the iron-bodied wagons lasted into BR days.

COVERED GOODS WAGONS

The three 10-ton covered goods wagons, Nos 4, 6 and 7, were all wood-bodied on wood underframes, and of these only No. 7 was identified as having been built by the Chorley Railway Wagon Co. in 1893. All were condemned by 1915, and they were replaced, two of them twice, according to information in the Condemned Wagon Registers, by GWR outside-framed covered goods wagons built in the 1880s. Only one of these survived the grouping, SWMR 4 / GWR 101546, and it was condemned in 1928.[27]

GOODS BRAKE VANS

The three goods brake vans, Nos 1–3, were stated by Hertz in 1908 to be of scrap value only. Two of these, and probably the third, were replaced by GWR outside framed brake vans built in the 1880s but none survived the grouping.

LEFT: GWR No. 1806 was another 1910 transferee, becoming SWMR No. 3. The engine is seen here at Neath shed in 1918, having been moved there two years earlier, and was returned to Duffryn Yard in 1920.
Courtesy Neath Railway Historical Society

BELOW: Back with its original number at Duffryn Yard, GWR No. 1806 was fitted with pannier tanks in October 1926 and condemned in November 1938.
Author's collection

NOTES

1. TNA: PRO RAIL 250/24.
2. TNA: PRO RAIL 639/9.
3. TNA: PRO RAIL 1110/430.
4. TNA: PRO RAIL 1057/1546.
5. TNA: PRO RAIL 1110/185.
6. TNA: PRO RAIL 254/343.
7. *Locomotives of the Great Western Railway, Absorbed Engines*, pp. K254–K256.
8. Fred W Harman, *The Locomotives Built by Manning Wardle & Company, Vol. 3 Broad Gauge & Works List*, (Century Locoprints nd).
9. TNA: PRO RAIL 250/24.
10. TNA: PRO RAIL 254/57.
11. See Chapter 7.
12. TNA: PRO RAIL 254/68.
13. TNA: PRO BT 31/15048/30591.
14. Potts & Green, *Industrial Locomotives of West Glamorgan*, pp. 71–2.
15. TNA: PRO RAIL 254/57.
16. TNA: PRO RAIL 254/68.
17. *The Locomotives of the Great Western Railway, Part 5 Six-Coupled Tank Engines* (Railway Correspondence & Travel Society 1958), pp. E35–E40.
18. TNA: PRO RAIL 254/68.
19. TNA: PRO RAIL 254/69-93.
20. See Chapter 7.
21. TNA: PRO RAIL 254/57.
22. TNA: PRO RAIL 254/349.
23. Mountford, *Register of GWR Absorbed Coaching Stock*, pp. 75–7.
24. See Simmonds, *A History, Vol. 2*.
25. TNA: PRO RAIL 254/57.
26. TNA: PRO RAIL 254/355–7.
27. TNA: PRO RAIL 254/384.

ABOVE: The third locomotive transferred to the SWMR was GWR No. 1546. Prior to this, the rear coupling rods were removed and the engine ran as an 0-4-2ST, as seen here at Gloucester in 1903 before being moved to the SWMR as No. 5 in 1911. *Author's collection*

BELOW: Ex-GWR No. 1546 as SWMR No. 5 at Duffryn Yard. *Author's collection*

SWMR No. 5 regained its GWR number at the grouping, acquired pannier tanks in October 1922, and lasted until 1935. The engine is seen here alongside the coaling stage at Duffryn Yard and facing south, this being the preferred orientation for engines for the run up the SWMJnR to Tonmawr and on to Glyncorrwg.
Author's collection